Wax Poetics Anthology
Volume 1

Wax Poetics Anthology, Volume 1
Copyright © 2007 Wax Poetics Inc.
All rights reserved.

ISBN 978-0-9798110-0-5
ISBN 0-9798110-0-7

Wax Poetics Books
45 Main Street, Suite 311
Brooklyn, NY 11201

waxpoeticsbooks.com

Printed in Hong Kong

PUMA®
puma.com

)**waxpoetics**
HIP-HOP, JAZZ, FUNK & SOUL

Preface

Towards the end of 2000, the idea of Wax Poetics magazine was born. The so-called crate-digging sub-culture was in full bloom, with many music fans actively participating in an appreciation for the music that came before them. We wanted to learn more about the past and help to recontexualize the present. So we began collecting stories from fellow record addicts and writers—from interviews with jazz legends and obscure funk musicians to contemporary disc jockeys and golden-era hip-hop producers. In December 2001, Wax Poetics Issue 1 was published and surprised even our closest contemporaries with its unique, singular vision and clean design. ¶ In the summer of 2007, after twenty-four issues of what has developed into definitive music-history journalism, we compiled our first anthology, culling articles from Issue 1 through Issue 5, which was published in the summer of 2003. We've incorporated new illustrations and photos but left much of the original feel, which, six years later, is starting to seem quite vintage itself. Enjoy this first volume of an even more concise vision of Wax Poetics.

Music Is
the Message

Idris Muhammad's Power of Soul

by Eothen Alapatt

I met Idris through Jimmy Lewis. I needed a drummer. We'd had a drummer on *Hair* when we were doing it downtown. He'd gone out of town, but he wasn't quite what we wanted anyway. So I asked Jimmy, "Who should we get?" He said, "Idris." He had worked with Idris as a sessioner and in the King Curtis Band. I think I had Idris come play with us, but it may have been that we went straight into rehearsals. He was great, right from the start. He had a great, strong beat. And he played in the right style. He actually was a jazz drummer but when he heard the music for *Hair* he didn't go the wrong way. He went right with it. He stayed in the band for four and a half years. He created a book of drumming, for when he missed the show. [Idris's subs] had to try to do what he did, and none of them could. He was so powerful; it was unbelievable! After he played that show for about a year, I said, "We've got to record this band; they're so good!" And then we did the *First Natural Hair Band* LP. "Ripped Open by Metal Explosions" is probably the most funky outing on the record but Idris had a lot of moments in the show that were really terrific. Towards the end of the show it goes into pure rhythm for about twenty minutes. Idris just kept it up, it was great. From one song to the other, with lots of breaks and interesting stuff. I used Idris for other projects, like the *Woman Is Sweeter* LP, and lots of demos. I used his wife Sakinah too. We all had a close relationship. But after the show closed, he moved out. He was traveling, playing with jazz groups and such. So I started with Bernard [Purdie] again. I'd kept in touch with him anyway during that time. For certain things, I used Bernard. The two are just different. Bernard is very sharp, you know. He plays a lot of interesting rhythms. Idris concentrates not so much on rhythm as on the beat—the actual four beats in the bar. And he generates a terrific momentum, like a train going down a hill. I don't know anyone who does that better than Idris. And in a show, it's overwhelming. By the end of the show the audience is breathless, because of this unbelievable drumming. They didn't know it, but I knew that's what it was.

—Galt MacDermot »

Where were you born?

New Orleans—that's my home. Sixty-one years have gone by so fast, I'm shocked. I was born Leo Morris. My father's family originated from Nigeria, and my mother was French. When I came into the family, there were seven of us. My three brothers, and one of my sisters, were drummers. The first day I went in to school, the teacher gave me a drum. She said, "Here's another Morris; give him a drum!" I went home with this drum and, man, my mother was mad! She said, "Oh shit, not another one! I got to buy khaki pants, a white shirt, a yellow tie, and a blue jacket so he can be in the band!"

Well, you had to follow the Morris's musical dynasty!

See, I was just a kid trying to play cowboys and Indians. I wanted cap pistols! But it was already written that this was going to happen. I lived in a neighborhood that was full of musicians and schoolteachers. Any day, you could hear music just walking the streets—somebody playing, rehearsing. Or you'd hear these marching bands in the streets. I think my attention focused when the bands in the neighborhood would play in the streets. I lived near two bars, a club, and a restaurant. The bands would do what we called a "dry run." They'd start rehearsing in a guy's house, then they'd come out of the house and go down the street, and people would follow them right into a bar. It was spontaneous. Someone would say, "Get the band a drink!" and then they'd move on to the next bar. This was my beginning in music, because the music was there. My thing was the bass drum. I used to hear this *boom boom boom*, and I'd run out the house and dance underneath the bass drum player. I can still remember the guy with the bass drum saying "Move your ass from under this drum, or I'll hit you with this mallet!" I was walking between the bass drum player and the snare drum player.

An important point regarding the precision that New Orleans's drummers embody—in marching bands, the drum kit had to be separated.

Well, you had a guy that played the bass drum with a cymbal at the top that he played with a coat hanger attached to a broomstick. That was the hi-hat. And then you had the snare drum player. These were bands that would play for funerals—or for any occasion. Back in those days you'd go to the same school from start to grade twelve. So my first professor was my musical director all the way through high school. And him and my older brother, "Weedy" Morris, were the first two Black musicians in Louisiana to be inducted into the Navy Band. My brother was the snare drum player, and my professor played the bass drum. While they were in the service, Weedy said, "When you get out, look for my brother and them." All of the drummers I met coming up in New Orleans knew him.

What led to your professional start?

It was one Mardi Gras day, and I was eight or nine. A guy came by the house looking for drummers. He asked for me—these old Dixieland musicians wanted me! They begged my mother; they said they'd take care of me. I played on the back of a flatbed truck. They set up three or four beer cases for me to sit on and gave me a kick drum, snare, and a cymbal. I knew all the songs, so I started playing. I was in the parade, and the kids from school saw me. One thing I'll never forget, there was this girl from school I was trying to talk to, but she would never look at me. She would come to school every day, all pressed and ironed. This day she saw me, and she said, "Hey, Leo!" I was playing drums in the parade! Then they slipped me a little wine, and at the end they were passing this money out: I got two fives. I said, "You get paid for this?" The man said, "Yeah!" That was it. That's when I decided I would be a musician. See, in those

days going to the movies cost twelve cents. And from then on, it was a different story with that girl. You know what I mean? I went home, gave my mom five dollars, and then I took all my buddies to the movies. I said, "Mom, I'm going to be a musician."

Did your parents recognize your nascent talent?

One day, my father told my mother, "Tell Sydney to stop playing!" Sydney was my older brother. My father had just come home from work, and he wanted to smoke his pipe and read the paper. So my mother went around back and saw me playing the drums. She didn't say anything and left. My father said, "Tell the kid to stop it with that noise!" She said, "You go tell him!" Well, he went back there, saw it was me, and he was shocked! He said that he thought it was my older brother. He had no idea!

You never had any formal training?

No. See, I'm a natural drummer. I'm a drummer that inherited the drums from my family. And my father was a banjo player. He played with Louis Armstrong back in the days. But we had so many kids that he became an interior decorator to support us. He couldn't do it just playing music. But he used to sing to us all of these songs—standards. From my father, I inherited a musical ability. That's where the musical part of my drumming comes from. See, my drumming is different from the rest of the drummers, 'cause I'm a musical drummer. I play the musical part of the song. I inherited a gift from the Creator. I can do things with the drums that no other drummer I know can do.

So when did you really start gigging?

I started going to my brother's gigs and waiting till he decided I could play a song with the band—maybe the last song of the night. The Nevilles are my family; we lived in the same neighborhood. So Aaron and I used to play gigs at Tulane and LSU with our music professor. We'd also go to see Arthur Neville's band, which at that time was called the Hawkettes.

The Hawkettes would later become the Meters.

Well, the band would play at the YMCA. We would go to the dance, and then I would sit in with the band, and Aaron would sit in with his brother. At the time, both John Boudreux and Smokey Johnson were drumming for the Hawkettes. I knew them both. They would come to my house to practice on my drum set, 'cause my mother had bought me a tape recorder. They'd practice and listen to themselves on the tape recorder. Smokey would play like Art Blakey. John would play like Max Roach. I'd listen to them for hours. Next thing you know, I could play what they both played. This started me practicing different things with the drums. Then John went on the road with Eddie Bo; the Hawkettes needed a drummer. So Arthur's father, who was their manager, said, "Go around the corner and get Leo." They said, "Well, he could play with us, but he doesn't have a set of drums!" I'm, like, fourteen years old. So my mother made Sydney lend me his drums. We traveled—Bogalusa, Shreveport, Baton Rouge. So I'm playing with the band, and the father said, "He knows all our music!" [Back] at home, I played with Eddie Bo, Earl King, and Lloyd Price. I went on the road with Arthur in 1957 with Larry Williams. We recorded some good records. Man, I was recording at fifteen years old!

Were you making good money?

My father asked me what I would do for a living. I said, "I'm going to play the drums, pop!" Once I started this thing I was making money so fast! Man, when I was living at home I was wearing clothes tailor-made on Rampart Street. I was clean!

What led you out of New Orleans?

Fate came through in this area. I came back with Arthur Neville,

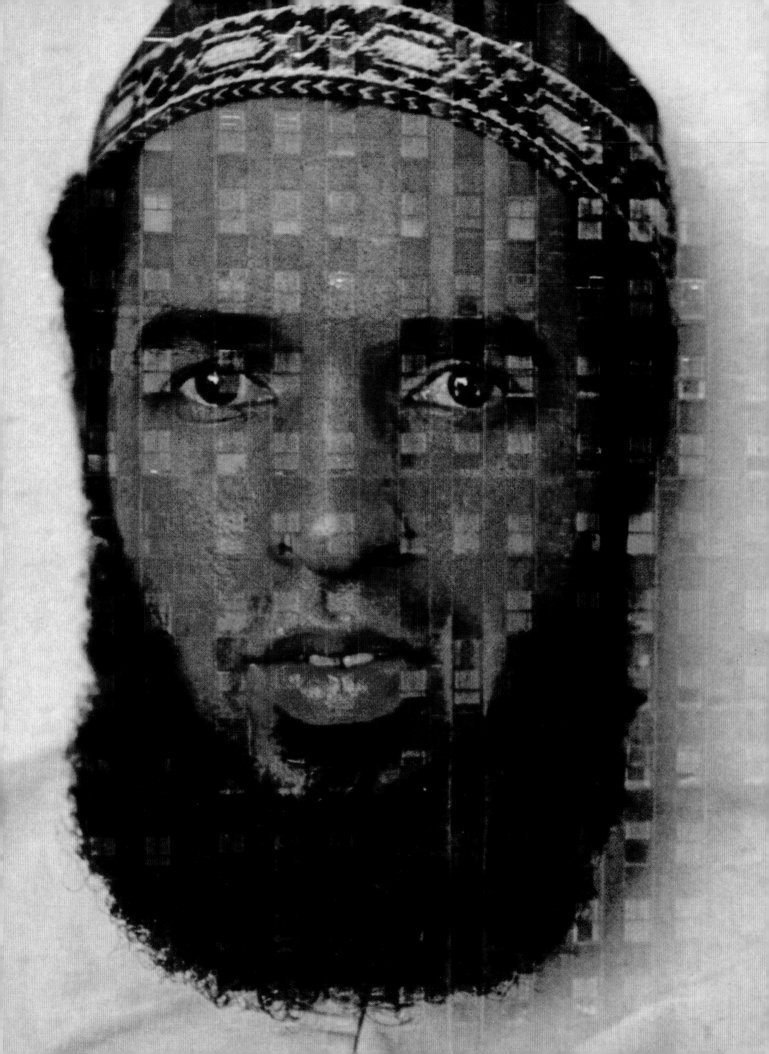

and the band wasn't working. I met this guy Joe Jones. We had a hit record, so I went on the road with him. Then I met Dee Clarke and Jerry Butler. They flipped over my drum playing! Once I was with Joe at a restaurant, and he told me Sam Cooke was sitting in the dining room. Joe told me Sam was complaining about his drummer. See, Joe had the gift of gab. He said, "I've been talking with him, and I want you to meet him." So we went over to his table, and Sam asked me to sit down. He asked if I knew his songs, I said, "Yeah." He started singing, and I started playing on the table. He hired me right there. He said, "Come to the Municipal Auditorium and play with me tonight." When he went on, I went on. I played that show without a rehearsal. And nailed it! I left town with Sam Cooke. He brought me to New York. My first trip to New York, and I was his personal drummer, man.

But you didn't stay in New York.

No, I came back to New Orleans, and another guy from New Orleans took my gig with Sam. I went back out with Joe Jones. But Maxine Brown took me to New York again. We were opening at the Apollo Theater. Jerry Butler was the star on the bill. But I was playing with Maxine Brown. She bought me my first brand-new set of drums. Jerry said [of our performance], "Damn, man, he got that burning for her. Maybe I can get that for me." So I played for him on the same show! I made a whole lot of money. I went to Chicago, and Curtis Mayfield started playing the guitar. I ended up being Jerry's musical director. Then I left Jerry and went with Curtis.

So how did you end up playing jazz again?

My wife, who was the lead singer with the Crystals, was living in New York. I was living in Chicago. I decided I would come to New York to be with her. When I got there, I had no gig, so I went to the Apollo Theater. I met with Reuben Phillips, the Apollo's bandleader, and let him know I was in town. He fired the drummer in the Apollo band and hired me! So I was in the band for about a year and a half. As I worked there, I was playing around town, sitting in with this group and that group. One day, I went down to this club called the Five Spot, and I sat in with Rashaan Roland Kirk. When I finished, this guy came up to me and said I sounded good—could I do a concert with him? His name was Kenny Dorham. So now I'm playing a concert at Town Hall with Kenny Dorham's band, Freddie Hubbard's band, and Lee Morgan's band. So I met all of these jazz musicians.

And you went on to infuse New York jazz with the diverse influences you picked up in New Orleans in your fledgling years.

I'm a natural drummer. I have some special qualities that came from the Creator which allow me to play all kinds of music. In New Orleans, you had to play for all different kinds of people. You played bar mitzvahs, you played at the universities, you played jazz, you played the street music, Latin music. I didn't know that my repertoire for music was so vast until I came to New York.

And jazz was changing from an intellectual music that had to be "appreciated" to a danceable, fun music again.

Right. The straightahead bebop took a step backwards to the music that was coming up that had a beat to it. I didn't know it at the time, but I was setting the trend for this music. I met Lou Donaldson at Birdland on 52nd Street. I was coming up the stairs, he was coming down the stairs. Bill Hartman, a trumpet player, said, "Hey Lou, that's the little drummer I was telling you about." Lou said, "Hey you, can you swing?" I said, "Yeah." He said, "You working this weekend? Gimme your number." And he called me. I went to Baltimore, and we played a gig. During the first tune we played, he turned around and told Bill, "We got ourselves a drummer!" Within two weeks, I'm in the studio recording with Lou for Blue Note. My first

record for Blue Note was *Alligator Bogaloo*. It was an instant hit. Oh, man, next thing you know Blue Note is calling me to record with George Benson, Lee Morgan, Stanley Turrentine. All of these guys.

Not surprisingly. You were a hit maker.

Yeah, my track record for R&B had already been set down. I had made hit records with the Impressions. I have a gift, man, that I can tune into your music. I can make your music better than what you thought you wrote. I had no idea I was doing this. But next thing you know, I'm recording with all these guys. I'm doing so well that I'm shocked. Everybody's saying, "This Leo Morris is a bad cat." I met Eric Gale, Chuck Rainey, Ralph McDonald. These were the session guys that were doing the R&B and funk stuff in New York. They latched into me, got me doing dates.

What were those Prestige and Blue Note dates like?

We'd just go to Rudy Van Gelder's studio and run through the song a few times. They might give me chord changes, but they never gave me no notes, 'cause they relied on me to play something to make the song happen.

You and Bernard Purdie supplied the backbeat to the entire soul-jazz movement!

[*laughs*] But Bernard could never play the drums that I played. He is a great drummer with his own style. But guys learned how to play the drums from me. There were things I was doing with the drums that guys took and made their trademark.

Like what?

That hi-hat thing that Bernard does. That *shoop shoop shoop*. This is something that I created. I was the drummer with Galt MacDermot for *Hair*. We played onstage with the actors, on the back of a flatbed truck. My drum set was set near the cab of the truck. I could only have one ride cymbal and the hi-hat. So I played all of this music off of the hi-hat, and I accented off the ride cymbal. After a year and a half I became sick, so they sent in a sub to play for me, and it was a disaster! After I came back, Galt made me get a book written up. Eventually, I had nine drummers subbing for me. This started with Bernard Purdie, Billy Cobham, Alphonse Mouzon. All these guys were subbing for me, 'cause this was the hottest musical on Broadway. So I'd created this thing off the hi-hat; Bernard comes by and looks at the book and says, "I can't play this shit, Idris!" And he leaves. Next time I heard that thing was on Aretha Franklin's "Spanish Harlem." I saw Bernard, he said, "Did you hear what I stole from you? This hi-hat lick." So guys were taking things from my drum playing and incorporating it into their style of drum playing.

And a lot of musicians were influenced by *Hair*.

I met Miles Davis two years before he died. We were playing a gig, and he asked me who I was playing with. He said, "Idris, you should get a band together and play some of that funky shit I heard you play in *Hair*. When I saw *Hair*, I changed my whole band. I knew there was money in that kind of music."

Wow, right around the time of *Bitches Brew*.

That's right! He changed everything to electric.

And got Jack DeJohnette to play funky rhythms—like you played. What do you know about the hip-hop movement?

They hear these beats, and they take a part of it and sample them. I wasn't hip to it till my son Idris Jr. showed me what these guys were doing. I've met some hip-hop musicians. These guys said that they could get into the stuff I did really fast, 'cause it's so clean, so natural—but funky.

Your drumbeat is instrumental to '90s hip-hop production.

That's the nucleus of the music, the beat. If they don't have the beat how can the rappers do their thing right? The rappers have told me that with my drumbeat, the lyrics go right.

On top of that, you had such a bangin' sound on your kit.

I have a unique way of tuning my drums. I learned this as a youngster, and at Rudy's [studio] on the [mixing] board. Rudy took my drum playing and put it up front and put all of the other instruments around it. So when you first hear my record, you hear the drum. On all of these guys' records! I learned to get my drum sound in the studio. So if I just meet an engineer, I know how to explain what I'm going for, so he and I will have a good rapport.

There's nothing worse than having a great drummer paired with a bad engineer. How about your equipment itself?

Well, there's a funny story about that. Art Blakey heard me play at the Five Spot the night after someone stole my cymbal bag. I was using cymbals some guy brought in, and he said, "Son, you sound real great but those pot covers you're playing on don't do you no justice!" He said, "I'll be back after you get off, and I got something at the house I think I can give you." So I hung out with him for two and a half days before I got back to my apartment. I ended up with the cymbals that I made all of the records that you're talking about on. I've had those cymbals for thirty-two years. I'm playing with them right now.

How do you feel about the appropriation of your music by the hip-hop generation?

I think it's a great music, man; look at the record sales. These guys sell so many records that they only have to have one hit.

But how do you feel about the movement artistically?

Yeah, I like it, 'cause it's another phase of the music.

Even though hip-hop musicians appropriate your music? And you're not necessarily getting paid for it?

It don't really belong to me, man; I'm only the creator. If you take something I create, and you do something with it, then someone else will take it and move it to another stage. And this is what happened with hip-hop. This is in my aura. I'm doing stuff for people to put out there so people can grab it. The gift the Creator has given me, I can't be selfish with. If I keep it in my pocket, it's not going to go anyplace. It doesn't matter if a guy stole from me. I'd say, "Well, what did you do? Okay, let me show you this." This is how I live.

That's a very humble attitude.

I watched people. I used to travel with the rock-and-roll shows. I watched stars. I got to the point where I had *Turn This Mother Out,* and it frightened me. I had a big record. I was opening for the Jackson 5, but the saddest point in my life was being a star and being in the dressing room by myself. And then the most sad thing was that the band was on the bandstand, and I had to wait for the police to escort me to the stage. I'm by myself. I'm used to being with the band. I was a sad dude, man.

I wish more people were as open-minded about their music as you are.

Well, you see, man, it don't belong to us. Secretly, whatever you have is gonna come out anyhow. If you think you are hiding something—you have a private vault that you have stuff in—when you leave this world your wife is going to open it up and sell everything. She's gonna sell everything in that vault! It's gonna come out anyway. So why not be free with it while you're here and share it with other people? 'Cause it don't belong to you. ⬤

Originally appeared in Wax Poetics Issue 1, Winter 2001.

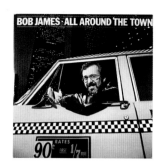

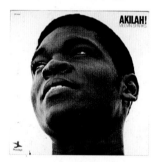

Pretty Purdie the Hit-Maker

by Eothen Alapatt

I've known Bernard since about 1966. I was sixteen when I met him. As a musician, Bernard came along when the music changed. Before him the beat relied on the shuffle. Purdie came along with a straight eight-beat—with the shuffle on the inside. See what I'm saying? And the sound just changed. He also came along when the electric bass came in. After '64, you didn't see acoustic basses with R&B groups. As the bass got more projection—and louder—the drummer could afford to be louder. And Purdie certainly was louder than any of those other cats that were down there! He had a strong, strong foot and a strong, strong beat that was perfect for the bass guitar. ¶ What a person plays means nothing if the time's no good, and Purdie is the king of time. The naval observatory can get their time from Purdie. They gotta call him! That's why me and him hit it off right away. When I first came down and hit the scene I was known as a very busy bass player. Not busy in terms of work, but busy in terms of notes! Mostly what I learned from Purdie was what *not* to play. I saw how Purdie would build a song. A little bit here, a little more next time around, throw your little zinger in here but don't overshadow the rest of the rhythm section. He played like a boxer in a boxing match. A boxer doesn't come out swinging like crazy at the opening bell; he picks [his opponent] apart gradually. That's what I learned from Purdie. He's the master of building. ¶ He is worth everything that everybody says about him. He's the man. In that particular groove of music, he is the man and has been and always will be. In the vein of music that you call rhythm and blues, I don't think I've ever come across anyone that is his equal. When he's in his element, forget about it! ¶ I believe everything that we hear today, no matter what it is, came from what Purdie set up. –Wilbur "Bad" Bascomb »

SONOR

You know, even though I've known you for quite some time, I don't think I've ever read any interviews with you. Most of the information I have on you comes from the back cover of the *Shapes of Rhythm* LP! Where were you born?

I was born in Elkton, Maryland—the seat of Cecil County. Maryland has twenty-three counties. Cecil County is one of them. Elkton is the biggest of the small, little towns, and that's where all the politicians and banks are. It's there that everybody comes to. It's also the place that had one [institution] where all the Black kids went to school, which is George Washington Carver. Every Black kid in Cecil County was bussed to the Black school. It was right near my home—a mile away actually—in Elkton. My family walked to school.

Was Elkton a cultural, as well as political, center? Did you grow up around music?

No, there were no musicians around me. I'm sorry—there was one, and he had a band. The Clyde Bessick Orchestra. This was jazz, but it was called "big band" at the time. It was called "dance music." I was five or six when I first took notice. I started playing with the band at age eight. My teacher at GWC, Leonard Haywood, was the drummer with the orchestra.

So you played in the school band, and Haywood was your instructor?

He wouldn't let me in the band at first. [*laughs*] I'm very serious. It wasn't so much that I wasn't good enough, it was about an age situation. I was too young to be in the band, but I was gifted enough to play. So in order to do what I did, he would allow me to be in the band only if I took up another instrument.

Which was?

The trumpet. The worst thing he could possibly do to me.

Why?

[*laughs*] Because I couldn't stand the trumpet! From trumpet I had to go play flute for a year and a half. I was seven or eight at the time. See, I always had rhythm on the drums. But he wouldn't let me touch the drums at school—he would only let me do it at his house. So I would go to his house, while he was teaching other students, and sit on the steps watching him teach other students. When he wanted an example, I'd jump up to do it. He would tell me to sit down and play what he wanted, then I would get [off the drum kit] and sit back on the steps. This went on for almost seven years.

Why did you go along with this? Most kids would have given up!

I always wanted to play the drums. I wasn't gonna let no one stop me from playing the drums. But Mr. Haywood had me play the trumpet and the flute, because he wanted me to learn music. But I didn't know that. I thought he was punishing me!

How fortunate that he started you on the path to becoming a musical drummer.

Of course it is, when you realize that twenty or thirty years later.

It takes a hip teacher to instill that musicality in you, without you even knowing what he was doing.

He was quite the hip teacher. Oh, he saw the gift. I had the gift. And that's what he used to say to me. I would get so upset, 'cause I thought that he was saying that to get me to shut up. You know, there were so many little things that he would say and do, but he never raised his voice. That's the thing that got to me. I would get mad and upset, and he would tell me, "You're still going to have to do it." I would say, "Why, why? No one else has to do it. And I'm better than any of the other students you have. I can play rings around them!"

He would say something like, "Yeah, but they're older." He always had an excuse.

Ah, the infamous Bernard Purdie self-confidence rears its head at an early age!

Oh, my confidence was there when I was four or five.

You said you played in Bessick's orchestra at age eight. So Mr. Haywood must have taken your latent abilities seriously.

Oh yes. I played on the bandstand. The reason is that every Friday and Saturday, Mr. Haywood had to play with the band. And he would get drunk. See, he liked vodka or gin. And he would give me this tall glass, supposedly filled with water, and I would hold it for him. And I would feed him from this glass, which was full of either vodka or gin. And it was great. [*laughs*] Because when the intermission came, he would sweat so much that he would go out to his station wagon, and he'd sit down and fall asleep. So I would finish the job. I would go back, and sit down, finish the job—[and everyone in the band] would know he was too drunk to continue.

Wow!

Yeah. I knew all of the Bessick songs. Every one of them. Because I knew everything Mr. Haywood did. I could mimic him with no problem. But it wasn't about mimicking. He wanted me to learn music. So I knew how to play—and interpret—whatever I sat down to do.

When did you form your first band?

I had my band when I was twelve years old. That was Jackie Lee and the Angels. I was the leader, even though my name wasn't Jackie Lee. I was definitely an Angel. [*laughs*] I also signed the contracts.

A businessman at age twelve?

Oh yeah, you had to be! The thing is, these are the things Mr. Haywood taught me as I was growing up. You had to learn how to manage. And I'm not just talking about managing money. I never looked at it as managing money. But managing to do the *job*. It was always a job. No matter what happened, I had to do the job. The first time I got paid, I became a professional. The first time I got paid, it was either eight or ten dollars. That was big money! I mean, that was super money, and I got paid to play the music. I was eleven or twelve.

So by the time you formed the Angels, you were quite the young veteran.

Oh yes. I would always be around for the Clyde Bessick Orchestra, and I was also playing in the high school band. This went on till the end of the '50s.

Then you enrolled at Morgan State University.

Well, I was out of school for a few months, 'cause I couldn't afford to go anywhere. So two members of the House of Delegates—Mr. Berkely and Mr. Stanley—got me into college. They knew me, 'cause I worked for them in Elkton. But I had to go to study business administration. The reason was that this was the only opening they had, so that's how they got me in. It had nothing to do with what I really wanted to do, but it was a way to get me into the school. They had a great music program at Morgan, one of the best in the world. I could only take one music class though. At first I could only do my major, my minor had to wait for at least a year.

But you must have at least joined the college band.

Yeah. I joined the band immediately. They knew that I could play. They also knew that I was good at what I did. We had two brothers there—I'm trying to think of their names. They played trombone and trumpet. Boy, they were awesome! They had their own band as well, so I joined. But I didn't know that they were either alcoholics or drug addicts. Turned out they did both. But

Photo by Beth Fladung.

they were phenomenal musicians, and everyone around town knew them, 'cause they were in their second or third years of college.

Sounds like you were a busy man.

I was also one of the photographers for all the freshman. And I worked in the cafeteria, 'cause I was there on a workman's scholarship. So I had to do those things, as well as excel in my studies.

You were hustling.

Well, you had to! That was the only way to get ahead! Outside of school, I was playing swing, the blues, R&B, country—whatever was necessary for me to do. And I started forming and playing in different bands. Within six months of being at Morgan, I was playing in three different bands. I was playing uptown, at the nightclubs. I could also play show music, 'cause I read music!

Thanks to Mr. Haywood.

Right. It was all easy for me to do. Because of that, I did what was necessary. That's when I ran into a man named Purnell Rice. He was the only drummer I ever knew that could play a roll on a pillow. He wasn't allowed to make noise in his house, so he learned how to practice on a pillow. I saw it with my own eyes, I couldn't believe it. I knew then I had to go back to the woodshed! [*laughs*]

How so?

That man's hands were so fast! He was much older than me; I would say he was as much as fifteen years older than me. He was playing strip music, all kinds of show music, anything that had to do with reading and interpreting music for people who danced.

So he was an inspiration during your college years?

He made me want to go practice. I could play the precision drumming, 'cause I played in the circus band when I was fourteen. That was never my problem. But I was never super fast. I couldn't do

the rolls anywhere near the way Mr. Rice could do them. He did the press roll like he was taking a piece of paper and ripping it—he was so smooth. But for me: "Your rolls are always like biscuits," he used to tell me. My rolls were a bit…

Slower?

Well, they were never super smooth. I had to do what they called the "buzz roll." But I would never be as smooth as him. To this day, I still do biscuits. Oh yeah, I love my biscuits. 'Cause they work for me. I don't try to be no super smooth cat! My little biscuits work!

When did you graduate from Morgan?

I only had two years at Morgan. I didn't graduate, 'cause I left and came to New York City in 1961. The band that I had, we had been playing well together. Everything worked out, and [the band members] wanted to go to New York to make a record. It was there that I met and worked with Mickey and Sylvia. We rerecorded "Love Is Strange" for their own label. That was my first session date, one week after moving to New York. I was living in the Bronx.

And you never left.

I mean, I got here, had a ball, and fell in love with this town. I was just a kid. I just loved what I saw.

Not to mention you had solid work lined up!

Man, Mickey and Sylvia paid me eighty dollars to work from noon until four o'clock on a Sunday. I got paid eighty dollars! I was rich! I was *rich*! I knew I was rich. I'd hit the big time. I went back to the Comet Club, where I was working nights, at 165th and Washington. We played for the door. And of course, I made all kinds of tips, 'cause I sang and danced as well. I did everything. That was what it was. I was a showman.

And then the session work started pouring in.

Photo by Beth Fladung.

That all happened from demos. There was a guy named Herb Abramson. He, I found out later, was the president of Atlantic Records. I met him 'cause he had a recording studio on the sixth floor up on 56th Street. I just went and introduced myself. I would go around and tell people, "I'm good. Hire me."

So the stories of you walking around wearing the signs that read: "Pretty" Purdie, the hit-maker?

All of them are true. I know now that I'm a master of self-promotion. But back then I'd just go ask anyone to give me a job! [*laughs*]

Like Rick Shorter.

I got in on the ground floor of New York sessioning. Rick was another person doing demos. By 1964, I had a reputation. I had made hit records! "Just One Look," Les Cooper's "Wiggle Wobble," "Hi Heeled Sneakers." That's how I met Galt [MacDermot]. That was the same year, 1964.

Do you remember the day that you two met?

Of course I remember meeting him! [*laughs*] The day that I met him—the strangest part is that I'm looking at him, and talking to him, and I remember saying to him, "Do you know what you're doing? Do you know what kind of music you're doing here?" He said [calmly], "Yes." I said, "But, do you really know what kind of music this is?" And he said [calmly], "Yes." I said, "But how would you know how to do this kind of music? I mean, this is African music, and funk, and pop—all in one!" I said, "I don't really think you know what you're doing! And if you do, that would make you a genius."

And?

He said, "Well, I do know what I'm doing." I said what I said because I really didn't think he understood. Man, *impressed* isn't the word. I was floored. I'm telling you, I didn't understand that the

man really knew what he was doing.

Yeah, I've seen the pictures! By looking at Galt, you wouldn't be able to tell that he was such a musical revolutionary.

I had never seen a White guy play that good—with sincerity—and know exactly what he wanted. He knew exactly what he wanted, and this is what he asked for [on demo sessions]. So I said, "Okay, I'll do it."

You two got along well?

We hit it off *immediately*. Absolutely immediately. At that time I was arrogant, but I didn't know I was arrogant. I thought I was just smart. He told me that I was arrogant. But I'm playing the music he asked for. He told me I was the first one to give him exactly what he asked for.

Can you clarify?

For me, I always had to play what was being dictated. That's how I learned to play. But this is where my gift comes in. My gift allows me to play anything with anybody, 'cause I hear where they want to go with their music.

Galt was perhaps the first person to document you as a musician—to focus on your abilities—with his *Shapes of Rhythm* album in 1966. That was an album made by sessioners—Galt, yourself, Jimmy Lewis on bass, and "Snag" Allen on guitar—for themselves.

Yeah! I remember that record. Galt would play some of a tune on the piano. I would turn around and say something to Jimmy—but I had to learn to keep my mouth shut; Jimmy actually threatened me a couple of times. Oh yeah! Jimmy would cut you or shoot you, it didn't matter which. He pulled his gun on me once! I'm telling you, that cat always had a gun and a knife. He was from the streets! [*laughs*] He was a street person.

Sounds like those must have been some stressful sessions.

No, not really. The sessions weren't volatile. Galt was the soothing image for everything. And Snag always said, "Yeah, sure man. Let's do it." Snag would do the backbeats, then play a rhythm afterwards. We always did what Galt wanted. Jimmy was the one who took longer to get it done. But eventually, since he listened to what Galt was doing on the piano, he would give in. That's why I would say to Galt, "You're either a genius, or you're crazy."

I think that "Coffee Cold," one of Galt's tunes that you recorded during the *Shapes of Rhythm* session, is a little of both. The rhythm on that song is far beyond the conventions of the time.

Oh yes, I remember that song. But the point is, I got that feel from Galt. Listen to what I'm saying to you, he was playing those types of rhythms on the piano. And these were African rhythms. This is why I didn't understand— why everybody didn't understand—what he was doing. He was playing African rhythms! After working with him for a year I discovered that he'd been living in Africa! I never thought to ask! Never even occurred to me to ask if he'd lived in Africa. All I knew is that he played [African rhythms] on the piano. And I said, "Okay, if this is what you want, I'll play it." You never expect to see someone—he had gray hair then—to play these kind of rhythms. How would he know?

As the '60s progress, you play drums on records that have influenced drummers from then until now. Like Aretha Franklin's "Rock Steady," and King Curtis's live version of "Memphis Soul Stew."

Well, I agree with you there. I'm learning that that's what [my drumming] has done. But to me it was just a job. When Aretha sat down at the piano, the whole arrangement was coming out of that piano, from her fingers. I just took it out. I just gave parts to different people in the band.

As one of the pillars of funk drumming in America, when did you realize that the funk rhythm had taken over American popular music?

I never looked at anything as being taken over. People misunderstand. I had no idea that I was setting a trend of any kind. I was just doing a job. It was just a job to me. This is what the person was playing; I was bringing out the rhythm. It was a job!

You were damn good at your job. It didn't matter if you played rock, folk, funk, or jazz—any record that you're a part of rings with your unique sound.

The drumming I played was simple to me, 'cause it was part of what the music was supposed to sound like. I know that people are saying all these fabulous things about me—that I changed the world, and this and that. It was a job. [*laughs*] I could not tell you that what I was about to play was going to change the music business. You get these ideas; they come from somebody, from someplace. They were not my ideas in the first place. I took what people had and made it work. That's what I was great at.

In WAX POETICS Issue 1, we interviewed your contemporary, Idris Muhammad. He said that you took a hi-hat lick from him.

[*laughs*] No, that's not quite so. I was doing that [lick] when I was twelve years old. I was doing that with the big band. It is my trademark. I was doing that in a fourteen-piece orchestra. My teacher, Mr. Haywood, told me what I was playing was eventually going to happen in music. "But not now!" he'd shout. "Don't do it now! Leave it alone!" [*laughs*] I didn't know what I was doing. I had to figure out what I was doing.

No matter how progressive your drumming became, you never left the pocket. I'm thinking of your drum breaks recorded on songs like Charles Kynard's "Sweetheart." You stay in the groove,

and we love you for it.

You had to. All my life, I was told, "Do not break the rhythm. Let people dance." That is why my solos are the way they are, I tried to make them danceable. I was trying to keep the music as tight as possible, without making big splashes or getting in the way. I didn't want to get in the way of the vocalist, but, yet, inspire the vocalist. I did that because I learned how to control my beats.

Speaking of beats, your first album on Date is full of 'em!

Mmm hmm! My manager at the time, Dave Kirkpatrick, was the vice president of Epic Records. At that time, I was producing for him, for Daedalus Productions. I did Peaches and Herb, Ronnie Dyson—and we also had Sly and the Family Stone. As quiet [as it] was kept, it wasn't Sly that was producing the records. For example, his first album—the only one that was a happening album—I did that for Daedalus. I didn't know I was supposed to get credit for these things. Ken Williams and myself, we had to fix Sly's albums, because he was tore up the whole time he was in the studio doing these things. We had to make his records happen.

How exactly would you "fix" his albums?

We would switch things over to eight-track or twelve-track. Keep what he had, and add little things to help support and to keep the music happening. I did the same thing [for] the Beatles.

You know, I'm sure Sly fans are going to contest your claim—much like the Beatles fans have contested you since you came forth a few years ago to dash their perceptions of their musical heroes!

Oh yeah. And you want to know what? I don't care anymore! About the Beatles situation? That was part of my job. I was the fixer! I've been fixing things since 1963.

Any other notable projects that you "fixed?"

We had the same thing with Eric Burdon and the Animals. Just about every European act that was being done in the '60s and the early part of the '70s.

How about the Monkees?

Yes, the Monkees. Of course! The guy who was their contractor was a drummer. But he stayed drunk all the time.

And alongside of all this, you found time to revolutionize both the sound and feel of funk drumming.

But I had a good engineer, see. Phil Ramone. He liked the idea of the echo chamber. We used an echo chamber, and we studied where to place the mic in relation to the snare drum. He kept the mic at a small distance from the drum, but he used the room itself as its own echo chamber.

Yeah, hearing you on your early records—and even the jazz dates you did for Bob Porter—you get the feel that you're seven feet tall!

Exactly. It's booming, but the looseness is what gives it the flow, and the feel to stay out of everybody else's way.

Were all of your solo ventures as successful as the session dates you did?

Yes, all of them were. I had good arrangers. I always had good arrangers with me. I would give them what I wanted, and then I'd let them fatten up what I had—with whatever they wanted to do.

Tell me about what has to be your most obscure release, the soundtrack to *Lialeh*.

[*laughs*] That was the first time I was going to have credit as a writer/composer. It was a small-scale movie; I scored the entire thing. We had ten thousand copies manufactured, and then they told me I couldn't do any more. They had to come to me to get my permission every time they were going to make a deal around the world. The ten thousand [pressed domestically] were made by my own company, which was Poor Boy Records. I sure wish I had kept some copies!

You know, an interesting parallel between the recording trajectory of both Idris and yourself emerges in the mid- to late '70s, with disco. I would have thought that since you are both such rhythmic drummers, you two would have fought against the disco feel. Instead you assimilated it.

When music is changing, and the feel of the music is changing, you go along with it. You don't try to fight it. You can still make rhythm out of disco, but it's all about *how* you do *what* you do *when* you play. In the late '70s, I went along with the program. I kept it tight, kept it funky, and then I loosened it up. Let the music breathe.

And the '80s?

The '80s were very horrible, but I was playing live. I was playing jazz with Dizzy Gillespie all over the world. I was with Gato Barbieri, I was with Roy Ayers, and then back with Aretha. I always thought back to the '60s and '70s, but I never let it interfere with the job I was called to do. You go and do your job. In the '80s, though, I learned how to use the computer. I was writing music with, and without, the computer.

In the late '80s, hip-hop sampling brought your drumming back to the forefront of popular music.

In the beginning I didn't take to it too well, 'cause Aretha got paid, or James Brown got paid. I had to accept the fact that I wasn't going to get paid, 'cause I wasn't the artist being sampled. I was the drummer. In the beginning I was upset; now…nah. No one can take away from me what I have, what I've learned, and what I've done. And I don't care what they try to do. The point is I've been able to survive all of these years. Over forty years in this business. I was able to learn the business, and play and survive in the business.

And the hip-hop generation regards you as one of the godfathers of the movement, much like James Brown.

I realize that now. That is a big thing to me now. I'm very pleased. This is why I'm working. I know what I'm going to do for the next six months. I'm running all over the world. I'm teaching, I'm giving lectures, I'm giving master classes, and I'm traveling around the world having a good time. Traveling two hundred and fifty thousand miles a year and loving it. And getting paid. I figure I have another twenty-five to thirty years. Oh, at least!

Ah, the regenerative powers of music…

You have to regenerate! You got to! I've only noticed my impact in the past fifteen years. And I'm beginning to enjoy what it's done for me. I don't have to go around patting myself on the back for my achievements. They're now being put in front of my face. And other people around the world are beginning to see what I've achieved. Which is why they've kept me working. This is my way of getting paid. But I also know that I have to give back. And as long as I feel that way, I'll still be compensated. I don't have a problem in the world when it comes down to playing this music. I've been very lucky and fortunate with my arthritis and stuff like that. I'm going to go ahead and enjoy myself. And love it. Absolutely love it. Yes, it was a job. It will always be a job. But…I can have fun…with my job. ◉

Originally appeared in Wax Poetics Issue 2, Spring 2002.

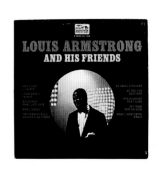

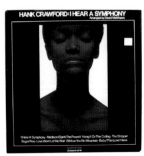

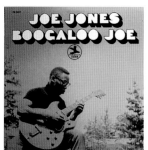

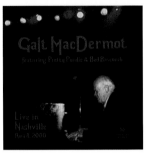

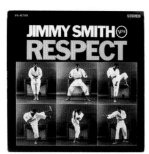

Clyde Stubblefield *the* Funky Drummer

by Cherryl Aldave

In the beginning, there was the break. The party people of the early '70s park jams saw it was good, and hip-hop was born. By most accounts, many of the breaks favored by those nascent b-boys and b-girls came from a single source: pompadoured funkmeister, James Brown. But by all accounts, the most sampled drum breaks from Brown's records were played by two drummers: Clyde Stubblefield and John Starks, better known as "Jab'O," which is his preferred spelling. ¶ Clyde, behind the thunderous bass and dancing snare on funk-fests like "Mother Popcorn," "Cold Sweat," and "Funky Drummer"—the song thought to be the most sampled in music history—joined Brown in '65 and left in '71. Jab'O (who formerly played drums for Bobby "Blue" Bland) also came on board in '65, and lent hard-driving, jazz-influenced grooves to Brown hits like "Get on the Good Foot," "Sex Machine," and "Papa Don't Take No Mess." Jab'O stayed on until '75—his ten-year tenure with Brown making him the longest continuous drummer of Brown's ever fluctuating lineup—and recorded more charting singles with him than any other drummer in Brown's career. ¶ Although neither receives royalties from the sampling of Brown's songs—Brown owns all the music—both remember their time with the mercurial soul singer fondly, and summarize it as a great learning experience. ¶ Today the pair, who say they're "like brothers," give drum clinics together and still actively tour and record. In 1995, their autographed drumsticks were inducted into the Rock and Roll Hall of Fame in Cleveland, Ohio. Recently, the two released a CD, *Find the Groove*, under the name the Funkmasters, and an instructional video, *Soul of the Funky Drummers*. In May of 2002, Clyde momentarily gave his sticks a rest when he was diagnosed with bladder cancer; a successful surgery removed the malignancy, and Clyde wasted no time getting back behind the trap-kit to pay mounting medical bills. When not on tour, Clyde performs every Monday night at the King Club (in his home city, Madison, Wisconsin). Jab'O, now living in Mobile, Alabama, can be heard Tuesday through Saturday performing at Red Bar in Grayton Beach, Florida. In this two-part interview, Clyde and Jab'O discuss beats, life, and Brown. »

Illustration by Brad Howe.

Clyde, where are you from, and why'd you start playing drums?

I'm originally from Chattanooga, Tennessee, and when I was about eight or nine, I went to an Armed Forces parade after school. I heard the drums and loved it. I came home from that parade marching, and started playing on boxes and tin cans. When I was about seventeen, I moved to Macon, Georgia, and started playing a lot with blues guitarist Eddie Kirkland. I was playing with [Eddie when] I met Otis Redding, and I played with Otis Redding off and on when he'd go out with Johnny Jenkins and the Pinetoppers.

How'd you start playing with James Brown?

I went to a club one Sunday in Macon and decided to sit in and jam with the house band. I didn't know Brown was in the audience, but, after, he came up to me and said, "I'd like for you to come audition for my band." I did, and that's how I got in. What's funny is, when I was a kid I delivered papers, and on Saturday morning before I'd pick up my papers, I'd sit in this bar and play pinball. Right by the pinball machine was a jukebox, and I used to play all the new Bobby "Blue" Bland records—"Turn On Your Love Light" and all that. I loved the drumming on Bland's records and I always thought, I want to play like this drummer. He's got the grooves that's happening! When I joined Brown I walked up to a drummer there and said, "Hey, how long you been here?" He said, "About two weeks." I said, "Who did you play with before?" He said, "I was Bobby 'Blue' Bland's drummer." My jaw dropped. It was Jab'O!

At the time, Brown had five sets of drums and five drummers onstage during a show. After my audition I made the sixth drummer. All drummers didn't play at the same time on each song; Brown would call on different drummers when one wasn't doing what he wanted. After a while, Jab'O and I were both thinking that we wanted to play more music, but with all those drummers there we couldn't, so we started knocking them off by playing better grooves. Brown fired one; that left five. Then he found out this other drummer couldn't do what Jab'O and I were doing so he fired him, and in a while it got down to just Jab'O and me. Every time a drummer got knocked off, we'd just look at each other and go, "All right!"

How much influence did Brown have on the drum patterns you and Jab'O played?

Brown didn't have too much influence on me and Jab'O's drum [patterns]. The rhythm section would go in the studio and start playing some grooves, and James would come in and put the horns on it, add lyrics to it, and that would be a song. Or he'd walk in and have a song playing in his head, but he didn't have an idea of how he wanted the drums to go. We'd sit down and start playing something, then he'd say, "Yeah," and start adding stuff. I can't take ideas as far as drum patterns. When [producer] Butch Vig—he lives out here in Madison with me—he called me up one day and asked me to come up to his studio to play on [Garbage's "Not My Idea"]. He said, "Just play what you want"—and that's the best way. When someone calls me for a session, I have to make my own pattern and then [they] fill it in with the song.

"Funky Drummer" has been sampled so many times. Are you tired of hearing it?

No, but I actually didn't care about that beat. People ask me to play "Funky Drummer" all the time, and I really don't know how it goes. It was just something I put together at that moment, and [people] took it and made a big thing out of it. There's a lot of other drum patterns in James Brown songs that I like better. "Cold Sweat," which is my favorite, "I Got the Feelin'," "Give It Up or Turn

(left to right) Bernard Odum, James Brown, Jab'O Starks, and Clyde Stubblefield at Criteria Studios, Miami, 1966. Photo courtesy of Alan Leeds.

It Loose." Those are drum patterns that I put together mentally. "Funky Drummer"—not much thought [went] into it.

Jim Payne's book *Give the Drummers Some!* briefly discusses the distinctive, quarter-note hi-hat style you first used on "Mother Popcorn" in an era when most drummers played steady, eighth-note hi-hat patterns. Was the use of that style in "Mother Popcorn" a conscious attempt to break the norm?

No, I just played what I felt. I don't know the difference between a whole note, half note, or quarter note. I don't read music. Notes look like Chinese writing to me.

But some of your drum patterns are available on sheet music. Who transcribed them?

Well, after I had played a few hits with Brown, some musicians from different schools of music wrote my drum patterns out. They could only write so much, 'cause I don't know what I'm doing, so they guessed at some of the stuff and whatever those sheets say, *they* know and I don't know. I'm like a chef or an artist; I add stuff as I go along. I might be playing a groove and decide I need a little more seasoning here, or some color over there. It's just a soul feeling.

I've read that James Brown could be difficult to work for. What was it like being a part of his band?

It was fabulous. We walked onstage to kick ass! We were like true soldiers: having fun offstage, but when we went on that stage, it was serious. Brown had a particular way he wanted things, and we wanted to perform the show the way he wanted it, so we didn't allow no mess from the band. The only thing I didn't get off on was the money he paid you. He wound up taking the majority of it back at the end of the week by fining you. If you missed a beat, or your shoes [weren't] shiny enough, or you did something wrong onstage, you'd

get a fine. Like, I'd be playing a song and I might get confused and hit a wrong beat. He'd turn around and do his fingers like five, ten, fifteen. That would be the fine and it came out of our money. We had to pay for our own dry cleaning and hotel out of our salary too—before we got our check. Other leading entertainers of the time did that too, or they would cuss out the band real bad. Brown was not a curser. If he was in one of his moods, he'd just fine you or tell you he was going to fire you, so I'm honored to have been around a person that didn't curse us out and treat us like a dog in that sense.

When you look back on your time spent with Brown, what are your fondest and least fond memories?

Playing with all the great musicians that I had a chance to play with, and the European and the Vietnam travels are my fondest memories. We did USO shows in Vietnam, and it was a gas to be over in the war playing music. It was an honor to go over there and entertain the American soldiers. But I still don't understand the war, and my least fond memory was when I was drafted. I was out in California playing with Brown, and the only way I got out of service was because Brown had a bodyguard who was a deputy sheriff. [His bodyguard] knew a lot of people in Washington D.C., and he called them on Brown's behalf and got me out of it. It's amazing, but other people owing each other favors got me out of service. It wasn't something I was really fighting against. If I had to go, then I would've went, but I just didn't understand it.

The rhythms you created for Brown's songs helped make him the most sampled artist in the world. How do you feel about being a part of that?

His music is the most sampled, but Jab'O's and my drumming is the most-sampled drums from his music, and [many] rap groups

used them to make their songs what they are. They knew it was James Brown's music, but they didn't inquire about who was playing the drums. They just paid James Brown the money, because he owns everything. He could put out a new album to this day and put some of our old stuff on it and we probably wouldn't know anything about it. I don't even know how many of his albums I'm on. Like the live recording at Madison Square Garden, he took songs from that and put them on an album called *Live in Dallas*. The songs would be switched around on albums, and sometimes he'd give the music to somebody else and they'd make a whole new song out of it. If we had been thinking, we probably could have gotten our drum patterns registered. I don't know how, but something could have happened so that we could have taken credit for them. Now I put all my patterns on sample CDs. A person can buy the CD and do what they want to with it, because they paid for the patterns. I can understand that. But if you're just taking a James Brown song and [lifting] my drum pattern off it, that's stealing.

Do you think that hip-hop artists and other recording artists should do more in terms of acknowledging the musicians they sample?

I think more of them should get on websites or magazines like this or radio talk shows and explain where they got their ideas. If they didn't use my drum patterns, then they used someone else's, but they probably don't acknowledge them either. Somebody sent me a list of all the people that's sampled my drum patterns. It's almost two hundred people and out of that many people no one's ever said, "Clyde Stubblefield." Sinead O'Connor came the closest when she came [to Madison]. I went to her show; she used "Funky Drummer" on one of her songs ["I Am Stretched on Your Grave"]. During the show she gave a shout out to "Madison's own original Funky Drummer," and the place just went crazy. As far as my name being on the record, I wasn't on there, but she gave me respect.

Do you like hip-hop?

I like the grooves of hip-hop. I play hip-hop with a group from Madison called the Crest. I play along to records. We might have a bass player or a guitar, but it's usually just me playing [along] with the records.

What kind of music do you usually listen to?

I mainly enjoy watching TV, but when I pull out something, I pull out a variety. I listen to country—people call me Clyde Pride, Charlie's cousin. I listen to blues, funk; I listen to a lot of the stuff I played on, so I can keep the feeling and get new ideas. Then I get tired of music and go watch TV for a long time. I don't let music be my life. Sometimes, it's too serious, and I don't want to get that serious.

How did the recent J.B.'s reunion album *Bring the Funk on Down* come about?

Fred Wesley was in control of the get-together, and he called everybody and asked [us] to bring two original tunes to record. We met up in Atlanta, Georgia, and I brought in a tune called "Born to Groove" written by Chris and Ann Plata, and a tune called "There's a Price to Pay to Live in Paradise" written by me and my wife, Jody Hannan. HBO had "There's a Price to Pay to Live in Paradise" up for [consideration] to be the theme for *The Wire*, but they used "Way Down in the Hole" by the Blind Boys of Alabama instead. But they did use a minute and forty seconds of the song in this episode where the drug dealers are setting up in this new section. It's playing in the background. I'm so proud for people to want my music on things like that. It's an honor, like when me and Jab'O were asked to put our sticks in the Hall of Fame. We never expected stuff like that, but the recognition makes us feel so good.

Despite your recent surgery, I know you're still quite active. What have you been up to lately?

Well, besides the Funkmasters CD, me and Jab'O have been doing a lot of drum clinics for our endorsers like Meinl cymbals, Vic Firth drumsticks, Remo heads, Odex microphones, and Yamaha drums. I recently did a session in New York with the Masters of Groove, which is Grant Green Jr. on guitar and Reuben Wilson on organ. Bernard Purdie used to play with them, but I think he's busy working on some other stuff so I'm taking over his position with them, and the album from that session's gonna be coming out soon. I also play with this group from [Madison] called the B3 Bombers. We recorded a hot CD called *Live at the Green Mill*. They are a great group and they have a totally different funk. Ben Sidran and his son Leo are producing a new album for me, and that'll be out in the spring. I've already been in the studio and recorded my part; now we're just working on getting other stuff on it. I still play drums [in the jazz trio] for Michael Feldman's *Whad'Ya Know?* radio show once a month, when the show [travels] to different cities all over the country. That's one of the greatest musical families I've ever been in, and we all have a great time together.

After I was diagnosed with bladder cancer—well, ten or twelve years ago—I went to a recording studio in Cottage Grove, which is a little town near Madison, and recorded some stuff but never went back to edit it or mix it down. The owner of the studio, Randy Green, called me recently and said he wanted to edit and mix all that stuff down and give it to me so I could use it as a fund-raiser for my cancer fund. He gave me the product and it is hot stuff. That's gonna come out in the next two to three months. Also, a lot of groups in Madison have put together shows where part of the proceeds are for my fund, and that's really typical of the people here—they are the greatest people I've ever met anywhere in my life. ◉

Originally appeared in Wax Poetics Issue 4, Spring 2003.

Jab'O Starks Don't Take No Mess

by Cherryl Aldave

"You're all man, Jab'O, you're all man." Now that's a compliment coming from anybody, but when it comes from the Godfather of Soul, you've got to be *somebody* that *nobody* should mess with. ¶ John "Jab'O" Starks is a bad man, no doubt about it. If the name isn't enough to clue you in—Jab'O, spelled to indicate Jab Oh!—he's one of the most sampled drummers in the world, and was behind the beats on more of James Brown's charting singles than any other drummer in the entirety of JB's career (his best friend Clyde Stubblefield holds the title of recording the most number-ones with Brown). Prior to joining Brown, Jab'O played drums for Bobby "Blue" Bland, lending his lightning snare, swinging cymbals, and meaty, insistent bass to Bland classics like "Turn on Your Lovelight," "Stormy Monday Blues," and "That's the Way Love Is." After leaving Brown in 1975, he traveled and recorded with B.B. King and currently resides in his hometown, Mobile, Alabama. ¶ Jab'O is quite gregarious, and an engaging conversationalist—just don't catch him when he's trying to catch some z's unless you want to get told! He doesn't hold back, and in this interview he speaks frankly and with authority on subjects from working with James Brown, to segregation, to how he feels about the state of contemporary urban music. After interviewing Jab'O and getting to know him a bit, I can't help but think about how well his personality fits the title of his last number one single with Brown—1974's "Papa Don't Take No Mess." »

What inspired you to start playing drums and how old were you when you started?

I can't tell you how old I was; I just know I was in the seventh grade of school. I'm from Mobile, and when they had Mardi Gras, I heard the marching band from Mobile County Training School. The drummer, Rudolph Files, I never will forget his name. Man, you could hear that whole drum section, and when he wasn't playing, you knew it. And as soon as he came in and started playing, it was just like, "Here I am. I am the commander of this drum thing." He took control and I followed that guy for like two miles just watching him play, and I said, "Man, I'd sure like to play like that."

And then did you get a drum set?

Nah, baby, in those years I couldn't afford a drum set. I couldn't even afford a snare drum. The school had a drum and I started beating on cans and pans and stuff at home and my mother raised the roof about me beating on everything. When I came out of junior high, when I was going to my freshman year of high school, during the summer before school started they had the guys that were trying out for the marching band and they [told them], "No freshman joins the marching band. You'll be part of the main band, but you won't make the marching band your first year." I went out for summer trials and I already had my mind set that I would be marching, I'd have a uniform, and I did and that was that. Then my band instructor said, "We're gonna get a little high school dance band and we want you to be the drummer." I was like, "Okay." We took the school snare drum and tied it to a chair; we took the bass drum, put it on the floor and put two bricks on [either] side of it; we went and got an old raggedy foot pedal from somebody; we took our marching cymbal apart and set it on an old stand and there we

where. My first set of drumsticks was made for me by an older man that was doing whittling.

Do you still have them?

No. I couldn't even tell you where they are. I finally got the shell and one of the tom-toms from my first little set from home, 'cause when I left home and went on the road with Bobby Bland, my mother told the guy on the next street, "He's not gonna want these drums anymore, so you can have them."

As a child, before you became a drummer, what did you think you were gonna be when you grew up?

Didn't know. My grandmother—she was the boss, and she had very different plans for me. My grandmother had plans that I was gonna graduate from college and more than likely I was gonna teach or somewhere in that line. My grandmother said, "You get the best education that you can get. Don't ask me how we gonna get the money; you figure out what school you want to go to, I'll see that you go to that school." That was Mama, that was her dream for me, and when she passed I had got to the third year in college. I didn't finish, you know. I wanted to play. I was fooling with music, and that's where I wanted to go.

Who are some of the great drummers that inspired you?

I had no formal training in playing drums, but I hear so much, and I pay attention to what other guys are doing and play it the way that I can play it. I heard shuffles from some of the best. Shep Shepherd years ago with Bill Doggett, or some drummers you would hear at blues gigs, and I couldn't do it the way they was doing it, so I did it my way, and that became my shuffle. I've heard quite a few drummers, and everybody has something different to offer. I've listened to Dave Weckl, Ed Shaughnessey, I've listened to what's-his-name that played with Count Basie: Sonny Payne. A lot of people. I just saw one of the finest jazz drummers I ever heard in my life, Elvin Jones, and I know Elvin personally. Elvin's seventy-five years old and still smoking. I saw him in January in Columbus, Ohio, 'cause we're with the same drum company, Yamaha. There's so many guys that don't have a name, will possibly never have a name. You just have to walk up in any city and listen to some guys play, then you can hear guys that's really smoking.

How'd you hook up with Bobby "Blue" Bland?

We had a local group in Mobile called the Castanets. I was playing with that group and Bobby Bland and Junior Parker came to town and went to Club Harlem, 'cause if you came to Mobile in those years, Tom Couch's Club Harlem, I don't care how big you were, if you were Black, you came there and worked for Tom Couch. Bobby and Junior was getting ready to break up. One was gonna keep the old band, one was getting ready to get a band of his own, and they wanted to hear us, so we went up and did an audition, and they left. I guess they was going back to Houston. They called back and asked if the band wanted to come on the road, and the guys were like, "No, we don't wanna go." They had their little girlfriends, and we were the hottest band in town so they said no. So they called back said, "Well, we didn't really want the whole band anyway—you reckon that drummer will want to come out?" Tom called me and said, "Would you like to go?" I said, "Yup! I sure would!" He said, "Well, get your stuff together, and they'll let you know where to come." I went and got a little plastic bag, put my clothes in it, and went to Houston to meet the band, and that's the way it started. That band changed after I got there—there were some personnel changes. I played a few gigs with them when Joe Scott, who did all the arranging for Duke/Peacock Records for Don Robey and a couple of other people, he took over to write for the

Illustration by Brad Howe.

March 1995 at a Chicago video shoot. Photo courtesy of Alan Leeds.

band, but that's the way it started.

Did Joe Scott or Bobby Bland have any influence on your drum patterns?

No. Nobody had any influence on my patterns. They'd say, "This is what we're playing. What do you hear to play this with?" And when I'd do it they'd say, "Yeah, we'll use that," and that's the way it was.

You went from playing local gigs to going on the road with one of the era's most popular stars. What was this like?

When I went with Bobby Bland it was really exciting. I had always played behind different artists—John Lee Hooker, Sonny Boy Williamson, Howling Wolf, Percy Mayfield, Gatemouth Brown. All of these people were brought into Mobile as a single artist, and the Castanets was the band that played behind them. With Bobby, I went on the road, and it was an honor. I had never traveled with a professional band other than our little group, especially someone with a professional name, and I had no problems. Bobby Bland, he and Junior Parker are the easiest-going people I've ever met. Bobby Bland is a real fine person. It was nice. I played behind quite a few people but when I was with Bobby Bland I did shows with most of your big stars. The Temptations—I had a cousin that was singing with them. Melvin, the bass singer. Melvin's from Mobile, the Drifters, the Chi-Lites, the Impressions, Otis Redding, Little Willie John, Maxine Brown, the "5" Royales… People don't even remember those people. Jackie Wilson…the last show that Sam Cooke did, we was on that show. It wasn't two months after that tour that he got killed. I knew all the old singers that was out there doing it. I knew Gladys and her brother and cousins, I just knew all of them. It was beautiful. I wouldn't give anything for the experience, for the people I met, the friends that I've got. Out there

in that world, all the Black artists, everybody got to know everybody. You had to. You ran into each other, you did shows together. I loved doing the Apollo and the Regal and the Royal, all of the East Coast theaters, till I got with James Brown. Then I got sick of them, 'cause I never worked that many shows in my life. James Brown was smoking. He could come offstage, you'd change clothes, and about thirty minutes later you're going back onstage again.

Like three shows a day?

Nah, baby, five shows. First time on the road we played the Carolinas. It was the first time I'd ever played in tobacco warehouses on the back of flatbed trailers. Then we got to play in the ballparks, then we started playing the big venues, but it was amazing. I learned a lot out there on that road with James.

How'd you go from Bland's band to Brown's?

Well, James Brown had heard me a couple of years before I even went with him. He came to hear us whenever we were in the same city, and he had been trying to get me to play with his band, but the Bobby Bland group was such a good group I didn't want to go nowhere. I didn't think I was ever going anywhere, but then I got married in '60, then a couple of years later the baby came. I needed to make more money. I had to get a raise, and they said, "We can't do that," and James offered me twice what I was making. I just told them in '65, "Well, that's it. I got to go. I've been offered better pay." And that's what it was about. I needed to make the money.

I know you're familiar with hip-hop and how some rappers are competitive to the point that it escalates to violence. Did these kinds of rivalries exist when you were playing with Bland and Brown?

No. You know what they did? They got onstage and said, "Watch this," and they did the best that they could do, then walk off and say,

(left to right) Bootsy Collins, Jab'O Starks, Johnny Griggs, and Clyde Stubblefield, 1970. Photo courtesy of Alan Leeds.

"Now you get with that." When James went onstage to entertain… I still say James can't sing a lick, but you don't beat James entertaining—you might as well do something else. You're not going to beat him being an entertainer. I used to watch Sammy Davis Jr.; that man could go onstage for an hour and a half with nobody but him and keep you spellbound the whole time. But that rivalry thing, I don't know where we get off having to hurt each other. There's enough hurt in the world, so why do we have to go around talking about killing each other, 'cause as soon as the war breaks out, you get over there, you start crying, scared to death but yet still you holler, "I'll kill you." What's the reason? Life is too short.

Do you like hip-hop?

I don't listen to a lot of it. Snoop Doggy, he did some things with Fred Wesley. Fred told me that Snoop knew who we were, and he wanted to do some things, and I said it was fine with me. I have nothing against hip-hop people. The only thing I have a problem with—degrading women and all the four-letter words. I don't see that as necessary.

Do you think it's easier to get involved with the music industry today or when you first started in the business?

It's hard to say. You had a lot of record companies that were grabbing artists and maybe putting one record out, but you still got a contract to hold them so they can't do anything else. Now, you don't really have to have talent for them to make you. It's about the dollar and how much they gonna spend to make you into what they call a star. When they make you, you're sitting down grinnin' and skinnin', but you don't have the perceptions of a businessperson and all of the money they spent. You gotta pay every dime of

that back before you make any money. So that means you got to go out on the road and the stuff that you got, if it doesn't show up [on the charts] six or seven months from now, what you had, or what you thought you had, they take that away! Think about Ray Charles. Ray Charles was not a dummy in the music world. They don't own Ray Charles; Ray Charles owns *all* his masters. I never will forget what Little Richard did. Little Richard was one of the first Black artists that incorporated his band. It was Little Richard and the Upsetters, but when you bought Little Richard, you had to buy the Upsetters separately, but he didn't come unless the Upsetters came, because it was his band! That's business, honey! Look at James Brown. James Brown had three offices when he was hot. When James was smoking, you couldn't book him, 'cause you didn't have enough money. You could promote him, but he booked himself, and that's business! Half of them now don't even know what they're making. You put all this stuff around you and you ride around in the car they done *leased* for you, and the next thing you know, you're not that hot person anymore. You have nothing and you wonder, "Where did it all go?"

How would you sum up your experience with James Brown? Was he difficult to work for?

My experience with James was…one of learning. I learned the entertainment business through doing some of the things he had me do, watching some things, listening to some things he would do. He was not difficult with *me* to work for, because we had an understanding. When I joined his organization, he explained what he wanted and what he didn't want. If you asked how much you were gonna make, he told you. If you didn't like that then you guys made an understanding as to what your fare was gonna be. A lot of people say, "If you didn't do this and that for James, he would fine you." I told him right off the bat, "I heard that you fine a lot of people. I don't pay fines." He looked at me real strange as if to say, "Well, what are you saying?" I said, "I don't pay fines. If you take my money, you're not taking money from me, you're taking it from my family. I don't go that route. You tell me what you want me to do and how you want me to do it, I'll do it, but so far as paying fines…" That was the understanding that we had. A lot of guys—even Clyde [told] me, "I didn't know you didn't pay fines." I was like, "No, I sure didn't!" You had to understand where James was coming from. The people that had to pay them fines, well, he told you that's the way he wanted it, and if they didn't do it that way, he fined them! I don't knock what he was doing, 'cause—figure this way—if you don't like what he's doing, then leave. When the whole band quit James, I would have left with the band, but I'm glad I didn't, 'cause so [many good] things happened to me afterwards. I had a contract with James. He broke his with me. I didn't break mine with him.

What was the contract for and what got broken?

I had a contract to work with James for *x* amount of time, then the contract also said that [he] was supposed to do this for me or do that for me, and a lot of it didn't happen. I called his attention [to it], and he said it [would] be taken care of but it never was.

What specifically wasn't provided to you that was in your contract?

I'd rather not go into all of that. I told him we didn't need a contract. I gave him my word, but he said, [*imitating James's rapid-fire growl*] "Nah, I gotta have this contract!" That was fine with me, but when the band left, I told him, "The only reason I didn't leave was because I had a contract with you." He said, "You're all man, Jab'O, you're all man."

Why did the band leave?

It was different things. It was the fining; it was the demands that he would put on different guys. Say you're off four days, we're gonna have rehearsals the second day that you're off, and that means people that lived in different places couldn't go home to a point, 'cause you had to stay there to do the rehearsal. Basically, they did not think that he was fair in what he was doing, so a lot of the guys gave him an ultimatum: "Either you change this way of doing it or we're gonna leave." James being James, he wasn't about to conform. That's when he sent for Bootsy and his brother and them. We [had] played Jacksonville, and the next show was in Columbus. James didn't want to lose all that stuff he had going so he said, "Okay, I'll give you guys my answer when we get to Columbus." We landed in Columbus, Georgia, the next day. When we got there everything was set up, the equipment that belonged to James, the amplifiers, but the guys still had their instruments, [and] they didn't take them out. They waited on him, but, at the time, you just didn't understand [that] James had sent for Bootsy and them the night before we even got to Columbus. He flew into Columbus and waited [while] his plane went to Cincinnati to pick those guys up. Then when he walked in, they said, "Well, Mr. Brown, have you decided?" He said, "Fellas, I just can't do that. I'm not gonna go that route." They said, "Okay, thank you…bye." They all took all their bags and instruments and they left. Everybody. The whole band except me.

How do you feel about so many of the drum patterns you played with Brown being sampled with little recognition and no financial compensation? Clyde told me Brown owns all the music.

It's an insult. You feel good that somebody thought enough about what you were doing to use [it], but I was always taught [that]

if you take something that does not belong to you, that's stealing. If you want what I have, the only thing you have to do is ask; [but] if we got paid for it, do you know Clyde and I would be pretty wealthy by now? But you don't even have the guys that'll put in their credits: "These patterns were taken from John 'Jab'O' Starks or from Clyde Stubblefield." All your artists, the first thing they'll talk about is "I want respect," but how can you get it if you don't give it? I'm not bitter; the good Lord has blessed me and I know it, but I just think musicians have been taken advantage of for so long that it's time something be done about it. So many years, a lot of your ideas have been used and, everybody comes up to you: "That's mine." That even happened with James. The guys in the rhythm section, we'd sit down and start playing a little groove together, and James comes in: "Yeah, I wanna hear, um…play that thing you were playing there. Yeah, I like that." And then he'd take that and try to add a tad here and there, but it's still your groove. Then he would say, "This is my stuff." We could go into that a long way but then again, hey.

You and Clyde are from the South; James is from the South. Why are most of the great African American musicians from the South?

Well…most of your Black families, somewhere down the line, that Black family is from the South. Regardless of what you say, you still have that Southern root in you.

A lot of people make fun of the South for some reason.

When you don't understand, you criticize. Ask them, "What do you know about the South?" *Well, it's segregated.* It is? It was… See, I came up in the segregated years, so I know exactly what went on. When I went on the road, I experienced it firsthand.

Will you tell me about it?

The summer of 1959, I went on the road with Bobby "Blue" Bland and Junior Parker. Before that I was playing in Black clubs ninety-eight percent of the time in Alabama. I went over to Mississippi and played on the coastline at colleges there…but you only got there in time enough to sit down and play, and they had little sandwiches and stuff they'd give you off in a little room that you'd use. You didn't do anything but play and leave. I never will forget, I went up "on the mountain," as they call it in Birmingham, and played at this golf club up there. The young man that had us up there, his father was a member. We were told by a White police officer, "I don't know who got you niggers up here. I don't know what you're doing up here. You got no business up here, but I tell you this much: one hour after you finish playing, I don't even want to know there was one of you niggers up here." We told the guy, and the guy's father ran the officer away from there and told him he would never work up there anymore, but that was a part of all that. When I first left home and went to Houston, Texas, to join Bobby Bland, I was told to get off the bus, get a taxi, and tell him you want to go to the Fifth Ward to Club Matinee. I [had] my plastic bag and my little ol' makeshift set of drums. I got in the taxi—he took me there, and I had never seen that before. It was in the Black part of town. It ran down after everything closed up over there, but that's where I saw a [Black] guy that had a tailor shop; the barbershop had five or six chairs in it and everybody was doing processes. I didn't have nothing but just a regular haircut. And [there was] good food. Some of the best food you ever wanted to eat, twenty-four hours a day, but it was still the Black part of town. You just didn't go over to the White part of town.

When [we] went on the road, we were playing the chitlin circuit. You played the entire South from Virginia down to Miami, all the way back across and around till you left Texas, and then you went to Arizona and California. It was a different world there. It was a little different on the East Coast too, but it was prevalent. There were the signs that said "colored water." I used to ask, "What color is it?" being comical, but it was colored water, colored restrooms. The colored restroom was used by men *and* women, *if* they had one. If you wanted a sandwich or something, they always had a sign that said "coloreds" that pointed to around back where there was a window where you were served from. There was some larger places that had a stool or two in the back, and somebody came from the kitchen, asked what you wanted, gave it to you, and you paid for it and left. There was the times you couldn't go into the department store and try anything on. Either you took it and left, or you didn't get it. If you were in town for a Black club owner, you played that job, but they would book you for a White club too. You went and played, then you left and came back. You didn't mingle. I never will forget—right out of Shreveport with Bobby and Junior—we had a dude tell us, "You niggers get that crap and get out of here!"—and he didn't call it crap. When we got through, we didn't even break our stuff down; we just loaded it up like it was and left, 'cause the man was serious.

They talk about the segregation; that's the way it was. Even with James Brown. I never will forget—Harley Beard was the bus driver—we left New Orleans, and at that time there wasn't interstates. Going from New Orleans to Memphis, you ran up Highway 61, and when we crossed out of Louisiana into Mississippi, there was a station that sold diesel on either side. We pulled in the first one, Harley got out, and when he put the thing in the tank, somebody said, "You got a bathroom?" He said, "I don't have no colored bathroom." Harley stopped the tank right there. I think he'd ran about two dollars worth of fuel in there. He paid him, and he said, "Hey, he doesn't have a *colored* bathroom"—and he underlined colored. The guys got right back on the bus; we pulled across the street. The guy at the other station, before we could say anything, he said, "I got a bathroom for men right here, for ladies right there, and if the ladies need some more room, they can go in my house, which is right here." Then he said, "Yeah, I get all of his colored business, because he does not have a bathroom that people can use. All I ask is leave the bathroom the way you find it. What else can you do but use the bathroom and come out?" We laughed at how he put it, 'cause that's the truth! What else can you do in a bathroom? We spent about four, five hundred dollars with that man in an hour.

Were there any other differences between playing for Black versus White audiences?

If you went to the West Coast or to the East, it was basically a mixed crowd anyway, but in the South you had a lot of Caucasians that enjoyed rock and roll. But you'd be surprised at how many folks love the blues. I want to tell you this, the blues, jazz, and the Black gospel, that's Black folks' music to the world, but do you know you can count the young Black kids today that know anything about the blues or the artists that did it? The first thing a young Black will tell you, "I don't like blues, 'cause they sad." Where you coming from, baby? How much swinging, good-groovin', booty-shakin' stuff do you get coming out of them blues? It's all there! I mean you can ask them to name a couple of blues artists. "Uh…B.B. King." But you can take a White kid, and he'll run them straight down the line! It's your music that you are giving away, and you don't know anything about it. And when these questions are asked, you look real dumb, 'cause you don't know. The older generation of Blacks in your Black homes, you listened to the Black music. You listened to Black choirs out of the church where most of the [Black] entertainers came from. Then the juke joints—every community almost had one, and if you

didn't hear some of them records being played on the jukeboxes, I don't know where you came from. You had to hear it, 'cause they'd have it going on the weekends, and you couldn't do nothing but hear that. Honey, if you don't teach coming out of your home, if you don't expose them to something other than a lot of the other things they hear you can't expect any better. I sit down sometimes and shake my head, and it's not only the Black kids. I just cannot understand how you can sit in a car and turn one of those radios up, and I can hear you a mile away. Not only the young men, the young ladies put the babies in the back and turn it up, and then you wonder why your child can't hear. That child cannot say his prayers, that child cannot say "thank you" or "please," but one of them tunes come on that kid can recite that entire tune and cannot even read or write his or her name.

In radio's early days, you didn't hear Black music unless it was on programs like the *King Biscuit Flour Hour*. In light of the struggle for mainstream airtime, what do you think about the state of urban radio today?

If you saturate me with this twenty-four hours a day, seven days a week, 365 days a year, I'm gonna start saying, "Oh man, I like that." What you have to start doing is getting away from that. There's more good music out there now then there ever was, and that's the reason I say if you don't like what you're hearing, open your mouth and say, "Wait a minute, why do you have to play this twenty-four hours a day?" If you stop listening to a lot of it and started listening to a different type of music, the radio will go to whatever you're going to. You control what they do. The rap artists—I don't put anybody down, but let me tell you one thing: it takes talent to sit down and write. Everybody can't write and the same stuff you write with the four letter words, you can sit down and write some of the most beautiful stuff. Look at Babyface, or look at Gamble and Huff. Look at all of the people that were writing before you got there were blessed with a talent to write some good stuff, and if you fail to do it, it's your fault. You're losing it, and that's what we're doing. We're losing it, baby, but that's the way it goes.

I know Clyde doesn't read music, but do you? Did you ever write out any of your drum patterns?

I wish I could write, and I can't, and the people that say that they can write my patterns, they can only write what they think they hear, 'cause I don't do the same things the same way all of the time. Basically, they say, "Well, I listened to this record, and this is the pattern he's playing on that record."

So you just remember them all? From all those songs?

I told you, I'm blessed. ⬤

Originally appeared in Wax Poetics Issue 5, Summer 2003.

For Sweet People
From Sweet Charles

by Matt Rowland

Nashville, Tennessee. Music City, USA, if you please. I certainly am pleased, because my hometown of the last seven years has proven to be a great resource for digging up and learning about music history. Contrary to popular belief, Nashville earned the title "Music City" way before it became a hub for the country-and-western recording industry. Fisk University's Jubilee Singers established the creative power as well as the commercial viability of African American music back in 1871, when choirmaster George White bravely took his septet of former slaves out on tour singing "spirituals" and smashing stereotypes about the potential for America's newly freed Black people. A huge success, Nashville's finest didn't stop until they had performed for the Queen of England and toured Europe. The music world would never be the same. ¶ A few blocks from Fisk lays Tennessee State University (TSU), where a certain drum major by the name of Charles Sherrell studied composition in the late '50s. Although his first instrument was the drums, Sherrell (aka "Sweets") picked up the guitar while washing Curtis Mayfield's Jaguar at the El Dorado Motel, where he did yard work. He switched to bass guitar while in the Air Force gigging at officers' clubs. Soon fate would lead him to Club Del Morocco down on Jefferson Street, where he would hone his performance chops in Johnny Jones's band alongside a young Jimi Hendrix, who was stationed at nearby Fort Campbell. Before long, Sherrell was touring with the likes of Aretha Franklin, Jackie Wilson, and the Drifters. »

Photos courtesy of Mickie Sherrell and the Joseph H. Davis Master Video & Film Collection.

By 1968, the soul music scene was changing for good. In July of that year, James Brown would come through Music City and recruit Sweet Charles, the first of a handful of Nashville musicians to join the Godfather's groove machine. After some brief consideration, Charles joined the James Brown Orchestra and—like the Jubilee Singers a century earlier—went out and changed the world.

Ever heard of a song called "Funky Drummer"? That's Sweets on bass there in the pocket with Clyde Stubblefield. "Soul Pride"… "Give It Up or Turn It Loose"…"Mother Popcorn"…"It's a New Day"…"Funky Drummer"…"The Payback"… Sweet Charles definitely stayed busy laying down the groove for many of the most seminal, monumental funk recordings of all time. After a break in 1971, he came back to join the J.B.'s in 1973, and stayed through the remainder of the decade. His 1974 LP on Brown's People label entitled *For Sweet People from Sweet Charles*, and a series of singles including the classic funky 45 "Hang Out and Hustle," gave Sweet Charles a chance to shine as a solo artist, writer, and arranger, thus securing his complete artistic legacy.

Mr. Sherrell's contributions to modern music are inarguable, especially when one considers that it was the electric bass that made this kind of music possible! Bassists like Sweet Charles and Larry Graham plugged into the funk vibe at a unique time when the bass player's newly electrified role was pushing dance music and rhythm and blues into a whole new realm. Within a decade of Leo Fender's development of the electric bass in 1953, the relationship of the rhythm section and the horns and other melodic instruments would fundamentally mutate into a new funky language. According to Quincy Jones, the electric bass forever "changed the sound of music.… The rhythm section became the stars." In other words, the bass player got down before the drummer would *ever* get some!

Knowing such a legacy had roots in my hometown, I knew I had to hook up with Sweet Charles the next time he came through. He now resides happily in the Netherlands, where he still records music and plays with the Dutch band Gotcha!, but was pleased to arrange a meeting in Nashville when he came to visit around holiday time. He brought along lifelong friend and James Brown bandmate, Joe Davis. Also a Nashville resident, Davis played trumpet with the James Brown Orchestra from 1968–1971 and was actually the first Black television producer in the city. These two soft-spoken gentlemen had plenty to say on music and life in the James Brown world, and I consider myself blessed to have had the opportunity to take it all in.

So tell me about growing up in Nashville.

I grew up around Pearl Street, which now is projects and stuff. I went to Beard School, Pearl Elementary School, Washington Junior High, and then Pearl High. And went to TSU for a minute.

How did you start out in music?

I actually started out playing in the first, second, third grade band. My music teacher was Andy Goodrich.

What was your first instrument?

Drums. Actually, I started to play the trombone, but that was too loud for my mom and dad.

Louder than the drums?

Yeah, because I really couldn't play it. It was a whole lot of *bllaahh*. Plus, the mouthpiece on the trombone at that time. It was so big, all up on top of my nose. So I put that away and started playing drums. At Pearl High School, I was drum major the whole time, also playing snare and timpani in the concert band.

What did your music teacher say about you back then?

If you're gonna stick to this for a future, you have to learn the basics first. And then study, experience, study, experience…keep learning, keep learning. Because you never stop learning. I'm still learning.

When did you start learning keyboards?

This organist at our church, Professor Scandricks, offered to give me private lessons at his house. I was out of school [TSU]. Before then, I was into concert music—Bach, Beethoven, Nocturne, you know. Because that was the kind of stuff we were playing. We went all the way through school together. [*pointing to Joe Davis*]

JOE DAVIS: Probably the most important thing I can say is that the man you're here to interview is the reason why I was ever included in a context like this, even though we came down the pike together. The teachers he was telling you about I was exposed to and trained by also. But had it not been for Charles, I never would have been exposed to that rock and roll, or rhythm and blues on the level of a James Brown. It's proven to be one of the best experiences of my life, even though I've gone on to have two or three other careers after that time.

So you were listening to classical. Who got you into that?

SWEETS: By playing that type music in high school and then listening to people like Roger Williams, when Ray Charles first come with the strings, Nat King Cole and people like that. I loved the sound of the music.

The arrangements…

I love arrangements. And I love violins. Because violins to me—it puts a cape on music. It makes it real angelic. It puts a spiritual thing into your body, if it's a good arrangement.

It comes through in your music. When did you get into the soul and R&B scene?

Curtis Mayfield and the Impressions were living in Chattanooga, Tennessee, but would record in Nashville. They would always stay at the El Dorado Motel, where I was keeping the grass cut and doing yard work. I washed his car and played around with his guitar. After that, I come out of school, my father passed. I went into the service to help my mom out.

That's in the early '60s?

Yeah. All this music was on the air bases that I was on. I formed a group. We were playing at the officers' clubs and stuff. That's when I picked up the bass. I said, "I think I can play bass."

So you moved from drums in the combo to the bass. How did you know that the bass would be an instrument that would take you places?

Because the bass to me is the foundation of any song. If the notes and the changes are played real good, you can feel the bass going through your body. That's when you touch people. When you feel that certain thang.

When was your first professional gig?

Some people came through Nashville looking for a backup band for Aretha Franklin and Jackie Wilson for the tour. So I knew this guy Johnny Jones who had a group called Johnny Jones and the King Kasuals. Him and Hendrix and everybody and Billy Cox [bass player with Jimi at Woodstock and in the Band of Gypsys].

So you played with Jimi Hendrix in Nashville?

Yeah. Club Del Morocco down on Jefferson Street. He lived here for a while.

That's hip.

Johnny found out I was pretty talented. I think it was through this friend of mine that also used to play with him, Waymon Reed [also a trumpet player with the James Brown Orchestra in the late '60s]. This would be 1967. They was playing everything. Had a good horn section, the Muscle Shoals Horns.

JOE: Johnny Jones is better known today as a blues guitar player.

Sweets and Maceo Parker lounging on the rooftop.

Really roots blues… *Real* blues. But rhythm and blues was getting bigger and bigger. Johnny Jones, he played it all. He was a band-leader. He organized groups and combos. Charles played with him, I played with him, locally and in an extended fashion—the chitlin circuit, as it was known back then. Johnny Jones had an organization that played at Fort Campbell, which was where Jimi Hendrix was enlisted. Hendrix was attempting to learn guitar, and Johnny Jones, Billy Cox, and those people were already at least semiprofessional, because they were entertaining the soldiers. And that's how they came to know each other. A lot of people credit Johnny Jones with being Jimi Hendrix's first guitar teacher.

SWEETS: We used to jam together in Club Del Morocco on Jefferson Street. Had to get out before five o'clock, because I was under age.

Man! So Aretha Franklin and Jackie Wilson came to town. Did you play on "Your Love Is Lifting Me Higher"?

I didn't play on the track, but in the show many times. It was a package show: Jackie Wilson, Aretha Franklin, the Drifters, Big Maybelle, Peg Leg Moffett, which was a guy who had a peg leg, right…but he tap-danced on one leg. Oh yeah, Curtis Mayfield and them—the Impressions.

Would you play with all those groups on that tour?
I think we did play behind all of them.

Did you graduate TSU?
No.

What was your concentration?

Arranging. Composition.

You played with the Past, Present and Future band in 1967?
Yeah, that group was a supergroup here in Nashville. I was a vocalist for the group. Every now and then I would play bass or drums on certain tunes that the drummer couldn't hack.

You had a 45 out…
I believe it was on Mecca. "Bones to Bones" was the hit, and then on the flip was "If I Only Had a Minute."

What made it a hit?
It was different. It was a different sound coming from White musicians. But that sound with my voice, it was different to people. It was a funk beat, sort of like hard-rockish beat, but the melody was sweet, the horns was *bat bat bat*, and then the way I was doing my voice…

So when did James Brown come and offer you a job?
July 1968. See what happened… He had me and my band [Past, Present and Future] to open up his show at Municipal Auditorium. He figured I didn't need to be there; I need to be over here. "You got too much soul to be over there! You're in Nashville. This is country; you're not going nowhere but to a farm." So I said, "Well, I'll tell you what… You give me a couple weeks to think about it." That pissed him off. Because he figured, "I'm James Brown. If I offer somebody a job, they should just jump right at it." But I wanted to think about it and think about my purpose for going out there with this guy that I didn't know, how I was gonna conduct myself. But I promised myself not to change me for nobody. So I said, "I'll just go out there as me."

If he does something that I think was disrespectful, I'll tell him.

When I first went out there, he had me sitting behind a set of drums. Waymon Reed told him I was a good drummer. He said, "He's a good musician." So the bass player he had, which was Tim Drummond [White bass player with the Dapps, plays bass on "I Can't Stand Myself (When You Touch Me)" and "Licking Stick – Licking Stick"], caught hepatitis [on tour in Vietnam] and came back. So James says, "You play bass?" I says, "Some." "We're going to find out. We're going to cut 'Black and Proud.' "

What had you heard about his style, his way of managing things?

Well, I heard that he was real, real firm on dress attire. I agree with that—with the fines and stuff. Because he used to buy all the uniforms, all the shoes, all the shoe trees, all the bow ties, everything. Everybody had their own stuff. He would get them cleaned. So if he would get them cleaned—I mean, you *should* look good onstage. Your stage appearance means a whole lot in show business. You go up there looking good, that's the first good impact you get on the crowd. And then you hit 'em in the jaw with the funk or the country or whatever…but if you look good, you're halfway there. Sometimes, the pay would be late. That used to bother me. To me, if the band hit on time, they should get paid on time.

What was it like playing on "Say It Loud – I'm Black and I'm Proud" in 1968?

Well, after I heard the words to it, it kind of frightened me, because you know at that time a whole lot of stuff was going on. Martin Luther King and all the riots and stuff. We've been playing, performing for all races of people—I've seen them in the crowd, you know. So [I'm thinking], "This is going to hurt him." Because you can't go to a concert and sit there and say, "Say it loud, I'm Black and I'm proud" if you're not Black or if you're not Mexican or whatever. You can't do that so you'd feel cheated, you know. That scared me. But James realized it too. Because all of a sudden his crowds started dropping off. He only did that song live maybe three or four times. Five at the most. Then he stopped doing it. For that reason.

How did the Black community at large at that time perceive that record?

The DJs of course went on it big time. It started selling. But I think that James made them stop selling the record. So we had to come up with some James Brown funk stuff. So that's when we did "Give It Up or Turnit a Loose"—stuff like that.

"Funky Drummer"?

Yeah. So we started cutting stuff like that. Then James went back to the DJs, played this, played this, and *boom*.

He just came out with the funk and blew everybody's mind, basically.

Yeah. Blew everybody's mind.

In that era, your first stint of playing and recording, you were on "Funky Drummer," which is one of the most sampled drumbeats ever.

I know it. I hear it all the time.

Often the musician's credits read, "Bass: Fred Thomas or Charles Sherrell." So you were both in the studio and whoever happened to be playing at the time…

Yeah, whoever played it more distinct and really brought the note out. Fred played real heavy, like on "Funky Good Time" [i.e. "Doin' It to Death"].

What song made you first realize the scope and power of what you and the James Brown funk movement were doing across the world? What made you first realize that nobody had created this funky sound before and that you all were making history?

"Mother Popcorn" was the song that I realized was a powerful movement in the James Brown groove machine. Heavy on the one with the bass drum. Bass guitar was on the "one and," horns on the "and two" of the beat, which made the track groovy and funky at the same time.

What kind of things did James Brown say to the band in order to impart his unique musical vision to the musicians in the studio when writing and recording? Because it seems to me that the song structures, the repetition of the beats on the one, the heaviness, the emphasis on the drums, the crazy way to play the guitar, all these things were a radical departure from convention. What was it like in the studio inventing this stuff?

Most of the ideas came from James Brown. He was a good dictator more than musician. He would make different sounds, and we were musically educated enough to turn the sounds he made into music. Myself, the drummers, the guitarist, we [were] like mechanics on a Rolls-Royce… Knowing how to make it run smooth. Being in the studio inventing this stuff was educational for all of us.

You split in 1971… Decided to take a break?

Yeah, if you want to call it a break. I split because of a business disagreement. Financial business disagreement. We were doing a thing in Vegas. And it was time to go home. James was in the casino gambling. We're outside waiting to get paid and go home. I got tired of waiting. I had a plane to catch, so I went in the casino and told his bodyguards, "Hey, we need to get paid. We need to go home." He says, "Don't bother me, I'm gambling." I said, "Okay." So I went out to the bus and got his bass, took his bass inside the casino and *busted* it. Right there. And says, "Can I get paid now?" And then I left.

And what did he do?

Looked at me like I was crazy. I left. A month later, Joe and Maceo and them left.

Yeah, that's history.

You know, if I work I want to get paid. Simple as that. I don't want nobody else's money. I just want mine. So to me, he was giving my money to those people. I wanted mine before they took it all.

You're gonna come back… But tell me more about that period. You worked with Marva Whitney and Lyn Collins. What was she like?

Marva…beautiful lady. Lyn Collins…beautiful people. No problem performing with them. The only problem that they had was satisfying Mr. Brown.

His perfectionism?

I wouldn't say perfectionist, because very few stuff that he did was with perfection. I mean whatever it is, is what it is. But I think it was the power…the power play of James Brown: You're gonna do what I say. I'm the boss. I'm James Brown. So he had that on the singers and some of the band members. He tried it with me a couple of times, but he saw that I wasn't biting, you know.

What was up with not getting any credit on the albums?

Like I said, with the power, with his name. He knew the people to play on. He was surprised that I had my music-business end on. Having stuff copyrighted, having my own publishing company. It just freaked him out.

That's one of the most important things.

That's the most important thing. But a lot of people were just so excited about being with James Brown, that he said, "Write me a tune." They'd do it and just give it to him. They wouldn't have no backup, no kind of legal protection like sending it to the Library of Congress or whatever or the publishing company. As soon as it's

Sweets singing at a Nashville R&B club in the '60s.

Sweets performing with the Majestics at Club Steal-Away in Nashville, pre-JB 1967.

finished in the studio, *that's* when you do it: the very next morning, when the mailman come.

Is that what you tried to do?

No. That's what I *did*. That's what I did. That part he didn't like about me. But he respected me for being like that, because most of the people out there let him get away with a lot of stuff. But just about all the stuff that I wrote and recorded with him together, we split publishing. I got mine. Except one tune, "Get Up Offa That Thing."

"…(Release the Pressure)"? That was 1976.

Oh man. Me and Jimmy Nolen come up with that tune down in Florida somewhere. Me and Jimmy Nolen come up with that. And James heard us playing it. He come into the dressing room, said, "What is that?" "It's a tune." "What is it?" "We call it 'Get Up Offa That Thing.' " "Yeah? Let me hear it! Sweets, you gotta help me with some words." "No problem. 'Get up off that thang / Dance and you'll feel better / Get up offa that thang / Try to release that pressure.'" Plus I'm singing on that cut with him! Answering him, you know. That's the only one… Him and Hal Neely [Starday-King], they did something with it and got it out there. Because the next day he booked the studios. Me and Jimmy Nolen, you know, cookin' and shit, then, *boom*, we cuttin' the tune. The next thing I know—'bout a week or two—it was out on the airwaves!

Before you came back to the James Brown camp in 1973, you were back with Past, Present and Future for a minute, back in Nashville.

Yeah, working with them. Working with a bunch of other people.

JOE: What we did together earliest after the group left James was the two albums we cut that were Nashville-oriented albums. Most of James's band left around the time Charles was describing in 1971 from the gig in Las Vegas. Although we stayed on the bus and went to Augusta [Georgia] and began to record there what came out to be the *Sex Machine* double LP. Part of the reason we left was because of the way we saw Charles getting treated. You know how members of a band kind of cult up together, and they feel like all for one and one for all. From time to time, James would have incidents with individuals. Like Charles said, he was a control freak and he liked for you to feel his power. And we would be watching as individuals somebody that was a part of our unit being misused and that kept us kind of down. We didn't like that. We all got fed up at the same time. Money was getting to be late; he had stopped paying for some things that he had been known to pay for, and things were changing. So we just decided we didn't want the unit tore up. We'd leave and go do something on our own. We met with James to discuss what we felt was fair treatment. And we disagreed. All we did was formalize a disagreement, and we left. We came to Nashville and cut an album. I feel like that was one place where my influence—right or wrong—was felt by a group of people that I held in high esteem: those band members. *They* were why I wanted to play with James Brown. I didn't necessarily want to play with or for or behind James Brown. I wanted to play with that damn *band*! That bad band! Just to tell the truth about it. So I identified more with them. I can appreciate James Brown. Like I said, it was the best part of my life. I have not [had] a high point like that since then, and I've been around, you know. I really treasured that period of time. But we left and we came to Nashville and we cut an album—Maceo and All the Kings Men *Doin' Their Own Thing*, which turned out to be the best album that we as that group did.

By 1973, it was the J.B.'s. What was it like playing with the new group?

SWEETS: It was all right. To me, I feel that the first James Brown

funk band that I went in had the baddest guitar player in the world: Jimmy Nolen. And Alphonse Kellum. And then me and Clyde and Jab'O and Melvin Parker [Maceo's brother]. With me coming back, those guys were glad to see me back, because I brought that *groove* back. I brought it back in there and kept it in there… until the milk turned sour again. You don't like drinking sour milk.

"Doin' It to Death." With the J.B.'s.

Fred played real heavy. My style of bass—I played notes and measures and bars where people wouldn't expect. I would play syncopation and then I would hold on the groove, and every now and then go somewhere where people wouldn't expect to hear something. That's the reason my style is different. It's not that I'm the best bass player in the world, because I don't think none of us will ever live to see the best, right? But I do what I do. I play the feel that God gave me, the gift to play and fill it up and make it different.

What led up to the *Sweet People* LP?

They released a couple things off the album as singles. I went out and did Soul Train a couple times. I did *Midnight Special*. I did Don Kirshner's *In Concert*. When I did *Midnight Special*, Wolfman Jack was the MC. The name Sweet Charles was given to me by James Brown and producer of *Soul Train*, Don Cornelius, because a group of ladies organized a Sweet Charles Fan Club in California.

Then James started asking me to do this, or do this, come up with a bass line for this and Fred Wesley and stuff. We went to Zaire and played for the fight—Muhammad Ali and George Foreman. They shot a movie of it; it's called *When We Were Kings*. It's a good one.

How did your record fit into the whole People vibe? It kind of stands out.

It's the only thing in there like it.

Right. Whose idea was it to come with an album like that?

Mine. Let me tell you how I got to do this album. At that time, Fred [Wesley] found out what a good medium—I won't say good, because I don't feel I'm good—I'm mediocre. I play what's needed. All right, so Fred found that out, right. So Fred said, "Sweets, we're going to run over these tunes. I know you know the lyrics." James's stuff. We're in A&R Studios [NYC] rehearsing these tunes. So while I was singing, the president of Polydor, Jerry Schoenbaum, walked in the studios looking for James. He heard me singing. He says, "Hey kid, what's your name?" I told him. He says, "My name is Jerry Schoenbaum. I'm the president of Polydor. You wanna do an album?" I said, "Yeah. With an *orchestra*." He says, "We can get what you want from the union. Come to the office after you finish with this. We're gonna have a talk." So I looked at Fred, I says, "You're going with me." Fred said, "Hell yeah! You know who that is?" I said, "He just told me: Jerry Schoenbaum." This was maybe in early 1974.

How did Dave Matthews get involved?

I knew Dave from Cincinnati. James always had Dave Matthews there at the [King] Studio. And then James had a group up there called the Dee Felice Trio. So it was Beau Dollar and those guys [the Dapps—James Brown's funky White protégés] and Dave Matthews, so I knew where he was at. So after I talked to Schoenbaum and told him, "I want an orchestra," he said, "What do you mean?" I said, "I want the harp, I want oboes, I want bassoons, I want French horns, and I want twenty-one violins. I want a full percussionist. I want Cornell Dupree on guitar. And if we can find Wilbur Bascomb or Gordon Edwards on bass."

So "Bad" Bascomb played bass? I just figured you played bass on—

No. Fred and I would sit in hotels all night drinking coffee, eating salads. We had manuscript paper all over the floor. I was all the way

Bobby Byrd and Sweet Charles hard at work in the studio control room.

over here; Fred was over here. I was writing what I wanted on this song, what changes, what riffs. Fred said, "Damn, Sweets, we need to call Dave Matthews if you want strings like that!" I said, "I want strings just like that. I don't care if you call Quincy Jones! I want *strings*! These peoples got *money*!" They come up to me, I didn't go to them. He said, "Okay, well, I'll call up there…" I says, "Call him! Tell him I want him. I want him for three weeks." It was me, Fred, and Dave Matthews in a hotel room with stuff all over the floor, drinking coffee, sometimes staying up all night, writing arrangements.

What was Dave Matthews like? A lot of people don't know much about him. He's a white dude from Louisville, Kentucky, right?

JOE: He's the funkiest, most *together* arranger/composer that I ever met through James Brown.

SWEETS: Me too.

People don't even know. There's a guy out today called Dave Matthews, and I'll say "Dave Matthews" and I'm not talking about today's Dave Matthews, I'm talking about *him*.

JOE: I know it. I remember running down to 328 Performance Hall [in Nashville], because I thought it was the Dave Matthews you're talking about, when this [new] Dave Matthews's career first started.

It sounds like the three of you really had a vision, and the musicians were following your vision. Because when I hear it, it sounds totally different than everything else to me. I'm hearing all those changes, like the little pause with the clarinets riff…

SWEETS: Yeah. Like on "Strangers in the Night." [*singing*] *Doo*

doo doo doon. Weird stuff.

One of my favorite cuts is "Dedicated to the One Love," which is like a 6/8 beat, but it's on the same album as "Soul Man," which is the heaviest funk beat. So you were really doing something different, bringing this sweet flavor with the really hard…

Yeah. And this other tune here, "Yes It's You." [*sings*] *"Doot. Chicka doo doot. Chicka doo doot."* They released that as a single and that thing went off! And they still playing that in discos all over Europe.

Were those the biggest records off this?

"Soul Man," "Yes It's You," and, believe it or not: "C'mon let me show you where it's at."

"I Like It Like That." Who did "Strangers in the Night" first?

You know, I really don't know. You see, the "Strangers in the Night" came from the time when I told you I used to listen to Roger Williams and people like that, Nat King Cole. And plus Dinah Washington—"This Bitter Earth" and all that shit. That's where the "Strangers in the Night" thing came to my brain. We *got* to do "Strangers in the Night." And Fred looked at me like I was crazy. I said, "We got to do it." You know, they played [that song] a lot too, because it was totally different than the normal "Strangers in the Night," the way Sinatra sang it.

What is it about singing in falsetto? How did you know that doing the whole *Sweet People* LP in falsetto was the right move?

Singing in falsetto is an ear-catching move, because you're not straining, plus you don't have to sing loud and hard. It's like people

Onstage with James Brown during the early '70s.

will listen if you talk to them in a normal tone, but if you yell at them, they don't. For the *Sweet People* LP, I wanted to sing to the people in a normal tone.

Let's see what else…

I wrote "Give the Woman a Chance" and "Treat Me Like a Man." The voice on the intro of the album was Fred Wesley.

The woman between the songs. Tell me about her. What's her name?

Vespa. She was the secretary at the recording studios. After we did the tracks, Fred said, "We need to put something totally different as a lead-in to each song. Think of something." So he called Vespa: "Vespa—come here, come here for a minute. Just put the phone on hold or whatever. Come here. Let me hear you say, [*whispering*] 'He's a sweet soul brother.' "

And she just…

"Say it exactly the way that you just said it. Can you do that again for us, please?" [*whispering*] "He's a sweet soul brother." *Boom.* And then after every song, he says, "Think of something else." And she starts, [*whispering*] "Tu amore. Je t'aime." …in different languages. And that freaked us out, but we let her go, because she was relating to other different races.

So what was the reaction to this album?

When we finished it, they were very pleased. I was truly satisfied with it. You know, sometimes when I listen to it, I say, "Oh, I should've done it like this." But it's today. I did this back in '74. So I

did it the way that I felt in '74. If I do some of these songs onstage, I do it exactly the way that I recorded it, but I put a little bit more *balls* in the song. You know, put the power in it. You up there with the horns and the guitars and stuff—you don't have an orchestra. But the band has still got to play the same arrangement and basically the same feel. But I have to bulk it up, you know.

It's the rarest People LP, isn't it? Was it moving units?

Man, you know what? When James did that deal with Polydor, that label [People] didn't have Polydor distributing it. To me, that really hurt the musicians and the artists that was on James's label. Because, say, if they wanted to release something off this album, they wouldn't call me, they would call the People label, which is James Brown. And then James would tell them do this and do this. If the thing was just strictly Polydor, then Polydor would have called the artist that James really [jerked] around financially. Taking what wasn't his, you know. But, it got me out there.

People was the most successful of any of his other little labels. It could have been worse. It's a miracle that it came together; it's pretty rare that an album with such a unique vision as yours and Fred Wesley's and Dave Matthews's would come out like this.

See, that shows the versatility in a musician, a bandleader, or arranger. You have to be able to—if you're going to classify yourself as an arranger—you have to be able to arrange any kind of song that they bring to you. Country, bluegrass, whatever… You got to be able to do that. Fred was good at it, you know. I was good at it, some

The mid-'70s, Sweet Charles Sherrell looking forward.

stuff. Pee Wee [Ellis]… And that's what freaked people *out* about this. "Fred is doing arrangements like *this*?" See, they was thinking the people that played with James is only people that can play funk! When you do stuff like this, this brings the truth out.

"Hang Out and Hustle." 1975. Did that have to do with the dance that was coming out?

No. At that time, that's when the disco thing started coming in, right? So I said, "I'm going to write a tune about me going to the disco, hanging out with my friends. That'll work." Yeah.

It's a pretty mean bass line. Did you play bass on that?

Yeah, I played bass on it. [*pulls out Naughty by Nature Poverty's Paradise*] This group here… You heard of that group? Did you know that they done "Hang Out and Hustle" on this album?

They sampled it? 1995.

I just found out about it three weeks ago. They got me singing "Hang out and hustle…"

Did you get paid?

No, I didn't. I called about this and asked, "Why didn't somebody contact me?" They said somebody *was* contacted. So what they did— they called James. So James okayed it, so I'm sure they wrote James a nice check. Because I was affiliated with the James Brown empire.

How did you get to the Netherlands?

The reason I moved to the Netherlands was because I had been going everywhere with James. And during the times that we played the Netherlands, it was a totally different atmosphere than playing

anywhere else in the world. People treat people like people. There's no guns in Holland. You don't hear sirens twenty-four hours a day. You barely hear a siren. If you do, it's because it's a bad wreck on the interstate. Plus, you don't see people's furniture and stuff set out on the street over there, because the government takes care of the people over there. You don't have nowhere to live? They give you a place to live, plus give you money. The tax over there is very high…but it's cool! Because you are well taken care of. You can go into any hospital without having to sit out and die out there in the lobby if your grandmama don't have American Express, you know what I'm saying? You can go to any hospital. No hospital turn nobody down. That's enough.

Give me one of the wildest memories from the late '60s, early '70s out on the road with James Brown—one of the highlights.

One of the wildest things that happened. First of all, James Brown—he's a strange guy. After all the stuff that I went through with him, I survived. Thank God. But if it hadn't been for James Brown, I feel there wouldn't have been a Sweet Charles. There's only one Sweet Charles. He took me all over the world. He gave me the exposure. The rest of what I do is left up to me. So I want to take my hat off to him for doing that. I want to make sure that's known. Now the wildest thing that happened. We did a job down at the stadium in Miami. Played after a football concert. Then we played a nice club right down where the boats are—the marina. Played two nights in this beautiful club in Miami, and the stadium. After the gig we was ready to get paid.

As usual.

Yeah, as usual. James was gone. He left that night after the show. Got on his private jet and took off. So then everybody was calling me, because they figured, "Man, Sweets will do anything. Anything!"

Was this before or after Las Vegas? What year was this?

This was in the '70s. Before I quit in '78. After I had written "Kiss of '77," so it had to have been around '78 or something. Everybody calling me: "Sweets, James and the payroll man—they're gone!" Gone! Didn't pay the band. So I looked out my window; I saw the bus still there, of course, and the equipment truck full of equipment. I had the room list of everybody. I called the guy that was driving the truck: "Come down here and bring me the key to the truck. I need to get a keyboard off the truck later on, and I got a song I need to write for James." He said, "Oh, okay, Sweets." Brought me a key, he said, "You want me to open it?" I said, "No, no, no, you go on back. I didn't mean to wake you up. I'll get it and I'll bring the key back." Called the bus driver: "Hey man, I need to get something from underneath the bus. I got to get some books that I'm supposed to give some DJs that's going to come by. For James." The bus driver came down and brought me the bus key. I said, "Go on back to bed." I took the keys to his bus and to his truck with all the equipment, put them in my pocket. I called him [James] and I says, "I have the keys to your bus. I have the keys to your truck, and it's going to be mine unless you bring that money down here and pay us. Why did you do us like this? Now we're in a hotel, we don't know how we're going to get out of here. But I have the keys to your bus—if I have to sell this bus and your truck with the equipment, that's what I'm gonna do!" And I hung up the phone. I took the band… I called this guy, the promoter that booked the other gigs for James. I called him and let him know what happened. I said, "Man, I now have the band. The name of the band now is the Nuclear Explosions!" And people…freaked…out. So of course he sent a couple of big guys down there to Miami to get me and get the keys back to his bus. Big guys. But I also talked to the promoter and told him, "Call the highway patrol and the state troopers and have them over here." I told him what was going down, and I said, "I have a feeling that James is going to send some goons down here to get me." When they came in, guess who met them at the front door? The highway patrol and the state troopers. "You boys here for something? You here to see somebody?" "Yeah, we here to see…" They said, "Yeah, we know. What you want? What you want? You got any money with you? Well, if you don't, get your ass back up. *Nobody* is touching Charles. If you don't have the money, get your asses back in them cars, and we'll escort you back."

How many guys was it, just two?

It was three guys. Big guys. One of them used to play with James. He's dead now. He was a drummer. His name was Clayton Fillyau. You probably seen his name. He was the drummer playing on that first James Brown *Live at the Apollo*. Big guy, good drummer. Him and a couple others.

What happened then?

So I talked to the promoter and said, "Look. The band is now called the Nuclear Explosions, so find a club for us to work so we can pay the hotel bills and move on." So he did. We worked a club down there like three nights, and he paid us. And then I contacted some other people in Guadalupe. Called them and had them to book us over there. I took the band to Guadalupe for like two or three weeks.

Where is that?

One of them islands.

In the Atlantic?

Yeah, it's a nice place. They have a Club Med. It was great.

What happened after that? What did James do?

Well, he sent me money. He finally sent me money. We didn't have no argument about it at all. No bad words. He sent the money. I gave the guys a piece. Returned the truck and the bus after we flew back into Miami from Guadalupe. They wired me the money. And so the band went back. He walked up, "Sweets! How you doing?" I said, "I'm fine, how you doing? Good to see you."

That's it?

That's it.

To wrap up… What is funky music? What is soul music? What were you feeling back then, because you all were inventing this rhythm that's now taken over the world. The rhythm on the one.

The rhythm that we created back then had a couple of things about it. It was heavy. It was good and danceable. The feel of the rhythm then was funky, and it was consistent.

You could nod your head to it.

Yeah, to where you could just be in a car and bang your head on the dashboard, you understand? James Brown's funk thing that we had was consistent. It'd just drive people.

Yeah, you could play James Brown records all day—

All week!

—and not stop nodding your head!

Yeah, so it's the type of rhythm that relaxes the mind. Plus, it makes you think. Because once you start doing this [*nods head*], you get into a different rhythm, and then you gonna think about something that's positive. So our groove was a groove that kept people focused.

I find it helps me focus, personally.

Yeah. It's all true. One thing I found out, when you tell the truth, you don't have to think about it twice. If you tell a lie, if you say it again, you gotta say the exact thing, and that's kind of hard to do. I want to thank you for taking your time out and contacting me. I've been around for a long time, thank God. I want to thank you for being into our music, our history. I want you to make sure that you mention [Joe Davis], because we grew up together. We went all the way, I mean *all* the way together. When I got wind that James needed a trumpet player, I told James, "I got a trumpet player in Nashville. This is my man!"

JOE: The real truth is that Charles Sherrell…everybody didn't know this, but he had a side job when he was working for James Brown. He was the unemployment bureau for the James Brown organization. And James had a penchant toward Nashville musicians. I guess he was caught under the "Music City USA" concept.

The rhinestones and whatnot…

JOE: He had a preference—because he had a good experience with people like Charles—for Nashville musicians. That made it easy for people like me to go out there and do well. But I still wouldn't have been able to do it without Charles. And every other musician who was from Nashville, who played for James at any time after Charles went out there, was recommended by Charles Sherrell. So Charles has always promoted Nashville as a city.

Nashville's pretty cool.

SWEETS: Yeah, it's a great place. ⊙

Originally appeared in Wax Poetics Issue 5, Summer 2003.

Live and Lowdown
with Marva Whitney

article by Josh Powers

Marva Whitney helped shape some of hip-hop's greatest classics without knowing it. The music contained on *It's My Thing, Live and Lowdown at the Apollo*, and her 7-inch releases on King and Forte have provided beats for the 45 King, Stetsasonic, Public Enemy, EPMD, and N.W.A., to name a few. As a featured vocalist for James Brown, she played with many of the musicians we now credit as the founders of funk, while contributing a singular vocal style to everything she did. Graciously inviting me to her home, Marva sets us straight on Mr. Brown, the mysterious MJC label, and the early days. ¶ "I started out in the church," Marva begins. "My mother and father, we had a group called the Manning Gospel Singers. Then from there I went to the Whitney Singers. She was a young lady, who worked with children, by the name of Elma Whitney. She still has one of the hottest gospel groups here in [Kansas City] and is known throughout the United States. I joined them and became a Whitney-ette, which was kids four through ten [years old]. Then you became a Whitney Special, and then, when she thought you were good enough, you became a Whitney Singer. I've played piano since the age of nine. One day, my mother stuck me out there at church, and I was scared to death, but I made ten dollars! Which was a lot of money in those days!" »

Before we get to your time with James Brown, tell us how you got into soul music.

I was the piano player for a girls' rock-and-roll group; I can't recall the group's name. I had been out of school for about a year, while the other girls were still in high school at Central High. One of the girls—her name at the time was Brenda Patterson—went on to marry Donald Cox; so as the girls started to get married, they lost interest in practicing and playing.

Now, my first break came from Bobby "Blue" Bland. His booker, Willie Cyrus, who was considered a heavyweight in those days, knew I was working with Tommy and the Derbies and had seen us and knew we could hold our own with the best of those who came through. Those were the times that we were playing with Dionne Warwick, Betty Everrett, Ike and Tina Turner. When they came through [Kansas City] we would be the opening-up group for them. I was going by Marvelous Marva, not Marva Whitney, at that time, because at that time the Derbies were on a level, and we had such a following that we knew you had to have a show. See, in those days, people expected to see beauty, to see something grandiose, so you had to have a *show*! We thought that we were just that good so we decided to go out to California, to make it big. We went out to California and just about starved to death! I tell you the truth! We found out the best places were clique-ish, and they wouldn't let us through. Now, my mother and father taught me that there is honor in work, so I went to a temporary agency out there and got work as a key punch operator! And we ate! Jobs were few and far between.

Now, we found out that a few doors down from where we were staying was a place called Little Richard Arms that was Little Richard's apartment building where he stayed. Through Bumps Blackwell, somehow [Little Richard] found out about us and saw us play. He fell in love with me. He said, "I got to make a trip to Detroit, but when I come back, I'm going to make you a star." *Okay.* He did exactly what he said, only he wanted only me and not the Derbies! The group said, "See you later, Marva," but I changed my mind, and we came back to Kansas City. So, before I got to James, I had two opportunities—with Bobby Bland and Little Richard—that didn't work out.

So when did James come into the picture?

I had gotten involved with a gentleman by the name of Clarence Cooper, God rest his soul; he left us about six months ago. He had set me up with a Mr. Ben Bart, who was the owner of Universal Attractions. They had the label called Smash, and James was at that time managed by Ben Bart. Mr. Cooper had arranged for me to have an audition with Mr. Bart so I could get under his management.

Now, one time, Mr. Brown came here, and a riot broke out! They got to arguing over who was the best dancer! So I'm sitting around, waiting for Mr. Bart, and they get to fighting. That was the end of that! I never got to get with Mr. Bart. So we go home, and there goes my chance again.

But Clarence kept up, and he had good connections. Now, James used to come to K.C. at least twice a year at that particular time, and the next time he came around, he played two shows on the Kansas side. I'm at home minding my business. I had no intent of going. I get a call from Clarence, and he says he wants me to come and audition to go out on the road with the James Brown Show. I said, "I ain't got no stockings, and I don't have any money!" He said, "Don't you worry about a thing." So I put on a dress, got pretty, and went on down there.

Now, I thought he would have me audition between the two shows. It gets to the middle of the show, and James don't call me. That joker made me wait till midnight, when the show was over!

Alfred "Pee Wee" Ellis was the band director at the time, and he was the one who had to tell if I could sing or not. So he takes me through the gamut. And they had it on a Mickey Mouse little tape; he went to give it to Mr. Brown. So [James Brown] listens to it back in the dressing room, and Pee Wee comes out and says that Mr. Brown wants to see me.

So you were about to get some heavy news!

Well, James said, "Can you catch a flight to Cincinnati tomorrow, to cut a record?" I said, "Yes, Mr. Brown!" But unbeknownst to me, I was supposed to be under Mr. Bart, with James producing, but James convinced Clarence that I should be managed by him.

So you went to Cincinnati...

Right. And that was the first time I'd heard about things being "in the can." The first songs we did in the can were "Saving My Love for My Baby" and "Your Love Was Good for Me." But see the thing about songs being on tape in the can is it may not be your key! James has an altogether different—see, I was used to things being rehearsed, but with James it was on the spot. So I get the words in front of me, maybe take the track down twice, if the key ain't right, that don't mean a thing, you got to get it. That was my time, so I tried to make the best of it. That's how we got started.

How was your relationship with James? He's known to be difficult; did you get along?

[*pauses*] Yes and no. James taught us a whole lot, and I'm most grateful. He taught us punctuality. He taught us that being together in dress, in what you say, in how you present yourself, was just as important as how you were on stage. I remember one time I had a wrinkle in the back of my dress, and I got a fine of fifty or seventy-five dollars! He was the kind that if the show started at eight, you were there at six thirty. Sometimes he could have a bad day. He didn't have to say a thing; you just got out of his way!

You know, James kept his eyes on the market, and if someone was rising up, he had to come back with something. Which is why we came up with "It's My Thing"; because the Isley Brothers were doing so well with "It's Your Thing"!

It's interesting that on the credits to "It's My Thing" the Isley's are given as the writers of the song, when your version doesn't really bear any resemblance to "It's Your Thing."

Well, at first, I was listed as the songwriter, but they didn't have their business straight, so it wound up being listed as an Isley Brothers song. Mr. Brown wrote the music, and, on the way to the studio, he told me to come up with the answer to "It's Your Thing," and I did.

Do you still keep in contact with anyone from the day?

Oh yeah. Martha High. Lyn Collins, who is a beautiful person, a real brain; she should have been an attorney! I speak with her almost every day. She is a real, righteous person. We've supported each other since we've known each other. Speaking of Lyn, did you know that *Think* was recorded here in K.C., at the caves?

The caves that the Custom Cavern Sounds label used to use?

Yeah! Right here in my hometown! In fact, if you listen real close on "The Big Payback," which was also recorded here, James says "Hey, Marva, the Big Payback!" because I was there.

You know I was on T-Neck? "Giving Up on Love" and all that was the best stuff I ever did, because it wasn't a James Brown production. It shows me on my own.

That's a hard one to find.

I know. I can't find it myself.

Can you tell us about the MJC [Marva, James, Cooper] label? Many don't know that Louis Chechere's classic "The Hen" came out on MJC before it came out on Forte and Paula.

That was Clarence Cooper, my former manager. I knew nothing about that until after the fact. He kind of just slid that out. I'd like to know about it, since my name is on it. I'd like to know if there were any other releases.

So would a lot of people. Tell us about Forte and Ellis Taylor.

Well, after King, I was in K.C. and Ellis was an engineer at Channel 9. He had Forte records. We got together, and that's when I became Marva Whitney-Taylor. I came to Forte, because, at that time, I couldn't seem to get anything else going.

That was the single "Daddy Don't Know About Sugarbear" backed with "We Need More" with Ellis "Gripey" Taylor.

Yes, and it's funny, when I went to England in 1988, everyone wanted to know, "Where's Gripey Taylor?"

Well, what's he up to?

He's retired. He kind of keeps to himself.

So the timeline for your releases would have been King, Forte, then T-Neck?

That's correct, but I also did an album for the Nashboro label, with Oliver Sain as the producer, in St. Louis, that was never released in the U.S., only in Europe. Incidentally, all my stuff is owned by Polygram, and they lease it out to other labels. Right now, Soul City records has rereleased *It's My Thing* and *Live and Lowdown at the Apollo* on vinyl and CD.

Now, I don't want to touch on any sore spots, but what are your feelings on being sampled? As I'm sure you know, you've been sampled by N.W.A., Public Enemy, EPMD…

"The 900 Number"…oh yeah. Myself, Lyn Collins, James Brown—we are the most sampled artists ever. And I never got paid. Never! Lyn had the same problem with "It Takes Two." That record sold over a million copies, and she never saw a dime. I'm glad that people like what I do, but I'd like to get paid.

Was that money going to James Brown, or was it a situation where the sample was never cleared, and there was no one to catch it?

Well, probably both. But myself, Lyn Collins, Martha High, we would like to get paid. But I have faith it will work out in the end. ◗

Originally appeared in Wax Poetics Issue 3, Fall 2002.

Make Checks Payable to Charles Mingus

by Karl Hagstrom Miller

Vinyl-heads can smell hard times. Crumbling economies, failed businesses, skyrocketing rents: each loose coveted vinyl from the crannies and basement storage units they have inhabited for decades. Plant closed? Let me check out the garage sales. Independent record store gone bankrupt? The mother lode. Hands tremble flipping through pristine plastic. The search for oddball records has two cardinal rules: read the transformations of class in the United States, and know that race has everything to do with these transformations. Don't be late. Hit the right place at the wrong time. We all know this. Suburban thrift stores are typically good for REO and Bob Seger. Gentrifying neighborhoods cause Pete Rodriguez or Doug Carn to float to the surface—for a song. Desperation is the friend of the record collector. Hipness depends on finding a population aggrieved enough to produce good music, suddenly pushed to the point of parting with it. ¶ Case in point: Catskill, New York. The sleepy town of Catskill shares little with its riverfront neighbor, Hudson. The latter's volatile swing from de-industrialized cement town to destination of White flight at least means people are on the streets. The main drag boasts high-end antique shops and the sure sign that the choice vinyl is gone: gourmet coffee. Hudson is currently the sight of a bitter debate about the return of a major cement plant. Many new arrivals fear that the clouds of white dust will drive away the tourists and settle like a perpetual blanket on their houses and cars. Many old timers fondly remember when cement jobs enabled them to have houses and cars. »

Catskill has not had Hudson's one-sided resurgence. Driving up Highway 9W in 1996, one first encountered the dormant cement plant. Main Street boarded up. Unemployment rampant. Catskill was a ghost. The only businesses doing any business were on the edge of town: a tattoo parlor and two unassuming junk shops, one selling antique housewares, the other stuffed to the gills with records. It was my favorite kind of shop: volume without design. I couldn't walk down the aisles of the small store. Dusty records and a few odd books were stacked precariously everywhere I looked. Slowly making my way through the merchandise, I unpiled half-filled boxes and loose platters to get to what was underneath. I kept asking the aging owner what he wanted for different discs, and after a series of similar responses I caught the pattern. Everything was eight dollars a pop. *Rumors*—dozens, at eight dollars a pop. Rufus—ditto. Twenty thousand or so records all priced the same. A virgin copy of *Gunfighter Ballads* made me hesitate, but, you know, one only needs so many versions of "Cool Water," and I have to *really* like a record to lay down eight bucks.

After about an hour of sifting through shifting piles without much to show, I came across a small collection of jazz discs. Several Miles reissues—*At Fillmore* was a bargain at the set price. Underneath were three records in unassuming tan covers with black printing. On the back of each, in small type, was the following message:

> This album can be purchased only by mail through the address below and any other form of sale is unauthorized. Send your order and remittance directly to: **Charles Mingus Enterprises, Inc., P.O. Box 2637, Grand Central Station, New York, New York 10017.**

Titles traced life on the road: *Mingus at Monterey; Music Written for Monterey, 1965. Not Heard…Played in Its Entirety at UCLA, Vols. 1 and 2*; and *My Favorite Quintet*, recorded live at Minneapolis's Guthrie Theater. Eight bucks apiece brought them home.

The three albums told two stories. One was the hard times that brought them to the proprietor. Junk shops often speak the passion of their owners: vinyl, artwork, military gear. But just as often they collect freight tossed overboard to ease the load. The thousands of albums witnessed people on the move—dislocated and traveling light, leaving the accumulated contents of their homes behind.

The second story was just as much about hard times. Charles Mingus Enterprises was the escape plan of a trapped man.

Mingus, who died of Lou Gehrig's disease at the age of fifty-seven in 1979, was one of the great composers of the century. Doubters and revelers can check out grand opuses "Half-Mast Inhibition," "The Shoes of the Fisherman's Wife Are Some Jive Ass Slippers," and "Far Wells, Mill Valley," among countless others. Or dive into the smaller group improvs. "Fables of Faubus" and "Meditations" were spontaneous compositions in his book, starkly different every time they were performed, crackling with new beats, growls—even fresh forms—inspired and executed in the moment. Elements of baroque and stride piano, Dixieland, Duke, gutbucket, gospel, and atonal wails swirled together in a single song, shattering conceptions of separate genres or styles. Mingus had the unique genius of playing music history and making music history at the same time. And his music swung—*or not*. It was accessible—*or not*—according to his extraordinary vision.

Yet, Mingus the great composer could not pay the bills. He perpetually struggled to make money with his music, even as he saw record executives, concert promoters, and younger, less visionary

artists—most of them White—taking cash to the bank. Mingus's life was a roadmap of the intersections of race and economics in the U.S. music industry. The very decision to pick up the bass—an instrument he would quickly push beyond the groundbreaking role pioneered by his hero, Jimmy Blanton—was motivated by race and money. When he met lifelong friend Buddy Collette, young and awkward Mingus was playing cello in his Los Angeles high school orchestra. According to his autobiography, Mingus caught flack from the elder sax player:

"How'd you like to make bread and wear the sharpest clothes in the latest styles?" Buddy asked… "Go get yourself a bass and we'll put you in our Union swing band…"

"Get a bass?"

"That's right. You're black. You'll never make it in classical music no matter how good you are. You want to play, you gotta play a *Negro* instrument. You can't slap a cello, so you gotta learn to *slap that bass*, Charlie!"[1]

Mingus took his friend's advice and got paid. He carted his bass around town, studying with jazz and classical players and practicing even as he rode the trolley back home to Watts. By the early 1940s, he was making dates and a name for himself around the jazz and early R&B scene down Central Avenue, the heart of Black nightlife in Los Angeles. When the wartime recording ban ended, the aspiring musician cast his lot with a series of similarly aspiring local labels. They were looking for jukebox hits. He penned pop-inspired dance tunes such as "The Texas Hop," and "Baby, Take a Chance on Me." Yet he also nodded to the off-kilter harmonies that would dominate his later work with the austere "Weird Nightmare" and brooding arrangements of pop songs "Pennies from Heaven" and "These Foolish Things."[2] Not your average nickel-in-the-slot selections. Mingus wanted to make money with his music, so he dove into the waters open to Black musicians of the era. He played bass. He played jazz. But he insisted on twisting both beyond convention to accommodate the sounds swirling in his head. He was not getting rich.

Mingus picked up the pace. He backed Lionel Hampton. He appreciated the exposure but was frustrated by what he considered his leader's Tomming, not to mention Hampton's insistence on maintaining the publishing rights to tunes Mingus wrote. He left. He needed to get paid. Prestige Records offered to record him for ten bucks and some coke. He left. He toured with Red Norvo and Tal Farlow—an interracial trio that did not make waves due to Mingus's light skin. Then a New York TV producer insisted on using union members. Black musicians had a hard time with the New York union. Norvo, after protesting, replaced him with a White guy. He left, but not without making the most of it. Filing a grievance against Local 802, Mingus won a $500 settlement. After his mother-in-law tossed in another $600, Mingus started his own label with friend Max Roach. They called it Debut Records. It was 1952.[3]

Debut joined a small but vital tradition of Black artists going into business for themselves. Almost as soon as Black musicians caught the notice of existing labels, (signified by Mamie Smith's "Crazy Blues" in 1920), Black entrepreneurs started up their own. They were putting the tenets of Black Nationalism into practice. Harry Pace and W. C. Handy founded Black Swan in 1921. They advertised in the national Black voice, the *Chicago Defender*, telling readers to buy "the Only Genuine Colored Record. Others Are Only Passing for Colored." Black Swan's bread and butter was the blues. Yet Pace and Handy were more interested in showcasing Black classical musicians—artists who were still systematically excluded from major concert venues and recording studios. Black Swan was about

access as much as art—money as much as racial uplift. After pulling in over $100,000 in 1921, Black Swan spiraled into debt. They sold their extensive catalog to a White-owned competitor three years later. Other Black-owned labels with names like Sunshine and Meritt came and went as quickly. Later, trumpeter Dizzy Gillespie gave it a shot with his own Dee Gee Records. Again, the label folded in a few years. It was hard to fight the majors.[4]

By the time Mingus and Roach organized Debut Records, the bassist had dived deep into bebop—the frenetic, modernist riff that reclaimed jazz from White swing kings by injecting it with equal parts church, Debussy, and improvisational fire. Bop was suffering the same cultural whiplash that had afflicted swing. One moment, Black innovators such as Gillespie, Charlie Parker, and Kenny Clarke were working under the radar, brewing new sounds in Harlem after-hours clubs. With the nation's ear still tuned to swing, they were not getting paid. The next moment, bebop was the rage. It was the soundtrack to White beatnik escapades, fashion shows, and Jiffy-Pop commercials. The innovators were still not getting paid. Debut offered a solution. As Roach recalled, "Nobody was beating down our doors to ask what we were doing. The only way to make records under our own names was to start our own company."[5] Ownership meant reaping the profits from the sale of one's music, not just the one-off payments per selection or the miniscule royalty rates offered by the major labels. It could mean a living. As Mingus quickly discovered, it also meant navigating an apartment overrun by product, licking a lot of mailing labels, and bothering record stores to pay up.

Debut had a nice run. They released several records by the likes of J. J. Johnson, Clifford Brown, and Quincy Jones. Their masterstroke became one of the landmark documents of the bebop era, *Quintet of the Year*, featuring Mingus, Roach, Parker, Gillespie, and pianist Bud Powell. Yet even this victory carried the mark of the trials that had convinced Mingus and Roach to go independent in the first place. Due to contractual obligations, Parker had to use a pseudonym. The local union asserted its control and tried to stop the release of the renegade recordings. And lacking the muscle of the majors, Debut could not get local distributors to pay for the product they had already sold.[6] Debut lasted until 1958, when it collapsed in a heap of uncollected payments and artists' royalty demands.

Meanwhile, Mingus had been gaining a foothold within the larger music industry. His compositional chops were expanding—check out 1956's "Pithecanthropus Erectus" or 1957's "Reincarnation of a Lovebird." He found his ultimate rhythm-section partner in drummer Dannie Richmond. His relentless gigging and recording for various labels, especially a young Atlantic, eventually brought him promising sessions with the behemoth Columbia Records. His initial release for Columbia was a breakout produced by Teo Macero, a Debut alum and future tape-splicer for Miles Davis's electric masterpieces. *Mingus Ah Um* gave the bassist some economic breathing room. With Columbia's marketing power behind it, the record sold much better than his previous releases. It even garnered a hit with album-opener "Better Git It in Your Soul," a rousing gospel-drenched shuffle complete with hand-clapping chorus and, not one, but two, drum breaks. "Boogie Stop Shuffle" hit even harder, recollecting earlier grooves such as "The Texas Hop." Mingus was a name. He started living well. Yet, once again, he found his label frustrating his success. Columbia disputed the sales figures for *Mingus Ah Um*, claiming the album sold a paltry three thousand copies. They suggested the album had been bootlegged.[7] Mingus was enraged.

He took things into his own hands. Charles Mingus Enterprises was going to do it right. He set it up as a mail order business. No majors. No distributors. No retailers. Nobody touching the money passing between the consumer and the composer. He took out ads in music magazines such as *Coda* and the *Village Voice*. They were as much editorial wail as sales pitch. "Among the causes of deprivation in which most musicians live are the avarice and corruption existing in the big business of record companies and their cohorts...I am doing something more to help free the next, younger generation of jazz music...LEGAL NOTICE: $500 for evidence which secures conviction of any person for selling these records..."[8] No bootlegs this time. He would not let it happen.

Mingus drew no dividing line between American racism and the economic exploitation he found in the music industry. The liner notes to Charles Mingus Enterprises' second release, *Town Hall Concert*, launched a thinly veiled attack on Columbia's John Hammond.

This Negro-discovering, self-endowed enemy not only to the black man, do I charge him and his efforts to further keep righteousness from my black donkey brothers, I charge this ham-am the enemy of all freedom, green, red, black, yellow, English, French: 'There ain't no white man except in America...' Why he wouldn't give a starving puppy a bone, let alone pay his taxes from the money he earned on this axis, as Birds blow their axes—can't get fair money or enough to-lax...John Doe relax? Schitt old John, Hamhead, is the ax and the tax.

Charles Mingus Enterprises would be different, he insisted.

After we pay the musicians, the band, as a cooperative group, will receive a minimum of 7–10%. We'll be the first company to do this and we'll find out why so many people can't sell our record under the table like John Hamhead said must happen... This will be the first American company to make a step to give justice to all employed. When we succeed, we will also practice fair employment—and not just blacks—we will employ an equal amount of human labor outside of the recorded music world—like secretaries, business executives—compared to the mathematician's statistics of integrated peoples in the NYC area, or any other city we expand to.

Referring to his band and concert organizer Mrs. Dupree White of the NAACP, he concluded, "With disgust for the American recording industry, I give you, the public, this day seven people set to free themselves in music."[9] It was a declaration of independence.

Charles Mingus Enterprises' first release was *Mingus at Monterey*, a double disc stuffed into a single sleeve chronicling his triumphant debut at the 1964 Monterey Jazz Festival. The album featured three sweeping works. A touching Ellington medley concluded with Mingus explaining, "I imagine I should say 'I love you madly' at this point, because if there is a recording the money will all go to Duke Ellington, which is about due him. I've stolen it." If there was any doubt, money was on his mind. Yet he was thinking music as well. "Orange Was the Color of Her Dress, Then Blue Silk" was followed by a big band arrangement of "Meditations on Integration." A bowed bass line gave way to rolling woodwinds. Mingus slowly built a soundtrack to an imagined epic by stacking melodies one upon another. Then he abruptly jumped into a vicious swinging ensemble workout under a crying sax solo. Mingus pushed the band through a dozen dazzling sections before breaking down into a smoldering conversation between his bass and Jaki Byard's piano. "Meditations"

CHARLIE MINGUS FINGERS THE RECORD HI-JACKERS

was an encyclopedia. Music history—jazz, classical, folk, free-form—integrated into one seamless score. The crowd went nuts.

Upon its release, orders rolled in for *Mingus at Monterey*. Even Mingus was surprised by the results. Small checks started stacking up in his apartment. He quickly prepared three more releases. *Town Hall Concert* and *My Favorite Quintet* featured his small ensembles. *Monterey* at times had the tension of a band about to collapse under its own weight. *Town Hall* and *Favorite Quintet* were spry, agile, able to soar. Without the added horns, the music opened up, and Dannie Richmond's astounding drumming came to the fore.

Richmond played with Mingus for twenty-two years. Mingus molded the former sax player into his image of what a drummer should be: elastic, organic, conversational. Together, they defined the Mingus rhythmic ideal and created some of the most breathing, funky grooves around. Richmond could play orchestrally behind the composer's written sections, emphasizing the form and holding together the often-disparate strands of melody. Yet it was under extended solos that the rhythm section really went to work. Check out "Praying with Eric" on *Town Hall*. They mixed it up constantly. Second line. Swing. Stop time. Double time. Latin. Polka. Some grooves lasted no more than a measure or two. Mingus and Richmond created a fluid yet shifting foundation for the horns to do their work—suggesting many later funk and hip-hop experiments with a flowing progression of changing beats. The two locked into a rhythmic embrace.

The fourth release by Charles Mingus Enterprises was another concert of ambitious large ensemble pieces. Following his 1964 success at Monterey, Mingus had big plans for the 1965 festival. He prepared works that would challenge "Meditations" in scope and

theatricality. They had names like "Once Upon a Time There Was a Holding Corporation Called Old America," "They Trespass the Land of the Sacred Sioux," and "Don't Be Afraid, the Clown's Afraid Too." Money got in the way. When several boxes of *Mingus at Monterey* failed to arrive at the festival, Mingus saw sure sales dissolve into missed opportunity. He blamed the festival promoter for the snafu and walked off stage in disgust after a twenty-minute set.[10] He had trouble building momentum.

A week later he presented the music at UCLA. He released the concert on a double disc titled *Music Written for Monterey, 1965. Not Heard…Played in Its Entirety at UCLA, Vols. 1 and 2*. "Meditations on Inner Peace" opened the show with a near twenty-minute drummerless dirge. It was not typical Mingus. After two false starts on "Holding Corporation," Mingus sent the extra horns backstage to practice before launching into a quartet tribute titled "Ode to Bird and Diz." The return of the chastised members brought a whirlwind of orchestral jazz, sounding like a circus band playing ragtime in a Weimar cabaret. It was aching and ambitious, if under-rehearsed. The show ended with "Don't Let It Happen Here," a musical adaptation of a poem by German anti-fascist Pastor Niemöller. In 1966, Mingus released two hundred copies of the concert, complete with liner notes linking Nazi scientific experiments to police brutality and the Watts rebellion that had occurred just before his UCLA gig.

That was it for Charles Mingus Enterprises. Four albums in two years. His life was falling apart. Mail requests for albums went unanswered. The Better Business Bureau logged complaints. He was evicted from his New York loft. Film crews caught him weeping as city workers loaded his belongings into a dump truck.[11] In desperation, Mingus dumped his dream of autonomy within the music industry and signed a distribution agreement with his friends at Fantasy Records. The reissue of *Mingus at Monterey* was accompanied by a heartfelt plea from Mingus for personal contributions. The UCLA tapes languished in the storage facilities at Columbia before they were tossed out during a general housecleaning. Mingus slipped from view, tired, broke, and confused.

The '70s would find him resurfacing. The publication of his sensationalist autobiography in 1971 brought press clippings. He got back in the graces of Columbia. Teo Macero came on board for an album of large-scale works. They recorded selections from the UCLA concert. "Don't Be Afraid" burned far hotter than the original. "Holding Corporation" was redubbed "The Shoes of the Fisherman's Wife Are Some Jive Ass Slippers." *Let My Children Hear Music* was something of a retrospective, touching on different aspects of his art: ballet scores, Latin tinges, blues. They even resurrected "The Chill of Death," a word jazz piece Mingus penned back when he was recording juke box numbers for independents in Los Angeles. The album covered it all, and recorded it beautifully. He was an elder statesman. He began to make money again, even as much of the earnings from record sales were going straight to Columbia.

Charles Mingus Enterprises became a footnote to his long career, an ambitious—some believed foolhardy—attempt to change the world. Mingus tried to reinvent the way music and money were made. He was only half successful. Charles Mingus Enterprises was a financial failure.

Record collectors love footnotes to history. Great artist plus failed plans equals expensive gems. The three albums I picked up in Catskill glistened. The discs had the luminous sheen of virgin vinyl. The covers were intact. They were well protected for several decades before they were dumped on the heap at the Catskill junk shop. They had the added value of being extremely rare, especially *Not Heard*. Think about it. Original recordings of major works by one of the nation's great Black jazz men. Political music from the era of Black Power. No distribution. Only a handful pressed before the masters were lost. The equation ends with a price guide listing for one thousand dollars. Dealers salivate at the sight of this stuff. Their blank expressions belie the questions rumbling through their heads. "Where in the world did he find them?" "Why wasn't I there?" "How much do I offer to make them mine?" The traffic in rare vinyl, particularly in Black musicians only belatedly celebrated by White enthusiasts, often makes far more money off the music than did the original artists. Their fly-by-night venture, their lack of distribution, their inability to get paid are all cash in the bank to the savvy collector. Desperation is the friend of the record hound.

I was not above financial considerations myself. I could woe afford to keep precious gems on my shelf. I dubbed the discs before selling them to a New York dealer and buying a laptop. ◉

Originally appeared in Wax Poetics Issue 1, Winter 2001.

NOTES

1. Charles Mingus, *Beneath the Underdog* (New York: Penguin, 1971), p. 52.
2. Mingus's independent label sides have been reissued on *Charles "Baron" Mingus: West Coast 1945–1949* (Uptown UPCD 27.48, 2000).
3. Gene Santro, *Myself When I Am Real: The Life and Music of Charles Mingus* (Oxford: Oxford University Press, 2000), pp. 74–75, 90–102.
4. Ted Vincent, *Keep Cool: The Black Activists who Built the Jazz Age* (London: Pluto Press, 1995), pp. 92–105; William Barlow, *Looking Up at Down: The Emergence of Blues Culture* (Philadelphia: Temple University Press, 1989), p. 128.
5. Ibid., p. 97.
6. Ibid., pp. 102–105.
7. Ibid., p. 240.
8. *Coda* (April–May 1965); quoted in Brian Priestley, *Mingus: A Critical Biography* (New York: Da Capo Press, 1982), p. 164.
9. Liner notes to Charles Mingus, *Town Hall Concert*, 1964 (Charles Mingus Enterprises JWS 005, 1966); reissued as Fantasy OJC-042).
10. Priestley, *Mingus*, pp. 166–167.
11. The eviction is captured in Tom Reichman's documentary, *Mingus* (1968).

Liberated Brother
Weldon Irvine

interview by Eothen Alapatt and Oliver Wang and intro by Oliver Wang

As a jazz player, leader, and, most of all, mentor, Weldon Irvine's legacy transcended generation and genre. Whether as Nina Simone's longtime musical director, an early adopter of the Rhodes electric piano, or an oft-sampled composer/arranger by hip-hop producers, Irvine was a consummate creative force and gifted musician. However, despite having been rediscovered and embraced by the likes of Mos Def and Q-Tip, Irvine's later days were marked by depression, and, in April of 2002, he took his own life. Eothen Alapatt and Oliver Wang collaborated to commemorate Irvine's life and times through his own words and Wax Poetics dedicated their third issue to his living memory. »

Photos by B+ from the "Umi Says" session for
Mos Def's 1999 album *Black on Both Sides*.

Can we start with some basic biographical info?

WELDON IRVINE: I was born in 1943 in Hampton, Virginia. I was raised by my grandparents. My grandfather was Major Walter R. Brown, the first commandant and dean at Hampton Institute, which was the college I attended. My grandmother was a pianist, and she also played bass violin. On my father's side—while he didn't raise me—in terms of the gene pool, it must have been kicking quite strong. [My parents are] deceased now, but my father was a musician, and he must have played over fifty instruments. He made his living as a vocal performer, and as an educator in the city of Baltimore. When he went to college he majored in English literature. Even though I wasn't raised by my father, would you believe that when I went to college I majored in English literature, and wound up making my living as a musician?

How did you get your musical start?

My first instrument was the voice. I was a boy soprano. And I sang like Frankie Lymon. But at around nine or ten years of age, I had my tonsils and adenoids removed by a surgical operation. That left me with this nasal quality you now hear, which meant that I no longer sang like Frankie Lymon. I didn't express myself musically until '55 or '56. I heard the rock-and-roll piano players, specifically Little Richard, Fats Domino, and later on Huey "Piano Legs" Smith. Hearing them, I began to dabble on the piano. This gave me my new voice, which, in fact, became the keyboard.

I understand that you're able to transcribe any music you hear?

The Creator blessed me with a gift to be able to see music in my mind, like it's on a printed page. So I write music—I can write anything I hear. But I didn't realize this at a young age. It's like people who have perfect pitch—they think everybody can play what they hear in their heads. But perfect pitch is a rarity. [My gift] is a little different. I can write anything I hear. But I just got the *Compton's Encyclopedia* to let me know how many beats a whole note had, and to get the lines and spaces right.

Did you hone your musical ability at Hampton University?

I had a triple minor—speech, drama, and music theory. While I was there, I was a member of a quintet; we went as the Bill Barnwell Quintet. Bill was the saxophone player. We won the Intercollegiate Jazz Festival in 1964 as the best college group in America. That was like the Olympics for me. Quite exciting, as an undergraduate in 1964.

How'd you get your start professionally?

Freelancing as a piano player, for whoever would hire me. I did a little bit of arranging. I guess the first guy that hired me was a saxophonist named Sil Austin, who had some prominence in the '50s. And then the next group of note was the Kenny Dorham Big Band. That was quite exciting. This was 1966. When that band broke up, I formed my own big band. Because, again, that was a vehicle for my arranging and composing abilities. So the Weldon Irvine Big Band was formed, alongside smaller ensembles. Trios, sextets, quintets. Some of the people in these various groups have become household names in their own rights. My first drummer was Billy Cobham, or Ron Jackson. Down the road came Lenny White. Trumpet players, I used Randy Brecker and Tom Browne. Saxophone players would include people like Bennie Maupin and Steve Grossman. Even piano players. George Cables was the pianist in the big band. We did double duty. I was also friendly with George Adams.

Where were you living at the time?

Geographically speaking, I resided in Jamaica, Queens. Over the years, most of my students have come from that area. So, in the '60s, it was some of those names. In the '70s and '80s, it would be people like Don Blackman, Bernard Wright, of course, Tom Browne.

How'd you hook up with Nina Simone, working as her musical director?

I saw Nina Simone when I was second year at Hampton. She was such a perfectionist, I said, "I'd give anything to just play one gig with Nina Simone." But I didn't think it would come to pass, because she was a pianist and I was a pianist. In 1968, she decided that she wanted to be liberated from the piano. She wanted to hire an organist. She auditioned for two weeks, hadn't come up with anyone. On the last day of the second week, I was maybe the last person that she saw, I came in, she said, "Look, turn that thing up, I don't want to hear any lip…" I went in, played one chord; she said, "You have perfect pitch. You're hired." Got the gig as her organist, became her musical director, collaborated on several songs to include "Revolution" and a song called "(To Be) Young, Gifted and Black."

That was a huge hit for Simone.

Yes. That blew me up. That was 1968. Nina had just gone to see the Broadway show by the same title, which was, in fact, the autobiography of the venerated Lorraine Hansbury. Nina was very inspired, having seen the production. She immediately wrote the melody. [*hums the melody*] But she told me she had somewhat of a mental block in terms of the lyrics. She asked me if I would give it a shot. She wanted some lyrics that started with "To be young, gifted, and Black…" and ended with "…is where it's at." I could fill in the blanks. She wanted it to be a song that would be inspirational to young Black children from then till the end of time. I thought it was like a charge, a spiritual commission. So for the first time in my life, I had a mental block. I labored with this concept for two weeks. Then one fateful afternoon, on the corner of 8th Avenue and 41st Street, on my way to the Port Authority Bus Terminal to pick up some girlfriend of mine, I was stopped at a red light. And all of the words you hear in that song came to me in a torrent. I must have tied up traffic for five minutes. New York taxi drivers were going crazy! But on a matchbook cover and some napkins, I wrote those words. I think they came from the Creator, through me.

You must have referenced your own upbringing in that song.

It wasn't fun.

All of the frustration and pain, all of this versed in song.

Yeah, I have a line that says, "I've longed to know the truth, there are times when I look back and I'm haunted by my youth." That line in itself was harkening to some memories that I had experienced as an individual, and even some ethnic memories in my genetic coding. When I wrote that song, I didn't read [the words] till a couple of days later. When I actually typed it out and read it, I was weak in the knees. Those sentiments were so heartfelt, the ones that came through me, that I thought they were speaking to the circumstances of generations of people.

I think it was one of the first pop songs to capture the essence of that cultural rebellion.

I had written "Revolution." I wrote that even before "Young, Gifted and Black." It was a take off on a Beatles song. The words on that are even more in your face. "Young, Gifted and Black" was a song of celebration.

At the same time that you're having such success with Nina Simone, you're finding your jazz compositions covered by well-known jazzers.

I was working with Nina Simone as a musical director and collaborator, as far as composing was concerned. But if you rewind to the jazz groups—like my groups—we were playing places like Slugs, the Village Gate, [places] of that nature. I had been writing songs for myself. As a composer, when I write a song, it's always my intention to perform that song live and hopefully record it and document it. Not unlike Duke Ellington—he wrote songs for the world to hear. In the '60s, I didn't have a recording outlet. So I'd write these songs and play them with my own band at the time. I'd had a catalog of songs since the '50s. It was what it was. As I established rapport with people like "Groove" Holmes, Freddie Hubbard, Stanley Turrentine, and word got around that I was the cat who was with Kenny Dorham, and was the cat with the big bands, they'd come to me: "Say, man, I'm going to make a record; do you have any songs?"

It was that informal, huh?

A lot of times I'd play [one of my songs] for 'em live, or I'd give them a tape or something, 'cause I would record the songs in a demo form for my own band. They learned that they could ask me, "Do you have a song incorporating this?" Or, "Do you have a song incorporating that…kind of like…between James Brown and Miles Davis." I would say, "Whatever you need, if I don't have it, I'll have it by tomorrow."

Which covers are your favorites?

Freddie Hubbard's version of "Mr. Clean" on the *Straight Life* album. I like his version better than mine. I also like the version of the song "Mr. Clean" that was done by Peter Herbolzeimer—that was a big band. And I like the version I rearranged for Bernard Wright [on *Funky Beat*]. Now, "Sister Sanctified," I recorded it but I prefer Stanley Turrentine's version to mine. "Young, Gifted and Black" has been recorded by so many people—Aretha Franklin, Nina Simone recorded it first… Dionne Warwick… But my favorite would be Donny Hathaway's. Those are some examples.

Tell me a little about your compositions and arrangements from the late '60s.

A while back, you mentioned to me that you thought my *In Harmony* album was more diverse than just rare groove. Well, I've always been one who is a fan of the philosophy of inclusion, rather than singling out one period of time and saying, "This is the joint." So my big-band arranging style covered styles that went back as far as the '20s and '30s. I would attempt to imitate some Duke Ellington, on up to the Thad Jones tradition. But also, I'd flip the script and go with some James Brown–type arrangements.

So you were blending funk and jazz early on.

I was doing that back in the '50s. It's cross-pollination. Anything I heard that I liked, I incorporated.

I've been doing this before anybody, but I don't have any discography to verify this. I coined my own term in the '50s—I said, "I'm going to do some 'rock jazz.'" Combining rock and jazz. I figured it could be done, because a lot of these early rock records were nothing but twelve-bar blues. That's from Louis Jordan into James Brown to Bill Haley, et cetera. Later on, when the Fender bass came along, that changed the emphasis of the beat. Its prominence gave the bass drum a different prominence, and the bands began to lock bass drum patterns with bass guitar lines.

Can you explain a bit further?

Of course. In jazz, you have the swing rhythm on the two and four. Now that was played with the hi-hat cymbal. In R&B [and] rock and roll, the two and four is on the snare drum. So you have the bass drum accenting the one and three. That kind of a thing. Again, because of the nature of my ears, I heard this shift in emphasis immediately, and began to incorporate it in my arranging and compositional techniques. But also in the way I played and emphasize different beats.

You put out your first two records, *Liberated Brother* and *Time Capsule*, on your own Nodlew label, and both are notoriously rare.

Initially, I pressed two thousand copies of *Liberated Brother*, and did a re-press of five hundred copies. I only pressed two thousand copies of *Time Capsule*.

Commercial success was not forthcoming, was it?

I would like to think that people were buying those kinds of records; I just didn't have distribution. I already had major credibility by way of my composing talents, by way of the artistic talents of people like Freddie Hubbard and Nina Simone. When I listen back to these records—my records—and then compare them to the records of the day, I think two things: one, they hold up well by comparison, and, two—these are my bragging rights—in a lot of instances, my reissues are more prevalent than some of the [records] that sold more than mine did back in the day. And because of hip-hop, the sampling availability continues as we speak.

Tell me about your deal with RCA, which you struck the same year you released *In Harmony*.

I got that deal in 1974, for my *Cosmic Vortex* album.

Some great tracks sprung from your RCA records. I'm thinking of "Walk that Walk," "Love Your Brother."

Funky as unflushed toilet stool.

And "Pogo Stick." You weren't scared to break down to the drums. This was in 1974, when hip-hop cats were first spinning breakbeats back to back. You were in New York City, were you aware of the movement?

I didn't know about them, but in terms of breaking it down, two of my all-time favorite breakdowns would be James Brown's "Cold Sweat" and Dyke and the Blazers' "Funky Broadway." We called them "boogaloo beats" back in the day. Those breaks—it was like being on a prairie, catching a calf, and branding it. Those beats got branded onto my brain. Not only the beats, but the breakdown concept. I've used it repeatedly in the past.

And you even busted a rap or two over the drums.

Having been an English major at Hampton in the '60s, and being an avid poetry lover—and being aware of the beat generation—I was feeling poetry over funk beats. Although hip-hop wasn't a term in mind, the concept was what was fueling the engine. I was somewhat inhibited. I was like, "You know, Weldon, no one's doing this and if you talk too much over this record it might turn people off." But I should have gone for it, I was feeling hip-hop—literally.

You weren't just reciting verse either. That's what makes those short utterances so remarkable.

I had a flow. I realized that, [like DJs,] if [the] articulation was not locked in—if they didn't have a flow—they were going to have a catastrophe on the dance floor. If you want the party to keep happening, you want to keep the beat of the dance floor. You have to have a flow, as you say in hip-hop. I recognized that. That's why I attempted to do it.

You spent much of the latter half of the 1970s as a playwright, putting out shows like *Young, Gifted and Broke*. How was the playwright's creative process different from that of the musician's?

Similarities between the playwright Weldon and the musician Weldon—first similarity is that I believe that in order to be a good playwright, your story has to have a beginning, middle, and end. And in terms of the entirety of your theme as how you develop it, in my composition, even if it's instrumental, I like to have a beginning, middle, and end. I like for the beginning to be enthralling. I certainly want to hook you from the jump and then reel you in. So in the storytelling process itself, I certainly realized that in the theater, of course, not only do you have a story line and plot development, but you have the characterizations themselves. I liken that to the

musicians that I may choose to be a part of my ensemble. The musicians are comparable to actors on the stage, and the parts that you write for them are comparable to the lines you would write for actors to speak. So this is a question that I've never been asked before, but, as I attempt to answer it, I do stand by my answers.

Your discography pretty much disappears once you enter the '80s. What happened?

When I was dropped from RCA, no one would touch me with a twenty-five-million-foot pole. I think I was blacklisted. Or whitelisted. Again, the things I was doing, not only in terms of what I was saying, but also taking the initiative in ownership, were things that the industry at large was not embracing. When you think in terms of what happened after the '70s and in the '80s, when disco began to proliferate, you saw a waning of the social consciousness that you had had in the '60s. With "Disco Fever" and "Love to Love You Baby," and "(Shake, Shake, Shake) Shake Your Booty." I wasn't trying to hear that. And I think—not to be disparaging about disco artists as such—but in terms of content, I don't think we're going to be talking about the content of any disco artists in the year 2030. By the same token, there was a certain repetitive nature to disco that, as far as I'm concerned, was setting back musical progress. When I was dropped from RCA, being one circumstance, and then the music changing, it was hard not only to sustain a recording career, but many of my protégés were also dropped, and the music kind of fell into a cave. I think hip-hop at least reignited a spark and a zeal in

the music industry and in people like myself and Roy Ayers, who were quite active in the '70s. We all somewhat fell off the scene in the '80s, and some of us have come back into favor through acid jazz and/or hip-hop.

Of the many people who've discovered your work in the last ten years, a majority have come through hip-hop. How was it for you for the first time to be discovered and sampled by hip-hop artists?

KRS-One, Blastmaster, I hope you're listening. I had *Criminal Minded*, and I was waiting for *By All Means Necessary* to hit the stores. I was first in line, bought the tape, put it in my tape deck and I heard "*Duh, duh, duh…* You're a philosopher. Yes! I think very deeply," and I stopped the tape. I said, "That's my keyboard in there." I played the whole thing, and Kris and Scott La Rock had sampled [Stanley Turrentine's cover of] "Sister Sanctified." It rocked my world. I loved it. Kris was the first one to sample me—and I'm a big hip-hop fan, a big KRS-One fan, so I wasn't mad at all. Took a while to get the check, but it's all good now.

Besides that, you've been sampled by the likes of Q-Tip for A Tribe Called Quest's "Award Tour," Ice Cube for "Look Who's Burnin'," and Casual for "Get Off It," not to mention many others. Were you paid royalties by these artists?

No. Q-Tip was the first to actually clear the sample through me. Everyone else was bitin'. But it's all good; no one owes me anything. I've been paid retroactively. After the Biz Markie situation, there was a ruling in court that stated you couldn't sample original works with-

out paying the writers and the publishers. After that case, I got on the phone and called the labels—not the artists. They didn't want to be stressed by any litigation, so they said, "Your check is in the mail."

Have you done all right, royalty-wise?

I'm not complaining. I want to say this to anyone [reading] this interview, any aspiring musicians, any active musicians, particularly writers. It's incumbent on all of you to have your business game tight. Sometimes things happen—inadvertently—in the studio, things like that. Things aren't signed, the participants aren't necessarily in contact with one another. Whenever something is created, writers have to protect themselves as writers. If you write in collaboration with someone else, take out a napkin, matchbook cover, or whatever, and say, "You wrote the words, I wrote the bridge, I wrote the verses…" Write the dates. It's just a covenant and a bond with the creative participants. You're protecting yourself. Many brothers and sisters are not taking care of their business.

Indeed. Who taught you the ropes?

My schooling on this was from Horace Silver. In the '50s, when I was in high school, I would take the bus to New York from Hampton. I might see James Brown at the Apollo, from 8:00 to 10:00 P.M. [Then at] 10:30 P.M., I'm at Birdland, checking out Horace Silver. At midnight, I'm at the Village Vanguard checking out Miles Davis, Wayne Shorter, Ron Carter. Next night it might be Sun Ra. Out of all of them, Horace corresponded with me, he took me under his wings. He said, "I want you to promise me two things. One, finish school before you come to New York, and, two, you're going to make it as a writer before you make it as a piano player, because your writing is better than your piano playing. So make certain that the first song you have recorded is in your own publishing company, so you make all the money. And he explained how to do it. He showed me that on all of his records, his publishing company, Ecaroh Music—which is Horace backwards—published his songs. That's where I got Nodlew from—Weldon, backwards. So my first recording, "Can't Let Her Go," on a Freddie Hubbard record called *High Blues Pressure* in 1968, was the first song in my publishing company. Thank you, Horace; you've saved my life.

In terms of sampling, do you ever take issue with how they're used?

Only in recent years, where they're clearing the samples. So many times, it was done [without my knowledge]. I didn't have the chance to scrutinize or evaluate. In some cases, I may have taken exception to a lyric or a direction, but, by and large, of those who have sampled me, I thought their rhymes were in good taste, and their utilization was on point.

A lot of composers/song writers like yourself don't validate hip-hop like you do.

I was a poet before I was a piano player, singer, or composer. So I always loved poetry. I listened to hip-hop. I knew about Cash Money and of course [Fatback's] "King Tim III" and Roxanne Shante and the Treacherous Three. So I was a hip-hop fan before I was even sampled. And I recognized the art form as valid, because the lyrics were poetic, and a lot of the original bands were *bands*. They were bands; they weren't sampling. So for me, I thought it was a continuum of what had gone on before, and I'm glad to [have been] a part of it then. And glad to be a part of it now.

Your reputation in the '70s was as an ensemble player. What are the similarities and differences between those whom you've worked with in the past and the younger cats you're working with now, like Mos Def, Talib Kweli, or Q-Tip?

In the '70s—and I was and am an ensemble player—when I came to New York from Virginia, I wanted people like Coltrane, Freddie Hubbard, Elvin Jones, Tony Williams, Ron Carter to be in my band. I wanted them in my band, because they were the best players among the best players in New York, but I knew it was very unrealistic for me to think I could ever get those guys to play with me, a veritable unknown. But I moved to Jamaica, Queens, and although I couldn't get Elvin Jones or Tony Williams, I did get Billy Cobham. [I got] Clint Houston and George Cables, and I played saxophone for a while. Later on, I got Marcus Miller and Bernard Wright and Tom Browne. So what I discovered was, okay, if you can't get Tony Williams and Elvin Jones, but you can get Lenny White, you've got Tony Williams and Elvin Jones, at least the embodiment of their styles in one drummer. So all props to the cats in Jamaica, Queens, you all know who you are. I'm fortunate that all of those guys played in my bands over various periods of time. They comprised what we call the Weldon School: I, being older than them, was mentoring them as a leader and a teacher. The main difference between those guys and the guys in hip-hop that I'm teaching now is those guys were players from the jump. It wasn't a question of me teaching them what a Locrian mode was or what a scale was, but it was a question of me fine-tuning which aspects of the music they found themselves deficient in. With these new guys, I'm giving them a grounding in music theory and basic technique and after they get that, then we'll explore, spending a lot of time in the blues in particular. It'll be up to them how deep in the swimming pool called jazz they want to go. But they'll at least have the working tools to express their musical ideas as they see fit.

How about for yourself? You've managed to stay active in the music scene for four decades now. Do you feel like you've been keeping up with the changes that have happened?

I hope that I'm evolving. It has been said about me that I've always been ahead of my time, and there may be some truth to that. Because when I'm sampled some fifteen or twenty years after the original composition, and I listen to the way my music is couched within the confines of hip-hop, I must admit that it sounds fresh to my ears now. It doesn't sound dated. So the question deals with evolution. I think I have a very sound grasp of the cultural lineage, particularly of the Black musical experience, from African chants, to field songs, to gospels, to big bands, to swing, to bebop, to R&B, to hip-hop to whatever the next flavor is going to be. So, being grounded in the past and wanting to be innovative myself, I came by a style that we now call the Weldon School. But this school extrapolates from things that came before, and there are so many different influences. You know, I've written over a thousand songs, so I think I evolved maybe around the time I was nineteen or twenty. Some of the best songs I've written I wrote in 1963, and I'm just now getting around to recording them. ⭘

Originally appeared in Wax Poetics Issue 3, Fall 2002.

Breaking Bread with Timothy McNealy

by Chad Burnett and Wilson Brooks

Geography is your friend. Use it to your advantage. If Detroit has the soul, San Fran has the psych, and London has the library, then Dallas has definitely got the funk. But just like anywhere else, it's no free lunch out here. Just because the history's here doesn't mean the Texas funk anthology is at your fingertips. However, with a little legwork and a lot of luck, it can be rather surprising what one can uncover. One day you're salivating over a super rare, super funky track off some bootleg comp, and the next day you're rapping about the tune with the original artist over a $2.99 breakfast buffet. Oh, the power of proximity! ¶ Timothy McNealy lives an hour away. He is the legend who has given us the beautifully funky "Sagittarius Black" 45 with the equally brilliant "Funky Movement No. 2" on the flip. Perhaps the best-known release on his Shawn label, "Sagittarius" is only a tiny piece of this puzzle. We get the big picture by taking a stroll through the mind of one of the Lone Star State's funkiest. »

Prior to the launch of your label, what were you participating in musically?

Well, I began playing professionally in 1956, at eleven years old. Several of us began quite young. My best friend was Michael Fugit. We lived in Sherman, Texas, and practiced in his parent's garage. We were using Sears [Silver Tone] amplifiers. The group was named Mike and the Six Sensations. We played for local club dances and were booked in other Texas clubs each weekend. Mike played bass. Charles Chamberlain played guitar and had a super feel for blues. Wallace Ray Polk and Ronnie Brewster played drums and were, what we called at that time, very funky. [Brothers] Charles and Fared Nibblet played tenor and alto saxes. I played piano and doubled out on slide trombone, something I had learned to play in public school. In or about 1963, after spending a short time in the Air Force, I returned to Sherman and rejoined the band. They had made a lot of progress and had a new band leader and trumpet player named James ["Bubba"] Fagin. Bubba had traveled on the road and had paid his dues, so to speak. His style was jazz, and with his knowledge, we all were able to add to our musical abilities.

Were you involved with any other record labels before (or after) the creation of your own imprint?

I am one of the original members of the Mustangs, the backup band for Bobby Patterson [Jetstar Records]. In fact, I helped form the band. Two of my friends from Mike and the Six Sensations [Mike and Ronnie] were the first to be chosen and I was the bandleader until Robert ["Bobby"] Simpson joined the group. Bobby had a degree in music, so it was natural that he would take the lead spot in our group. I still played organ and helped record most of the tracks. I also contributed some vocals on a few of the songs. In fact, on the song "I'm Leroy, I'll Take Her," Bobby is talking to me. At about the same time that Bobby Simpson started fronting the Mustangs, I was looking elsewhere to keep my music abilities polished. I remained a member of the band until around 1970, when John Abdnor Sr. [of Abnak/Jetstar] dismantled us.

And one time [after the dismantling of the Mustangs] my band changed names to the Upsetters. We were well known in Dallas at that time. We had sessions under that name, although I don't remember much about what was recorded.

When was Shawn established? Have you always had sole ownership of the label and all of its publishing?

Shawn Records was founded in 1970. It was basically for my own personal use, primarily as an instrument to get my own music out. I have always owned it and my publishing [Sledge Publishing]. No one other than myself has ever owned any part of it at anytime.

What is the significance behind the label's name?

Shawn is the middle name of my oldest son. His name is Timothy Shawn McNealy.

Did the distribution for Shawn Records, through H&W One Stop, ever reach outside of Texas? Were there any other means for the distribution of your records?

At that time, H&W was the largest record dealer in the area. With a limited finance, I needed Walter Jackson, the owner of H&W, who was also a friend of mine, to help. He did, and that was the extent of my distribution. As far as out of state, I received news in 1972 that someone, even then, was black-marketing my records. I was a small company and had limited access to making an investigation.

"Funky Movement No. 2/ Sagittarius Black" had a regular slot on the radio. Do you recall the stations from which your music was heard? What about radio stations in neighboring states?

It was played quite a bit here in Dallas. I don't recall the call letters, but I know that Houston, Austin, New York, California, Washington, and Jersey were just a few who had them on a regular playlist.

Your singles "KC Stomp" and "Funky Movement No. 2" seem to be the scarcest. We only know of one or two copies of each to be in existence. Were these 45s pressed on a significantly smaller scale than the other Shawn releases?

By the time I got my record company going, the cost of doing business was tough. Not a lot of money was there to press up a large amount of records. And even for a small company such as mine, things were hectic.

Do you remember how many copies were pressed for these two songs?

I only pressed five hundred copies of each.

In regard to "Funky Movement" (Shawn 0156), we've heard it alleged that you don't remember cutting this specific song to record. How much truth does this statement hold?

I remember it, but it was not one of my favorites. If I heard it, I am sure I would remember much more about it.

[*We pause so that Mr. McNealy could recall this 45. Immediately after pressing play the memories start rushing back.*]

Oh yeah! I remember it now. That is definitely T-Bird Gordon on the horn. I haven't heard this in years! Back then we did a lot of track separation, so both the lead and backing vocals are mine. This was one of the main songs we would perform in the clubs at that time.

Tell us a little about the scene back then. The clubs had to be hoppin' at that time.

I guess one of the most exciting times was at a place called Soul City. It was out there on Greenville Avenue. It was like a little Las Vegas club with the curtains and the big railing where people would sit around and order drinks and what have you. Then they had a floor space with tables that was right at the stage. And when the curtain opens you do your show. We were booked in there seventeen weeks straight in a row. And while we were there, we were booked with acts like Dobie Gray, about the time he had his hit "I'm in with the In-Crowd." Also, Eddie Floyd came through, and we did stuff behind him. I remember Jimmy Smith came in and performed, and we also got to play behind the Coasters. That was some of the most exciting times.

We were also doing a lot on the college scene. In Austin, we would go there to the university to perform for the sororities. We did that a few times. Then there was a time I was playing at Club Sands with Fred Alexander, who later played with Lakeside, and I remember we called our backing band Liquid Funk. After this I was playing at Rickshaw, which was a club over in North Dallas. It was heavy. When T-Bird Gordon was playing with me I called my band the Sweat Band. In fact, the Sweat Band was the band that played behind me when we recorded "Sagittarius Black" and "Funky Movement No. 2." So at one time in Dallas I had a pretty good name for myself. Folks knew I could play, and, if I had a band, it was going to be together.

You also recorded the 45 "Do It/ What Would You Do," by Mr. B, aka Bernard Miller, who was an FM radio DJ in Dallas.

Mr. B was a young exciting radio jock that was hot on the FM station. One day I got a telephone call from him asking if I would help him record. Everyone I asked about him said that he was a good guy but that he could not sing. I was always a sucker for the underdog and open for a sob story, so I wrote and produced his material on my label. By doing this I learned I was strengthening my place in the radio programming. I also wrote some other songs at that time that I could never find again, and I'll leave it at that.

On your best-known 45, "Funky Movement No. 2," I believe in

SAGITTARIUS BLACK BAND
SHAWN RECORDING COMPANY

Backup Rhythm Section • Timothy McNealy
Sledge Publishing Co.
Photo By: T.McNealy © Copyright 1972

the beginning of the song, you shout "Lookout, Soultex!" Was this directed towards the Dallas-based label?

Believe it or not, I said, "Look out, Joe Tex!" Joe was hot during those times and just mentioning his name was a ploy to be used.

Oops. We were hoping that would be our transition. You knew Soultex owner Roger Boykin, who produced the Texas Soul Trio.

Roger and I met at clubs during the '60s where he was playing. It was mostly jazz, but very good jazz. We became good friends at that time and have remained close friends throughout the years. [In the] later years I asked him to play with me in the "What's Goin' On?" session. This was my interpretation of Marvin Gaye's hit tune, and we both enjoyed it. Actually, it is still one of my favorite songs. Roger and I still keep in contact.

Did you see Soultex artist Booker T. Averheart perform?

In the early years, I had an opportunity to play several gigs with Booker T. Averheart. I didn't know him very well but he was a nice guy. I have not seen him in many years. I'd love to know what he's up to.

Your good relations have definitely lasted throughout the years. We've heard you on Mr. Boykin's 730 AM Dallas radio show. But besides Mr. Boykin's bands, who were some other notable local acts that were making noise around the same time you were?

[Rev.] Jimmy Filmore, Little Hamp, R. L. Griffin, Jolly George, Big Bo Thomas and the Arrows, Freddie Empire, Little Ernie, Big Jack Dixon, the Warm Excursions with Robert Whitfield, the Other Brothers, et cetera. During the '60s and early '70s, there were so many local artists battling for a spot and name recognition.

Digging a little deeper, did any local bands have any influence on your own sound?

There was a group by the name of Les Watson and the Panthers. I believe Willie Weeks was the bandleader's name. Those guys put on a real show. We began to hang out together, and from this connection we both learned a great deal.

Did you ever travel out of Texas to perform? If so, where?

I traveled to many states, but the most exciting times were here in Texas. At that time, I was more into my music than the girls, even though I still had more than my share. It was an amazing time! While with Bobby Patterson, we were booked as the backup band in Houston for Bobby Sherman, who at that time had his own teen television show. This was definitely a crazy experience for us. So many women were there to see Bobby.

Seems to me that at this time, it was expected of you to know a lot of material. Did you have to learn the popular artist's songs in case a tour hit your town and needed a rhythm section?

Yes, we played a lot of shows for a lot of people. In spite of all that was going on, we looked at this as an opportunity rather than an inconvenience. We enjoyed performing for these artists. One of our hopes was to get recognized by a big-time producer and to get paid. We did have time to create our own tunes though. I'm telling you, it was a job back then. We would come to work at 8:00 A.M., have a fifteen-minute break and a thirty-minute lunch, and the day would be over at 4:30 P.M. It was work! ⬤

Originally appeared in Wax Poetics Issue 2, Spring 2002.

Manzel Breaks It Down

interview by Dante Carfagna and intro by Andrew Mason

Manzel. The word is akin to a secret incantation among those obsessed with drum breaks: pronouncing it with understanding means one has graduated to an inner sanctum of beat lore and arcane knowledge. The etymology of the term is obscure; most know only that it refers to the artist listed on a legendary 7-inch called "Midnight Theme" that few have ever laid eyes on. Yet even the most casual hip-hop listener has heard the Beat innumerable times. Released in the late '70s as a 45 on Fraternity—a Cincinnati label best known for the work of Memphis guitarist Lonnie Mack—the song "Midnight Theme" is a mellow mid-tempo funk instrumental featuring soulful interplay between piano and synth. Pleasant but unremarkable, save one thing: the tune is led by four bars of some of the crunchiest open drums recorded. The sizzling half-open hi-hat, punchy kick, and a popping snare caught the ears of New York City's breakbeat-hungry underground and soon found their way onto the primal *Octopus* bootleg breakbeat series in the early '80s. First flipped by deep drum break pioneer Prince Paul in 1988 for De La Soul's demo cut "Plug Tunin'," the rough rhythm resurfaced in 1991 when transplanted Brooklynite Lawrence "DJ Muggs" Muggerud made it the backbone of a Cypress Hill B-side called "How I Could Just Kill a Man." »

Manzel's only other release was another 7-inch on Fraternity show-casing two instrumentals, "Jump Street" and "Space Funk." The latter tune again features a tasty and unusual four-bar rhythm break at the head, this time beginning with two bars of reversed tape before the straight beat kicks in. The beat and a snippet of the phenomenally fat bass riff were used on "No Competition," an Eric B. and Rakim track from 1988's *Follow the Leader* LP, while the short drum break and organ stabs of "Jump Street" powered Ultramagnetic's "Ain't It Good to You," released the same year.

The two singles have remained among the more elusive breakbeat celebrities, with even hard-core diggers and producers unable to add the originals to their roster. In 1988, New York's Downstairs Records re-pressed the second Fraternity release, but the limited quantity meant this too was thinly spread amongst aficionados (note the timing of the Ultra and Rakim releases though). Things brightened considerably for the drum-break-loving community when Kenny "Dope" Gonzalez took matters into his own hands, contacting the man who set this whole thing off, keyboardist Manzel Bush. Now a Lieutenant-Colonel in the U.S. Army, Mr. Bush (no relation to the commander in chief) granted Gonzalez access to the original master tapes of his '70s sessions, and in late 2002 the first official pressings of "Midnight Theme" and "Space Funk" in over twenty years began surfacing.

Wax Poetics contributor Dante Carfagna takes Lt.-Col. Bush back to his musical youth and memories of the nascent Midwest funk scene.

Can you tell us a little bit about your background?

I was born in Lexington, Kentucky, in 1952. I was lucky, in that music has always been a big part of my life. My parents insisted that I take piano lessons, but I always wanted to play football, you know? [*laughs*] In those days, primarily in the early '60s, music lessons were about $2.50 per hour. I would listen to the radio, and play the latest tunes by ear, tunes like "Baby Love" and "My Girl" and "The In Crowd"—Ramsey Lewis, you know? So I wouldn't practice my normal lessons, and ultimately I'd get into trouble, and finally I got bounced to a local piano teacher in the hood. Anybody who grew up around [Lexington] in that time frame would know this lady. She was a profound impact on me, and her name was Miss Mamie Grimsley. This lady was a person that was choir director, everything, she taught everybody's parents and everything. You couldn't get away from her. You know Joe Clark, the *Lean On Me* person? He didn't have anything on this lady. She influenced everyone, and me in particular, because she helped my ability to concentrate and produce under pressure. 'Cause if you didn't play, your backside would get fired up; this was corporal punishment days, right? [*laughs*] And with that she only charged about seventy-five cents, and that's if you had it. She would take in the students that would be referred to her from parents, but again most of them would be like me—guys that started out downtown at the regular music stores. And if you weren't playing, hey, we're gonna send you to her. I look back on it now, and that really paid off.

Was there a point where you decided that music was what you wanted to pursue professionally?

Well, I think there was. Another key influence for me came from my cousins, the Higgins brothers out of Lexington. They were, and they remain, excellent musicians—Norman and Jonathan on drums and Bennett on sax. They played all styles of music. I'd go over there on Sundays after church or whatever, and really get imbued with all kinds of music and things to do. These guys were super folks, because they were family-oriented, and they introduced me to the music of Charles Earland and Brian Auger and Jimmy Smith, just

to mention a few. It was really profound on me, 'cause they were profoundly talented musicians, and they *didn't do drugs*. They didn't have to, because they could really play. They were on call for traveling musicians who came into the area—you know, Roy Ayers, the Count Basie orchestra, all of the different road groups that would come in. When you were in Lexington, and if you were a musician of note, you stopped over and paid your respects at [the Higgins] house. I saw them being friends with such a diverse group of people, that I said, "Hey, this is kind of cool." Another thing I really enjoyed with them, was these guys drove *really fast cars*. [*laughs*] Anyway, they really exposed me to some of that fat organ sound, and I was really fascinated with that organ sound with the walking bass lines. So, in 1969, I went to a local teen club, and I saw some kids about my age playing in a little group. I hadn't given it that much thought—being with a group—but I went there, and I saw these guys playing. The name of their band at that time was the Senators. I noticed that they didn't have a keyboard player, and I basically knew all of the songs they were playing, so I said, "Hey, I might want to check into this." I worked up the nerve to talk to my folks and talked them into cosigning for a new, red Farfisa combo organ and a Fender Super Reverb amp. So, that was my first rig.

And you began playing and gigging with the Senators?

Yeah, I worked up the nerve to invite them over. I invited Larry Van Dyke on guitar, Skip Wilson on bass, George "G-3" Johnson on drums, Jimmy "Hump" Campbell on percussion, and had them come over to my house for a jam session in my garage. We also had a couple of guys who were brothers, their names were Charlie and Cecil Mealing, on vocals, and boy we *jammed*. It became *the* event in our town to come to our garage sessions. I mean, it was unbelievable.

I recall Charles Mealing fronted a group called the Mercy Men as well.

Right. The time frame for this, when [Mealing] came out, we came out together, is like '69. Eventually, we had personnel changes, and he went to play with the Mercy Men. In '69, we all came out together and jammed and entered local talent contests, and won 'em. We then changed the name from the Senators to the Soul Syndicate and the O' Jays.

Like the vocal group from Cleveland?

Yeah, but at the time we didn't think about all that, you know. We went on the road from about '69 to around about '72, and again we had some personnel changes along the way. Steve Garner came in on drums as G-3, our original drummer, went off to college and everything. Steve was a real gifted drummer, and he brought some *real* funky drums in there. His idol was Bernard Purdie. I recall that he and I would listen to all the different Bernard Purdie records. Purdie did a drum break [version] of "Cold Sweat." There's a break in the James Brown tune, and Purdie did some things in that drum break, and we all went "*Whoooaa*," you know. [*laughs*] Steve and I really became close as we went through and figured those kinds of things out. I was saving up to get a Leslie tone cabinet for my Farfisa then, because I wanted that rotor sound and didn't have B-3 money, you know. I figured out a way to do that and got that rigged specially through my little Super Reverb and got a cool sound. But Steve, he loved the horses. You know being from Kentucky, he kept trying to get me to come to the track and bet what he did to pick up some quick cash. [*laughs*] We still remained good friends with all the folks we came in contact with musically. G-3, the original drummer, had a hot rod—a 427 Chevy Chevelle—and I mean that thing was the *truth*, so we made some good money that way too. [*laughs*]

So while gigging did you tend to stay in the Kentucky and

southern Ohio area?

Uh-huh. We branched out a little while later to Chicago, but pretty much we were in what was not quite the chitlin circuit, but it was close to it. We would follow [groups like] the Ike and Tina Turner Revue. As a matter of fact, we used to open up for Exile, which was a kind of pop group or whatever in the Kentucky area, at the Fireplace, a type of lodge in Lexington. We used to play Club 68 down in Lebanon.

And Joe's Palm Room?

I played a gig in Joe's Palm Room. My cousin Bennett was a regular at Joe's Palm Room. Primarily though we played a lot of clubs, proms…when I say clubs, I mean private clubs—Elks and people that had private social clubs, that kind of thing. We really had a good time. And I *did* go to the track with Steve, I bet what he bet, and shortly thereafter I got a new Hammond B-3. [*laughs*]

Can you recall any other groups in the Lexington area that were doing the same kinds of things you were doing?

One group that was really, really hot was called the House Rockers. They were like the forefathers, if you will, of our group. They were an older generation of guys who really had the local club scene down. They were local legends. Snooky Robinson, I think that's what his name was, a tenor sax man, fronted that group. Later we, in some of our personnel changes, got a guy to play trumpet when we added horns to the group, and he was one of the original members of the House Rockers. His name was Les. Our bass player, his father, was named Geno. Geno Wilson was our road manager and, man, we had some times. A lot of fun and a lot of growing up, you know, on the road. One of the people we came into contact with was a guy you may know, a guy by the name of Butch Yates.

Of Leroy and the Drivers?

Yeah! Butch came into our group—he and a female singer by the name of Angie Dee—they both had toured with Ike and Tina Turner, as part of the Revue. I guess this was probably around '72 or '73, somewhere around there. She was touring with us, and she had Butch come in, and we had this guy named Les, and we were doing a lot of Sly and the Family Stone–type things. A lot of things we played were sort of like—you heard of Sharon Jones and the Dap-Kings?—it was along that kind of stuff. Butch, though, he was a lot of fun—he was something else. I lost touch with Butch over the years, but finally got in touch with him about a month ago after all these years. Matter of fact, while Butch was playing with us, he was recording "The Sad Chicken."

No kidding.

Tell you the truth, that was another influence, because here's a person that went into the studio and did something. He didn't just talk about it, he went in and did it.

He must have been a little older than you guys.

Yes, he was. He was older than we were, so we looked up to him. I mean this guy had all sorts of things going on—not only was he a super saxophonist and musician, but he had a *chopper bike*. You know, an *Easy Rider* chopper bike? C'mon, kids looking at that? We'd be like, *Butch*, you know. [laughs]

Did you ever go into the studio with the Soul Syndicate?

We had a variety of different name changes over the years. I believe we went from the Soul Syndicate to Touch of Funk and later to Hot Ice. The nucleus of the group stayed together, with Larry Van Dyke on guitar, myself on keyboards, Skip on bass, and Steve on drums. We had different horn players and vocalists come and go. We saved our money, and we did go into the studio, in Louisville, Kentucky, probably around 1973 or something like that. We went to

[Fultz] Studio, and we recorded "Jump Street." We recorded that, and we just kind of held it. I think we did a soul vocal or some other kind of song, but we kind of held on to it.

And later when you hooked up with Shad O'Shea, you issued it?

Yeah. We just kind of put "Jump Street" in the can. Larry Van Dyke and I wrote that one. He's doing some really great wah pedal work on there, it's classic now.

That would explain why "Jump Street" sounded like it was recorded many years earlier than "Space Funk." So how did you get together with Shad O'Shea and his Counterpart Studio?

Well, we searched through the phone book, talked to a few people and basically went around and visited different studios. Fifth Floor in Cincinnati, Queen City, Jewel, all those places. I kind of just went in there. What I do, is I try to sense a vibe, you know? The thing that impressed me the most about Counterpart is that they had all kinds of instruments there. They had a B-3, a couple of Leslies. I didn't have to haul anything, you know, lift anything. [*laughs*] They had a real nice drum booth, so Steve just brought a cymbal, his snare, and his trusty Speed King foot pedal. When we got there they had all kinds of ambiance and lighting. I mean, I don't know if they had the fog machine or not, but it was just like being in the club. They would turn the lights down, and it was just a blast. I got married in 1975 to my college sweetheart—we went to Moorehead State University—and she said, "Go back in the studio, put these tunes down!" So I said, *"okay!"* So we went in for about a week or so in April, about 1975, if I'm not mistaken. I was experimenting with synthesizers then. I really had always loved left-hand bass, you know, walking bass and keyboards and stuff, so that's what I decided to do. They had sixteen-in and twenty-four-out; I think it was a Crown board, full DBX. We took a long time to mic the drums though, we really paid attention to that—the hi-hat in particular. I was looking for a real crisp distinct sound for the hi-hat, you know, to cut through. If you listen to "Midnight Theme," the opening drum piece on there, you'll see that's what we did.

Who was the engineer at Counterpart for these tracks?

I can't recall his name right now, but he was super. There were two engineers, I believe. When we laid down "Space Funk" up there, it was really cool, because again the environment in there, and we had already worked out the song structure, and we were on a break, and the engineer was messing around and said, "Listen to this"—and that's how the reverse drum at the head was born. He played the drum part backwards, we started listening to it, and we said, "That's pretty cool." So Steve layed down a few other things, and we put it all together, and that's what you hear on the head there.

So you cut "Space Funk," "Midnight Theme," and "Sugar Dreams" all in that week in April?

Well, actually, we did "Space Funk" earlier, and we came back later and did about eight tunes. On the CD are the tunes nobody has heard before, we just put them in the can and kept them. They're really special, because we tried, on purpose, other than on one kind of house/dance-type of track, to make them timeless. Recently, when Kenny Dope came over to meet me, I actually played him some of these things he had never heard and he went, *"Ahh,* man." [*laughs*] 'Cause this was his stuff, you know?

You recorded these tracks in 1975, and they were issued in 1978?

Well, "Space Funk" came out in '77, and immediately got super, super airplay. This was a national release—I debated about doing a national release, but went ahead and did it. Immediately, folks were calling. It broke out big-time in New York, because of the block-party people. Up and down the East Coast it was really taking off.

Manzel Bush today, retired Army Officer.

It was reviewed in the June of '77 *Billboard*, I believe—you'll see a blurb in there. I was just knocked out, we were on there with the Doobie Brothers and everybody. I was going, "Whoa, man, look at this!" We were really excited, it was doing very well, and lo and behold, the movie *Star Wars* came out. Back then, radio stations only really featured one instrumental, it wasn't the smooth-jazz stations that they have now, [*laughs*] so unfortunately being on an independent label we couldn't go up against the big boys. So [Meco's] Star Wars theme kind of knocked us out of the box. The interesting thing though, was that it still kept being played, it went underground. I lost track of it for a pretty good while around 1978, because I was on active duty [in the Armed Services]. I was in Ft. Hood, Texas, and Army business kept me out of what was happening at the time.

Twenty-five years later, what are your views on hip-hop and sample-based music?

Well, I think hip-hop is generally good. I don't mind the sam-

pling; I take it as a compliment. I am just knocked out that our music has been able to reach as many people and influence so many folks around the world. I'm completely knocked out about that. From a legal standpoint, things have to be worked out appropriately; steps should be taken to address all that. I don't have a problem with all that [sampling]; I'm in good company. There's all kinds of folks that have been sampled, and as long as you get credit for it and compensation, what's not to like? At one point in time, a lot of the kids were not playing instruments, they were sampling and so forth, so perhaps folks will go back and actually sit down and play the live instruments and do the recording—you see signs of that now, and that's great. I think the music spectrum is open to everybody, so as long as you adhere to some rules and regulatory procedures, everything's great. ⭕

Originally appeared in Wax Poetics Issue 4, Spring 2003.

Fania Rising

by Karl Hagstrom Miller

You say you're in a band? You make your own beats? Who cares. The world is full of musical geniuses who never got the attention they deserved. They channeled joy and angst, absorbed vast vinyl collections, practiced till carpal and tunnel became everyday words, and still failed to make a splash outside the bathroom "echo chamber" in their home studios. You are a cliché. ¶ It doesn't have to be that way. Stop perfecting those sampled flute loops. Come up with a business plan. How do you get your label started? How can you harness the power of the press? How can you fill Yankee Stadium with ticket-buying fans? Repeat how others have done it. ¶ You could do worse than following Fania Records. The label that became synonymous with salsa in the '70s started humbly in the back of its founder's car. In just over a decade, Fania commanded a fat majority of the Latin music market, went transnational, and boasted a corral of superstars including Willie Colón, Ray Barretto, Larry Harlow, Bobby Valentin, teen dream Héctor Lavoe, and the man who started it all: Johnny Pacheco. The Fania All-Stars sold out annual concerts at Yankee Stadium. They played the Rumble in the Jungle. They built an empire. Major labels salivated, cried, and eventually got wise. ¶ Here is how Fania did it—broken down into bite-sized morsels for easy digestion. Theirs was not an overnight success. The label harnessed the limited means at their disposal. They played it smart, at least in terms of their own interests. Check it out. Maybe your label could be next. »

STEP ONE: GET YOUR MUSIC TOGETHER

Johnny Pacheco was no musical neophyte when he started Fania in 1964. He had been a player for quite some time, practicing, writing, and getting paid. Born in the Dominican Republic in 1935, Pacheco was around music from an early age. His father led the famous Santa Cecelia Orchestra and encouraged his son to play. The family moved to New York in the mid-'40s, and young Pacheco soon took up the accordion, violin, sax, and clarinet. He studied percussion at Julliard. He picked up the flute. He was in demand. He put time in with the big Latin bands: Pérez Prado, Tito Puente, and the suave, campy Xavier Cugat.

Latin dancing was big in the 1950s. Everyone had mambo fever. Latinos dug the heritage. White folks dug the grace. Arthur Murray told them it was alright—and where to place their feet. Bands were often booked in several halls a night. They played White-society gigs one minute, Latin clubs the next. Bandleaders such as Prado and Puente were steeped in the tradition, yet much of their output during the '50s Latin craze was geared toward the White mainstream. "Marilyn Monroe Mambo" anyone? Appealing to the White majority was double edged. It brought the cash. It got the Victor contract. It bought groceries. Yet it could alienate the core Latino audience—lightly swinging the Havana Hotel while Fidel was making his move. Pacheco knew the bargain he was making. He would do it again.

The year the casinos were kicked out of Cuba, Pacheco started a revolution of his own. Joining Charlie Palmieri's Duboney Orchestra, he helped spearhead the *charanga* craze. The charanga was smooth. It simmered. The lilting 3/2 clave rhythm remained, but violins and flute replaced mambo horns. The sound was fresh in 1959, even if it echoed the 1930s vibe of Cuban sensations Arcaño and Cachao. Palmieri and Pacheco made something new by turning to an older style. They debuted on United Artists Records. Following their mentors' crossover model, their disc featured charanga takes on Cuban tunes as well as U.S. standards "Moonlight Cocktail" and "Mack the Knife." It was a big hit. The band defined the local scene. It ran into trouble as Palmieri and Pacheco began booking conflicting gigs. Pacheco decided to book a band of his own. His charanga band debuted on Alegre in 1961. The record sold, but the bandleader chafed at making money for someone else's label. He was also aware of the music industry's track record with Latin dance crazes: once the novelty wore thin, so did label interest. He had seen it happen many times before. The international Latin market was little better, dropping the same conservative flavors throughout the Spanish-speaking world. Connie Francis and Vicki Carr were queens. Pacheco had put in his time, got his chops in order, and knew how to make and market Latin music. He was ready to really strike out on his own.

STEP TWO: FIND A PARTNER WITH CAPITAL

Pacheco met lawyer Jerry Masucci when he was in need of legal help during a divorce. The Brooklyn native and former police officer had been turned on to the Latin sound during a business trip to Havana. After getting to know the up-and-coming flutist, Masucci dropped five thousand dollars startup money and Fania Records was born. Their first release, Pacheco's own *Cañonazo*, carried the number of Pacheco's birth date, 325 (March 25). The pair packed product in the trunk of a car and visited Latin record dealers throughout New York. The label began to grow. Pacheco handled musical decisions. Masucci covered the business end. Together they would build Fania into a powerhouse. They just needed something for the kids.

STEP THREE: FIND A SEX SYMBOL

Free from major label contracts, Pacheco was also free from the majors' love of the Latin-tinged ballroom. No more "Mack the Knife." Time for a fresh face for Latin music. Fania found it in a seventeen-year-old Bronx kid named Willie Colón. The young trombone player had already concocted a punchy, powerful sound. Colón's band attacked the groove with glee. Percussion sizzled. Horns went splat. Vocal *coros* were excited, breathless. It was almost—but never quite—out of control. Throughout, the prominent bass kept things grounded—evidence that Colón had imbibed the lessons of R&B. He was in good company.

While parents swayed to the mambo, a young generation of Nuyoricans sampled Motown, Stax, and Atlantic. Deep grooves and party tunes. The result was boogaloo. Often sounding as much soul as Latin, boogaloo popped congas and timbales into funky, easily sung anthems. Veterans laid the groundwork. Bebop conguero Ray Barretto hit in 1963 with "El Watusi." Mongo Santamaria, after boiling with Prado, Puente, and jazz/Latin fusionist Cal Tjader, released "Watermelon Man." The tune witnessed the twisted trail of boogaloo: a Cuban conguero, fresh from dropping deep into traditional drumming on *Mongo* and *Yambu*, cuts a driving version of Herbie Hancock's hard-bop anthem, itself a product of young jazz lions soaking up the Latin scene. If boogaloo sported a jazz pedigree, few of its major proponents flaunted the fact. This was party music meant for quick comprehension and consumption. It was loose and spacious, infectious and disposable.

Willie Colón could boogaloo with the best, but on his early Fania discs he went one better. Colón developed a new look for the Latin music star. Boogaloo flew in the face of Latin traditionalists. It was willing to trade the sacred clave for a syncopated R&B four. Tito Puente scoffed: "kiddie music." Yet even as they broke new musical ground, the boogaloo "kids" still dressed like their elders. Barretto's band donned dinner jackets. Pete Rodriguez wore cardigans when he wasn't in tails. Colón changed the image of the music. He went gangster. Perhaps taking a nod from Joe Cuba's *Wanted: Dead or Alive*, Colón plastered his early Fania discs with depictions of the criminal life. *El Malo*, *The Hustler*, *Guisando (Doing a Job)*, *Cosa Nuestra*, *Crime Pays*, *The Big Break*: Colón rode fancy cars, cracked safes, and buried bodies in the East River. The bad boy image worked. Colón's persona was as dangerous and fresh as his music. He sold records. In a sea of button-downs playing to the crossover market, many Nuyorican kids saw Colón as the real deal. And in Spanish Harlem during the late '60s and early '70s, authenticity meant more and more.

STEP FOUR: SUPPORT LOCAL ACTIVISM

In 1969, the year of Colón's third Fania release, Puerto Rican activists formed a chapter of the Young Lords in New York. Encouraged by the example and support of the Black Panthers and Chicago's original Young Lords Organization, the New York crew was a multiethnic coalition promoting Puerto Rican self-determination, nationalism, and cultural pride. "¡Jíbaro sí, yanqui no!" They took over a church that would not house their breakfast program. They occupied a hospital demanding a treatment center. They wore military gear. No cardigans. The Lords galvanized a generation of Nuyoricans fed up with everyday poverty and racism. They dug Latin music.

The Lords' enthusiasm for Puerto Rican culture touched several Fania artists. Salseros got heritage conscious. They cut back on the boogaloo and rewrote Afro-Cuban traditions by highlighting unique Puerto Rican contributions to the music.

Colón and Baretto helped revive the *plena*, a rural ballad style many saw as one of the few genres indigenous to Puerto Rico. Check out Colón's *There Goes the Neighborhood*—plenas galore and the added pleasure of old-school player Mon Rivera on trombone. Some Fania artists also began writing lyrics about politics and history. Channeling the P.R. zeitgeist, Barretto declared the importance of Latin culture to the American mainstream. While most in the country were still tripping on Santana, Barretto said it was *all* Latin music. In the '60s, he explained, "the whole basis of American rhythm…changed from the old dotted-note jazz shuffle rhythm to a straight-ahead straight-eighth approach, which is Latin."

Barretto's understanding of Latin music, and his playing for free at Young Lords' benefits, endeared him to the Party. Barretto did the right thing. Others did not. In 1971, the Lords wailed in their newspaper *Palante*:

> [M]any bands refused to play because the Party couldn't pay them. These bands are very money-minded and even though their music is fine they don't give a shit about the people. Many of our people cannot afford to pay $5 or $6 for tickets at rich-owned (usually White-owned) music casinos. All the money at these dances goes into the pockets of greedy disc jockeys, promoters, and bands. None of it goes to the people… These bands have our people, mostly young, dancing while they reap in all the profits. This music pacifies us and keeps our minds away from the realities of life—poor housing, poor health care, brutality from the police, poor jobs, etc. The music they play is almost all non-political and doesn't give a message or any education or how to "move" on these conditions.

Barretto, the paper insisted, knew the score. "Bands like Ray Barretto give these messages to our people. These bands comprehend the necessity of change. They do not need to play for money because they have love and respect for our people, which will help them to survive." Publicity like this literally could not be bought. Barretto's support of the Lords did help him survive, just as he helped the Party make ends meet. It also helped make Fania look like it was part of a movement. Some of the most recognizable names in the organization wrote liner notes for Barretto's Fania releases. Felipe Luciano testified on 1972's *Que Viva La Musica*:

> He has grown, you know. This Ray of light of late has grown more conscious of his blackness/browness and his continental origins like Africa. Listen to Ray behind the trumpets, snatch him lurking behind the piano, lay in the cut and smell Ray cooking. P.R. Bar B Cue.

Supporting the Lords helped give Barretto street cred. It brought new fans to the shows. Fania was a new kind of Latin label. It cared about the people, not crossover. Didn't you hear the Young Lords swoon?

STEP FIVE: CREATE A SUPERGROUP

Ray Barretto or Willie Colón could fill a dance floor in New York. When they appeared together, they left crowds waiting in the streets. In 1968, Barretto dropped *Acid* and *Hard Hands*, the funkiest Latin soul discs in his collection. Colón issued *The Hustler*. Pacheco was still going strong. Larry Harlow, "El Judio Maravilloso," added vocalist Ismael Miranda to his band. They began to garner hits. Jerry Masucci, ever publicity conscious, scheduled a few Latin jam sessions at an East Village club called the Red Garter. He

filled the stage with Fania stars and hopefuls. He brought in ringers Tito Puente and Eddie Palmieri. It was a showcase, bigger than the sum of its parts. The band was loud and relentless. The dance floor dripped sweat. It was a mob scene.

Fania released the show on two LPs by the Fania All-Stars. They hoped the records could introduce the rest of the world to the sound that was causing New York Latin music lovers to lose so much sleep. It was a keen marketing move: an all-star concert that promoted the label as much as the individual artists. It kept the publicity and potential profits in the family. Established acts combined efforts, and lesser knowns could bask in the glow. Yet it was not a new idea. Latin labels Alegre and Tico had done it before. *Live at the Red Garter* sold well in Fania's hometown. Like its predecessors, the record failed to sell elsewhere. Masucci tried again.

STEP SIX: MAKE A MOVIE

In August 1971, Masucci booked another All-Stars concert at the Cheetah on 52nd and 8th Avenue. Fans packed the house. The line outside twisted for ten blocks. The police were called out for crowd control. The Fania All-Stars jammed through the evening. Pacheco directed the show. Larry Harlow played keys, Bobby Valentin bass, and Willie Colón headed up the trombones. The cadre of singers included Ismael Miranda, Héctor Lavoe from Colón's band, and the great Pete "El Conde" Rodriguez. The players had fun. They joked with each other and traded moments in the spotlight. The mood was joyful and loose. The crowd ate it up.

Masucci filmed the show. He created a feature length movie by combining the footage with portraits of Puerto Rican life in Harlem and the Lower East Side. *Our Latin Thing (Nuestra Cosa)* premiered nationally in July 1972. It did what all the Latin all-star groups before could not. It demonstrated the power, joy, and groove of Nuyorican music to many who had not heard it before. The movie got press. It was reviewed in *Rolling Stone* and *Time*. The movie showed people not only playing salsa but enjoying it. The Cheetah audience caught as much screen time as the players. They laughed, cheered, and dazzled with precise and creative dance steps. The crowd's excitement was contagious. Clubbers throughout the land took notice. So did major record labels. The movie was Fania's debutante ball.

The genius of *Our Latin Thing* was its ability to speak to different constituencies at the same time. The mainstream press and its readers saw the film as a dance party. Strong grooves, fresh steps, style: the film signaled a possible future for disco. The New York Puerto Rican crowd went to the film and saw themselves. *Our Latin Thing* featured Nuyorican lives. Kids playing on the sidewalk. Impromptu concerts in the park. Ghetto poverty and junkies. Alternately beautiful and disturbing, the images of street life in *Our Latin Thing* at least avoided the stereotypes that had dominated depictions of Latino culture on the silver screen.

It is difficult to imagine a film getting positive coverage in both *Palante* and *Billboard*. *Our Latin Thing* did. The Young Lords' paper celebrated the film's depictions of the barrio. "Time was when the only time you saw Puerto Ricans in the movies were in films like *The Young Savages* or the racist classic, *West Side Story*," Lord Pablo "Yoruba" Guzman's review began. "*Our Latin Thing* has some progressive qualities—it's the first commercial film that comes closest to showing the Puerto Rican reality (although this is contained mainly to young Puerto Ricans in New York). It shows where we must live, which, when magnified many times on the screen, raises a lot of consciousness particularly among a Latin audience." The film was better than its predecessors. Guzman criticized it, however, for not linking barrio culture to the struggle for liberation. "As long as we're making music in the parks, the movie makes ghettoes like the Lower East Side look good," he lamented. The film was good, but not good enough. Guzman would soon come around to Fania's side.

Billboard gushed. *Our Latin Thing* hit at the perfect time to attract the attention of the national music industry. It thrust Fania artists center stage at the very moment the majors were entering the theater.

STEP SEVEN: MAKE THE MAJORS SALIVATE

The mainstream record industry noticed the growing Latin market as early as 1968. *Billboard* led the campaign, noting consumer hunger for clave. Morton Levy, president of Roulette Records and Latin subsidiaries Tico and Alegre, spoke to the magazine. "With all of this talk about rhythm and blues," Morton told the magazine, "you have about twenty million Latin Americans in the United States starving for Latin music, plus another 400 million around the world who are Latin and moving into middle-class environments in many countries." Levy insisted that a breakout Latin disc could sell 800,000 copies nationwide. The industry took note.

After paying it only passing attention, *Billboard* began actively promoting Latin music in 1972. The magazine published a supplemental booklet titled "The Latin Explosion" in its November 25th issue. It was four months after the premiere of *Our Latin Thing*. Latin music had arrived in the big leagues. The supplement discussed the rising tide of local and regional Latin scenes, noting the growing number of clubs featuring Latin dancing, rising Latino buying power, and even the sales potential among the politically conscious. Pan American Records head Harry Frenkel explained, "Everyone has heard of Black Power, but now we have Brown Power." For *Billboard* and its readers, Brown Power meant buying power. *Billboard* divided the supplement into profiles on several regional hotbeds of Latin music. Chicano and Tex-Mex music blossomed in Texas and California. Miami and Chicago were home to strong Cuban and Puerto Rican scenes. Yet New York reigned as the center of the Latin Explosion according to the journal. New York had the clubs, the radio stations, the recording studios, the labels, and the fans.

Latin music insiders did not need *Billboard* to tell them they were on to something. They did need the magazine to tell everyone else. Disc jockeys, club owners, and label heads took out ads congratulating the magazine for hopping on the bandwagon. "Caytronics Welcomes *Billboard* to the Fastest Growing Area of Our Industry, Latin Music." "The Cheetah Salutes *Billboard* magazine for its insights and awareness of the Latin Music explosion." Others used the *Billboard* supplement to preach the possibilities of crossover. Masucci told readers, it's "going to take the right product to really break the market nationally… Latin musicians have to realize that they must experiment with American music and use it for their own development." He insisted that White folks could be persuaded to buy salsa as long as Latin musicians met them halfway. Stop singing so much Spanish. Demonstrate the vitality of the Latin dance scene, and work "American" elements into the musical mix. The long descargas in *Our Latin Thing* accomplished the first two. Masucci's Fania All-Stars would eventually achieve the third.

"The Latin Explosion" marked something of a turning point for Fania and the New York Latin scene. Prior to its arrival, the label had put most of its efforts into developing a strong following in the Nuyorican community that had spawned many of its stars. *Our Latin Thing* went nationwide but its sound and images were purely local. With *Billboard* attention, Fania began pushing outward, looking for the special combination of sound and style that would break Latin

music and produce the mega-seller that Morton Levy had predicted in 1968. Some believed this campaign was a denial of the label's Nuyorican roots. An increasing number, however, saw crossover as a new political strategy.

STEP EIGHT: MAKE FRIENDS WITH THE PRESS

Fania might not have made it to the top without Izzy Sanabria. The graphic designer joined fortunes with the label in the early '70s. Their stories cannot be told separately. Sanabria created most of the label's memorable album covers, pushing the look of Latin music beyond stereotypical shots of smiling stars, orgasmic but nameless women, or White dancers getting their groove on. Sanabria wailed, "Most Latin labels just won't admit to cover strength. It is time for the Latin industry to utilize its talent to the fullest and to begin to create trends, instead of just copying them." His album art did just that. Bold graphics, psychedelic imagery, and integrated liner notes displayed the unique character of each album. His work got Fania albums noticed in the record racks.

Sanabria was also an aspiring media mogul. He was MC for the Fania All-Stars. He produced a television show called *Salsa*. In 1973, he started a humble pamphlet listing upcoming Latin shows in New York. The pamphlet was in English—perfect for second and third generation Latinos raised in the U.S. but interested in Latin culture. When a small ad for one-dollar subscriptions flooded his mailbox with requests, Sanabria was in the magazine business. Sanabria's *Latin NY* became the mouthpiece of the New York salsa scene, promoting local artists and clubs and even going a long way toward establishing "salsa" as the catchword of the movement (but let's not forget the influence of Cal Tjader's *Soul Sauce* or Charlie Palmieri's *Salsa Na' Ma'*).

Sanabria was on a mission. He believed salsa could be a trojan horse, integrating Latin culture into the mainstream and bringing Latino people along with it. It was a turn from the socialist revolution touted by the Lords, but it was not a complete denial. Sanabria used *Latin NY* as a platform for promoting positive imagery of Latin culture. He reprinted articles from the dominant press and used their Latino stereotypes as fodder for his own editorials. When *Oui* featured what he called "spic chic" pictorials, Sanabria took aim. "We must be careful that we are not exploited and that we are represented in the media in a manner which will contribute to the enhancement of our image." Let them be wowed by Latin chic, he insisted, but keep it positive. "Let them imitate us. It's the biggest compliment we can receive… America eat your heart out wishing you had what comes naturally to us… Let there come over America and the world a Latin influence which will keep us in demand forever." Salsa held the keys to this kingdom. Boogaloo, Latin soul, and the Latin hustle filled dance floors. Where the Lords failed, salsa could deliver.

Sanabria pushed hard. He turned *Latin NY* into a glossy covered gem. He helped Larry Harlow lobby the National Association of Recording Arts and Sciences for a Latin Grammy. He encouraged other Latin labels to take marketing lessons from the rock world. He created an awards show of his own, showering congratulations and statuettes on New York's finest. It was a bid for respectability. It worked. Salsa was a sensation.

Fania benefited from *Latin NY*'s campaigns. The voice of the salsa scene featured legions of ads, reviews, and artist profiles promoting Fania artists. The *Latin NY* Music Awards left very few Fania acts out in the cold. In 1976, the label ran an ad boasting, "Out of 30 music categories, the Fania family reaps 20 awards." It could have been rigged, but that's almost beside the point. *Latin NY* and Fania rode each other's coattails. They cooperated. They brought salsa to

the masses and took the proceeds to the bank. Were they selling out? Or were they changing the joke and slipping the yoke? Get America's feet moving and its hearts and minds will follow? The artists dug it. Barretto cheered the possibility of escaping the low-paying "cuchifrito circuit." The majors encouraged it. Columbia signed the Fania All-Stars. Even the Young Lords got onboard, as Pablo Guzman went to work for *Latin NY* before joining the Fania staff. *¿Que viva la revolucion? ¡Que viva la musica!* Fania had arrived.

Eight basic steps to industry domination. Can you follow? Fania's was not an easy road. It was a multi-front attack—a balancing act.

Play well. Make it fresh. Pay attention to the hopes and desires of your community. Keep core audiences happy, while pushing outward. Know a reason why expansion matters. This was the formula for Fania's rise. It says nothing about its ultimate fall. For that, a few words of warning must suffice. Avoid formula. Beware of merengue. Dance with them that brung you. And never, under any circumstance, title a record *Crossover*. ⬤

Originally appeared in Wax Poetics Issue 3, Fall 2002.

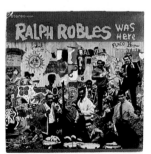

The Poor People Music
of Clive Chin

by Wilson F. Karaman

To label Randy's Studio 17 a mere component of Jamaica's musical evolution would be a misstatement. For the better part of a decade, Randy's *was* Jamaica's musical evolution. In a time of social unrest and global political instability, the modest studio constructed by Vincent Chin at 17 North Parade in Kingston served as a major catalyst in redefining the sound of reggae music. In particular, the early and mid-1970s productions of Clive Chin, Vincent's eldest son, harnessed the rebellious atmosphere of the day and, in doing so, ushered in a new era of progressive music on the island. By bringing gritty instrumentals and socially conscious lyrics to the people, Clive seized control over a musical revolt that transformed reggae into the predominant medium for sociopolitical protest. ¶ The story of Randy's begins in 1959, when Vincent Chin first opened a retail shop on East Street in Kingston. Capitalizing on a newly developing indigenous music industry, Vincent sold independently produced Jamaican records to an increasingly interested public. By 1962, his operation had outgrown its storefront, and the business was moved to its ultimate home over on North Parade. Jamaican autonomy, achieved in August of that year, prompted a further substantial growth in the record industry as people lined the dancehalls in celebration of their new liberation, and Vincent sought to profit by venturing into the realm of production. At the time, recording studios were few and far between, with only a handful of studios renting recording time to freelance producers. For several years, Vincent did his recording at the legendary Federal Studio, scoring with vocal hits by the likes of Lord Creator, Toots and the Maytals, and Alton Ellis. By mid-decade, however, increasing fees and lack of available studio time led to a shortage of recording opportunities for many producers, Vincent Chin included. By 1965, Vincent set in motion a remodeling agenda for his storefront, which included plans to construct a studio above the retail area, and by the fall of 1967, the studio's new foundations had been laid. »

With regard to the original recording equipment, Vincent employed Bill Garnett, one of the engineers at WIRL studios, to construct a custom board and console. The initial set up involved a quarter-inch, two-track Ampex recorder, and was operated by Garnett himself. Since recording time was at such a premium in Kingston, however, Vincent's plan to use Randy's strictly for his own productions quickly proved unfeasible, and the studio was subsequently rented out to other producers. Meanwhile, in order to keep costs down, Vincent involved the help of his family members in running the studio, including Clive. Still a schoolboy at the time, Clive would head to the studio most days after school to help out according to his father's wishes. It was through this rather forced apprenticeship of sorts that Clive would develop and hone his studio skills, which, a couple years down the road, would help mold a new era of Jamaican music.

A turning point for the studio occurred in early 1970, when the chief engineering post changed hands. One of Clive's older schoolmates, a man by the name of Errol Thompson, had been working as an apprentice under engineer Sylvan Morris at the famed Studio One on Brentford Road. After a recommendation from a friend of Vincent's, Errol was offered the job at Randy's. Upon his arrival, he reconstructed the board to suit his taste, and the studio upgraded to a half-inch, four-track recorder, which allowed for more versatility in the recording process. With Thompson at the controls of a new board, and the young Clive increasingly active in the production process, one of the most important associations in reggae was quickly taking shape.

Reggae music of the late 1960s had become increasingly popularized, as a substantial rift developed within the Jamaican record-listening audience. Sound systems still ruled the urban dancehalls, with DJs providing a live running commentary on metropolitan plight, but it was the more rural, wealthier areas of the island that accounted for the majority of record sales. Thus, the mainstream hits of the day took on an increasingly soft, even pop-like feel; organ hooks frequently set the melody, and an emphasis on clean production emerged. In fact, period productions by the likes of Lee Perry and Rupie Edwards, while commercially successful, were notable for their rather explicit lack of real political commentary. By the early 1970s, however, this stylistic monopoly would come crashing down.

The end of the 1960s gave way to increasing unrest amongst Jamaica's urban dwellers for several reasons. Political tensions were already running high with the escalation of the war in Vietnam, and a universal unease continued to grip the world as the two nuclear powers of the day, the United States and the Soviet Union, fought proxy battles across the globe. This uneasiness translated very directly to a Jamaican people who had, in nearly ten years of independence from Great Britain, still not reaped the promised fruits of freedom. The nation remained quite poor, and infighting amongst the ruling conservative party, known as the Jamaican Labor Party, resulted in very little reform or economic stimulus. Meanwhile, intensifying protests in America about the country's involvement in Vietnam sparked similar discontent with regard to domestic policy in Jamaica. The minority People's National Party took an increasingly hard-line leftist stance, openly attacking the perceived complacency of then Prime Minister Hugh Shearer and blaming the conservatives for the country's economic woes. The result was a progressively hostile political climate leading up to the 1972 Parliamentary elections, and an underlying tide of rebellion in the streets. "It was a time of pure revolution," Clive Chin recalls. "The people was in need of change, and this is when I begin producing. The people need a new way of expressing themself. They need a music for calling attention, a boom-shack-a-lack music."

While the content of Randy's productions did indeed expand farther into the political sphere in the early 1970s, the pace of the music nonetheless preserved its popularized uptempo feel. The Lee Perry–produced *Soul Rebels* album by Bob Marley and the Wailers brought tremendous exposure to the production capabilities of the studio, and while important in introducing the record-buying public to a new lyrical ambition, it still retained a similarly commercial instrumental backing. Furthermore, because the studio was contracted to outside producers a vast majority of the time, commercial potential was a prerequisite for any song released on the studio's house labels (usually Impact). As Clive recalls, "Impact was the hit label. My stepmom had the last say on rating the tunes, so she pick the songs that will sell. She not concerned with politics, because politics wouldn't sell!" In fact, until Clive finally ventured into the production arena on his own in late 1971, the vast majority of politically based songs failed to pass auditions at Randy's.

Around this time, the house band at Randy's, known as the Impact Allstars, featured a relatively stable lineup of renowned musicians. The typical lineup included Aston "Family Man" Barrett and Lloyd Adams anchoring the rhythm section on bass and drums respectively, along with Alvin "Reggie" Lewis on rhythm guitar and "Bongo" Ossie Hibbert playing organ, and either Earl "Chinna" Smith or Ronnie Williams rounding out the arrangement on lead guitar. In early 1972, however, Clive brought one of his school friends, a young Horace Swaby, over to the studio during off-hours to record a melody penned by one of his classmates, Dennis Wright.

Staged press photo for *This Is...Augustus Pablo*, with Clive Chin posing behind Pablo playing melodica. The Wailers, who played on the album, could not appear in the press photo due to a contract with Island Records.

Mixing down an Augustus Pablo session in 1973. (left to right) Dennis Thompson, an assistant engineer; Errol Thompson (on phone), the head Randy's engineer; Clive Chin (in background); and Augustus Pablo. Photos by Balfe Bradley and courtesy of Clive Chin.

Although he had already scored a hit with his haunting melodica on "East of the River Nile," Swaby, who recorded under the name Augustus Pablo, remained a relatively minor player amongst the island's musical ranks. This standing, however, would be short-lived following the release of what would become one of the most groundbreaking tracks ever produced during the reggae era. With the Allstars providing a killer rhythmic backdrop, Pablo tore his way through a jolting, highly improvised melodic line.

The completed track, titled "Java," signaled the beginning of a new chapter in Jamaica's musical history book. The slowed tempo of the rhythm section, coupled with Errol Thompson's raw, understated mix, resulted in a vastly different sound than any the public had been accustomed. It was the first song to employ the "rebel rock" sound, and it set a new course for the vast majority of productions to follow for the rest of the decade. "That tune just blow up," Clive remembers. "Yeah, 'Java' was a big tune for me, because it was something new. This was poor people music, and it capture the rebel feeling that most people have then. It's a very down-to-earth sound, and the city people, them could relate to it." By this time, the studio had upgraded the recording equipment again to one-inch, eight-track, which allowed Clive and Errol Thompson a much more defined sound. By recording the bass directly through a microphone and getting Pablo's melodica on a separate track, Thompson was able to create a very eerie mood for the tune. Clive originally released "Java" on his own side label, Checker, but the immediate demand was so great that the cut was quickly pressed up on Impact and distributed in mass quantity.

With the upcoming elections of 1972 providing an ample backdrop, the focus of popular music on the island began to change, and change rapidly. The success of the new instrumental sound developed by Clive, as well as the relative acceptance by the public of politically oriented songs, created an environment ripe for a combination of the two. Artists on both sides of the political fence flocked to Randy's to voice their opinions, often resulting in rather scathing personal attacks and indictments. Among others notable for political substance, the Junior Byles–voiced "King of Babylon," produced by Lee Perry, thinly veiled its likening of Prime Minister Shearer to an evil king presiding over a corrupt land. Yet despite the building political interest, Randy's productions, other than Clive's, remained relatively tame. "My stepmom not into political songs, or the Rasta tunes at all. She pass up [Fred Locks's] 'Black Star Liner'! So I haffi press the more political tunes myself, on my own labels." Over the next couple years he would produce many crucial hits in this vein, employing the vocal talents of such well-respected performers as Dennis Brown, the Heptones, and Freddie McKay, in addition to lesser-known artists like Senya, Ta Teacher Love, and even Ducky Simpson's first incarnation of Black Uhuru.

The Randy's sound, through Clive's productions, developed into a veritable blueprint for conveying messages of social unrest and the hardships of poverty. Defiant vocal cuts like Senya's "Children of the Ghetto," Sweeny's "Won't Come Easy," and Hortense Ellis's cover of "Woman of the Ghetto" tackled tough social issues that had, by and large, previously been ignored in mainstream music. While softer "country reggae" sounds were indeed still receiving attention for their market value in terms of rural music fans, an alternate economy now existed within the production industry in the form of rebel rock. Clive released scores of productions on a plethora of labels, including One Way Sounds, Checker, Giant, Demon, Hot Shot, and Tan-Ya (named after his little sister). In addition to producing vocal cuts, Clive continued to work with a small core of musicians to polish his sound, and Errol Thompson, drawing from the rhythms laid down by these musicians, put together one of the very first dub albums, the elusive *Java Java Java Java* (aka *Java Java Dub*).

Randy's maintained its dominance as the premier studio in Kingston through mid-decade, which provided in-house recordings an immediate spot in the public eye. Clive took full advantage of this situation by reeling off a string of raw hits, including Dennis Brown's seminal "Foot of the Mountain," a Heptones' version of "Guiding Star" (accompanied by a scorching Pablo instrumental), and a remarkable Alton Ellis cover of the Cornelius Brothers' "Too Late to Turn Back Now," where Clive had his musicians build a new rhythm independent of the fast-paced original melody. The result was a bouncy back-and-forth beat with a surprising underlying edge, due in part to Clive's instrumental arrangement, which lacked a rhythm guitar—he instead employed a cheese grater to match Pablo's keyboard on the upbeat.

Meanwhile, Clive had also succeeded in bringing instrumental sounds back to the forefront of the industry. Following his success with "Java," Clive recorded one of his more notable full-length records with Augustus Pablo's *This Is…Augustus Pablo*, which essentially consisted of a collection of cuts featuring Pablo blowing his melodica over the more popular studio rhythms. Several other instrumentals, including a Hortense Ellis B-side version, "Guns in the Ghetto," and Tommy McCook's saxophone run on the "Java" rhythm, titled "Jaro," as well as the Impact Allstars treatment of the popular "Mission: Impossible" theme, also gained attention from the public.

By mid-decade, several new studios opened in the Kingston area, including the brand new Channel One (constructed by the Hookim brothers), Joe Gibbs Studio, and Lee Perry's musical shrine, the Black Ark. Although it remained technically open until 1979, Randy's began to lose steam in 1977, when several members of the Chin family relocated to New York (including Clive). Clive would return occasionally over the next two years, presiding over Senya's "Rootsman" session in 1978, and several 1979 Rico sides originally intended for the *Man From Warieka* album. These titles rounded out the Randy's catalog, and the studio officially closed its doors in 1979, perhaps prematurely yet undeniably legendary.

Protest and social strife were the underlying cornerstones of urban life for Jamaicans of the early 1970s, and, thanks to the vision of Clive Chin, the people gained a primary outlet for expression through music. This outlet was made possible first and foremost by the success of Randy's in essentially cornering production in Kingston. As Earl Morgan of the Heptones recalls, "Everybody record at Randy's. If yuh nah record deh, nobody know you." With the majority of the industry's attention and resources concentrated on Randy's, Clive assumed a very powerful position at the dawn of his producing career, and indeed used this position to his advantage very effectively. He combined conscious lyrics with deep, brooding melodies to create a brand new sound. In doing so, Clive introduced the general public to the potential power of music as a social force, and thus effectively carved out a new path for the industry, one that would be followed by countless subsequent producers throughout the 1970s. The rebel rock sound was a raw and determined voice, and it belonged to the poor. ●

Originally appeared in Wax Poetics Issue 2, Spring 2002.

King Tubby and the Birth of the Remix

by Wilson F. Karaman

When Byron Smith accidentally left the vocal track off a dubplate bound for Ruddy Redwood's sound system in 1967, he inadvertently stumbled upon one of the most profound innovations in recorded music history. Through this development, the tiny island of Jamaica gave birth to the art of remix, long before DJ Herc and friends patented the concept on American soil in the late 1970s. Following Smith's unanticipated introduction, remixes came to rule the better part of the next decade in Jamaican dance halls, thanks particularly to the contributions of one man, the late Osbourne Ruddock. Ruddock, better known by his alias King Tubby, revolutionized and standardized the post-production mixdown. In doing so, he helped initiate a transition whereby the engineer's role became of equal importance to that of the musician in the creative process. Satisfying patrons at the local sound system dances was not an easy feat; doing so required the freshest sound around, and Tubby's remix experimentations were unparalleled in their creativity. Indeed, with his studio in the Waterhouse district of Kingston, he became the recording ambassador of dub music, and the engineering advances pioneered by Tubby and his apprentices laid the groundwork for hip-hop's infancy in New York City later on in the decade. ¶ The road to dub's creation began in Kingston's dance halls as early as the late 1940s, when the first sound systems appeared on the scene. In the years leading up to this time, weekly dances in the city generally featured strictly live music, usually in the form of a single dance band churning out sets of jazz or traditional folk music. After World War II, however, a transformation in economic production occurred whereby the United States, having mobilized its factories for wartime production, began mass-manufacturing consumer goods. As a result of subsequent American exporting, the Jamaican general public suddenly had access to items like shortwave radios, on which they could receive transmissions from New Orleans and other Southern hotbeds of rhythm and blues. This led to a shift in demand from the record-buying public, whereby the more up-tempo, gritty sounds of boogie and shuffle became the order of the day. »

Seizing on the opportunity, several dance promoters began setting up basic turntable and speaker units at the dance halls and bringing local shop owners and record collectors in to spin the latest hits from America. Though technologically crude at their initial inception, the systems quickly developed into the most popular form of dance-hall entertainment. As the 1950s rolled along, system operators began to take on personalities similar to American disc jockeys, whereby they would introduce each record with slang catchphrases and exclamations. Meanwhile, since dance promoters dealt with far less overhead from paying a single DJ as opposed to an entire band, they had more money to improve the featured sound setup. Promoters began employing local technicians to construct larger, more powerful systems, capable of broadcasting sounds throughout a radius of several blocks. Huge mobile speaker units were brought in for the larger dances, and local powerhouses like Duke Reid's Trojan Sound, Sir Coxson Dodd's Downbeat Freedom Sound, and King Edwards's Giant Sound quickly established themselves as the top dances of the day.

At root in the battle for sound system supremacy lay the age-old DJ archetype of, quite simply, the rarer the better. While the big sounds would send representatives up to America every week to pick up the freshest American tunes (a distinct trademark ability of the larger sets), these tracks were generally available in the Southern United States and, as a result, not necessarily particular to any one set. Thus, while the bigger dances all featured relatively rare songs, no system was able to establish a real market dominance due to lack of exclusivity. The end of the decade, however, saw Sir Coxson recording local singers for restricted play on his sound system, and the idea quickly spread. By the mid-'60s, Coxson Dodd and Duke Reid had each constructed their own studios, with Dodd constructing his infamous Studio One at 13 Brentford Road, and Reid adding Treasure Isle Studio to the second floor of his liquor shop on Bond Street. While various other producers of the day would rent out studio time at both spots to cut their own tracks, the fact that Dodd and Reid controlled the studios gave them a huge leg up on the competition.

By the dawn of rocksteady in the mid-'60s, the studios had become veritable factories of rhythm for the related major sound systems. Twenty-four hours a day, session after session would be cut and promptly waxed on acetate using in-house equipment. As the rocksteady era rolled along, Treasure Isle increasingly became the dominant studio, and Reid expanded his mission. Instead of keeping all of his tracks exclusive and waiting for songs to break in dances controlled only by his own sound, Reid began shopping cuts around to other systems, including Ruddy Redwood's Supreme Ruler of Sound. If a rhythm blew up at another dance, Reid could still exploit the situation since he owned the tune and could therefore release it in a larger pressing to the general public. Such was the case in 1967, when Reid's chief engineer Byron Smith was in the midst of cutting an acetate of the Paragons' hit "On the Beach" for Redwood's sound when he accidentally left the vocal channel off as he ran the tape. The result was an essentially instrumental version, with the vocal only faintly audible in the background of the other channels. When Redwood switched over from the vocal cut to the instrumental version at his dance later in the week, the crowd went wild, shouting along in place of the absent lyrics.

In this way, the concept of remix made its rudimentary entrance in the world of music. Following the success of Smith's accident, instrumental versions started appearing on the B-side of released 45s. This not only benefited Reid's wallet (the new craze led to a dramatic revival of sales), but in fact touched all of the sound systems, as the instrumental cut allowed each sound to showcase the talents of the system operator. Rather than simply introduce each cut before the track began, DJs could now run through their typical strings of jive over the rhythm track before switching over to the vocal. Certain smaller sounds began to gain prominence not only on the strength of their rhythms, but the entertainment value of the DJ in charge.

One such system to benefit from this phenomena was the Home Town Hi-Fi in Waterhouse. Essentially a minor side project of Osbourne Ruddock, then a freelance electrician, the sound typically played smaller parties in one of Kingston's toughest neighborhoods. This changed, however, when Ruddock, who operated under the alias King Tubby, employed a friend of his named Ewart Beckford to DJ his sound around 1969. Better known as U-Roy, Beckford quickly made a name for himself as one of the top live entertainers. As the Home Town's popularity began to rise, Ruddock became increasingly interested in upgrading his sound in order to compete with the larger dances.

Drawing on his expertise as an electrical engineer, he fashioned a new amplifier for his set. The central speakers of the sound were modified to include 16 ohm woofers and a powerful bass boost capable of shaking the floors. As one of Ruddock's apprentices, Phillip Smart recalls, "The speaker was so big, it can't run with the electricity in the dance. So man would run up the light poles on the street and take power from there to run the sound!" The most notable variation, however, occurred when he built a reverb delay unit into the back of the amplifier, which he attached to a switch on the top. When turned on, the amp would produce an eerie echo effect on any sound that traveled through. According to Smart, the effect was intense: "U-Roy drive up on his bike with Tubby's new speaker, an' it have the reverb unit built up, but him kept real quiet about it before that session. But when him introduce the first riddim, him call out, 'You're now entertained by the number one sound in the land,' and it echo. Man, the dance ram hard! He chat with an echo all night, the people couldn't get enough!"

This proved to be a key turning point for Tubby, as the success of his amp in the dance hall provoked him to attempt similar electronic manipulation in the small studio he had recently set up in the back of his house. Originally, the studio featured a rudimentary, essentially homemade eight-channel board and a basic acetate press, which Tubby used solely for remixing rhythms and pressing cuts for his sound system. During this quest for advancing his sound, however, he recognized the necessity of a more durable board and thus arranged to purchase an MCI four-track console from Dynamic Sounds, another local studio. He then acquired a new Presto dub machine capable of cutting approximately five minutes of tape onto a 10-inch pressing, which perfectly suited his sound system needs. His arsenal of mixing equipment at the same time came to include two Ampac four-tracks, a two-track, and a Fisher spring reverb unit, which allowed him to recreate the echo effects that had previously proven so successful at dances.

The key to Tubby's studio sound, however, lay in the minor alterations he made to the equipment. As Phillip Smart remembers, it was a very deliberate process: "Tubby always plan way ahead, and once he set the board it was done, he nah touch it again. But first, yunno, he mess aroun' with the console, an' the reverb, an' his amplifier, an' t'ing. Get in there and adjust everything. His studio was a completely unique sound. Even the engineer tone in the console, unique to Tubby's." The four tracks allowed Tubby great versatility in mixing down the rhythms, as typically the drum and bass, guitar and keyboards, horns, and vocals were separate tracks. Thus, any

channel could be faded in or out of the mix at any time, and Tubby could alter each track with echo or other effects individually.

As his popularity spread, more and more producers began leaving tapes at Tubby's studio to be remixed. Increasingly creative additions (and subtractions) began showing up in the mixes as Tubby and a handful of apprentices including Lloyd James ("Prince Jammy"), Hopeton Brown ("Scientist"), and "Prince" Phillip Smart continuously stretched the studio's boundaries. Sound effects like thunder, forest sounds, and gunshots could be edited into the mix right from commercial records, or, with a little ingenuity, actually created in the studio. "Yeah, for a couple a dubs we need a bigger crash a thunder, so we tek the spring [reverb unit] and drop it 'pon the floor," recalls Smart. "It make this huge crash, an' Tubby record it an' mix it right into the song." Other effects, like the engineer's tone, filtered and run through an echo, became trademark elements of a Tubby mix. The tape itself could even serve as an effect, with a quick rewind simulating the popular dance-hall technique of a "false start" of sorts, where the DJ would lift up the needle or spin the record backwards in order to provoke the crowd and start his string of lyrics again.

By the mid-'70s, the popularity of dub had spread to the point where a 7-inch, previously styled after American releases to feature a hit tune with a second, less commercially viable vocal side on the flip, would almost exclusively be issued with either a remixed dub or a DJ version of the rhythm as its B-side. In this way, remixed sides effectively came to be recognized as songs unto themselves; the remix engineer could create an entirely new musical entity by altering and rerecording material that already existed. The creation of music no longer ceased when a band ended its session, but instead became contingent upon an engineer's reconstructive impulse. Entire dub albums began to see release starting around 1973, including Herman Chin-Loy's *Aquarius Dub*; Keith Hudson's *Pick a Dub*; a collection of rhythms from Randy's studio called *Java Java Java Java*; and Lee Perry's seminal *Blackboard Jungle Dub*, mixed by Perry himself and King Tubby.

The remainder of the 1970s saw dub evolve as engineers—particularly the crop of apprentices on hand at Tubby's studio—honed

their craft. The rise of newer recording studios like Joe Gibbs and Channel One, and the ascending popularity of the so-called "flying cymbals" steppers reggae, patented by Bunny Lee's Aggrovators outfit and modeled after the fashionable Philadelphia soul and disco scenes in America, added a diversity to the style of Jamaican popular recordings and, as a result, introduced new avenues for dub exploration. Phillip Smart recalls the challenges of mixing down an Aggrovators track: "Man, Bunny riddims tough! Tubby have a fix-pitch mixer, so yuh need even levels or yuh can't master right. But the flyin' cymbal t'ing is tough to get flat enough, so I make a fair share a mistake, but that's how we learn." The advent of 12-inch singles furthered the opportunity for creative engineering, as the longer sides allowed engineers to run a loop of the rhythm and go straight from the vocal cut to the dub, essentially turning the two sides of a 7-inch into one extended mix.

Dub continued to rule the dance halls until the end of the decade, when a new crop of freelance DJs like Josie Wales, Charlie Chaplin, and Jah Thomas emerged to steal some of dub's dance-hall thunder. Much like their American counterparts, these DJs featured impressive improvisatory abilities, and would "rap" in rhyming couplets over standard popular rhythms. Their talented vocal stylings again brought the focus of dances back to the DJ and relegated the music to background rhythm once again. Yet the contributions of King Tubby and others in establishing the version as a tool for further musical experimentation is undeniable in all the subsequent mutations of Jamaican, and even American, popular music. The first American hip-hop record to break onto the national scene, the Sugar Hill Gang's immortal "Rapper's Delight," was itself a version of Le Chic's popular disco track "Good Times." Jamaica's insatiable dance-hall patrons demanded innovation for their dollar, and the island's engineers, led by the great King Tubby, responded with a revolutionary new art form. Remix engineers have transformed the music industry at large in years since, but it was King Tubby's Waterhouse Studio that, to paraphrase the great U-Roy, first succeeded in originating without imitating. ◉

Originally appeared in Wax Poetics Issue 3, Fall 2002.

Joel Dorn's Gig of the Universe

by John Kruth

When I was a kid, baseball was my game. But I couldn't care less about scorecards or ERAs and RBIs. The math on the back of baseball cards was wasted on me. I just dug the game and the players' personalities. That was until the Beatles played Ed Sullivan and then suddenly everything changed. Sports instantly became a thing of the past and rock and roll was here to stay. A few months later my sister's beatnik boyfriend came boppin' over to the house with some MJQ and Herbie Mann records tucked under his arm to provide the smooth soundtrack to their make-out marathons. The music drifting down the hall from her bedroom door opened up another world to me. Oddly enough, one thing carried over from my love of baseball to my new obsession with collecting records. For some reason I viewed musicians like baseball players and their producers seemed to be the equivalent of managers, for instance, Phil Spector = Billy Martin (although Billy Martin was often out of control, he was never accused of murder). I soon memorized the names of the producers as well as the artists I admired. There was George Martin with the Beatles and Joe Boyd, who produced the great British folk-rock records of Richard Thompson, Nick Drake, and the Incredible String Band. Then there was Joel Dorn, whose name appeared on the back of my favorite Atlantic sides by Mose Allison, Rahsaan Roland Kirk, Yusef Lateef, Les McCann, and Eddie Harris. (Kudos also go to Mickey Most for Donovan's discs and Tony Visconti for his sweet and crunchy production of T. Rex!) »

For some reason, I pictured Dorn as a cross between Leo Duro-cher and Casey Stengel—undoubtedly an old crusty streetwise dude saved from a life of crime by his love of making records. I was certain that Dorn, like both legendary baseball managers, was always ready to go toe-to-toe with the record company (the ump) over his musician's right for complete artistic freedom, even if it meant being tossed out of the game.

When fate led me to his door a few years back while writing *Bright Moments*, my biography of Rahsaan Roland Kirk, I found my imagination was not too far off. With a white beard and buzz cut, Joel looked the part but was hardly as gnarly as Leo or Casey. But there were more than a few occasions when I heard him threatening somebody on the phone to watch their neck, or he'd slam it in a car door if they interfered with his mad methods.

In recent years, Dorn steered the doomed 32 Records to a couple pennants. His short-lived expansion team, Label M, sadly bit the dust just weeks after 9/11. After spending some time combing the beaches of St. Petersburg, he's back with his new label Hyena. (Hey, if you can't laugh at the record business, you don't belong in it.) Hyena has released a handful of live discs by Les McCann, Eddie Harris, Rahsaan Roland Kirk, and Cannonball Adderley previously available on Dorn's earlier Night Records.

Let's start at the beginning. How did you land a gig at Atlantic Records?

JOEL DORN: There are few dates in my life that I remember but June 1967 is one of them. That's when I got my job at Atlantic Records. Because I had fallen so heavily under Ray Charles's spell, I had been hounding [Atlantic director of A&R] Nesuhi [Ertegun] since I was fourteen, writing him letters, calling him, and everything. I didn't just wanna make records, I wanted to work at Atlantic! It took me eleven years to get the job, after bein' a disc jockey and doin' independent stuff that they distributed—two Duke Pearson records, [Rahsaan Roland Kirk's] *Here Comes the Whistleman*, and a couple of Rufus Harley records.

Atlantic was a small record company but it was the best record company in the world—ever! There were two golden periods when Atlantic had its fastball—from the late '40s to the late '50s, and then the early '60s to the mid-'70s.

By the time I joined Atlantic, Eddie Harris was already there and had recorded a version of "Listen Here" on piano. That was on *Mean Greens*. He did "The Shadow of Your Smile" in the same groove he used on "Exodus," but it didn't really catch on.

I got a question for you that might be hard to answer.

If it's about Eddie it's *gotta* be hard to answer. Eddie was always hard to deal with. You had to work with him on his terms. He was angry but not in the traditional sense, like "the angry young Black man." Angry in a different kind of way. Not a bad guy. Very charming, very funny, very bright. A good father, a solid guy who saved his money… He was driven by some kind of manic need to distance himself from his hits and always re-prove himself. He was in a passive kind of war with most of the planet. You'll never know how brilliant he was, even if you listen to all of his records.

When you talk about records by Eddie or Les that didn't come across, what could you as a producer do to help 'em get across?

Just make 'em comfortable, so they could do what they did best, maybe compliment it a little. Look, I'm not a musician or a producer in the traditional sense of the word. I don't have *any* skills, but I *do* have abilities. I came out of jazz radio back when DJs were personalities who ad-libbed commercials to sell everything from hair tonic to cheap wine. Jazz at that time was a hip thing to get into after you

grew up a little bit. For cats comin' out of high school who were into pop music or R&B—the next place to slide to was jazz. Back then a lot of jazz was crossing over into the pop market. Ramsey Lewis with "The In Crowd," Nina Simone with "Porgy," Etta Jones with "Don't Go to Strangers," Ahmad Jamal with "Poinciana," Dave Brubeck's "Take Five," Eddie Harris with "Exodus." Three or four times a year, a jazz record would take a certain route, starting on jazz radio, crossing over to R&B, and then ultimately pop. My show was hit oriented in a dumb kind of way. It was the most accessible jazz—stuff like Ramsey and Mongo [Santamaria], "Fathead" [Newman] and Hank [Crawford] and [Jack] McDuff and Jimmy Smith and Les, but also included Trane and Monk and Mingus, Bird, and Lady. So I didn't compromise the integrity of doing a real jazz show.

Kind of like the tracks you put together for Hit Jazz back on 32 Records.

Right. It was not so much what I did as a producer, as it was a stomach thing, an instinct thing. A bell rings in your belly. I'd go hear these guys in the club and listen to their records, and then make suggestions: "Maybe you could build on that…" If I have a way of making records, it's to bring the right people to the studio under the right set of circumstances, to do what they do. I'm not one of those guys that if you make a record with me you're going to get my *thing*.

Like someone like Creed Taylor, who put his sonic stamp on everything he touched.

I don't even know how to do that! [*laughs*] But I do know that if you put your money on good horses, they're gonna win more than they're gonna lose. I just felt that these people could be bigger and better if they were recorded properly. That's of course without knowing how to make a record! [*laughs*] As a DJ, I got a lot of response from the listeners. The phone in the studio let me know what records people dug.

It was such a different time. People really took the music seriously. The clubs were filled with discerning listeners.

All these guys were wailing! You had Blakey and Yusef and Trane, Miles and Monk, and all the organ players. Everybody was working. You could go see McDuff and Jimmy Smith and the tenors—Stanley, Fathead, Hank…and guys like Oliver Nelson and Charles Lloyd…

Stop, I'm gonna cry. Let's get back to Atlantic.

With Eddie, I knew he could have a hit record any day of the week if the conditions were right. He'd come close a few times. My first gig at Atlantic was—after Nesuhi hired me, he went away for two weeks and left me an assignment. Eddie Harris was having major dental surgery and might not be able to play for a while. So before he went in for surgery he recorded like twenty or thirty songs in three days. Arif [Mardin] had just gone from being the studio manager to a producer and went in with Eddie and his working group to cut the stuff. There were boatloads of tapes. Nesuhi left me a note that said to go through them and see if there's an album there. The engineer, Bruce Tergeson, and I listened to all the tapes. There was one track that was twenty-eight minutes long that he felt could be good if it was edited properly. So I said go ahead and edit it. I didn't know how to do it! First he took it down to twelve minutes and I said, "Whoa, there's something here." Then he took it down to about seven minutes.

We're talking about audiotape and razor blades here.

Yeah, old-fashioned editing. It's no nobler than using computers, it just takes more time and involves another kind of skill. So the first record I put together was *The Electrifying Eddie Harris*, which was a top twenty record on the charts. It came out in the fall of '67. Eddie had this thing, the "Exodus" groove that he put like five thousand songs to. The other thing he had was the "Freedom Jazz Dance" groove, where all the songs go *whoop* like Stanley Turrentine.

What was working with Les like?

When I first came to Atlantic, Nesuhi asked me if I thought we should sign Les. I said yeah. He had been on Limelight, which was a deluxe-packaging wing of Mercury. He also had a couple records on the Pacific Jazz label that did pretty well, like *The Shampoo*. But Limelight records didn't capture him. The sides on Pacific Jazz captured his Ramsey Lewis/gospel piano-jazz style. But even the live records he made never really captured what he was about. Les was a great entertainer and a much better jazz player than people gave him credit for. He was also an unbelievable ballad player. Chicks loved when he sang slow, beautiful ballads; but when he sang 'em on records, I just didn't like the way he sounded.

I got to know Les when I was a disc jockey. He's one of my best friends now. He was plenty nuts in those days. He was like *twins*! He was funny in interviews. At the club he was as funny as he was a good musician. He had a terrific group. He'd set up a vamp and wail on it. I had seen him *kill* people in the club. But in conversations with him he told me that he hated the studio. He said people were always yelling out take numbers, stopping him for no apparent reason, or yelling at him to play more commercially.

The first record we did was *Much Les*. We just did what I thought he was trying to do all along, like "With These Hands" and "Doin' That Thing," and it worked. I actually did something that turned out to be smart. I didn't know the rules so I didn't know I was breaking them. Les said he hated when he'd get somethin' goin' and someone would be waving his arms to let him know they were running out of tape. What I did was set up two eight-track machines, and about a minute before the tape ran out on the first, we'd start the other. I knew Les could reach a broader audience, beyond jazz. It was just about makin' him more comfortable in the studio, and givin' him plenty of canvas and all the paint he needs.

How did the music change when Les went electric and started throwin' synthesizers into the mix?

It was pretty much just an extension of what he already did. The second album we did, *Layers*, is a minor classic among electro-freaks and engineers. I think it was *the* first thirty-two-track record that anybody made. We just put two sixteen-track recorders together. They were hand-cued. I didn't know that you couldn't do it. We just hated runnin' out of tracks. So I said to Bob Lifton, the engineer, "See if you can get two machines to run at once," and he found a way. That caused a lot of trouble at Atlantic because—

You're Joel Dorn.

[*laughs*] I really thought I was doin' somethin' cool. I thought it would be somethin' great for Atlantic. But they got pissed off. They said I was pissin' money away on this thirty-two-track shit. I might've spent some extra bread, but, y'know, it might've taken Columbus an extra week to cross the Atlantic! They were acting like I was spending their kid's college money or somethin'. It ended up that it became the industry standard. People started lockin' machines together. The only other guy I knew who was workin' on somethin' like that at the time was Leon Russell. He had a sixteen-track and eight-track hooked up together.

What's the story behind *Invitation to Openness*? That first track, "The Lovers," is a fantastic jam!

Invitation to Openness came about after Les called me up saying he dreamt he went into the studio to record and all the technical

stuff had been taken care of before he got there. All he had to do was sit down, start playing, and everybody would pick up off what he was playing. He didn't wanna hafta think about anything. I told him, "That's a good dream. I can help you with that one." He wanted eight or nine rhythm players and only one horn. He wanted somethin' different in the horn department. So I suggested Yusef [Lateef] on oboe.

I had seen Yusef play those oboe blues with [Cannonball Adderley]—numbers like "Trouble in Mind" and "See See Rider." So I said, "How about Yusef?" And he said, "Perfect." So Les got there around nine. The cats had already been there since seven thirty or eight o'clock. We had sounds on everybody. Everything was cool. Les's stuff was set up, his piano and whatever keyboards he was usin'. When he came in, we put the lights down and the guys that smoked, smoked. The guys that drank, drank. The guys that did nothin', did nothin'. And then it was just gone. At a certain point the room just lifted off the floor. That was "The Lovers."

Didn't you use a harp player on that session too?

That was Corky Hale, Mike Stoller's wife, who was working with Tony Bennett at the time. After the session, we were listening to the playback at train-whistle level and everybody was getting' off on it. Corky was there, havin' a ball when all of a sudden she looks at her watch and says, "I'm supposed to be at the Waldorf with Tony Bennett, and I'm late!" She was gonna need a helicopter to get from 60th Street to 49th Street to make it to that gig.

Didn't Roberta Flack sing a couple numbers on one of Les's

records?

Yeah, a couple duets with Les on an album called *Comment*. Rahsaan had turned me onto Roberta originally. He called me from DC and said I got this girl you should record, my bass player, Steve Novosel's wife. So I said, "What does she sound like?" He screamed into the phone, "She sings like a colored lady!" and slammed the phone down. [*laughs*] That was the last time we ever spoke about it. Then about a year later Les called me about her.

How did you get Les and Eddie together for *Swiss Movement*?

Here's what happened. The Atlantic studio and offices were in the same place at 1841 Broadway. I was walkin' into the studio as Eddie Harris was walkin' out. We bumped into each other in the doorway. "Hey, how ya doin'?" "How ya doin?" He was holding his latest invention, a trumpet with a saxophone mouthpiece. He later lent it to Rahsaan who used it on "Bye Bye Blackbird" where he imitated Miles. I asked him to play it for me, so I could hear what it sounded like. He had some crazy name for it that I can't remember. He played it without a mute, but because of the saxophone mouthpiece, it sounded just like Miles in the late '50s when he was usin' the mute all the time. Around this time, Nesuhi had met a young guy, who worked for the Swiss tourist board, named Claude Nobs who put a small festival together in Montreux as a tourist attraction. He had some great artists. The gig didn't pay much, but Claude treated everybody like royalty. So the record company sent the artist over and paid for the gig and transportation. In return, they got a video from Swiss television and an audiotape of the performance for the possibility of making a live album. Neshui was the first record exec to support the festival. He didn't care about the live record, but he dug Claude and wanted to support his festival.

It was decided to send Les's group and Eddie's group over. So I'm talkin' to Eddie, and he's showin' me the trumpet, and I said, "Listen, you're goin' to that festival in Switzerland; here's what you do, while Les is playing, go up on stage with the trumpet and play some blues. Les will fall in behind you, and it'll crack everybody up. Maybe something will come of it." Eddie had just had a big hit with "Listen Here." Les had a moderate hit with "With These Hands."

Three or four months later, I get this tape in the mail from the festival. It was a finished two-track, right off Swiss radio or television. I put it on to see if Eddie picked up on my suggestion. The air conditioner was broken that day. I was in the mixing room, and it was so hot I had to keep the door open. We put the tape on. Now all the doors were open to the studios, because it was a hot day in the middle of the summer, and the next thing I know, four or five people are standing at the door. A minute later, there were seventeen people at the door of this little mixing room.

Sounds like that scene with the Marx Brothers in *A Night at the Opera*!

Right! "Compared to What?" came on and people started dancin' like lunatics! I called Les. He said Eddie came by and they started talkin' and had a twenty-minute rehearsal and they went on. If you want to know what jazz is or what it's supposed to be? It's guys gettin' together and lookin' at the same finish line from five different starting points. It was a pure jam session.

It'll still sound fresh in the year 3000.

Exactly. It's odd, live records either they happen or they don't. It was just one of those things. In the Zen sense of production, yeah, I told them to get together and, yeah, Nesuhi sent 'em to the festival and paid for it. I never thought of them as jazz musicians. They were categorized as *jazz* and worked in the jazz world, but both of 'em were totally capable of transcending that.

After the success of the record, Les and Eddie started to tour together. They were like the comedy team of Abbott and Hardy! Les would just go on stage and play. Eddie would practice endlessly. He'd play upside down and backwards before he was comfortable. And then after the set, Eddie would go back on to show everybody that he could play piano just like Les.

Rahsaan and Yusef played music that got people crazy in the clubs. Sometimes they would take it outside and play something abstract, like Yusef playing Tagalog music from the interior of the densest forests of the Philippines.

Let's talk about your role as a producer.

Tell me what it was so I can do it again! [*laughs*]

Well, Joel, you created an atmosphere on jazz records that had never really existed before. Those swirling audio collages on Rahsaan's *The Case of the 3-Sided Dream in Audio Color* gave the album a sense of time and place that could only be found on something like *Sergeant Pepper's*. There was a continuity on *Yusef Lateef's Detroit* that was like cinematic montage.

Funny you should say that. Fellini was a giant influence on me, as was Magritte and the surrealists. If you asked me what some of my favorite records I produced are, you would think they'd be the hits like [Flack's] "Killing Me Softly" or [Bette Midler's] "Boogie Woogie Bugle Boy." I have affection for those records, but nobody could get in the way of this other stuff I was doin'. I was lucky enough to have some hits so I could pursue making records with Rahsaan and Yusef and Les. And then when I got the chance I signed guys like Jimmy Scott and Oscar Brown.

Talking about surrealist painters, Nesuhi must have been a big influence on you.

Tremendous.

I saw Nesuhi's collection of paintings at the Guggenheim.

At my best, I'm basically a charming bum. Nesuhi was a *real* gentleman, a quality guy with elegant taste. He exposed me to a lot of this stuff. Though I didn't need Nesuhi to get me crazy behind Fellini. He opened up a lot for me in terms of art. He was a brilliant but egoless producer. All of his great work was done with Trane, MJQ, Mingus, Ornette, Ray Charles… He had exquisite taste and captured people doing exactly what they did. I attempted the same thing, but I'd often add to what they did, although it didn't always work.

Well, Yusef's *Part of the Search* was definitely over the top.

When Mac Rebennack [aka Dr. John] walked in and saw Yusef and Doug Sahm playing together—this was back in his junkie days when he had extra ears—he looked at me and said, "What is *wrong* with you, man? You just went too far this time!" [*laughs*]

That's for sure! Let's get to Yusef.

The first record we made was *Complete*. As a disc jockey I remember all the different cuts from all of his albums that appealed to people the most, so I said let's do one of each—the honking tenor thing, the oboe blues, the exotic East Indian thing.

A Whitman's sampler.

Exactly. The second album was called *The Blue Yusef Lateef*. He was one of the few guys who could play *all* kinds of blues, not just eight-bar or twelve-bar or sixteen-bar blues. He could find blues in everything. Yusef could play blues from Neptune. He'd let me bring in Buddy Lucas to play harmonica or put background vocals on by the Sweet Inspirations. He was a highly revered guy, much older and much more experienced than I. I wanted to make him more commercial—but on his own terms.

You brought him to Atlantic after he spent the last five years or so on Impulse. His best albums from that period were actually

recorded live.

The live records were done in Philly, which was probably his biggest town. I'm not tryin' to focus on myself here, but back then every jazz musician had a guy in each city if he was lucky. In Philly, I was Yusef's guy. I was Rahsaan's guy. I was Fathead's guy. Hank's guy.

Yusef Lateef's Detroit was a simple concept. I wanted him to play with guys that would give him a broader appeal—the cream of the studio guys—Eric Gale and Chuck Rainey. They were at the height of their powers, playin' for people like Aretha and Wilson Pickett. I wanted to record Yusef with these guys, but he wanted to use his band. So we compromised and recorded with both at a small studio called Century Sound. If it didn't work it would seem idiotic—like Yusef Lateef records with oil *and* water! But this weird amalgam came out of it. Suddenly one and one was three! The R&B guys were intimidated at first. To them, Yusef was like Trane or Mingus. Richard Tee was like, "I don't know how to play that shit." But in the end it just came down to a bunch of guys getting together and playin' music.

It was a great mix of electric soul/funk and acoustic jazz.

Once I got his confidence, after the first two albums, we had a more facile working relationship. I was able to get him to do more conceptual things like overdubs he'd previously been reluctant to do. I'd say, "Why don't you overdub some horns on this?" And he wrote an arrangement for three trumpets for "Russell and Eliot." I'd say, "Here's the next idea—I want you to do musical portraits of what it was like to grow up in Detroit."

Kind of like the original concept behind *Sergeant Pepper's*, where the Beatles created a sonic scrapbook of their youth in Liverpool. I imagine that was an important record in your life.

Whoa, I'll tell you what was an important record in my life— "Hey Jude" because of that tag. I loved Ray Charles's tag on the live version of "I Got a Woman." In gospel music a tag could last fifteen minutes. I was in a car smokin' a joint when "Hey Jude" first came on the radio. The DJ thought they'd gone too far. I thought it was cool! I didn't give a shit about the Beatles when they were doing that cutesy early shit. They had catchy melodies, but I didn't want to hear Paul McCartney go *whooo!* I'd put Little Richard on! After *Rubber Soul*, I got the joke. Actually, King Curtis turned me on to them.

It's surprising that Yusef would go along with your arrangement of "Hey Jude!" on *Gentle Giant*. That was wild. Instead of a long fade-out you opted for a long fade-in. It takes almost a minute before you can actually hear anything at all and nearly three minutes before the tune gets up to full steam!

Yusef's got big ears! He heard the whole planet in cinemascope! We had to do something other than another arrangement of "Hey Jude."

It's one of the most recorded songs in the world.

The original blows everything else away.

How many records did you cut for Atlantic with Yusef?

Seven or eight, but I think his greatest record was *Eastern Sounds* on Prestige. But *Detroit* really worked! Yusef put these compositions together based on Detroit landmarks like the intersection of Russell

and Eliot or the amusement park at Belle Isle. The way he colored it with those trumpets—I don't think I ever overdubbed three trumpets on anything in my life! And then he's got three of them doing that bent Ellington stuff! I never thought of those as jazz records, although that's where they got played.

Yusef abhorred the word *jazz*. He called it "autophysiopsychic music."

Yeah, and Rahsaan *called* it "Black Classical Music." It's funny how people attribute mystical qualities to Rah's *The Case of the 3-Sided Dream*. Here's a mystical quality for you—Rahsaan and I were both leavin' Atlantic together. I had worn my welcome out. The way the company was goin' they didn't need guys like me anymore. It was headed in another direction, and I wasn't smart enough to dig how to stay with it. But Rahsaan still owed Atlantic two albums. I asked Nesuhi if I could cut both of the albums at once so we could be on our merry way. He said yes. I had $21,000 to make two albums. We ran out of money at a record and a half. Rahsaan wanted to know what we were gonna do. I said, "I dunno, I'll think of somethin'." And I came up with this idea purely out of necessity. Everybody went, "Wow, the three-sided dream—I get it! You get it?" Well, here's what you got… It was supposed to be a four-sided record but I had used all the money up and only had three—an album and a half with different versions of the same song. Y'know when you're desperate and you just come up with somethin'? I went to Nesuhi and said, "I have a really radical record here. It's called *The 3-Sided Dream*." He looked at me like I was nuts, as if to say, "Go do your best work somewhere else!" [*laughs*]

I brought in the other rhythm section again, Richard Tee, Chuck Rainey, and Eric Gale. Rahsaan, of course, held them in contempt. He was tryin' to get them to play stuff like "Giant Steps" and they're just tryin' to figure out what he's doin'. The sound montages were created to simulate Rahsaan's dreams and to fill time. People either said it was the worst piece of shit or the greatest album they ever heard in their lives. I say it's neither. It was an escape record. That was the reality.

Hal Willner called it the *Sergeant Pepper's* of jazz. Sorry to keep bringing up the Fabs. But if you listen to a track like "Good Morning Good Morning" with the roosters crowing and the foxhounds howling and sounds of the crowd and the orchestra tuning up and then listen to the dream sequences you edited—there are some striking similarities.

If I were to do it again right now, it wouldn't be a three-sided record.

Well, it was definitely a time of excess.

I was high on reefer in those days. I mean, all the time—like, for fifteen years! I wasn't alone. I was twenty-five years old and had the gig of the universe. ●

Originally appeared in Wax Poetics Issue 5, Summer 2003.

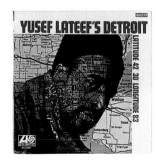

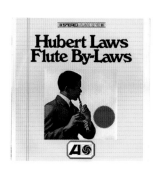

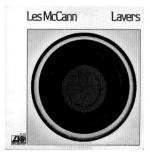

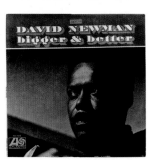

Hip-Hop and It Don't Stop

The Memoirs of Prince Paul

as told to Andrew Mason

I've been collecting records from the time I was five years old. A lot of guys probably say that, but I still have some of the records I got back then. I bought [King Floyd's] "Groove Me" when it came out, [James Brown's] "Hot Pants" when it came out…*Spider Man*—the one on Buddha Records that had a rock band on it. Everybody in my house bought records, so it just seemed like the thing to do. In hindsight, I guess it was a little strange for a five-year-old kid to bug his folks over a record. I wanted toys too, but I would cry over a record. I had a Mickey Mouse turntable, where you put his arm down on the record to play it. My mom told me that even when I was a baby, I would cry whenever the music box in my crib would run out; she had to keep winding it up. ¶ I'm the youngest in my family. When I came along, my brothers and sister were teenagers, and I was familiar with whatever they were playing around the house. My father was a hard-core jazz fan, like Thelonious Monk, not easy listening stuff. My mom was really into true soul music: Al Green, Marvin Gaye, Syl Johnson. ¶ The first time I heard anything remotely hip-hop, I was ten years old. Back then, I was shuttling between Amityville, Long Island, and Brooklyn, where my grandmother lived. I remember hearing about Herc, Bambaataa, DJ Flowers, and, around '78, I heard of Flash. That's when I started trying to DJ. Flash was always the guy. Back then, everybody played the break off Karen Young's "Hot Shot," Cameo's "Serious." I'm talking about just throwing in stabs, not scratching at all. Then when scratching came in, that's when I first started hearing about [Grand Wizard] Theodore, and him battling Flash. »

Photo courtesy of Adler Archive.

I would go to jams in the parks, and everybody would be dancing, but my whole focus would be on the DJ. Not that they were doing tricks or anything, but, oh my God, just the records they played. That was when they used to cover up the labels on everything. But the DJs weren't that bright, because back in the crates they would have the sleeve sticking up. I would be looking behind them, saying, "I *have* that record!" Pleasure, "Joyous"—had that. "Down on the Avenue," Fat Larry's Band—had that. Dexter Wansel, "Life on Mars"—had that, or my brother had it. Whatever he had, I considered it mine! [*laughs*] I had a lot of those same records in the house somewhere, and watching those DJs inspired me.

When I got into the sixth grade, I put a crew together with my friends that lived across the street, the Eveready Crew. They told me, "We're going to start a crew, and you're going to be the DJ." That's when all the teasing began. Think about it: this little kid in sixth grade trying to be a DJ. Everybody called me "Fake Grandmaster Flash"!

Initially, DJing was just for the love of the music, and to get recognized. I wasn't a jock, I didn't play sports, I wasn't supersmart, didn't have all the girls. DJing was a way to make people notice me. For a guy who had been nobody, faded into the cracks in the wall, it made me stand out.

Time passed and I progressed as a DJ, and by the ninth grade, I was considered one of the best in my local circle. At that time, I didn't have 1200s, of course; I was using B1s and this big silver Gemini mixer. I gave that to the [Hip-Hop] Hall of Fame people. And what bugged me out was looking at the other stuff they had there: Flash's mixer, DST's mixer—we were all using the same model.

For a while in junior high school, I used to spin for Biz Markie; he was my MC. This was in '81 or '82. Back then, he was called Bizzy

Bee. Yeah, there was another Bizzy Bee, but this was the Bizzy Bee of Long Island! He would come over religiously after school, and we would make mixtapes and go back and forth, tipping each other off on beats: "You got this? You got *this*?"

We had a whole little scene out there on Long Island. Rakim was coming up. He had a group called the Love Brothers. They used to call him Pop, or the Love Kid Whiz. They used to battle another group called Supreme Force [who later recorded for Nia], which was Freddy C [Freddy Foxx] and Chili Dog, who was down with Groove B Chill. If you went further west out to Hempstead, you had Chuck D and Bill Stephney with the *Mr. Bill Radio Show*. I remember going out to a high school in Central Islip to battle Diamond J, who later spun for EPMD. Back then, Parrish was in a group called the Rock Squad.

I was into all the tricks—under the leg, with the mouth. A lot of people don't know that was my primary thing. I used tricks to beat people, and that's how Biz and a lot of other people got down with me. It's called turntablism now, but if you hear a lot of my scratches from back then, they were ahead of their time. In "Just Say Stet," for example, I was breaking up words [*sings the "fun-ky" from James Brown's "Funky President"*], trying to invent stuff. As insane as people think I am on production—you know, thinking up ill stuff—I put that energy into my scratches, like, "*No one's ever done that before!*"

I also thought differently from a lot of people, at least DJing-wise, and that made me stand out. I would play things like Herb Alpert's "Spanish Flea," "Batman's Theme"—awkward songs, weird stuff just to bug people out! That comes from listening to Bambaataa; he was ill like that. What I didn't realize was that he had power and juice, so he could play stuff like that and people would listen. Who's going to dis Bam? He was the man! He ran a big portion of the Bronx;

Photo courtesy of Adler Archive.

he could play whatever he wanted to! Not with me. I'd throw these records on, and people would go, "He's buggin'!" and say I'm being stupid and all. But I had a lot of records that people weren't running, especially out on L.I.—you just wouldn't hear them. I collected anything and everything, and had all this obscure stuff to cut back and forth. I still have beats today that I've never heard anybody use.

I was out on the *Deep Concentration* tour with Peanut Butter Wolf and Cut Chemist, and we went record shopping in Florida. I found so many old-school breakbeat records. I'd blatantly put it in front of their faces, and they'd go, "What's that?" I was like, "*Perfect! They don't even know what it is*!" That was a good gauge. "You don't know this?! Okay." And I'd put it aside, not say anything more. There are a lot of records from that time that got overlooked; only the popular ones are really known about.

When comps like *Ultimate Breaks* came out, it was kind of cool, but, at the same time, it made me mad. For real collectors and DJs, it was traumatic. You know, you're there covering up your labels and all that, and those breakbeat records exposed a lot. There would be stuff on there that I had that *nobody* had. *Super Disco Breaks*, the *Octopus* joints—they would come out and I'd be like, "*Ahgh!*" I can't front; I bought them, still have them, but some of the records I had that made it special when I rocked the party were on there, and now anybody could go buy it. To me, as far as beat collecting, breakbeat compilations ruined everything. It just took the fun out of it. I'm glad I'm not as emotional and sensitive as I was back then when that was my forte. In those days, I was like, "*Man, that's wack.*" But you just try to stay one ahead, one up. Especially when I started working with De La. It would be like, "Y'all are thinking of using this; well, let me show you something you weren't even *thinking* of using—something that's right in your face!" There's a lot of stuff like that.

SURGEON ON THE MIX

I met Stet at a DJ battle in Brooklyn. I was a total b-boy back then— Kangol like LL had, Lees, green-and-blue Nikes, and a name belt that said PAUL on it. At that time, the group consisted of Daddy-O, Delite, Grand Supreme, and Wise. Daddy-O had these long braids down his back. They wore all white and had some spikes like the Furious Five. When they rolled up on me, I thought it was a gang. They were like, "That's him!" Mind you, I'm a teenager, probably sixteen, and they're saying, "You got it! You got it!" I said, "Got what? Hey, I'm not from around here!" They said, "You got what we're looking for!" They had just done the *Mr. Magic Rap Attack* show and won a contest, and they wanted me to be their DJ. Although I was living in L.I. at the time, I was down. I'd send them tapes of different records, beats, and stuff, and we'd meet up on the weekends and rehearse. I had no idea at the time what I was getting into. We were supposed to sign with Sugar Hill, but the contract was bad. We ended up signing with Tommy Boy, where the contract was also bad, but not as bad as the Sugar Hill one. Everybody was worried that I was too young to sign; I think I was seventeen or something.

DBC came in, and he was a keyboard player; he played by ear. Wise would beatbox, and I would scratch over that. When we did "Go Stetsa I" from *On Fire*, we had a drummer friend of Daddy-O's [Nawthar Muhammad] come in and play. Once all the elements were together; we were like, "*That's insane!*" That was where the idea of the hip-hop band came from. It wasn't until afterwards that we met Bobby [Simmons, aka Frukwan]. The first tour, we went out with two DJs (they gave DBC a set), and Wise was the human beatbox. That was the LL Cool J tour for Def Jam in 1987—my first tour. When we were embarking on the second album, we thought of getting the live drums officially into our act. We already were known for having a great show. We had a keyboard player—which nobody really had at the time—a DJ and human beatbox, and the drummer just made it complete. That's when we started saying, "We are the hip-hop band." It was first stated on "Go Stetsa," but that was when it became a reality.

Making *On Fire* was my first time in a "real" studio. I didn't know what I was doing back then, and I remember watching Bob Power really closely, actively trying to figure stuff out. He kind of broke my spirits by telling me, "You'll never learn this by watching me." I was like [*hangs his head*], "Oh…okay." *I'll figure this out on my own.* As far as producing, I really didn't know what it was. All I knew was that I made beats, and I knew what I liked and didn't like. Daddy-O was really running the show at the time. I just put my two cents in.

Everything was innocent at the time. I was going to school, trying to graduate college and get a regular job. The band was just a hobby, fun stuff, you know? I'd always worked a side gig, even in the midst of making records with Stet and De La. I worked with Nationwide Metric—a metric nut and bolt company—General Accident Insurance Company, a lot of places.

Ironically enough, I had a music appreciation course in college. Everybody there was into rock, Duran Duran, whatever was popular at the time. I was kind of in my own world. We had to do a project, and people were doing things like making a guitar, or doing a report on the origins of rock and roll. Now, in music appreciation, you are supposed to appreciate all music, and hip-hop was not respected *at all*. I announced, "I'm doing rap music," and everybody turned around and just gave me a nasty look. Now mind you, I'm one of maybe two Black kids in the class. The other guy turned to me and whispered "You're blowing it!" [*laughs*] The teacher said, "What, 'rad' music?" I said, "No, R-A-P. Hip-hop." The teacher sighed, and was like, "Okay." I put all this thought and anger into that report and ended up getting an A+. I used illustrations, wrote about the culture, how there's graffiti, dancing, there's the DJ, the MC. I wrote in the first paragraph that "those who are close-minded won't get it," psychologically setting it up so that you wouldn't want to be the close-minded person. I remember I used to get *dissed* though. Rap got no respect.

The guys in Stet were real dismissive of college and told me, "You don't need to do that; we're going to blow up!" I was like, "Man, we ain't blowing up nothing!" 'Cause I had seen the money we made, and I knew I had to go to school and get a job. The irony is that I took that approach, and I'm still here making records, while they had to go and get regular jobs. I don't mean to make it sound funny, but it's just ironic, because our philosophies were totally different. I never cared about who was wearing the gear or who was doing what, and that got to be their focus, following trends. *Three Feet High* was a total rebellion against that whole mentality.

THE MENTOR AND HIS THREE SONS

I met Mase through a record my music teacher from high school was trying to put out. His name was Everett Collins, and he used to play drums on tour for the Isley Brothers. There was a rapper named Gangster B who had a group called Play Hard; his song was called "Cold Waxin' the Party" [eventually released on Alexadon Records, 1988]. That's the first record with Mase's voice on it. You want to search for a record? Try finding that one! This was when I had first joined Stet, and he had me come in and program a beat on the Sequential Tom drum machine. They wanted me to do this backwards beat like how the Beasties did on "Paul Revere." I thought,

"*Nooooo!* I can't do that, that's wack!" I mean, "Paul Revere" is a great song, but to bite, especially in close proximity to when the original record came out, that's not my style. But they persuaded me, and so I programmed it. They were loving it, but me and Mase were sitting there like, "Oh, this is wack!" So Mase says to me, "I've got this project called De La Soul, and whatever you want to do, we're down." I'm like [*grins fiendishly*], "Word?"

Mase came by the house later that day with a really rough tape of "Plug Tunin'." They had done the beat collectively. Immediately, I thought, "This is really ill; it's just missing a few things." I dubbed some stuff over it, kind of redid it, and told Mase that I wanted to meet the guys.

When they eventually came over, I was like, "*You*?!" Especially Dave [Trugoy]. I was always a big nerd in school, but he was way nerdier than me. Pos—I knew his brother was a thug—so I kind of gave him credit, like, maybe he was a thug too, but he was just as nerdy! It was so weird; they were the guys you'd least expect to rhyme. I played them what I did, and they were all into it. I used Manzel, "Midnight Theme," from the 45. The other thing we used was a record that belonged to Pos's father [the Invitations' "Written on the Wall" (Dynovoice)]. Tommy Boy had a contest to see if anyone could discover what that song was, and nobody ever really came to the table. It was also a 45, and the irony of it was that on the side we used, it said "Plug Side." They were already calling themselves Plug One and Two; I thought they were crazy! They told me, "You know, when you plug in the mic?"—and had me say that in the beginning [of "Plug Tunin'"] to kind of set the concept up.

Everybody pooled their money together, and we made the demo at Calliope. I had thought, "Let's just do it right, twenty-four-track and all." I don't know what made me think that; it was just the blind leading the blind! "Hey, let's waste money!" Who knows—I just wanted to act like I knew what I was talking about. I was only twenty! I'd be in the studio, not really knowing much, but having heard stuff in sessions with Stet, and I'd say things like, "Yeah, let's compress that," not really knowing what I was doing! I had a crazy imagination about how to get stuff done, and it just kind of worked out.

So we did the demo, and I gave it to Daddy-O, 'cause he was the guy with the juice back then. I used to look up to him, you know. He was so smart, and he knew everybody. He was shopping this guy named Frankie J at the time, a keyboard player. I gave him the demo to take with him, and every place he went was like, "*Ehh*, Frankie J, but *these* guys…" So all the attention got on them. It was funny though, I brought De La to the studio one time to watch Stet, so they could familiarize themselves with how the process works and all, and Stet were like, "Why'd you bring these guys here?"—really making them feel bad. When I was making their demo, I asked Daddy-O if he wanted to get down with me, because I really respected him, and he was like, "Nah, they sound too much like Ultramagnetic."

But I had him keep shopping it, and a lot of people liked it. We got offers from Profile, Geffen, and Tommy Boy. I wanted to go with Profile. They offered a lot more money, and they had Run-DMC, plus I had already dealt with Tommy Boy through Stet, and I didn't want to go there. Geffen was offering us a big chunk of money for its day, more than twenty thousand. But De La liked [Tommy Boy President] Monica Lynch, so they decided on Tommy Boy.

When "Plug Tunin'" started getting plays, Merce [Pos] and Dave were amazed. I had made them not tell anybody that they had a record coming out until it was released, because of the pressure in the neighborhood, people bothering them. I just remember them being happy. They were the most thankful guys back then.

That's how I became "The Mentor," "Poppa Prince Paul." I really didn't know much, but I would tell them just about anything to keep their spirits up. You know, like, "Don't worry about it; our first album's gonna go gold," this and that. With Stet, I was the youngest member, and I always had difficulty getting my point across. They would say, "Ahh, young boy doesn't know what he's talking about." So I wanted to prove to them, and to myself, that I really did know what I was talking about (even though I didn't!)—that I really had a voice. Plus, I had been telling De La the whole time that it would work out, and I realized that I really had to make it happen!

SKIP 2 MY LOOPS

As far as beatmaking in De La went, everybody had a ton of ideas about what to use. My role was showing them how to put things together. They had a general idea of what they wanted to do—it could be just a couple records—and I'd take it and completely over-produce it. [laughs] That was my whole thing on that album: over-production! I was like, "Yeah, that's cool, but let's add this"; "Man, that snare doesn't really work, add this," et cetera.

Pos would bring in records, Mase would bring in records, Dave would bring in records sometimes. It's like a little competition, and I think that's how that album elevated. "You think this is hot? Well check *this* out"—you know? There was a lot of ego involved, us trying to outdo each other, and I would not be outdone! Watch me put this together. "Yeah, that part's cool, but let's loop this part." That was my role, literally telling them exactly what to do. I used to give them homework assignments at the end of every studio session: "Okay, when we come in tomorrow, you need your sixteen bars for this. Bring in this record; I know you got it, Pos. Mase, you're going to need to do scratches on this." I was a control freak, and still am to some extent. That's probably why we don't work together now; I want things exactly the way I want them.

At the time I started working with De La, sampling had just become popular. But I didn't want to do what everybody was doing at the time, just have a loop of one thing with maybe some scratches on it. I was going to layer my samples, have horns; everything's going to match, everything's going to be in tune. That, in my opinion, is the claim to fame of that record. Not just obscure samples, but how layered everything is. Some of that I bit off the Bomb Squad. I also listened to Dre, with "Eazy-Duz-It." I listened to all of that, and thought, "I'm going to take it to the next level, flip it a little extra." One, by using different records; two, by layering different stuff that you wouldn't even think about using together. "Say No Go" is a perfect example. There's so much in there: Sly Stone, Hall and Oates, the Emotions, and everything's in tune.

The bulk of the De La records came from battling for beats between me and Pos. A lot of times, we'd be in the studio, a loop would be playing, and we'd throw stuff on the turntable to see what would work and try to blend it in. It's a DJing thing. "Eye Know," with the Mad Lads and Steely Dan, came out of that.

I am a goofy guy to begin with, and I just brought that out of them in the studio. They would ask me, "Are you sure?" and I'd just encourage it all. Like with the Barry White thing ["I'm Gonna Love You a Little Bit More, Baby"], I always wanted to use that. We were in the studio with Q-Tip, Red Alert, MC Lyte, a whole bunch of people were there that day. I looped it up, and said, "I want to call this one…'De La Orgy'! Everybody go in the booth and just moan!" They were still kids; I was still a kid—we were just being stupid, having fun. I always wanted to do stuff like this, but with Stet, it wouldn't have fit. [De La] looked up to me. It was a different role. I opened up a side of them.

You know, "Whatever Paul says goes; he made Stetsasonic." I just lucked out that I had somebody to be my little robots at the time.

They inspired me too, because they made me do things I wouldn't have done either. They were so into: "We will not be seen as this; this is corny"—you know, elements in the culture at the time that they weren't having. It gave me that attitude as well; they brought that out of me, and it's stuck with me to this day.

I got a weird vibe from the people in Stet after the success of De La. Daddy-O has always been the leader of Stet, and I'm cool with that. I don't mind being the DJ in the back. At that point, though, when we would do interviews and things, people would focus on me, and he was no longer the man. I could see the guys in the group get a little upset, and I didn't want that. From that point on, things just got really weird. That was in between *In Full Gear* and the last Stet album. We just stopped calling each other, and Stet broke up unofficially.

FROM THREE FEET HIGH TO SIX FEET DEEP

After *Three Feet*, I was getting approached to do so much work. I remember, immediately, Serch approached me, like, "You know how you did 'Buddy,' with other cats rhyming on it? We want to do something like that," and that became "Gas Face." Kane, Latifah—it just went on and on. If I was as popular now as I was then, I'd be a millionaire! But rap was so new back then. I was making good money, but in comparison to now…it's like Dr. J compared to Jordan. You're still ill, but the times and the money are different. It was surreal though. I remember there was this truck I wanted, a Dodge 4×4, and I thought, "I'll just do a remix, go straight to the dealer." I wasn't one to splurge money, but it was strange to think all of a sudden I could do a remix and buy a car!

I didn't intend to make any more De La Soul records. It was going to be this record and then let them do their own thing. I told them, "You're on your own; you know how to work stuff in the studio," but they really wanted me to work with them on the next record. They considered me part of the group, Plug Four. I was flattered, and we did the next one.

I remember, with *De La Is Dead*, just trying to keep everything under wraps. I'm a private guy, and I don't like a lot of people knowing what I'm working on, or listening to too much stuff. It was hard due to the popularity of the first album; everyone was curious to see what we were coming with next.

De La got so big so quickly; it was strange. People expected one thing out of them and didn't necessarily get it. The first album was a lot of my personality, and they weren't necessarily like that. They got kicked off the LL Cool J tour for fighting. "Your boys just beat up this person…" Yo, I'd hear that all the time. "Pease Porridge" came out of a real incident. So, with the second album, you hear a lot more anger. I still wanted to keep the vibe of the first album, but I had to respect the fact that they were growing.

With *Buhloone Mindstate*, a lot of times, it was just Pos and me in the studio. Mase contributed a lot on that one as well, but separately. That's how that album was constructed—really fragmented. You could tell we were moving apart at that point. The stuff that came out on the *Clear Lake Auditorium* EP, for example, they did that on their own. I was there to record the vocals, but that was it. When I think about that album, the vibe was almost gloomy. Everybody was doing their own thing.

What really hurt me at the time was when Serch was starting his solo record. He told me he was talking to Russell [Simmons] and told him he wanted me to produce some songs. Russell said, "Paul? Why you want to use him? He's played out. He's out of here." I got

sad for a while. A lot of stuff seemed to be going wrong at that time. People were saying my De La stuff wasn't as good anymore. I had put a lot into Dew Doo Man Records, and that stuff never came out. People like Pete Rock and Large Professor were coming up, and my stuff hadn't been out there in a while. I felt like I was getting dissed, and that's when I began to put together the Gravediggaz.

I sat down, depressed, angry at the world, making all these dark songs. I just thought I would put together a whole bunch of undesirables, rebelling against everybody again. First I contacted RZA. I [had] met him at Calliope, doing "Ooh We Love You Rakeem." He had a loop, and I programmed a beat under it as a rough idea of what to do, expecting he would change it. The next thing I know, the record came out with my beat on it. But at the time, he didn't really have a lot going on; he had just gotten out of some trouble with the law. Poetic was homeless. Frukwan was making clothes or something. We were all Tommy Boy rejects! The concept of the group was to pool our resources and uplift each other.

We got together at my house. RZA brought Genius and Ol' Dirty with him, who at the time was called A-Son. Everybody just freestyled, got to know each other. This was before Wu-Tang had coalesced. It's funny, in hindsight, Wu asked me if I could do some beats for them, but I turned it down to focus on the Gravediggaz project. When RZA first played me a tape of his beats, I didn't know what to think. It wasn't even as polished as the stuff he's done that became popular. It was some really awkward stuff. Back then, he often sat down and asked me questions about producing and mixing. I lent him the record he used for the beat under "Wu-Tang Clan Ain't Nuthing ta F' Wit" [Biz Markie's "Nobody Beats the Biz"]. He tried to keep it, too! I had to go over his crib and snatch it back. [laughs]

RZA recorded stuff really rough—kind of like how I did in the beginning with De La—not really knowing what he was doing. At that point, I was becoming a technical-head, working with sequencers on the computer, trying to get stuff to sound a certain way. Watching RZA really brought me back to the raw guts of the music and not the technology behind it. I owe a lot to him for bringing me back to that.

It took a long time to get a deal for Gravediggaz, even though, to me, that demo was incredible. Everyone was getting discouraged and wanted to quit, but finally we were signed by Gee Street. By this time, RZA had pressed up "Protect Ya Neck" on his own, and that was making some noise, so he wasn't as into it as he had been. Gee Street wasn't even going to sign him as part of the group, in fact. It's ironic, because after Wu-Tang blew up, he became the focus of the group.

The second record [*The Pick, the Sickle and the Shovel*] wasn't really supposed to happen. When we got together, I made it clear to everyone that this was a one-shot thing. I think what happened, though, is that Poetic and Frukwan mismanaged their money. RZA took off, and I wasn't feeling like a Gravedigga no more. That was when I began working on *Psychoanalysis*. RZA and I didn't really want to do this new Gravediggaz album, but we felt like we were letting the other two down, 'cause that was all they had going on. But RZA had just formed a production team, and I came up with the idea that RZA could hand the production work to his boys, get them work—we don't leave Poetic and Frukwan stranded, and it would be good all around. So I didn't really do anything at all on that album.

PSYCHOANALYSIS AND BEYOND

Psychoanalysis was a record that nobody was supposed to hear. [WordSound Records CEO] Skiz had talked to me a while back and told me eventually he was going to have this label, and when he did, would I do an album for him. I agreed and forgot about it until a few years later [when] he calls me and says, "Remember that label I told you about? I want you to do the record for us." He was only going to press up about a thousand copies, so I said, "Okay, that's cool. We'll split the profits, and that'll be it."

Even though the Gravediggaz had done well commercially, the reviews were pretty critical, calling it a "horror-core fad" and things. I was fed up with the whole music business, too, and had been thinking of just moving down South, opening up a Jiffy Lube or Dunkin' Donuts, just getting out entirely. This record [*Psychoanalysis*] was supposed to seal my fate. Everything on it is—I won't say horrible—but it's not meant for people to like. It's me and a bunch of my friends from high school on tracks that nobody ever liked—a lot of really old four-track and eight-track recordings. The irony of it is that it resurrected my career instead of burying it. People actually liked it. Chris Rock called me, said he had heard it, and asked me to work with him. I couldn't believe it. Then there was a bidding war between Tommy Boy and Gee Street over who was going to pick up *Psychoanalysis*! I was like, "You've got to be kidding!"

I met Automator when he asked me to do a remix for Dr. Octagon's "Blue Flowers." We started talking and had a lot of things in common; we were using a lot of the same drum machines, watched the same TV shows. In fact, that's how the name *Handsome Boy Modeling School* came about—from [Chris Elliot's short-lived TV show] *Get a Life*.

My next record is going to be me biting everybody's style. That's the concept. Biting in 2002 is no longer a crime, so I'm taking advantage of that. You will hear all those things that you've never heard me do before. It's called *Politics of the Business*. I tried to make it sonically as close to a Jay-Z record as possible. Smoothed it out! I even made beats on there using no samples whatsoever. I wanted to make an album that's DJed right and won't slow the party down, where I can play it out when I'm DJing, and people will hopefully stay on the floor! It may be my best record, but my least favorite, 'cause it doesn't embody me as much.

I try to come from the heart when I make beats. I have an understanding of what makes a radio hit, but for me to just copy that style would be a little insincere. There's always a twist to it. I just do what I like and what I feel; I rarely compromise. I think that's real important. When people look back, when they look at my entire body of work, it gives a good description of who I am, and I'm proud of it—my son and his kids' kids can be proud of. To me, that's it. I'm not going to bling it out if it's not me and I can't back it up. I do crazy records, fun records, stuff that I think is creative, and fortunately I have a following that appreciates that. I've gone against a lot of people's advice, fired a lot of people. I've always gone against the grain, thinking that every time I make a record, it could be my last. But I just do it anyway, 'cause I can't make those regular records.

How far-fetched is making rap records and staying in business for any length of time? It's so trendy. One day you're hot and the next you're not. I never would've thought I could be in it for this long. I never planned on being a producer. I never planned on making records. I never planned on making music a career. It all evolved from loving music and loving the art. To this day, it amazes me that I wake up and make records. How wild is that? ⬤

Originally appeared in Wax Poetics Issue 2, Spring 2002.

Two Brothers with Beats

by Joe Keilch

When I asked Mr. Walt how many records they had, the answer was short: "Oh my God." Between a three-story house in Bushwick and a second apartment elsewhere in Brooklyn, they got a lot of fucking records. So many that they can't even count. But Walt says he's the organized one and knows where every record is. I witnessed one argument where Walt accused Evil Dee of not knowing where Public Enemy's "Shut 'Em Down" was and heckled Evil as he tried to find it. He found it. ¶ Two-fifths of the production crew Da Beatminerz, the Brothers Dewgarde—jokesters Mr. Walt and Evil Dee—have made an indelible mark on hip-hop, from Black Moon's *Enta Da Stage* to Smif-N-Wessun's *Dah Shinin'*. And like so many people, their record collection started with vinyl given to them by their parents. But as they began working in record stores, they started taking records much more seriously, not to mention buying a lot more. Mr. Walt worked at Music Factory in Jamaica, Queens, for seven years (check ATCQ's "What?": "What's Music Factory without Mr. Walt?"). Evil Dee did his record store time at spots like Music Hut in Harlem, Brooklyn's Beat Street, and the Brooklyn Bargain Bazaar, where he learned the mixtape game from DJ Johnny T. ¶ As Walt puts it, "I love shopping for breaks, [for] records. Been doing it twenty years and won't stop." Evil agrees: "Ain't nothing like the feeling of buying a record, coming home and finding a break on it." Walt elaborates, "Got so many records, been doing it so long, now we're record collectors. It's more than just a beat. Buying every Beatles or Pink Floyd record just 'cause you don't have it." I found out that, to the brothers, every record is precious, and no record leaves their collection lightly. During the interview, they argued when divvying up promo records. Walt considered giving me a copy of the new Usher album, and he wanted the one Ghostface 12-inch (with "The Watch" on the B-side) for himself. Both times E wasn't having it; the records stayed in his collection. »

Photos by Beth Fladung.

CONVENTIONS

They spent years buying the pricey and hard-to-find records at conventions but ended up very disillusioned. One particular dealer was the straw that broke the camel's back. He had a copy of Bob Azzam's *New Sounds*—with "Rain, Rain, Go Away"—but wouldn't discuss selling it, wouldn't even open his table until Prince Be of PM Dawn was ready. Understandably, they got fed up with the rampant favoritism and the constant reminders of the competition. "At the end of the day," Walt says, "I'm giving you the same green money as PM Dawn, as Kool Herc. Why you gotta act like that?"

Then there were the dealers who jacked up prices when a record was a hit. After Busta Rhymes used it, Seals and Croft records were going for forty bucks. And, as they point out, it's wack from both a collector's and a producer's standpoint. As a collector, there's no reason to pay that much for a common record. As a producer, it doesn't make sense to pay that kind of money for a record that was murdered and is now unusable. In essence, the dealers "saw green; [they] realized, *I can make money off this hip-hop thing.*" Ultimately, the dealers didn't have respect for the music or the record. And now conventions have become circuses, Evil tells me. He realized this when he got his first invitation to a record convention with an MC battle: "*Aaaah*, it's over."

BUYING TRIPS

They've been all over the world buying vinyl, but trips to New Orleans and Japan are especially memorable. On a trip to New Orleans in the mid-'90s, the routine was this: two vans—one to take Evil Dee, the Boot Camp Clik, Ol' Dirty Bastard, and, occasionally,

Kool Keith to do radio interviews, and the other to take Walt, Baby Paul, Posdnous, Pete Rock, and EZ Elpee record shopping. When they'd reunite at the end of the day to hit the clubs, Walt's first words would be, without fail, "Look what I got!"

"Usually Walt buys mad records," Evil Dee says, "but in Japan I bought so much records and *lost* so much records." A box of vinyl shipped via FedEx got caught up in customs and disappeared. They still lament the loss, but haven't slowed down. They still go out every week in NYC to find new joints. "I got spots I can't tell [Evil] about," Walt says. Evil replies, "He's gonna knock me out and take me there." It seems like for now they are done spending big money around the world and at conventions—it's strictly the dollar bins for the brothers. "If it has a rhythm to it, and we can mess with it, that's it," they say.

EQUIPMENT

It's well known that Da Beatminerz's studio of choice is the world-renowned—and real fucking grungy—D&D Studio. But they've also always had a studio in the house, the aptly named Dewgarde Crib of Hits. In 1989 or '90, it began with a little four-track studio. Before upgrading to a high-speed duplicator, they'd also added a six-foot-high stack of tape decks to keep Evil Dee's mixtape production rolling. Then, along with the money from Nervous, came some serious equipment. Now, the back half of the bottom floor of their Bushwick home is filled with turntables and a mixer, an SP1200, an MPC2000, an Akai S950, a Roland Juno 106, a Roland digital recording system, a mixing board, and a lot of records. Mr. Walt also has an MPC3000, an SP, three Akai S900s, an S1000, several mixing boards, and a Juno 106 at his apartment—along with a lot

more records. The S950 and the SP are the workhorses, they tell me, while the MPC is mostly used for pitch bending, sampling voices, and stereo sampling.

They've talked about making the kitchen in the Crib of Hits smaller and putting in a vocal booth, but, as Walt puts it, "Mom won't allow it." They do all their preproduction work at the house before going to D&D and are increasingly mixing down more in-house. Evil claims he's the "technical Beatminer," to which Walt responds, "Equipment, *shwipment*." Evil then quips, "Walt doesn't make beats no more—plays a funky trombone."

RESPECT

As hard as it is to believe, these cats had to earn their respect within the beat community. But even as far back as "Who Got Da Props?" they were getting theirs. Evil remembers getting props from Pete Rock because P.R. had always wanted to flip the Ronnie Laws record but could never make it work. Obviously, that's a big compliment. "Then they found out Walt was my brother," Evil says. "*Ohhh*, my whole secret was revealed. Everybody was like, 'This cat knows his beats—Mr. Walt from Music Factory is your brother?' It was out the bag."

One memorable entrance exam to becoming part of the beat community came when Diamond tested Walt on the drums that they had used for "Bucktown." The reputation-ruining rumor circulating at the time was that they'd stolen them from one of two places and didn't actually own the record. The first possible source was Apache's "Hey Girl"—Large Professor had used the same drums and left them open. And the second was Da Beatminerz's remixing of a Tribe Called Quest song that had the same drums. Q-Tip

accused Walt of stealing the drums off their two-inch reel. And, because sampling from hip-hop records was considered a mortal sin, the beat-heads were bugging.

As Walt puts it, "Diamond was the type of cat who'd try to run game on you to see if you knew what you were doing." They ran into each other one time and Diamond asked Walt if he used so-and-so—naming the wrong artist—for the "Bucktown" drums. To which he responded, "Diamond, it's good you're testing, but, c'mon, this is *me*." They know they had to be initiated into the beat community, but Walt has to wonder, "Why can't we just [have bought] the record?"—instead of being accused of stealing the drums.

SAMPLES

But they had the records. "I had all the DJ records," Evil says, "and Walt had all the beats. I had my little beats but nothing extravagant. You open up Walt's door, you hear *aaaahhhh* [the sound of the perfect beat]. I told everybody this, too. I would go beatdigging in my brother's room and find stuff and loop it up. Then Walt comes home, [and I'd say], 'Look what I made.' That whole Black Moon/Smif-N-Wessun, that's me digging in Walt's stuff."

For the brothers, making beats has increasingly become a race. "You're just racing to see who's gonna come out with it first," Walt says. "Hoping that the other person's sample isn't gonna be so big that you can't ever touch that sample again. Something like 'I Know You Got Soul' or 'Put Your Hands Where My Eyes Can See'? C'mon, it's over!" He recently got beat to the finish line. He was working on a Black Moon song for a *High Times* album and was chopping up the same Toni Braxton sample that ended up in Redman and Method

Man's "Part Two." Walt was "shanghaied again. It was like someone was looking in my window like, 'Oh, Toni Braxton.' Yo, it was so uncanny. No fucking way. I couldn't believe it. Just coincidence. In this game, if you've got an idea, hurry up with it."

Evil mentions, "I get shanghaied for beats by my own brother." ("That's right," Walt interrupts.) "I'll be looping something up," Evil continues, "and the record will disappear. [*laughter*] And Walt'll be like, 'Wanna hear this new beat?' That's the record! 'No it ain't!'"

PRODUCTION

These cats got tricks when it comes to making beats. Somewhere in all our collections, we've got a record that looks like someone ice-skated on it. When Walt's sampling something that is too clean (didn't think there was such a thing, did you?), he grabs an ice-rink record and samples surface noise, clicks, and fuzz to lay over top the too-clean sample. But their main trick, Walt says, is simply to "listen to the whole record. That's when you find the shit you missed." Evil agrees: "I buy records just to listen to it. The beat for 'Bentleys and Bitches'—I bought that record to listen to, 'cause I like Norman Whitfield as a producer."

DJ PREMIER

Both admit that DJ Premier catches them sleeping on things in their own collection. "Preem comes to our house," Walt says, "and looks through records. 'Oh, this is what I used for such and such.' I'm like, 'I had this record and didn't use it before you did? *Aaaahhh!*'"

"I think the funniest record Preem used," Evil remembers, "that he pulled out on me—and I looked at him like, *you asshole*—was the

Les McCann for '10 Crack Commandments.'" "I hate that!" Walt yells. "Asshole," Evil jokes.

KEYBOARDS

When we discussed the current trend of keyboard-driven hip-hop, Mr. Walt and Evil Dee gave props to the Neptunes for creating their own sound. And although Walt knows how to play, they only use keyboards to enhance sampled bass lines. "I can't turn my back on [sampling]," Walt says. "It's gotta have a sample in it. Regardless of what I tell [people buying my beats], it's gotta have one. I can't turn my back on that type of music. Even though what we sample isn't original, it [becomes] original, 'cause we take it and flip it into something else. But there's no originality if you're using the same sounds as Swizz Beatz."

THE FUTURE

Da Beatminerz have had the mixed fortune of being involved with two of the most well-known record labels in the rap game: Nervous and Rawkus. They've since moved on—a little jaded but a lot wiser—and, even without the backing of an established record label, aren't slowing down. But, most importantly, they're chilling with their family (Moms lives upstairs from E's apartment and the studio, and Walt lives with his son and girlfriend), keeping heads bobbing, and keeping people around them laughing. ◍

Originally appeared in Wax Poetics Issue 2, Spring 2002.

Diamond D Taps into the Past

by Reeve Holt

Diamond's 1992 *Stunts, Blunts, & Hip Hop* remains a shining example of an album crafted by a beatdigger in a time when sample clearance wasn't the pariah of the music industry, and his overall body of work places him among the upper echelons of producers in hip-hop history. On the eve of the ten-year anniversary of his classic LP, even as crates increasingly take a backseat to keys, Diamond "D" continues to evolve with the music itself, and is still getting his fingers dusty. His personal hip-hop chronology speaks to what talent, knowledge of records, a strong crew, and being in the right place at the right time can get you. »

Photos By Beth Fladung.

DIAMOND D... RAISED IN FORREST

Diamond, born Joseph Kirkland, was raised in the Bronx's Forrest Projects, and as a kid, there was "something about Forrest Projects, a lot of crews would come over there and just play music." These crews included many of hip-hop's pioneers, and while the biggest local DJ was Supreme, legends such as Grand Wizard Theodore and Grandmaster Flash also came through to play. Not surprisingly, Diamond caught the DJ and beat bugs early. Though at ten years old he couldn't go too far, he could go downstairs from his family's third-floor apartment to hear DJs and MCs rock, and down his hallway to practice on his neighbor Magic Mike's bedroom set. Mike first taught Diamond to DJ, and "had a couple of beats too," such as "I Can't Stop" by John Davis, and the Magic Disco Machine's "Scratchin'," which young D would cut up along with roller-skating joints like "Good Times" by Chic, "Bounce, Rock, Skate, Roll" by Vaughn Mason, and—his all-time favorite to run doubles of-"Catch a Groove" by Juice.

By 1982, at the age of twelve, Diamond had some curved-armed Pioneer turntables of his own, and a quickly growing knowledge of beats that he gained from listening to old tapes and older DJs. He particularly enjoyed picking the minds of such cats, "trying to get names," and they respected him, because he had records. While the prospect of getting on sets and playing outside excited him, and occasionally manifested, "just kicking it with niggas and just trading names back and forth" was more than enough for Diamond. Having begun buying and boosting records, hitting local shops and ones in Manhattan, Diamond also caught the tail end of New York institution Downstairs Records's existence (as he had with the park jam era). There he would read titles off the bootleg 45s on the wall, which often had the real title with the wrong artist—such as "Funky Drummer" by Yvette and the Kids—and spend money on records he just "had to have." Diamond's favorite mission of this period, however, remains the time in '83 he was able to rack J. J. Johnson's *Willie Dynamite* from under the watchful eyes of Music Factory's 400-pound gorilla, proprietor Stan Platzer. Diamond still laughs as he recounts how he brought the album home and "just went crazy"—and at the memory of "that old White motherfucker Stan, who knew *all* the beats."

HE'S DJ DIAMOND D... AND I'M THE MASTER ROB

Also living in Forrest at the time was Diamond's boy, Rob, who stayed on the eleventh floor of his building, and an MC by the name of Diamond David, or D, whose name the young Mr. Kirkland was really feeling. He liked the name so much in fact that he eventually dubbed himself DJ Diamond D, because, well, it just sounded hot. As he explains, "Because he was rhyming back then [and] I wasn't rhyming, I was just DJing, I was like, 'Okay, you the MC [named Diamond]; I'm going to be the DJ.'" For the inquisitive types, however, Diamond's line "But my name ain't David/Hell no/And for the bullshit you can save it" on "What You Seek" (*Stunts*) wasn't based on any desire to separate himself from the original D once he had started rhyming, but rather just something to rhyme with "save it." Curiously, Rob also ended up with a stage name—Master Rob—that another MC, the Fantastic Five's Master Rob, had already established as his own, but neither this nor Diamond's shared namesake impeded the eventual formation of the two neighbors' group, Ultimate Force.

I TOOK A BLUES BREAK... AND I BROKE IT

By 1985, Rob and Diamond had already begun working on their act when Rob began seeing Jazzy Jay in Forrest. Jay, who was big at the time on the strength of his production on joints like LL's "I Need a Beat," was talking to a girl who lived in the projects. Rob happened to know the object of Jay's affection and, as Diamond succinctly puts it, "[We] struck up a conversation with him, he brought us by the studio, he heard us, and we got signed to [Jay's label] Strong City." This process wasn't necessarily as quick as Diamond makes it sound, but was accelerated by Jay's intrigue and respect for D's knowledge of breaks. "Jay was surprised at the knowledge I already had about beats," says Diamond. "That's how I got cool with Jay, you know, when I first met him I hit him with a couple of names of some joints that I knew he had, like the "Blow Your Head" album [*Damn Right I'm Somebody* by Fred Wesley and the J.B.'s]. Me being so much younger than him, he took an interest in me—you know, somebody [so young] talking about the *Three Tough Guys* [LP by Isaac Hayes]."

Being around Jay, Bambaataa's right-hand man, further increased Diamond's knowledge of records, and he hung out at Jazzy Jay's studio "awfully a lot." Consequently, he was learning how to program watching Jay, and, as time progressed, would "do like Quincy Jones do, produce but don't touch no equipment, [telling Jay] 'I want the drums to go to this pattern, put this sample here, bring these horns in here.'" This collaborative process helped create the sole Ultimate Force release "I'm Not Playing," which Diamond brought the record to sample (*Cold Feet* by Albert King) and "basically arranged," while Jay programmed and was credited as producing. "I'm Not Playing" made some noise when it dropped, and was the clear standout on Jazzy Jay's 1989 *Cold Chillin' in the Studio* album. Along with Diamond's subsequent production on other Strong City projects and fellow Forrest native Lord Finesse's debut LP, the single's success garnered Ultimate Force major-label attention. Capitol Records eventually showed the greatest interest in the duo, but a solo secret of Diamond's served to derail his and Rob's project, and set him down a different creative path.

EVERYBODY WANTS A DEAL... HELP ME WITH MY DEMO

Working at the studio, Diamond had met and was influenced by more artists than just Jay, and one, Grand Puba, played a major role in the eventual direction of his career. Puba had been around the studio since Diamond first arrived, initially working on his Masters of Ceremony project and later on Brand Nubian's first record, and "really knew records." Like Jay, he consequently furthered Diamond's knowledge of beats. Perhaps more importantly though, "being around Puba and listening to [him] put together that first Brand Nubian album" provoked D to start rhyming himself. Inspired by Puba's writing and rhyme schemes, Diamond subsequently wrote and recorded what would become his demo, "Best Kept Secret," on the spot at Jay's, using a loop ("I Can Hear You Calling" by Three Dog Night) that Puba had in fact first used on MC Lyte's "I Am the Lyte." Puba missing a Tribe Called Quest session at the studio also fortuitously led to Diamond's inclusion on Tribe's classic *Low End Theory* (on "Showbusiness"), which introduced him vocally to the masses before "Best Kept Secret" dropped.

Diamond had the "Best Kept Secret" demo version with him in 1991, when meeting to discuss the then imminent Ultimate Force deal with an A&R rep at Capitol. As he explains, "I [was] down there, and I play 'Best Kept Secret' for the A&R. I'm like, 'This is some shit that I'm trying to get jumping off, too.' So he heard it, and he was like, 'Yo, you need to put this on the album, and you need to rhyme on some more tracks,'" even though the completed Ultimate Force album was already in the A&R's hands. Rob resented the label's interest in his DJ, however, as he was the focus of Ultimate Force, and

when Capitol told the two they would only be signed if Diamond rhymed on the LP, despite Diamond's objections, the deal soured. Mercury Records was also interested in the project but again wanted more contribution from Diamond vocally, and Rob was not willing to go along. As a result, Diamond subsequently signed a deal as a solo artist, and the completed Ultimate Force album was shelved to a DAT that he still has at the crib.

SEE I WRITE MY OWN RHYMES… PRODUCE MY OWN SHIT

Having been signed, and having put the Ultimate Force project to rest, Diamond began recording *Stunts* in '91 using an MPC-60, and, for the first time, programming his own work. Some of the breaks Diamond used in crafting the album, such as the loop taken for the

title track ("Almustapha the Beloved" by George Duke and Billy Cobham), were originally intended for the Ultimate Force project, but most were new, and many actually came from his beatdigging cohorts. The coproduction credits on the album evidence this, as Diamond gave them to anyone who had thrown him a record, regardless of their actual involvement in the production process. However, this was more a courtesy based on career moves than on any beatdigging code of honor. "If [someone] gave me a record, I put coproduced," he recollects. "That was my way of showing love, even if a nigga never stepped in the studio, because I wasn't paying niggas back then, so niggas [at least] could get a credit on a project." The result of his efforts, and those of his collaborators (both big and small), was an album widely acknowledged as a classic—a fact that

he is humbly proud of. As he puts it, "I'm proud that it hit niggas like that. I mean, it didn't just fly out the gate; it was more or less word of mouth, you-know, but I was definitely appreciative."

SO LET'S GET BUSY… AND DIG IN THE CRATES

"The word of mouth" that gained *Stunts* acclaim resulted from the fact the LP epitomized the second wave of hip-hop production—of which Diamond was an integral producer—and in many respects this is what made, and makes, it a legendary full-length. The second wave involved layering new, often as-yet-unheard breaks together, employing a DJ's aesthetics and a beatdigger's attention to detail (and crates). It was a direct result of what Diamond labels the "second level" of breaks. "It's like two levels of beats," he asserts. "It's the old

school level of beats niggas collect, and then it's the new joints that niggas back in the days wasn't up on. For example, the Little Richard drums ["The Rill Thing"]—that was recorded, like, in '72, but none of them niggas had doubles of that record. Flash, Bam, Herc, none of them, they didn't know about it, so, like, beats to them would be like the Blackbyrds, the Incredible Bongo Band, Babe Ruth, groups like that. Niggas wasn't outside in the park cutting up Lonnie Liston Smith's *Drive*, you know, or didn't have doubles of the Les McCann [*Layers*]."

For Diamond, and many others, the second level of breaks, and digging for them, began in earnest upon hearing the seminal works of Prince Paul and Hank Shocklee. As he states, "I know for a fact when 'Rebel Without a Pause' dropped that a lot of niggas knew it was some James Brown record, but they didn't really know [where Shocklee took the sample from]. I didn't know, and that made me step my game up, 'cause I thought I had all the James Brown records, and I knew I didn't have it." Around 1990, he eventually did come across a 45 of "The Grunt" by the J.B.'s at a girl's house in Forrest (and still counts it as one of his most prized records). By that time, though, Diamond had already begun digging for the second level of breaks heavily. And he had company.

THE SHOW B.I.Z.... DOWN WITH D.I.T.C.

Diamond's direct company came in the form of a crew of fellow beatdiggers he had known and been working with and around for a long time. One of these cats was Showbiz, who grew up across the street from Diamond. Diamond first met Show in '83 at a park jam after having heard he was "nice on the turntables," and upon meeting him quickly discovered Show knew a lot of records—in fact, they "pretty much knew [records] the same." The two have been running, digging, and collaborating together ever since. By 1990, their beat missions had gotten serious enough that Showbiz bought out the entire stock ("piles of records," says Diamond) of a furniture store on Prospect Avenue in the Bronx that both had previously hit hard. This buy resulted in some staple records (such as Jack Bruce's *Things We Like*) that would ultimately be sampled by their crew.

By around 1991, Diamond and Show's amalgamated musical family consisted of themselves, Andre the Giant, Lord Finesse, and Fat Joe (who subsequently made his somewhat inauspicious debut, "living hard like a penis," on *Stunts*), and they decided to officially label themselves Diggin' in the Crates. Although he cannot recall who exactly dreamt up the seminal namesake, Diamond credits his man Latief from Brooklyn with being the first person he heard use the term "digging"—saying "let's go digging" when they went shopping for breaks. The genealogy of the crew's adopted name notwithstanding, the title stuck, and has obviously now evolved into common parlance in the vernacular of beatdigging culture.

"Let's-go-digging" Latief was one of many beatdiggers/makers down with—if not an official member of—Diggin' in the Crates at the time, including other production luminaries such as DJ Premier and Mark the 45 King. While Diamond and Premier had worked on Finesse's first album together and gotten to know each other at Jay's, Diamond met Mark, as he did many producers and beatdiggers, through breaks. As he recounts, "At Hunter College, Queen Latifah gave a show [in 1991], and during the intermission I'm in the crowd, and I hear somebody cutting up a breakbeat from the first generation—Melvin Sparks's 'Gotta Get Some,' what older niggas call 'Apache Two'—so I'm like, "Yo, hold the fuck up." So I make my way up to the DJ booth, and it was Mark, and I was like, 'Yo, what you doing with that Melvin Sparks record?' He just started laughing, [and] that's how me and him became cool." During this period and the years that followed, Diamond met and befriended many other beatmakers similarly, through shared digging knowledge as well as mutual respect for how they or he had flipped a sample.

YOU GO OUT WITH THE OLD AND IN WITH THE NEW... I'M WELL SITUATED 'CAUSE I KNOW WHAT TO DO

A second album, *Hatred, Passions and Infidelity*; a label-nonsense-induced hiatus; an infamous proclamation as to his mic skills ("by far I'm the best producer on the mic"; Fugees' "The Score"); and various D.I.T.C. and other projects later, Diamond finds that such cultural interchange between beatmakers has waned, in correspondence with the significance of digging to much of hip-hop produc-

tion. "The music now is not digging-orientated at all," he says. "You know, [now] it's like, 'Who gives a fuck where those drums come from.'" And, he jokes, "Now you can be like, 'Yo, I got that same keyboard tool! That's on Bank A!'" Diamond blames this attitude mainly on the fact that "the industry as a whole has moved away from samples significantly," and says the declining state of beat culture on the whole is based seventy percent on the industry climate and thirty percent on the simple fact that many young producers don't know and/or own records, or care to. But, unlike some seasoned artists, Diamond is objective about this fact and the current state of hip-hop. As he rationalizes, "How could I be [bitter]? I mean, if you was eight years old when my first album dropped, you're eighteen now. At eight years old, you're not collecting records, you're in the park playing in the dirt." When asked to name a current producer who's wack, he laughs hard and requests to move on (after providing the broad answer that "a lot of producers are wack," but asserting that he's not a hater). He does use a Triton keyboard (albeit mainly to replay bass lines) alongside an MPC2000 and an MPC3000, and is not disenchanted with hip-hop's more recent sample-less, easy-digging manifestations. As he puts it, "I'm not mad about that, 'cause it don't make no nevermind anyway. I like that 'Pass the Courvoisier' record [by Busta Rhymes]. I don't give a fuck where those drums came from—it's hot."

Diamond has a similar attitude towards the present, often highfalutin world of digging. He's never even looked at eBay, and pragmatically accepts some of the ridiculous prices that float around as the natural outcome of demand and rarity coupled with the simple fact people will actually pay such prices. Although, as he observes, a lot of the records on the wall in stores like New York's Sound Library are up there "for a long time." While he does occasionally pass through such stores himself, Diamond nowadays does his digging about once a month out of state with Kid Capri, who he has been digging with since '95. Capri has a serious collection according to Diamond, as do his D.I.T.C. brethren Finesse and Show. Diamond recently cut a lot of the fat out of his own crates, and now has about forty, but he assures that they're "a solid forty." He currently digs mostly for the second generation of beats, having copped most of the first level a long time ago, but still finds gems like the "Midnight Theme" 12-inch (by Manzel) that his man Breakbeat Lenny put out, and the "Shack Up" 45 (by Banbarra) he recently caught.

While, as noted, Diamond has no problem rolling with the fickle industry tide, he does see some hope for the future relevance of digging and beatdigging culture to moneymaking hip-hop, and consequently hip-hop on the whole. Citing the success of Jay-Z's sample-based hit "Girls, Girls, Girls," he is aware that label executives and A&Rs will be open to samples if their impact is felt by artists and the masses. Diamond has already felt the weight of that song's success in dealing with A&Rs, and his contributions to this industrial reawakening can be found on Busta's *Genesis*, as well as projects by Pharoahe Monch and M.O.P., among others.

Ten years since *Stunts*, twelve since his first significant work on Finesse's first full-length (*Funky Technician*), fourteen since Ultimate Force's "I'm Not Playing," and twenty since he first started going back-to-back on his own turntables, Diamond considers himself lucky to have achieved longevity in the often fleeting world of hip-hop and to be able to still work with A-list artists. Perhaps most importantly though...he's still digging. ◐

Originally appeared in Wax Poetics Issue 3, Fall 2002.

Give the Engineer Some

by Andre Torres

After hearing the first saxophone on Public Enemy's "Rebel Without a Pause," Scotty Hard realized he could be anything. ¶ Already discontent with the music scene in Vancouver, Canada, his hometown of nineteen years, he moved to New York City in January 1989 with the intention of getting down with the thriving hip-hop scene. He remembers, "I came into it from that level, seeing it as a new form of music that was really innovative." ¶ Over a decade ago, Brooklyn-based producer/engineer Scott Harding, aka Scotty Hard, introduced the duo New Kingdom to Gee Street, producing the two critically acclaimed albums that followed. He has since engineered a range of albums, from the Brand New Heavies' *Heavy Rhyme Experience* to Chris Rock's Grammy-winning *Roll with the New*. And at the turn of the century, he coproduced and engineered the first two Blue Note albums from jazz-funk trio Medeski, Martin and Wood. ¶ Harding had started his trade rather casually, through years of playing guitar in bands in Vancouver. There's always one guy in the band who knows how to hook up the equipment, and Scotty was that guy. This skill and experience led to some engineering jobs, but the small scene always left him hungry for more. Once in New York, though, Scotty hooked up with friends like Bob Coulter—who was working with Stetsasonic as one of their "Stetgineers"—and got busy. "That was around the time Daddy-O, Prince Paul, and those guys were really hot," Harding recalls. "So they were doing a lot of remixes. When I wasn't working, I'd go hang out with Bob at Green Street [Studios] or Chung King or wherever he was working." »

He initially wanted to work at Calliope Studios, the D&D of its day, but at the time they couldn't guarantee him any work. After all, cats like Coulter, Bob Power, and Shane Faber were already putting in much work behind the boards. Through Bob Coulter, however, he got a gig at the legendary Chung King House of Metal. But after not getting paid one too many times, he decided to leave Chung King for the greener pastures of Calliope. It was at Calliope that he got a chance to work with a laundry list of artists from hip-hop's golden age: Stetsasonic, Ultramagnetic MC's, Major Force Posse, De La Soul, the Jungle Brothers, Jazzy Jay, Brand Nubian, Black Sheep, Fat Joe, and the list goes on. "The first session I ever did," Scotty remembers, "was for Tone Loc for the 'Tone Phone' [a 1-800 number sponsored by MTV]. He came in wearing, like, a white mink coat. It was ill."

But it wasn't all champagne, caviar, and bubble baths. "I started working at Calliope in April of '89, doing, like, every session. You had no assistant and got paid, like, ten dollars an hour," says Harding. "You'd get in there, and you'd have to take money from everybody. They were hard-ass about shit back then. If you booked time, you had to put half the money down to reserve your time, then I'd collect [the rest of] the money at the end. So I'm like, 'Okay, well, you owe $192.75 and that's 8.25% sales tax.' I mean, you had to figure this all out before the session started, so you're already in this kind of weird position of taking these people's money.

"It was a real ghetto studio," Harding says of Calliope. "Something was always going wrong. I remember one time, I was doing a session with Resident Alien, and the fucking tape machine just started smoking. I mean, smoke just started pouring all out of it!" But out of the smoke came a long-lasting friendship. "That's how I met Prince Paul," he says. "I was working on Resident Alien, which was a group he put together for his label back then with guys he knew from Long Island. A fat guy, a tall, skinny guy, and this little guy with a little arm. They all had green cards that said 'Resident Alien,' and he goes, 'Those three guys look like aliens!' So that's how his mind works."

Collecting money and extinguishing tape machines weren't the only extra work required at sessions, Scotty explains. "You had to either help people make beats or make beats for people." People usually think of the engineer as a studio tech who sets up microphones and records the sessions, but Scotty tells a different story of that era. "In the early days of hip-hop, even the guys who were producers didn't really know how to produce. They didn't know about getting tapes to the studio or over-dubbing; they'd just be like, 'Sample this record.' That was back when no one could afford any technology, which is totally different from now, where every motherfucker you know has Pro Tools at home. Back then, you had an eight- or twelve-bit sampler, and a couple of people might have had an SP-12, because this was even before the SP1200. We had an [Akai] S900, which is like ten seconds of sample memory. And guys would come in, and they'd have a pile of records, and they'd say, 'I want to use this and that,' and you'd loop that up and figure out if it was the tempo they wanted it in. So you ended up being sort of an engineer/programmer, even producing sometimes: 'Hey, maybe you should double that.' Or if something was out of tune, you might mention it. But I learned how to shut up. Sometimes, if something's totally out of tune or fucked up, it's not really your job to do that. But on the other hand, somebody'd come back the next week, and they'd be like, 'My man said the vocals was out of tune. Why the fuck you didn't tell me?' So you're damned if you do, damned if you don't."

But, Harding remembers, there were cats who had it together too. "I always thought Mr. Lawnge from Black Sheep was really good—besides being a great DJ—but at locking his beats up too." And, Harding adds, "A guy like Prince Paul really knows what he wants, the whole record, and the whole sound of it. He just gives me the track, and I mix it. I mean, Paul was one of the first guys I remember even bringing a disk in."

Sometimes Harding's extended involvement paid off. Mark the 45 King's remix of pop/R&B singer Lisa Stansfield's hit "All Around the World" would become Harding's most commercially successful session, but not before the record exec passed on 45 King's initial remix. "Because all Mark thought was, 'Yo, I got a beat on it!'" Harding explains. "When he hooked the beat up to it, that was all he thought [a] remix [was]: 'Yo, it's all about that! It's all about the snare drum!' The guy from the record company came in and wanted a full-on remix. I understood what he was talking about. So while

we're doing all the edits, Mark is just sitting there smoking, with this little globe radio around his neck. There were a million edits; I used two reels of half-inch for the one song."

But Mark the 45 King is no fool, and somewhere down the line, it really is all about the snare drum. Scotty has witnessed the evolution of hip-hop's drums over the course of the last decade: "After the DMX and SP-12 era, a lot of people were just using all loops," he says. "All of the early Calliope, Jungle Brothers, [and] De La stuff is all just drum loops. And the earlier you go, the more closely associated they are to all the stuff off the *Ultimate Breaks & Beats* records. Then gradually people started getting other records. Like someone would come in and be like, 'My dad has this Kenny Burrell record, and there's a beat on it.' So you'd build everything around a beat."

Scotty continues to drop gems on the golden era: "I know Louie Flores was down with Ultramagnetics—he did a beat on Tim Dog's record. I remember Tim was like, 'I'm putting Louie on; he's from the Bronx.' But Louie did a lot of the edits on the *Ultimate Breaks & Beats*. Sometimes, some of those break records were just one bar, and he would make them into two bars, mainly just so people could use them." Speaking on the longevity of the series, Scotty adds, "Even when we were doing the Ultramag record, which was way after that era, Ced would still be like, 'Let me get the "Pussy Footer" horns.' You know, just using that old shit."

Scotty's seen it move firsthand from the simple programming of the early beat machines to the looped beats spurned by the *Ultimate Breaks & Beats* series, to the highly complex arrangements achieved today, not necessarily to his liking. "Most of the stuff you hear on the radio, the drums are programmed. I remember talking to [Dan the] Automator about that. He was like, 'No one's using drum loops anymore.' And I realized, 'Yeah, you're right.' I don't really dig all of this really jiggy, fast stuff that almost has that drum-and-bass sound with all of that really highly programmed drum shit. It's not raw to me. There's nothing raw about that. That's what I like about the whole New York style of it; it's just more ill. I've always been more into that."

That ill, raw sound is what Scotty shoots for when he's behind the boards. "I think it's cooler to emulate records from the '70s instead of

emulating records from now. I think that's what I try to do when I engineer shit and make drum sounds, make it sound kind of old. This guy, Garth Richardson, who does stuff like Rage Against the Machine, came into a session I was working on. His dad used to produce the Guess Who, and he's like, 'Wow, my dad used to get drum sounds like that!' And I'm like, 'All right, thanks, that's a compliment to me.'

"I came at it from this musician point of view, always playing in bands. I think that's one reason I've always had good luck with all the jazz records I've made. My brother plays trombone, I used to play in jazz bands, and most of my records are jazz records, so I always knew what instruments sounded like. Whereas, a lot of engineers who came up in the '80s, everything was drum machines. But on the other hand, there's guys who made records twenty-five years ago, and if you brought a drum machine into the studio, they'd be freaked out."

It's not only drum machines that freak some engineers out; the mere sight of a session with Wu-Tang Clan is enough for some to head home for the night. Scotty sheds some light on the mystique of the Wu: "I met RZA through Prince Paul from doing the Gravediggaz. We got along pretty well with RZA, and I had done a couple of other late-night remix things. He probably just liked me because I could stay in the studio for fourteen hours, because I'm a fucking idiot! Because those guys would always show up, like, eight hours late." But Scotty seems to understand the process. "That's his whole style; it's like chaos. His shit is really dope. He's kind of like a conceptual artist in the sense that the idea is more important than the execution." Scotty remembers working on "It's Yourz," one of the more memorable tracks off *Forever*: "I mixed this song, like, five or six times. I remember RZA really liked it. When we were doing [the remix for Björk's 'Bachelorette,'] he was like, 'Make it like "It's Yourz"!'"

In the fickle world of hip-hop, few make it three years, much less a decade. But Scotty Hard has been able to keep himself, and his sound, fresh. Talking about his recording style, he reveals a bit of his secret to longevity: "That's what I do, just sort of get in the mood and do it as a performance, just spontaneously." ◉

Originally appeared in Wax Poetics Issue 1, Winter 2001.

The RZArrection

by S. H. Fernando

I've known RZA since about '93, when Wu-Tang first exploded out of the underground with the extra classic "Protect Ya Neck." Loud Records had me write the press release and bio for that, and I remember talking to a young Prince Rakeem on the phone for the first time, and being somewhat confounded by all the mystical Shaolin lingo he was spouting with almost religious fervor. This dude is definitely on some next shit, I remember thinking even then, because his intelligence and originality cut through the rough ghetto exterior with razor-sharp intensity. I eventually met the RZA at Firehouse Studios in Manhattan where he was working with Prince Paul on the Gravediggaz debut album, and the braided figure in scuffed up Tims and stained hoody seemed to have a very regal air about him. It's no wonder he's the undisputed Abbott of the Clan. ¶ As a producer, RZA forced our ears to accept new sounds. Sometimes we didn't like it at first—as in my initial reaction to a track like "Glaciers of Ice"—but eventually we were strung. As an MC, he flung lyrics with metaphysics, forcing us to actually think about and decode what he was saying. Though few people think about it in today's era of corporate rap, the RZA also pulled off a serious coup in the industry, signing his group to one label and spinning off solo deals for individual members on a variety of other majors. At one point, the Wu-Tang bat could be found flying on practically any major-label release that was soaring up the charts. ¶ Well, times have changed, but the RZA really hasn't since I've known him. He's still a committed hip-hop head who's constantly working and pushing the envelope. Though the spotlight's not on him at the moment, it suits him just fine, because it gives him time to develop his new roster of artists—names you probably never heard of, like North Star, Division, Suga Bang Bang, and Tekitha—and build up his label Digital Records, as well as to just grow and mature as an artist himself. He's got two studios—36 Chambers in Manhattan's garment district for his new students and the other at an undisclosed location for the Wu-where you'll usually find him working and holding court into the wee hours. »

Photos by Beth Fladung.

Have a lot of producers today bitten your style?

Guaranteed. I mean, but bitin'—niggas don't really use that word no more, 'cause everybody bitin' now, so niggas don't use the word no more, nahmean? They call it more like the nigga inspired me or whatever. But I think I inspired a whole generation of music out there really. From the top of the game to the bottom of the game niggas know when the RZA came through. I opened their minds up to a lot of shit, man. Niggas wasn't thinking about music how they thinkin' about it nowadays, pre-when-I-came, and shit. 'Cause I gave niggas a chance to open that seventh seal in their mind about music. Added mad shit to hip-hop. Now shit is an ocean right now.

You think the game is kind of stale right now?

Not really to me. Maybe the TV side of it, but I think hip-hop is flourishing right now, man. Especially sound-wise. I feel really good about a lot of artists' shit right now. I think the whole hip-hop generation has matured, man, for real. Niggas is nice out here. Especially producers.

But everything sounds so clean and glossy.

It's definitely more polished and more radio friendly right now, because hip-hop is now one of the biggest commercial-selling musics. Hip-hop is the driving force of the music industry. Even *NSYNC and all them muhfuckas use hip-hop to fuckin' guide their careers to the next level, so it's all over the place. But you got some niggas coming real clean and polished and you still got some grimy niggas out there too, and now that hip-hop is so widely expanded ,everybody got a chance to fuck with it like that. The whole problem with lyricists was there wasn't a balance before. Now I think there's a balance, man. Only problem I may have a little bit right now with

the game is that, yo, niggas actin' like they tryin' to front on Wu when we helped trigger it, y'know? I don't know who the culprit is. But Wu is the kind of people that spoke out against a lot of shit, and we really gave a lot of information about hip-hop, for our generation. And so you got a lot of clones out there makin' money, and they ain't even like that. That's just how it is though. I'd rather see a nigga clone me than clone them other faggots they was cloning before, nahmean? Even R&B niggas got braids and scarves wrapped around they heads. [*laughs*] It's superficial, it's a look, but it's a look that, yo, you couldn't walk into a restaurant and be respected as a man a few years ago. I was in China and shit, about three weeks ago, and I went to a hip-hop club—yo, muthafuckas, everybody, had a do-rag and a jersey on. Everybody. It was like a video shoot in that motherfucker. If you walk up and see twenty Chinese kids with do-rags on, singing the lyrics to "Tramp," and they don't speak English, you gonna bug the fuck out, man. So, hip-hop is big, and we helped expand it to those places, know what I'm saying? I'm proud of it. I mean you hung out with me many times when we was catching trains and car services, now you in the backseat of my muhfuckin' G-500. [*laughs*]

You don't think that Wu has lost their place?

I don't think Wu has lost their place and shit. I think like so many niggas imitated us and shit that other niggas had chances to replace us in their own way. But you can't replace the Gods, man. You just know that as soon as the Wu shit come out, really, it's always our victory.

What do you think about all these songs with the high-pitched vocal samples, because that's an innovation you really intro-

duced?

It's like this. When Loud was in control of things and had a lot of power and some labels weren't really strong like that and shit, you wouldn't even find that sound over there at Loud. But people who was listening to that, got influenced by that and started makin' that sound. And now it's mainstream. You probably feel like I feel, like the person that invented that or the person who brought that to the forelight; you don't hear his beats on the radio no more. But all great producers have been the same way. How about Dr. Dre? He went through a period of time when you couldn't hear none of Dre's shit on the radio either, nahmean. He basically went back to his lab and he was making all kinds of shit, and he came up with a whole flock of new shit. I feel like that's where I am too, man, as far as me as a producer. I feel like I'm in my studio, man, and I got a hundred songs done. I just feel good now. I feel like the old days where I had a lot of music in store, built a lot of music. I think that last album I released for Wu-Tang, *Iron Flag*, showed people that, yo—I made almost every beat on the album and showed you I'm diverse with my sound, yo. I can make any sound, and I'm an engineer and all that shit. So I know, people that really into a nigga really know that this nigga is the master of what he do, whether it's business, lyrics, or production. He really wear all hats well enough to do that, but I'm foremost a musician and artist. Now I feel like I got more of a chance to be that than ever. To a degree, even though I got my own label, my own studio, you know? But I don't think niggas stole my sound, 'cause the sound was there. I brought it to the light. But niggas always gonna respect what I did for the game. I made a lot of niggas eat in this game.

Was there a time you ever got burnt out and stepped back from the game for a minute?

I think this is the time right now—I'm stepping back. Yeah, I'm chilling right now, like fuck it. [Wu-Tang Killa Bees'] *The Sting* was already a year old before it came but it was a good album.

Why did you sit on it?

Well, 9/11 was big for the industry. When Loud went over to Sony, y'know, things really changed, man.

Don't you think something is missing from hip-hop right now?

Yeah, I ain't gonna front. I think the realism is missing. Realism is missing, y'know, but I got that and I'm not quitting. It ain't over for me. I'm really gonna do it right this time for y'all, so don't worry about that. The cure is coming, as far as consciousness and as far as from the heart of a man, and the heart of how God speak through us, and all that. But the people's minds ain't into that right now, and the market is not into that either, so everybody's like, "Yo, let's chill for a minute on that, let's just go party—pussy, drugs, and sex." But at the same time, that life is real, man. We can't party our life away, drink our life away, smoke our life away. It's a phase, man. But you really want to know what time it is really? It's 1992. That's what time it is. So just get ready, 'cause whatever wave I'm bringing, its coming in the same form, 'cause nobody else is bringing that wave.

Who do you like on the production tip?

I think everybody got nice right now. Just Blaze is fuckin' niggas up, Neptunes is fucking niggas up, son.

You like the Clipse's "Grindin'"?

I make a hundred of those a day, but even though it don't come

from me, at least the world could accept it and respect it. But I'm glad niggas like the Neptunes put that beat out, because I got hundreds of those now—that's that first one. They play on keyboards all day like I play on keyboards.

How are your chops these days?

I'm on it, man, believe me.

What are your new toys?

MPC4000, Korg Triton, Zoom's MP-7.

Tell me about the whirlwind replicator.

Yo, man, I invested a lot of money in that, but I wasn't really able to sustain it, man. It was basically like you could take any beat you make and scratch it and cut it like a DJ. But I didn't get to freak it like I wanted to, man. That's why I don't even get mad, 'cause I was doing it in my house for ten years before niggas knew I was doing it, then I got a chance to do it for ten years for the world to see it, and then I'll wind up in ten years in my house again and then my son may come out ten years later and say, look what me and my dad came up with. 'Cause my son is already playing chords at seven, when I didn't know about no fuckin' chords till I was fifteen, sixteen, seventeen.

How much of your time is spent on music these days?

If I wake up and smoke a blunt by noon, I ain't comin' out my house. I make beats till 5 o'clock. So I don't smoke sometimes. For the whole first half of this year, I ain't smoke. I went cold turkey. That's why I got a lot of product done.

So you can make beats without smoking.

Yeah, I mean, all them beats you heard [tonight], those are sober beats.

Aren't your beats a lot different when you smoke?

Well, now that I've learned music and shit, yeah, the beats are different. If you a sampler, smoke before you sample—that's the secret. But if you a musician, and shit, it don't matter.

How about smoking digi [angel dust]? Was "Sub Crazy" on the first Meth album a digi beat?

Nah, that was just weed.

What made you do a beat without a drum track?

Through the weed I heard the pulse of the sounds, nahmean. [*hums it*] I had the Juno back then.

Of that first round of Wu solo albums every album really was a different chamber.

Yeah, man, and right now I'm a grown man with it, so now I can actually go back into any chamber at any given time. That's the good thing about it. I think people was feeling me, 'cause they didn't understand what the fuck it was. Once they got a taste of it, they had different variations they wanted, and I think I never stayed in one chamber for nobody and that probably offended a lot of people, 'cause they was like stay *Cuban Linx* or stay *Liquid Swords*, and I never stayed. But I left a spot for someone else to stay in. I brought the soul, and that's the strongest thing I brought, the soul chamber, and some of the biggest selling hip-hop albums of all time have that soul in it.

Even with Dre, who's probably one of the best that ever lived and shit as a producer. I mean, he has one of the best ears of our generation. You know that. I mean, that muhfucka's shit sound like, "Who the fuck EQed that shit?" But I know that when I came out he listened to my music and shit, that he added soul to his shit. He know how to play music, he know how to play keys or he got a keyboardist and shit. So he could do it like that. But when I heard his music and shit, you could hear my stuff evolve too, it wasn't just like make that louder, turn it up, we spent time on the EQ with it.

So each one teach one.

When I see him a couple times in life and shit, he like, "*You a bad mutherfucker.*" I was like, "You a bad mutherfucker." Same thing with the Neptunes, y'know. Them niggas said, "You the best that ever did this." I said, "Respect, y'all niggas is killin' it." It's all good, y'know. So I may be older than some and younger than some, nahmean? I'm younger than Dre, so he probably like, yo, new nigga put me back on it. A young nigga like, yo, an OG put me on it, y'know. Marley Marl put us on to a lot of shit, you know that. Pete Rock put us on to a lot of shit. Prince Paul, y'know? Respect to all y'all niggas. But I know what I did too, though. I know what I did. So it's all good, man. It's great. It's beautiful that we all could even have that chance. Timbaland, too, man. Can't sleep on Timbaland. Timbaland had the craziest riddims when he came with it. So I'm proud to be a part of this shit like this, man, this hip-hop shit. 'Cause I love this for my life. I know when I was younger I was more egotistical like nobody could fuck with me. You know that. That was my motto. I still feel like, individually, nobody has, like, embodied hip-hop like I've embodied it in our generation. I ain't gonna front. I know that as a producer, a lyricist, a businessman, a video director, a film director, a designer of fashion, a warped talker, and *still-able-to-get-some-bitches*-type nigga—ain't never met a package like that, son, in hip-hop. I know I'm good. So I'm good for hip-hop and proud that hip-hop had me for one of they peoples, man. It's like a lot of rappers is more, like, large and, like, lifestyles of the rich and famous, because they basically contain themself, but we still got hundreds of niggas from the hood, and me personally, I'm still very grassrooted with my people, man. ⊙

Originally appeared in Wax Poetics Issue 4, Spring 2003.

The Wild Style of TRACY 168

by Andre Torres

It was two weeks after I was supposed to go to print, and I still couldn't get in touch with TRACY 168. A week later, I'm lying in the bed battling a violent case of the stomach flu, and the phone rings. It's him; now he's ready to get down. And such is the dance when you get in the ring with TRACY 168, or as his voice mail says, "TRACY the *Artist*." It had been going on for nearly six months, and I was growing weaker by the day. But I was up against the wall, I didn't have a Plan B; somehow I knew TRACY would come through in the end. As I watched him work two days later, I realized there was no other way for this whole thing to go down. It had to come to this. It was the culmination of six months of being sucked into the vortex of a man who virtually lives on the edge of reality. Not on the streets, he is the streets. This is what you get from the man who literally invented the term "Wild Style," not to describe a way of writing on a wall or train, but as a way of living life. It has meant feeling the rush of painting whole cars, top to bottom, outside and *in*; racking up as a means of survival, and fleeing from cops at secret lay-ups that only he and a few select others were even hip to. It has also meant being there when his childhood friend, RC, only eleven at the time, broke his neck trying to run from 5-0 while playing on the back of a train. It has meant seeing countless writers go on to bigger commercial fame using styles he and his peers created, while he still proudly runs with the rats. But this is the burden of TRACY 168, a true artist in every sense of the word. It's not the tragic tale of the talented artist who never "made" it. TRACY 168 makes it every day, not for the fanfare, but because he's got no other choice. He was born to do this shit. But take a look at any of your Graffiti 101 books, and you'll see more attention paid to cats that were still wetting the bed in 1974—when TRACY, CHI CHI 133, LEE 163, and SUPER KOOL were revolutionizing culture—than you will about the legends themselves. Throughout time, history has a way of being written by those who want to tell the story the way they saw it, or heard it happened. In the mythological realm of graffiti lore, it's easy to see how sometimes it becomes just that, His-story. Over coffee and toast, TRACY 168 pulled a few photos from his extensive archive and went back, images flooding his mind with some sweet and some not so sweet memories, in hopes of shedding a little light on the man I know as, "TRACY 168—Wild Style—*woo woo!*" »

TRACY 168 and RC, first "flame," 1971–72.

This is a TRACY and an RC. By the early '70s, the graffiti movement had already started a few years prior. Everybody came from everywhere; it was little cliques. You got Clinton High School, which had like PHASE 2, LIONEL 168, SWEET DUKE, LEE 163, those guys. Washington Heights, you had Brooklyn—DINO NOD, EX VANDALS, "A" TRAIN, BOP, and those guys. And in the Bronx, Highbridge near Yankee Stadium, was ours. It was CLYDE, me, FJC IV, RC 162, CHI CHI 133, SANTOS 108, CHARLIE 158, BOBBY 172. Then we started guys like CHRIS 170 and BONANZA, and it spawned off into RIFF 170 and guys like that; they were all a little bit after that.

We found this lay-up that was very important to the graffiti movement, because it had a catwalk. It was in Brooklyn. I wasn't just a graffiti artist and painter in the Bronx, I was from Manhattan and the Bronx. I'm Irish/Italian/Puerto Rican—that's who I am. I lived in Manhattan on the weekends, and, on the weekdays, I was in the Bronx, so I was all over the fuckin' place anyway. So this lay-up that had a catwalk was in Kingston, and it was a damn gold mine. The thing that made this a goldmine was that it had a catwalk. You had ten trains, which is a hundred cars, and they only ran during rush hour, so it was a sure thing that they would run without being buffed. So they ran with the windows too, which is the greatest thing on the earth. This picture here is like one of the earliest flames that had ever been done. It's like a "Latin" thing, flames. What I'm really getting at here is RC 162 was playing on the train in 1973, later on, and he was the first casualty of the graffiti movement. He actually fell on the back of a train with me and M-G I and was killed instantly. Now, that's the day I realized we're not playing a regular game here. This is not like Nintendo, where you get an extra life or you get another chance. I always thought that I'd see him again, so that was a tragedy, a real trauma on me as a child, because that was my graffiti partner. He was only eleven years old, and for him to lose his life for this art form—I won't let him die in vain. What I'm getting at is that we risked our lives to do this artwork. It wasn't just the safety of some fuckin' loft and showing our pieces in some museums. Instantaneously, we would bring the artwork to the people. But the thing is, I lost my friend, and I realized, "Wow, this is no joke!" You got trains that weigh tons coming at you; the tunnels are no joke. The tunnels—that was my world—I ran shit under there.

TRACY, first shadow, 1973.

So after a while, my name was on every damn train; it was pretty wild. It was me, SPIN, STOP 700. STOP 700 was Cooper, Ronald Cooper, he was in my class. I was hanging out with Brooklyn writers. I was hanging out with Bronx writers. I was all-city already; it was kind of cool. The Bronx was flipping out, 'cause they didn't know which yard I was in, and they couldn't perceive that I was in Brooklyn doing these pieces. 'Cause who would go there? The Tomahawks were running rampant over there. Gangs were running all over the city. It was like *The Warriors*. So we became kings instantaneously, then it was just about piecing. The thing grew fast—design, styles. One thing you did that was very important was make mistakes. If you're willing to take a fuckin' chance by painting, and going up there not worrying about the paint, and just going up there and doing some kind of design, I mean, that's the move. Now sometimes a mistake would become a good thing. Here's where I did the first shadow. What happened was me and PRIEST did a piece, and I had an orangey thing going on with the black 3-D. And what happened was I dropped the black 3-D behind the name, but I didn't cut the edges in the angle of the three dimensional, and it looked like it fell *behind* the piece. The sun was so bright that day, somebody went, "Wow!"—'cause it looked like a shadow was cast behind my piece. So they came to me to tell me they liked my new "shadow piece," and I go, "Yeah, that's what I did." So a lot of the things I did were told to me by other writers—I had no fuckin' clue. So I created the shadow by someone telling me what I did. Sometimes in a lot of pieces, I have no clue what I'm doing; I just know it looks good. They tell me what it is.

P NUT and SONNY 107 taking a "taxi," 1974.

We didn't really have much money; we used to take the trains all over the city. We were like *Tom Sawyer* kids, adventurous. But a lot of times, our train didn't get there, so we would have to take the "taxi" as you see in this photo. This is a regular way of traveling for a graffiti writer. This is P NUT 2—from the *Welcome Back, Kotter* fame; that's his piece in the intro—and SONNY 107.

CLIFF and TRACY, first whole train inside and outside, late 1973–early 1974.

In time you always wanted to have a partner, partners were very important. A partner was always somebody you knew who would take their name in a place where you didn't want to go. And always try to carry their own weight, so you don't want a partner who ain't got no juice. You would always get a partner that you know would carry your name in areas and places that you know he would do his job. So if you're going to be a partner with any writer you gotta make sure he's established as a fuckin' graffiti artist, and he has some balls, and he has style. Something. I started a group called Wanted; I had the first clubhouse. It was Woodycrest and 166th Street with seventy-two members in 1973. I had seventy-two members of the best writers in New York City. I must have been the most dangerous fuckin' writer at that moment. But my main thing is that I was always an artist. We took these dull, boring-looking subways, and we turned them into these beautiful rolling stock of rainbows. We took the shit and made it beautiful. It gave people something to look at on a gloomy day in the city. When the mayor would take his trips down to Florida—there's a transit strike, or there's a garbage strike—we're just stuck here, so it's to help take your mind off of all the horrors of your life. There's artwork, which is kind of cool. It was the positive thing that came out of the negative thing of gangs. We were all like diplomats; we came in every color. There was no such thing as color in this. We were all the same, because we were all artists, and we were producing positive stuff. It was beautiful.

Back to partners, sometimes they're not working up to their caliber, but they've got a lot of potential. So I would aim them. I wasn't a teacher; I was a sensei. So I would take a guy that had potential like CLIFF 159, and I aimed his stuff from a regular tag to really piecing. Cartoons—I was known as the first cartoonist too. You did big pieces, 3-DS; everything was almost done. There had to be something else, and what I did was created cartoons to enhance my name. The reason I used cartoons is because, if you remember, cartoons never die. They live forever. So cartoons are really establishing the fact that my name will live forever, I guess we were all looking for immortality.

Here CLIFF 159 did a piece with me, a top-to-bottom; I think it was brilliant. CLIFF was very good. He was a master writer; he was all-city already. He wore this little raggedy coat. The guy was like all-city from Manhattan! We did a whole top to bottom, on the outside. And then at the spur of the moment, we came up with an idea to do a whole top to bottom, a whole car, on the inside for the passengers that ride that train at that moment for rush hour. It was mostly still wet when the train went running from Kingston, and everybody had to stand, and just look at my freakin' name and his name! That was the first whole car, inside and outside. A funny story with the inside piece is that LSD 3 boarded the train after one of his LSD-hit-taking-tab-sitting-down-getting-high-all-night [binges], and he told me he walked in the train, and saw my name on the whole car with CLIFF. And he says he didn't understand how he could see through the train. He says, "I would look at the train; I could see your piece; I couldn't understand how I was seeing your piece through the outside." He didn't realize it was on the inside. It fucked him up; he thought the acid was just very good.

Wild Style at 196th Street, 1979.

The WILD STYLE is my name. LOVESTER ONE is my name; I was born on Valentine's Day. HAWAII 5-0. A lot of people mistake it, but what it was, was that I got a lot of the writers that were the best, and I took them from Wanted, and I established this group called Wild Style. Wild Style was a design that I came up with, and a lettering. But it was just a way of life to me, the way I lived. I had no rules; I was wild, like, untamed. But I had style, which was class. So that's how I lived, and I would almost try to teach other people how to live like this. So whenever you'd see a TRACY that was off the hook, that people would go, "Oh shit! Wild Style!" People thought it was the lettering, but it was just mechanical lettering. Anything where all the letters were connected was more like a mechanical lettering. It wasn't Wild Style, it was mechanical lettering. But it's okay, I actually feel honored, because a culture has actually been started behind what I've done. I'm, till this day, still fighting the authorities.

Wild Style, I invented it. What makes it mine is that if you look at it, it's all capital letters except for the *i*. Only a graffiti writer would say, "I'm going to use a capital here, and a small case here." It's out of context. See, these people who come from Madison Avenue said, "That's not right, fix that *i*, it gotta be capital." They're so structured; they wouldn't live with that. It bothers them, but it looks good. So when this guy approached me one day, and asked me to do a low-budget film—Charlie Ahearn. So him and Fab 5 Freddy approached me in the skating rink, Bronx Graffiti, and I said, "What is this about?" He says it's going to be a documentary based on hip-hop, and I said, "Okay, that's cool; I can relate." And it would help children; it would more or less be out there just to help broaden the horizons of all the people. So I said, "Okay, you can use it." There was no money, really; it was a low-budget film. I said if there's any money to be made, take care of it later. It still belongs to me; it's just that they used it for a title.

TRACY 168's design at full size on the train, early 1974

Lettering is lettering; you always have to do something with lettering. What made Wild Style mine—the funny thing is, I worked in an advertising agency. I designed Northern bathroom tissue, I did Tanqueray gin. I worked everywhere twice. I mean, I was always creating, so I knew the ins and outs, because I used to work under this professor, Jack Stewart. Jack Stewart taught me how to copyright my name and design, and trademark everything. So he was like a mentor to me, and this guy was like "who's who"—Cooper Union, Boston School of Design, Rhode Island, everything. So he taught me how to protect myself by drawing a copyright, and I taught that to all the writers. I'm always innovating to protect this graffiti. The funny thing is the first people to turn on you are usually writers.

This is in Professor Jack Stewart's studio, and it's a picture of a painting of a design I was gonna place on the train the following week, and I give homage to PHASE 2 on it. The main thing is to look at me and understand that I was in charge of my own life, and that's kind of wild. I was out of control, they said, because I don't live by anybody's rules but my own. But I wasn't an evil person. The whole idea is, don't push me too far, I'll knock a muthafucka's head off. I was *that* guy. But it was because of the art form I lived. You can't go in the train yard without thinking you might get mugged or jumped for your paint. I would knock a fuckin' guy's head off, but only bullies. And now I find myself fighting corporate America. The graffiti art form is very important to Madison Avenue now; it's a billion dollar industry. So they can't have a guy who grew up like I did owning something so important and so powerful; that's dangerous to them. Five judges called me a vandal this week, which is kind of funny, because if I'm a vandal, what the fuck am I doing in the New York Historical Society, who bought my paintings last week. It's kind of contradictory: this place buys my paintings, and they've got fuckin' George Washington on the wall, and this week they're calling me a vandal! That's the humor of it all. So the reason why I kept it so basic with the two colors is to show the lettering. I find that if you ain't got a real talent for doing letters, and your letters are not correct, you use more color, to camouflage. It's like putting garlic on bad fish; you're trying to cover up a fuckup.

TRACY 168 in Jack Stewart's studio, early 1974.

TRACY 168 on wall, 1998.

This is '98. I redid an old red and white TRACY just to show how a masterpiece, a burner, something that is perfect can withstand the test of time. I just updated something old, fixed it up, something old made new. You always just redress it; it's like putting clothes on an old piece. Everything repeats itself every twenty, thirty years. Clothes, everything—they come back. So I was showing everybody how an old piece from '73 could be re-dressed and stand on a wall, and people wouldn't know the difference. So it's kind of good and scary. People really aren't educated on what the hell it is, but at the same time they're introduced to something that's very old. It's like bringing an old record out, and listening to James Brown for the first time. No one ever heard him before, and they're like, "Wow, this is the greatest thing!"

Creativity's important, the truth is important, and the one thing I won't tolerate is taking this thing and changing the truth of it. That's why I'm here. I'm going to make sure the truth stays the truth. The only thing real about this is it comes from the heart, from your soul and shit.

Three-dimensional TRACY, 1984.

This is a 3-D TRACY to show how colors mix and match, and this is Federal Safety Color by Rustoleum. Sometimes it feels good to get a new different kind of paint; we used to use a lot of Red Devil by then. The idea is to use as many different designs as possible. You've got a lot of the drips going on; drips were very in. The outline is black, which I found a lot of times if you just left it alone without an outline it looked a lot better. Sometimes outlining would kill the piece. The good thing about having five letters in your name, I could always stick something in the middle. The *A* could have been an Alvin and the Chipmunks *A*, it could have been Captain America's head, because he had an *A* on his forehead. I could always stick something in there to replace my letter *A*. Here I have a star, sometimes I have a circle, sometimes I have a face. A TRACY face with the glasses. I have this character with sunglasses I use a lot.

Jungle Wild Style mural, 1992.

I used this Wild Style picture to show a neighborhood destroyed by a world that didn't give a fuck no more, and everybody's just living for themselves. So at the corner, I did a Wild Style in, like, a jungle, because we're living in a jungle. And the leopard represents how we have to survive this jungle. If you look at the street sign, it's a street cross, it's a cross of death. How many people gotta die to get out of here? And you gotta make it over the wall, and through the wall, and through hell to make it and reach for the stars. And then everybody's bitchin', everybody's saying, "Me, what about me?" But what the fuck have you done to make this better? The whole idea is to try to help each other, to get over that wall to make it to your stars—reach for your star. We should help each other, everybody's so into "me, me, me," and it should be more about us "us, us, us," helping

each other out. That would be so freakin' cool—that I miss.

I always did murals. I didn't believe in doing nothing, but what I felt like I needed to do, like paint. So I did a lot of murals. I'm like the first guy that perfected those murals for the city of New York. So I could make a living, so I could have some money in my pocket. And part two was a lot of guys started dying from drugs, from the crack and the dope in the '80s and '90s. So I started doing murals for people that died. Clyde Master was my first RIP memorial wall, I think. And from then on, I got one after another. I actually made it look like the day the dead would walk the earth. I made the Bible come alive; it's kind of wild. So I created this mural here to try to tell them, "Stop!"—before it's too late. "We have to try to help each other make it. Stop bitchin', let's do this. Go for the stars, let's make this work."

TRACY with rocket on 7 line, 1974.

Every line was easy to get to. The only line that wasn't really a regular line was the 7 line. This is the Flushing–Shea Stadium line. I mean, I lived in Yankee Stadium, and I don't want to be a traitor, but I'm actually a Met fan. What happened was I got bored. I hit the Ds; they went all-city. I hit the 4s; they went all-city. But the 7 line was an odd train. It only went across 42nd, really, and it shot through Queens. It was an odd train, and the color was odd. We had a background already painted for me—aqua turquoise. It was like a Federal Safety color, so all you had to really do was go and add a piece to it. It was actually having fun, and then also attacking an area where maybe I'll find some new artists that can stimulate me. Nothing like branching out to see if maybe I'll find a new style. And

I did, I found KANE, FLAME, a lot of guys that got up, pretty good with styles. The threat was there, which means they came at me full force, which is kind of cool. I brought RIFF, CHI CHI, BOP, P NUT, ZEST; all the masters from the Bronx went out there. It must've blew their heads, because it wasn't just painting there; it was killing them motherfuckers with masters. By the way, we did the first ten whole subway cars ever. That was our mission to do the 7s, to do the first whole train. What happened was the cops came with helicopters. We did it, they broke it up, and the first that got credit was KANE, I think, or LEE tried to get credit for it. ●

Originally appeared in Wax Poetics Issue 4, Spring 2003

Real to Reel with Charlie Ahearn

by Jeff Chang

When Charlie Ahearn, aka "Charlie Video" and Fred "Fab 5 Freddy" Braithwaite came together in 1980 to make *Wild Style*, neither had any idea just how important the movie and moment it documented would become. ¶ In fact, their own partnership was rife in symbolism. Freddy, a spraycan and video artist, had grown up in Do-or-Die Bed-Stuy, born into a family deeply steeped in currents of Black activism and jazz. Charlie, and his twin brother John, had come from the upstate New York suburb of Binghamton to be a part of the edgy East Village art scene. Both Freddy and Charlie began circulating in the boroughs during an era when New York City was bankrupt and in flames, when racial segregation was severe and degradation was everywhere. Their meeting helped hip-hop break out of the Bronx and move to the radical White downtown clubs and galleries. ¶ The rest is history. Indeed, it is amazing to consider that in the two years between the beginning of the *Wild Style* project and its theatrical release in 1982, hip-hop moved from a local Bronx youth subculture to a global youth culture. *Wild Style* captured the moment and, in turn, became a vehicle to spread hip-hop worldwide. ¶ Charlie has remained close to hip-hop culture over the years and has released and oral history and photo book of the old school, entitled *Yes Yes Y'all*. As a project of cultural recovery, it could have the same impact of *Wild Style*. At the least, it will undoubtedly shake up many preconceptions and puncture many myths about the old school. I spoke to Charlie Ahearn about *Wild Style* as he prepared for the book's release and for the twentieth anniversary of the movie's release. »

Charlie Ahearn (top) directing the Fantastic Five on the basketball location for *Wild Style*, 1981; photo by Cathy Campbell.

How did you begin the path toward *Wild Style*?

In 1976 and 1977, I was involved in a group of artists called Colab that were basically dropping out of the art world and trying to find a new way to make art and a new way to show art in the city. There was just the whole idea of "get the hell out of the art world, get the hell out of art galleries, and find a way to be creative in a larger sense." And that also meant being socially active and aware. There was a lot of radical social movement going on, and I was downtown and I naturally gravitated to Smith Projects as being the place to go. It's actually way down by the Brooklyn Bridge. I was making films and showing them in the housing project there. The way to be an activist, an art activist. That was the idea.

When I was there working like that, kids came to me and said they wanted to make a movie with me and they were into martial arts. So I spent two years making a film called *The Deadly Art of Survival*. It was shot in Super 8 and the whole thing cost two thousand dollars. While I was doing that, there were murals everywhere in that neighborhood by Lee Quinones. I would ask kids in the neighborhood, "Who painted these murals?" And they'd go, "Lee!" Like it was the most obvious thing, 'cause he's so famous. And I'd say, "Okay, where can I find him?" And everyone would go, "I don't know, he's around but he's kind of secretive. He's hard to find." So that became the character later for *Wild Style*, this iconic character of the graffiti artist as someone who is very underground, kind of like a political radical would be underground. In other words, he does all this stuff but he's not actually known by anybody. And that was a lot of what our art movement was about was working kind of

anonymously. Doing a lot of artwork, but not being famous, was really the kind of thing that we were doing.

Nineteen seventy-eight was a big year for him, wasn't it? He had big trains that year.

Yes, I think he was coming off his train career and was moving towards murals at that time. He sort of went from being king of the subways to being king of the murals and then the gallery thing. And he's still doing murals. He's done great murals. So anyway, I made this film called *The Deadly Art of Survival*, and Colab was giving this art show in Times Square called the Times Square Show. It was in an abandoned massage parlor. What happened was Fred Braithwaite came to a screening of the *Deadly Art of Survival* at that show. And he was amazed when he came there. Jean-Michel Basquiat was in the show, Keith Haring was in the show, Kenny Scharf. So Fred was becoming aware of these other artists, and so he wanted to meet me. He had seen posters for this movie around Lee's neighborhood, and he had been working with Lee organizing art shows.

So Lee is from the Lower East Side?

Yes, he's from Smith Projects; that's where he lived. And what I forgot to mention is that he came by a few times when I was shooting the movie, and he had this big Afro, and he was this skinny kid with a motorbike. And I'd say, "I want to work with you on this movie." And he said, "Bet." And I said, "Well, how can I get to you? Do you have a phone number?" "Nah, I'll just be around." And then he'd never be around. He was becoming elusive!

So he was kind of mythical.

Right, right! He was mythical! [*laughs*] Fred told me that he

A Cold Crush Brothers party at the Hoe Avenue Boys Club, circa 1980, with Caz, Easy AD, Tony Tone, and Almighty KG. Photo by Angelo King.

wanted to make a movie with me and said we should make a movie about this graffiti thing, and he said he knew Lee Quinones. So I said, "If you can bring Lee to me, come by tomorrow, and I'll give you guys fifty dollars," because I wanted them to do a mural outside the building. I gave them fifty dollars; they came by the next day. And I said, "Okay, you know, like, here we are, the three of us." And that became the beginnings of the idea of *Wild Style*.

So you were all talking about doing this movie together?

Fred and I were, and then Fred said that he'd agree to bring Lee. He said he knew Lee, and he was gonna bring him back, 'cause I hadn't seen him in a while. And he brought Lee to the Times Square Show. I gave them fifty dollars for paint, because they were gonna do a mural, which they did. That said "Fab 5"—that's what it said on the outside of the building, and that was definitely the beginnings of the movie. And right from that start, I began going with Fred to the Bronx. Actually, it was June 20 when I met him. Because I've got slides; all my slides have dates on them. And it's amazing how, in early July, I was already going to club after club up there. And the first thing that I went to with Fred—Fred had been sort of up in the Bronx that spring—and he had brought Debbie Harry and Chris Stein up there to meet Grandmaster Flash, which later became the "Rapture" song.

So I went to this park, and it was in a place called the Valley in the Bronx. It's North Bronx; it's in a large park, and it was dark in this park. I remember there was a reggae band playing, and the other side was hip-hop music. And we wandered to the hip-hop music. So Busy Bee was there, and he says, "What are you doing here?" and I said, "I'm Charlie Ahearn, and I'm here to make a movie about the rap scene." And he takes me by the hand, and he leads me out on the stage where there's a microphone, and there's an audience there.

This is the first time you've been to the Bronx?

No, my brother had already been living in the Bronx for a couple of years. I had been going to the Bronx to show *The Deadly Art of Survival*. I'd been going to Fashion Moda for two years, since '78. The Bronx was a hip place to go if you were an artist; everybody was going up there. But this was not the same.

It was a different scene.

It was a totally different scene! High school kids—and it was wild. And it was dark, and Busy Bee leads me out onto stage, to the microphone—and you gotta understand, everybody who is anybody in hip-hop is *right there*! The Funky 4 were there, Mercedes Ladies, all these people were all in the audience right there. It's not a big scene.

Who was DJing?

Breakout. So he puts his arm around me, and he says, "This here is Charlie Ahearn, and he's my movie producer. We're making a movie about the rap scene." Boom! That's all it took. In other words, it's not like there's a whole line of batteries of managers and attorneys and producers. It's just these guys are there, and I'm there, and what do they want to do—are they gonna look at me and go, "No!" They're not gonna look at me like that. They weren't suspicious at all. As a matter of fact, I never got asked, "Are you really a movie producer?" I never really made a movie in my life—I mean, aside from this movie *The Deadly Art of Survival*, which was on Super 8. I'd never written a script. I really had no connection to the movie business whatsoever, any more than I was just one of these guys that

Grand Wizard Theodore at the T-Connection, 1980. Photo by Charlie Ahearn.

K. K. Rockwell, Lil' Rodney Cee, and Busy Bee (center) at an outdoor jam, 1980. Photo by Charlie Ahearn.

Debbie Harry on the set of the "Rapture" video, with Jean-Michel Basquiat and Fab 5 Freddy, 1981; photo by Charlie Ahearn.

was making movies, and I was showing movies in punk clubs. I was not like a real moviemaker. I didn't know anything about it. I had never been to film school or been in the film business. But everyone accepted me as a Hollywood movie producer right off the bat! [*laughs*] Just 'cause, who knows?

And I didn't really have any money. It's not like I arrived in a limousine or something. I was just there. It's a matter of innocence on all sides. I didn't question whether they were rap stars! I took it all on face value that whoever I was meeting was the most important. Busy Bee became one of the stars of *Wild Style*. Funky 4, I became very tight with them. That was how it got started. And they brought me back wherever. People would hand out flyers wherever you were. And whatever was on the flyers, wherever I was, I would always go to those clubs the following week. Very soon after that, I got into the practice of bringing slide projectors, because I was always into this activist idea that if you're a filmmaker, wherever you're going, you're showing them.

I would bring a slide projector and show them over the DJs. My main haunt was the Ecstasy Garage. That was like DJ AJ, Mean Gene, and Theodore, but there would always be guest visits from the Cold Crush and of course, the Fantastic Freaks were always there, and Busy Bee was always there. Those were the stars of hip-hop as I knew it.

And the slides were basically of the clubs that you were going to?

Yes, yes, yes. I was also going out to the subways. The main visual was graffiti, the slides were about graffiti. And b-boying, interestingly enough, was something that was so—the first year that I was out and about, it was so absolutely not there. It was not there. Contrary to what everyone says, it was definitely the most important

thing when hip-hop began, but it died out and disappeared. I never saw it in any club I was in for a whole year in the Bronx. It was brought back by the Rock Steady.

Can I take you back to the making of the movie? How did you put the finances together?

Like I told you, *The Deadly Art of Survival* cost two thousand dollars. That was all pizza. That was the main budget. If you had two pizzas, it was easy to keep a collection of twenty kids around. If you didn't, they'd be out of there.

So it was a lot more pizzas for *Wild Style*.

[With] *Wild Style*, I was working in 16mm with a crew that—you know, I was confused about how big it should be. It was basically like a documentary crew. I think we had six to eight people total, the whole crew. That's nothing. There was no makeup person, no wardrobe person, no design person. There was a script supervisor, sort of, which was fine with me.

My style of directing at the time was so laid-back that I would do one scene a day. For instance, like when we shot in the subway yard, I had to put over a quarter of my entire budget to go toward paying off the MTA. I'm sure they never wanted to do that again. They allowed us to come to the yard. I paid them in advance. The night that we went there, it poured rain the entire time.

What yard was this?

It was in Brooklyn; I think it was New Lots. Lee didn't show up that night. I think he had second thoughts about whether he wanted to be on camera, because he was very religious about the dos and don'ts. He was okay for regular scenes, but I think he wasn't sure about being

Lee Quinones (bottom), star of *Wild Style*, in 1980; photo by Charlie Ahearn.

shown painting on camera. So we had Dondi do those. And he was great. We just put a do-rag on him and shot him from the back. But I needed close-ups from the front so I set up a scene under the Brooklyn Bridge. Because it was raining I couldn't shoot most of the stuff I wanted to shoot, so we basically just concentrated on long shots of him going in and out of the yard. Which we used, and it was fine.

Did the script come out of the casting?

The main thing was that, in 1980, graffiti was the thing—that was the story. For me, Lee was a logical choice. I didn't really think so much in terms of how could I make a successful movie, but I wanted to make a movie that had a simple story. 'Cause my idea was Bruce Lee movies. In other words, a simple hero, a simple story. Lee was gonna be the hero. And it's like a comic book. What is his problem? He's in love with this girl but she doesn't know he's the famous graffiti artist. That's it, that's all the movie is. And, in a way, it reflected exactly how I saw things—in a comic book fashion. He was dating Pink at that time. Pink was hot. She was out in the subway yards, I thought she was very attractive. She was kind of cute, and she was very street at the same time.

I couldn't get Lee to be in the movie for the entire year that I was organizing the movie. He wouldn't be in the movie. And he didn't want to be photographed. 'Cause he was real. He wasn't a movie star. When we shot the scene where he goes to the art collector, and he's supposed to be in bed with this woman—that could have been something else entirely. Pink found out that he was shooting this scene. She showed up at that apartment. She sat right between the camera and Lee the entire time. That's why he was so nervous! And,

like, you know, it was hard to direct!

This was supposed to be "popular art."

The whole thing of *Wild Style* was, yes, it was about making this movie that was gonna be shown in a movie theater, but it was all a process. It was just a very activist time. In other words, you could bring change to a lot of people by doing something like an art show. And then later it was brought downtown to Negril by Ruza "Kool Lady" Blue, and then the Roxy was the big blowout of the whole thing. Actually, the first two big evenings there, I did slide shows just like I did in the Bronx. I did 'em at Negril, and I also did them at the Roxy.

So there was this shifting and mixing that was very exciting to people, and of course the graffiti artists—they were meeting each other from all boroughs. The racial thing was a big deal. Mixing a lot of Black, Puerto Rican, and White people downtown altogether is very combustible, because people are coming from very different types of areas. So people get used to the idea that people can hang out with each other. And graffiti, at the time, was such a dynamic thing, because it was all-borough. It meant that it wasn't about your little local neighborhood; it was about the entire city every time. You were [always] going all-city; that's what you were supposed to do. So why shouldn't art be all-city? Why should it be about a little tiny neighborhood? That was the idea. ◗

Originally appeared in Wax Poetics Issue 3, Fall 2002.

Yarns of Yards and the Movie that Must Be Stopped

by Robbie Busch

Henry Chalfant moved to New York City in January 1973. He was a stone sculptor and had to commute from his uptown apartment to his downtown studio on Grand Street in Soho. Every day, he took the train and became increasingly entranced with the evolution of the graffiti he saw. He was amazed by the transformation from very rudimentary tags to whole cars, tops to bottoms to characters. The Soho art scene was leaving him cold with its emphasis on minimal and conceptual art, which he found interesting, but not very visual. He kept watching the growth of this subway art and thinking that someone ought to be documenting it. He finally took it upon himself and began taking pictures in 1976–77. He remembers, "I really couldn't stand it any longer, because it was getting better and better. The trains were getting more beautiful." ¶ Henry was new to NYC, though, and didn't have a real awareness of outer boroughs where they had elevated trains, so he was having a hard time trying to figure out how to document it. One day he took the train up to 125th Street and realized that the trains did go outside. He began to explore Baker's Field and the Bronx where the 2 and 5 lines had a very active graffiti presence. He collected photos of trains for two or three years before he actually met any graffiti writers. »

Henry Chalfant and Tony Silver. Photo by Robbie Busch, 2003.

In 1979, Henry met his first writer, NAK, who was DAZE's cousin. He told NAK that he knew who his cousin was and that he had many pictures of his work. NAK told Henry that he could meet his cousin, and other writers, at the writer's bench at 149th Street/ Grand Concourse. So Henry went that afternoon, after school, and the world of graffiti opened up to him. He saw a mass of kids with black books, trading style and looking for fame. His photos gained him a unique access to the community. He would become one of the few early champions of this new and exciting art form.

This interview was conducted at Henry's studio in the West Village on March 26, 2003. It was a reunion of sorts for the Style Wars documentary filmmakers, Henry Chalfant and Tony Silver, and some of the legends of the graffiti world who were featured in the movie: RAMMELLZEE, FROSTY FREEZE, LADY PINK, and DEZ. A follow up interview was done with Henry on May 28th, 2003.

How did you and Tony first meet?

HENRY CHALFANT: My older sister was roommates in college with Joan, Tony's first wife. When I went to college I spent a lot of time with her family in California; they were a sort of home away from home. Kathleen, my wife, and I moved to New York in 1973, and Joan had been living here for a number of years, so she was one of the first people I looked up. That's when I met Tony.

Did you stay in contact with each other?

HC: No, not really. We had dinner a few of times.

TONY SILVER: Cut to seven years later, there was a famous piece in the *Village Voice* by Sally Banes, with photos by Martha Cooper, entitled "Physical Graffiti: Breaking Is Hard to Do." It opened my eyes to the existence of something happening in the neighborhoods in the city with kids inventing their own ways of expressing themselves, their own art forms. It was written about as an alternative to violence. The city was, in many ways, in shambles and was at the

end of a major gang-violence era.

So, I was fascinated with the story [of] this dance form that was really something else, but was also a dance form. Kids were creating something for themselves that didn't belong to anybody else.

Henry's name was mentioned at the bottom of the article with a notice that there was going to be this performance [at the Common Ground art space in Soho], the first-ever public performance of this kind. I thought it was probably the same Henry.

HC: The first day that we had a dress rehearsal that was open to the public, Tony approached me right away and said, "Look, I think this would make an interesting film. Would you like to work with me on it?" It's interesting, at that point I had already been in touch [a little bit] with Charlie Ahearn. I was gonna supply him with photos and things like that. When Tony proposed a documentary, that was more interesting to be involved with.

More interesting because it was closer to the reality you were seeing?

HC: That and more of a role for me. With Charlie, all I was going to do was give him photos. With this movie I was going to have a more creative role.

TS: My idea was a small film, maybe a half hour, about this idea of expressing this energy in this kind of way. We were all living with graffiti in New York, but I came to this as an outsider. Henry was not; he had been documenting graffiti and other aspects of what we now know as hip-hop for quite a while. Through the presentation at the Common Ground, Henry really brought these elements together, conceptually, so that people outside of this world could understand that in some way this is all one thing.

So, on this wonderful night [after the show] Henry, Kathleen, and I got drunk together. I was thinking, "What is this film? How do I write a proposal? Where do I get the money?" Kathy launched

TAKE ONE, FROSTY FREEZE, BABY LOVE. Rock Steady Crew outside United Skates of America, Queens, NY, 1981. First *Style Wars* shoot.

into this riff, much like your presentation that night, Henry, "Do you realize what it takes to go into the yards? And risk death and arrest and rival crews with fifty cans of paint and create a masterpiece on the side of a train in a few hours and get the hell out with your life?!" I saw it at that moment as theatre, it was an opera, and I realized that what we had been living with in New York for the last eleven to twelve years was a real-life epic drama between these kids doing their own thing and "everybody else." It was a war. The movie was out there, with production values and everything; we just had to go shoot it.

I was fascinated by the idea of the bench. When Henry first mentioned the bench to me I imagined something like the Algonquin Round Table. [*everyone laughs*]

So, who was the Robert Benchley of the bench?

RAMMELLZEE: That's the way it was! You got good conversation and people arguing with you. Right? And if you knew how to strategize, you'd talk 'em out of it. If you didn't talk 'em out of it, you'd hit a wall…hit a train. See 'em the next day if he was lucky!

HC: It was great, because it was where you would go to see things, where you would go to meet people, and where you would go to have these discussions about what was good.

TS: Yeah. I was right. So, the first time Henry took me there we were supposed to meet some people; they had gotten the word. SKEME and DEZ were supposed to be there, but they didn't show up for a long time. We were standing at the south end of the platform, and I was peering into the tunnel. All of a sudden these two figures start to dimly emerge walking towards us. I thought they were workers, but it's SKEME and DEZ. They're walking along idly chatting about trains and this and that. They had walked all the way up there, and it was then that I really got it…on another level. This truly was a world that was absolutely pure in it's own way, and

the rest of the world didn't know anything about. The magic of that was amazing! I don't know if it came through in the movie, but that's what I wanted to show.

I think it does. Especially the way you have a classical approach to shooting the trains that intercuts with the handheld hip-hop style you shot with the breakers and the kids at the bench and the way the music plays off of those different types of images.

TS: One of the things I really wanted to do was integrate the photography and the music, so that you felt the movement of the trains. We had two amazing cameramen, Burleigh Wartes and Jim Szalapski. Burleigh did that shot of the 6 line, where those three white trains pass each other, from a rooftop at Whitlock Ave.

The first shoot we did was at the Inwood playground with the breakers and that same day we shot [the up-rockers] at the United Skates of America competition. The playground was just a demonstration, but the scene at USA was the real scene! I had brought in some crew to work for free. Henry had a little bit of cash, which I didn't have at the time. So between us we were able to do some filming. But that footage just sat for four or five months, while we looked for more money.

How did you get the funding to make the movie?

TS: It took a long time. I had never done this before. I would get these amazing responses, "This is fascinating! Extraordinary! Remarkable, what you are trying to do! How come nobody has ever tried to do this before?" And then, "I'm afraid I can't help you." I had this completely wacked idea that the National Endowment for the Humanities could fund this. I knew that [Harvard sociologist] Nathan Glazer had written some pro and con things about this and I got in touch with him. He thought that what we were doing was very interesting and said that he would be an academic advisor for our grant proposal. After that, we were able to get this

DOZE at United Skates of America, Queens, NY, 1981. *Style Wars* film shoot.

DEZ and crew, East Harlem, NYC, 1982.

RAMMELLZEE tag. Photo by Robbie Busch, 2003.

immense apparatus of scholars [including Columbia philosophy professor and art critic Arthur C. Danto and ethnologist Barbara Kirshenblatt-Gimblett of NYU] behind us who thought that this was a great project. I was warned by staff people at the NEH that this would never fly. But, I sent it in anyway. It was a huge proposal with many letters of support. It finally went in front of the NEH in early 1982 and was killed by one person [Gertrude Himmelfarb] who was the wife of Irving Kristol, one of Glazer's fellow neoconservatives. Glazer later told me that he made a personal appeal to the council, but she wouldn't do it. She was the one who described it as, "The film that must be stopped!"

HC: The big problem with the delay in fund-raising was that the whole thing was changing so fast.

TS: I remember, even then, you had some fear that it wasn't happening anymore. That nobody was going to the bench…

HC: When I took you, it was a few years after I first had been there.

When you made the film you hadn't been there for a while?

HC: No, I went there all the time. It's just that I think it was probably thinning out a little bit by the early '80s. Also, it was popping up in other places. There was a lot of benching going on at the Brooklyn Bridge stop and places in Brooklyn. There was a plot at one point to steal the bench and bring it to my studio. [everyone laughs] It never happened; I wish it had.

PINK: It's still there.

HC: Yeah, but it's different. It's one of those new ones. They used to be the slatted benches.

PINK: After a while it became hot, because it was so popular that's where the police would always go. New spots had to be found. I think by the time I visited in the early '80s, there were just toys

sitting there, nobody of any reputation or fame.

When did you first go, RAMMELLZEE?

R: 1980. Sittin' there with KEL FIRST and I was told that I shouldn't be there, because I was coming from Far Rockaway, Queens. I said, "I know I'm not supposed to be here, but I'm gonna be here anyway. And if anyone's gonna take me they can come and get some." We got to talking and I did a piece in his book. Very few people ever saw my pieces on the outside of trains. Most of the time I was doing EG [EVOLUTION GRILLER THE MASTER KILLER]. I only wrote on the train sixty times on the outside and sixty times on the insides: INDS 20, BMTS 20, and IRTS 20. Basically, I was doing warlord material, coming from Far Rock with SONIC 002. I had a crew called IKO-NOKLAST PANZERS, which was A1, B1, and C1. These guys came from Mitchell Projects, uptown, in the Bronx. I met A1 in F.I.T.; I'd call him and he'd come downtown. As he was hittin' down this way [to downtown Manhattan], I was coming with DONDI and NOK from Brooklyn…the New Lots yard. Through INK 76 and SONIC 002, I met ROTO and SNAK and we would come through Brooklyn in the opposite direction on the RRs and the GGs. Then I met DEAN and GEAR and that was another way of coming across. So, the trains just kept switching around. It was good publicity.

FAB FIVE FREDDY called me up at my house; he got my number from DONDI, and said that I had to come to the city to look at this guy Jean-Michel Basquiat. I asked him, "Why? He's just somebody who writes on a wall. He's not a train hitter. He's nobody special." Freddy said, "They're making him special."

I was sitting in my underwear chillin', so I said fine and got up to meet him. I went and met him in front of Lee's handball court on Madison Street in the Lower East Side. I didn't even know what

Tony Silver, PINK, QUIK, KaySlay aka DEZ, Henry Chalfant, and FROSTY FREEZE. Photo by Robbie Busch, 2003.

Fred looked like; he's sittin' over there in the park with his black shades on, doin' like this. [*RAMM poses like Freddy with his arms crossed and everyone laughs*] I said, "What's up, man, what's up? I gotta go back home." He said, "We need you to do something, we need you to check this guy's character out." I agreed and we figured out a way for me to meet Jean-Michel. I didn't meet him the first couple of times. Toxic [CI] and AI got to him first and told him that RAMM is coming to interrogate you. I said, "You wasn't supposed to tell him that. That was supposed to be a private thing."

But, he let me in the house. I had him rockin' in the chair for about two hours, 'cause he didn't know equations, he didn't know what a burner was…he didn't know nothin' about why we was writing on those trains. Why they were called rolling pages…pages of rolling thunder. He didn't know nothin' about that. I had him rocking. I had him rocking.

At one time, he pulled out a pocket full of money, man—seven thousand dollars. I said, "Fuck money, man." He went and threw a punch at me. I caught that shit and kissed it. [*everyone laughs*] I just laughed at him, he just sat down and started crying and shit. He said, "You don't care about money." I said, " I didn't write on the damn trains for no money. I make more money doin' what I'm doin' for a real living." I had a very good union job; I'm a diver by profession.

This all started happening at an art critic, Edith de Ak's, house. She had told me I want to know your little world, and I said all right. I was sitting with my bodyguard, coming from Far Rock, and asked her if she wanted me to stay in her house. She said, "Well, I live with another girl." I said, "Yeah, fine." So, I gave Gussy some money to go back to Far Rock. Before he left she yelled at him, "Does he always talk like that?" Gussy said, "Yeah! That's why they call him

the Ramm-ell-zee!"

That lady let me live there for almost nine to ten months, and she wrote this article on me in *Art Forum* ["Train as Book, Letter as Tank, Character as Dimension," May 1983, p. 88–93]. I didn't mind the pretty girls. It was not bad at all.

HC: What he was talking about, how he met up with all of these people, is so much a part of the graf scene. As opposed to what came before, when people were confined to neighborhoods. The scene opened up so that writers from Far Rockaway to uptown and the Bronx were getting together in New Lots and actually forming crews together. This is an amazing change from the gang era, which was just preceding this in the '60s and early '70s. Then you wore your colors and battled from one neighborhood to the next. You couldn't really go to other places. It was dangerous. If you were alone and did not have some sort of affiliation with some sort of clique, you were vulnerable.

Graffiti was a whole different scene. Part of the connecting thing about the trains, passing from one borough to the next, was that your reputation would precede you. That way you are already known, so that if you do run into somebody in the yard and they find out who you are, they probably already have respect for you from what they've seen of your work.

[*At this point DJ KaySlay aka DEZ comes in to Henry's studio.*]

When did you first start writing?

DEZ: When I first started I was kind of young. I was thirteen. I was in junior high school in 1978, and that's when I started.

How did you start? Who got you into it?

DEZ: There was artists around my block that used to hit the 6 train. There was SLY 108, MC 324, PUMA 107, and TS; they was called

DOZE at United Skates of America, Queens, NY, 1981. *Style Wars* film shoot.

THE SQUAD. On the west side of Harlem, PART had a lot of people; he had a lot of walls. ZERO, CIA…there was graffiti all over the place. I always liked to doodle on paper in class. I used to smoke a joint, y'know what I'm sayin'? Everyone was workin' in class and I was day-dreamin'…doodlin'. There was a lot of gangs uptown, back then, and they used to write on the wall. I used to see them with the spray can, defacing property. I wanted to deface property too. [*everyone laughs*]

So how did you go from the page to the wall or the train?

DEZ: Basically, I discovered that I had a little talent. I had a straight hand. I started with that stick letter *s* that everybody started out with and then I just tried to draw the letters that I seen. After a while, I got the marker and start outlinin'; after a while, it became repetitious. I used to get on the subway and see the pieces and be like, "Damn! I gotta figure out how to use the spray paint." I used to tell my mother that I wanted to buy this or that, but then go get two cans of spray paint. So I went to the back of the schoolyard and just kept practicing.

RAMM: I don't know how many times I told my mother I was goin' to buy new sneakers! [*everyone laughs*]

DEZ: I didn't know about the trade or rackin' or none of that stuff yet. It was new to me, and I wasn't runnin' with no crew. J.H.S. 13 [Jackie Robinson Educational Complex J.H.S.] is now the graffiti hall of fame. That schoolyard had PART burners on it, KAY 56 had pieces down there, FLINT. It wasn't a graffiti hall of fame [then], it just had scattered pieces all over. It was all old-school tags. I would just stare out the windows at the schoolyard and at lunch I would go down there and look at the pieces.

It was like your museum.

DEZ: Exactly. There was a lot of graffiti artists in the school. FED 1

and MASE was in there. Around that time we was king on the inside of the 6 train. FED 1 had an alliance with SEEN from UNITED ART-ISTS; they was kind of cool, so every now and then he would go and paint with them. He wouldn't be doin' the burners, but he'd be goin' through the inside. One time, I literally begged to go, he took me and I was like, "Yo! We gotta start doin' this!"

I got some paint one time and I tried to do a throw up. Nobody told me that it's supposed to reach the window or when it comes through the platform— [*everyone laughs*]

PINK: I did the same thing!

DEZ: When it came through everybody laughed at me and that kind of burnt me. I got kicked out of J.H.S. 13. At [my next school], there was an artist, PAUL 1, he was from Harlem River Projects. That's where the 3 yard was at. He seen me in school one day throwin' a piece—by then I was nice with the design. He said, "Yo, I got a yard in my project and we cannot get busted. I look through my window and there is an actual yard!" He said, "I don't got no style. I just tag. But if you come up there…" So, one weekend I met up with him. He was sayin' "what's up" to the conductor; later, he would buy a little thing of vodka for us. It was like we was home! We didn't have to run or anything. It was incredible. Even Martha Cooper came into the yard with us one time. It was crazy.

TS: Is that the photograph with the baseball bat?

DEZ: Yeah.

TS: Is that where you met SKEME?

DEZ: Yeah. SKEME was from the neighborhood.

HC: He lived on top of the 3 yard.

DEZ: Paul's building looked at it, but SKEME's buildin' was on top of it! SKEME was watching us paint one day; he was looking

Rock Steady Crew, 204th St. in Inwood, NYC, 1981. First *Style Wars* film shoot.

through the gate. PAUL told him, "Yo, get away from the gate!" If somebody's lookin' through the gate, then that means somebody's in there paintin'. When he left I was like, "Who's that?" and Paul was like, "It's some toy, but he paints some characters." I said, "Ah, man, we gots to pull him in, yo!" 'Cause I was like a letter man; I could do a character, but I wasn't the best.

How did you start, PINK?

PINK: I started tagging up an ex-boyfriend's name when I was fifteen. He got grabbed for graffiti and got shipped to live in Puerto Rico. In missing him, I was just tagging up his name all over. Hanging out with his friends, [I] learned the ropes of how to use spray paint and do a little style with the letters. But, not until I went to the High School of Art and Design in 1979, did I meet graffiti writers of all different colors and incomes from all over New York City, the Bronx, and Brooklyn. They all went there. I met three hundred graffiti writers in one shot. By the end of my first year there, I was tight with the best guys, like DOZE, SEEN TC5, and ERNIE. We were pretty much running things in that school. We got to meet some graduates from that school, like DAZE and TRACY 168. A lot of people got their start there, it's where you were either made or broken. Like DEZ, I had to beg to be taken to the train yard. These guys were not about to take some little female and endanger the whole mission. I was taught the ropes just like every other toy was taught, how to carry your own bag of paint and run and climb, and steal your own paint. You got taught things by masters like how to conduct yourself in the graffiti world.

In the underground, there were not a lot of females. In the '70s, there had been, like, BARBARA 62 and EVA 62, who actually bombed more than some guys. Guys are not quick to admit. Females in the

'70s had to link up together or with crews and go out and bomb like that. But by the time I started there were no females writing. I was the only female writing out of, like, ten thousand dudes in NEW YORK CITY. So, I instantly became famous just because I was a female. So, of course I had to back that up with some actual work.

RAMM: And you *damn* well did!

PINK: I had to go to the train yards. There's no faking that. No matter how much guys want to slander, "Oh, she was just doing some guy to get her name on a train."

DEZ: Nah, you was there.

PINK: I had to take them all to task and go painting with different groups from all over New York: Black kids from the Bronx, White kids from Far Rockaway, and Spanish kids in Brooklyn. I had to go painting with all different crews to prove to them that I was painting my own stuff and not just having some boyfriend, some guy, do it for me. I think I was a feminist at the age of sixteen. The more you said I couldn't do that, the more I'm gonna prove you wrong. After a year or two, I became aware that even younger girls were looking up to me as being a strong woman. So, I couldn't fail. I had to keep going and hold my head up for all of my sisters.

The film does a great job of showing the external and internal forces that were impacting the community. It must not have been long after you finished shooting that this "golden era" of graffiti would crash in on itself. You had a unique perspective. Can you fill in a little bit of what happened after the film was done?

HC: Around 1980, the community really started to change for all kinds of reasons. One of the things that happened was the art world became interested in it; that opened things up for people to start making money from it. Graffiti artists could make canvases and

put their work in galleries. The b-boys were finding the same thing. Rather than being a street culture they became performers who got paid. That changed things profoundly. People started to question their motivations for doing it. "Do we want to be gallery artists? No! This is boring and stupid." Then they would go back to the trains. This is happening at the same time that the Transit Authority was increasingly able to buff cars, take trains out of service, and even repaint the whole fleet. And in the midst of that was CAP and the cross-out wars.

So, by 1985, what you began to notice was that there were fewer and fewer young kids that were into it. There was a new kind of street culture that was emerging that was far more destructive. There were gangsters and crack. The drug dealers were kids.

A turning point that I saw was in the early '80s. I remember going down to the Roxy for Rock Steady and I ran into this guy from their neighborhood, Outlaw, on 18th Street and 10th Ave. I was saying, "Isn't this great! They're all making money. It's all good." He snorted and said, "That's chump change! I'm the one that's making money." He was selling drugs on the corner.

Of course, the writers had been doing drugs in the '70s and '80s. They were doing grass and zootie; it was part of the scene. But, the kids that were getting respect in the mid-'80s were the teenage drug dealers that were running things. They were getting a lot of money and supplying a lot of money to the younger kids.

There was still a respect for the master painters, but it wasn't as intense anymore.

So it just dried up?

HC: Yeah. Photography was part of the reason why it dried up too. If you were a young kid and you wanted to get style, you didn't have to go to a master painter anymore, you could just look at my

books. In fact, that was a bone of contention with some of the writers. Some of the masters felt angry that I was letting in all of these people to look at their work. All the toys were sitting in my studio, day in and day out, copying master style and then things would emerge that were obvious bites. It was always hard to bite in the old way; it's hard to copy something that's moving. But, if you sit and study it, you can reproduce it. So there was a certain amount of antagonism that I got.

But, at the same time they must have been honored that you were preserving their art.

HC: Sure. There was always more than one thing going on. I would never hear that complaint directly from an artist; I would always hear it thirdhand.

Was the movie accepted in the community after it came out?

HC: Everyone of that particular generation accepted it as being the truth…as being a good portrait of what it was. I think the reason for that is that it is a well-made film. Tony was able to capture the drama of what was happening and translate it to the film. And I think that the writers—and I emphasize the writers of the generation that it was about—thought it was true.

Why the emphasis on them?

HC: The older generation feel that they were totally left out. That their work was not given its due. Which is true, it wasn't about that, and it could have been more about that. The main reason it wasn't was because I didn't have pictures of their work and didn't know them as well. In the film, we do have photos from Jack Stewart and John Narr for the historical overview of where graffiti was coming from. But, we were focused on what was happening in front of us. So there is a little bit of bitterness from the older generation, because

DUSTER UA on the 2s and 5s passing over Hoe Avenue, the Bronx, NY, 1981, during the filming of *Style Wars*.

the film and the books became so successful and didn't give proper due to the older work.

How did you feel, FROSTY? When did you first see the movie?

FROSTY FREEZE: I remember you showed it at 57th Street, in the [Sidney Janis] Gallery. That's when I first seen it. And then Henry told me you were having the premiere at the Embassy Theatre on 46th Street in Times Square. I remember, 'cause it was at the same time that they were holding auditions for *Beat Street*, and it was a little after they released *Wild Style*.

I felt good about it. Seeing myself and others getting the exposure at the time when nobody knew what was going on in terms of the talent side of the b-boys, the graffiti side of the art form, and the DJing and MCing, partially. At that time, there was a lot of unity in the community, and a lot of things were happening fast. For me and the other Rock Steady members, we did it for the love and fun of it and it kept us out of a lot of trouble, streetwise, with gangs and stuff like that. It really united us, and we were able to take our act out on the road. So, for us, it really paid off.

PINK: *Style Wars* came out right after *Wild Style*, and the immediate reaction from the graffiti community was that they liked *Style Wars* a whole lot better. They didn't like *Wild Style*, 'cause it was edited and very…artsy. *Style Wars* was a very straightforward story. It explained everything to you very clearly with visual pictures and some really groovy music. It was all there, so that we could relate to it much better. Everyone liked it so much more, that I was like, "Damn! I'm not even in that!" [*everyone laughs*] I know I'm standing right off screen. I was there. And now I'm in it, which is really cool.

After you showed the movie in the theaters there was the one-hour version scheduled to air on PBS in Jan. '84. But, Channel 13 [WNET in NY] only showed it once. What happened and how did it gain its cult following?

HC: People had bootleg copies. They taped it whenever it was shown, and it was shown more often outside of New York. The executive at Channel 13 [Hugh Price] was the one who pulled the additional shows in New York City.

I heard that he didn't like the movie because of the music. He thought it put the graffiti artists on too much of a pedestal?

TS: Yeah.

HC: It was only shown once in the city. The Long Island Station, 21, played it more times. And it got shown numerous times in other cities across the country, so people got to see it that way. Sometime in the early '90s, there was a Discovery Channel showing of it. Everybody had been asking us to put it out on VHS, but it wasn't until the mid-'90s that we overcame the hurdle of getting enough money to pay for the music rights.

You only show a little bit of breaking, MCing, and DJing in the movie. How did you decide to focus on the graffiti more than the other elements of hip-hop that were going on around you?

TS: Well, it was difficult, and I regret now that there aren't at least glimpses of some of the things [we saw]. For example, Henry took me to DEZ's house. He lived with his mother, at the time, in the East River Projects [102nd Street and 1st Avenue], and he had his own DJ set up in this tiny little bedroom in this immaculate apartment. It was wonderful, but it was like overload. What we were working on was all I could handle. It's really too bad, but it is what it is.

Wild Style had already been shooting for a little while when you guys started. Was there any communication or tension between the productions?

CRAZY LEGS at United Skates of America, Queens, NY. *Style Wars* film shoot, 1981.

FROSTY FREEZE, KEN SWIFT, friend, and KIPPY DEE. Rock Steady Crew at United Skates of America in Queens, NY, 1981. *Style Wars* film shoot.

HC: There was certainly communication. Charlie and I continued to be friends. I mean Rock Steady was in his film, and it was I who had found Rock Steady. I think Charlie had come to the rehearsal event—I'm not sure if he did, but he certainly knew about break dancers from what Martha [Cooper] and I had put together. That was fine, I encouraged them to be involved. I didn't think our productions were competitive, because his was a docudrama and ours was a documentary. At the time, it seemed like they would be good companions and they have been.

TS: I loved *Wild Style*. I remember the first screening I saw, I started to cry. I saw it twenty years later and the same thing happened. It's a beautiful thing. But, at the time I was very worried and jealous, because Charlie was filming while we were looking for money.

HC: Around 1983, when Charlie was finished, and we were still editing, there was a little bit of tension. [*laughter*] We thought, "He'll come out with it and that will be it! They'll have seen it, and nobody else will want to see anything else about it."

Did it feel like a race at any time?

HC: It really didn't feel like a race until '83 when Charlie was in the New Directors/New Films Festival [at the MOMA], and we were still only halfway through our nine months of editing. Editing with a lot of doubts as to whether we could pull a real film out of the material. We had a lot of constraints to get all of the material down to an hour for the PBS broadcast.

PINK: On the six o'clock news, shooting at Art and Design, they made it nice and concise, "Graffiti writers—disgraceful bunch!" [*she sighs*]

RAMM: I think the word has a lot to do with the problem of the incident of actually writing on trains or walls. The word "Graffiti"—

scribble scrabble—it sounds decadent. The word "Illuminationist," the person who actually does the illuminations of the letter's chassis, this is more important. Wind Tunnels—instead of just saying we writing in subways. Subways of what? Subways of a planet? Subways of another culture? Say "wind tunnel," say "illuminations"—we have monks. Monks been doin' letters on greeting cards and schools and churches for centuries. I'm a monk! One of the baddest assassins that ever rode a letter that can fly! It's a way of describing it to *these* people, like some of these guys and cops in the movie. Say it to 'em the right way, use the better word, illuminationist, instead of graffiti [artist].

PINK: Next time we're facing a judge we can tell them, "We're illuminationists, not vandals. Therefore, I shouldn't go to jail." That'll work?!

RAMM: Yeah! They don't arrest the church! If you use the dictionary to the best of your ability, you have more of an arsenal. We don't have to use curses all the time. We can use large words. It may hurt them more than they think they're hurtin' us. And that's how you get 'em, by being profound.

PINK: Fuck yeah. [*everyone rolls with laughter*] ◐

Originally appeared in Wax Poetics Issue 5, Summer 2003.

Subject Matter of the '80s

by Dave Tompkins

Raw Dope Posse. Nobody remembers Raw Dope Posse, because nobody knew Raw Dope Posse. But if you're going to call yourselves the Raw Dope Posse, then you better sound like it. You better wear it on your sleeve with hydraulically raised letters, and once out of the sleeve, it would be in your best interest to wear a hole in the speaker. Volume 10, a rapper with a great name and blaring eyebrows, once said, "There are only so many dope-ass names going around." ¶ Raw Dope Posse sounds more like crew than group, some icebox-magnet letters stuck in a paragraph of shouts, where entire blocks are condensed into a corner, including the guy who shaved the name of Raw Dope's only 12 inch, "Listen to My Turbo," into the back of their heads. ¶ "Listen to My Turbo" could be a rear-window redneck slogan, right above "Fear This" and next to the sticker of Calvin taking a mischievous whiz on Earnhardt's NASCAR number. "Listen to My Turbo" is a Burger King parking lot on a vague summer weeknight, where the bass turns defrost lines into a sawtooth frazzle, boldfaced by the bug-zap glow of ground effects and nervous windows. »

Photos by B. Lloyd.

Cut for Show Jazz Records in 1988, "Listen to My Turbo" is the only release from New Jersey's Raw Dope Posse. The "J" on the Show Jazz logo is a microphone, the envy of the alphabet. Nikki Rap-N-Scratch is the other group on this tiny label, a sister-brother or lover-lover duo with a pair of binoculars for a logo.

Nikki says he likes bowling but went "Rambo" at his prom. Rap-N-Scratch, she's pictured on the cover scratching on the wrong side of the turntables. This record sounds like it was bootlegged at the prom, wired in a cummerbund, but at least they got a picture sleeve out of the deal. But did Show Jazz spring for the binoculars that appear in front of Rap-N-Scratch's mixer?

Raw Dope's small-fry budget must've gone into sweat suits and studio gear. Though fifteen years old, "Listen to My Turbo" could stop current producers in their tracks and make them drop in pauses for chin-strum. Hip-hop wasn't supposed to sound like this back in 1988, having ditched electro for James Brown. Not "Planet Rock"-by-Numbers electro, but the hard-sample mutant productions of Kurtis Mantronik, back when getting electrocuted was a part of learning the equipment, when Kurtis blew up two drum machines while making Just-Ice's "Cold Getting Dumb," baffling the Sam Ash sales floor. I once saw "Cold Getting Dumb" make a Jetta literally go battery brain-dead in an intersection in front of a Baptist church.

Likewise, Raw Dope Posse deserves a jumper cable endorsement from Jed Clampdown.

The beauty of "Listen to My Turbo" is that it's off the hook, literally. The beat is a busy signal with a crushed bell and a drumstick rolling its tongue. Then the horns show up and start frying wallpaper, to be sure that nobody confuses phone for a brass section. (If James Brown's on the line, don't tell him Raw Dope borrowed his snare and whooped its ass.)

Raw Dope's lyrics brag about their hardware, claiming "drum computer." I love it when rappers talk about drum computers, like Fresh Gordon before he hooked up the old-school community with free long distance. The guy in charge here is Kid Gusto and "Listen

to My Turbo" is still worth speed-boat money even if dude is caught with T La Rock's style around his ankles. Title-holder of the big-word belt, Terry "T La Rock" Keaton, declared himself "reason for a very nice day" on his 1983 Def Jam hit "It's Yours," a gift essentially, with bass levels tested in producer Jazzy Jay's car before the song was officially allowed out of the studio. Recovering from a severe head injury sustained on his front stoop in 1994, Keaton spent the remainder of the '90s reclaiming his memory and the legend of his own mind, discovering verses that the generation he influenced already knew by rote, whether conscious or not. "I don't really know what somebody said/but some musical rhythms can mess with your head." That famous couplet took on new meaning, won, and returned it to T La Rock with its head on a platter. As if to say, No, really, this belongs to you, sir. As if ownership were a matter of recall.

It's only right that Keaton hear "Listen to My Turbo"—instrumental first, before hearing an imitation of himself. Plus Raw Dope Posse deserves more of a name, more of a life than their limited blip pressing permitted.

Up at his Washington Heights apartment in Harlem, Terry Keaton agrees. He nods repeatedly with headphones full of Raw Dope Posse. He points across the room, past the photo of the Sleeping Bag Rap Pack, Just-Ice, Tricky Tee, T La Rock, Mantronik; past his television, which shows a 1997 CNN interview with an elderly woman he befriended in Brooklyn's Haym Solomon Nursing Home, where Terry Keaton awoke without his name. A roomful of absentminded grandparents celebrates his recovery and discharge while a bar mitzvah stomp plays in the background. Wide-eyed in the camera, the woman is concerned. "Why are we celebrating? If he's leaving, I'm not celebrating!"

Keaton will be missed. While mumbling the hallways with his lost verses, he was often recruited for bathroom trips, bed adjustments, and memory collection. Mistaken as an orderly but soon recognized as a friend, Keaton became known as the "Lyrical Saint of Haym Solomon." T La Rock says, "I saw these nurses working

there and wondered. You make friends with these people, and the next thing you know, they're dead."

Next to the TV, where the woman has now faded to snow, his point of reference lands on the phone. He jabs along with Raw Dope's busy-signal beat. "I hear a lot of edits goin' on." (Giggles.) "Sounds like some T La Rock stuff."

On cue, Raw Dope's DJ flies in the vocoded voice of Fab Five Freddy saying, "This stuff!" Keaton points from phone to his tape deck, like, "Did you get that?" Tape deck's recording meter pumps *hell yeah* into the red. (No matter what, one must always have the hip-hop presence of mind to cop a dub.)

While in the hospital, Keaton was fed T La Rock tapes by Greg Nice and Tony Tee, an old friend from Stillwell Ave. Ring a bell with "Breaking Bells" or "Bass Machine," its edits courtesy of Chep Nunez, who died in a tragic fire in 1990. (The loss of a friend, both painful and easy to remember.) At Soloman Haym, ghosts with gauzy memories often dropped by Keaton's room in their mottled robes and fuzzy slippers, listening to this six-two rapper get reacquainted with himself through a beat-up Magnavox. "They'd remind me of stuff I'd forget about," Keaton says. "I couldn't even remember my own song. I probably couldn't even lip-synch on time, like Milli Vanilli. These old people, they were more into 'Lyrical King' than 'It's Yours.' 'Lyrical King' was more laid-back. 'It's Yours' had all that scratching. Plus, you couldn't get that much bass in a nursing home."

Over near the tape deck in Keaton's Harlem apartment, by the blinking answering machine, there is a calendar. In fact, there's a calendar in every room, and, nice or not, each day is marked for life. The answering machine logs the important ones, like when Jay-Z called and explained a line from his smash 2001 hit, "Izzo." He was "overcharging for what they did to the Cold Crush," paying dap and debt to old-school heroes over a summertime Jackson 5 melody. On Keaton's machine, Sean Carter clarifies. He's also overcharging for what they, a myopic music industry, did to T La Rock. Overcharging for what they did to T La Rock's brother Special K, once

down with the Treacherous Three and then down and out. Though neither will smell Jehovah's windfall, the phone call means something, a good reason to wake up and listen to your own records.

Now for the A-side of "Listen to My Turbo."

Speak, memory.

Kid Gusto declares, "Subject matter of the '80s!"

We give each other a funny look.

Subject it to what?

Keaton says, "There's some Kool Keith in there."

Raw Dope says, "Boisterous turbulence!"

I say, "Maybe that's Kid Gusto."

Raw Dope says, "Accumulate data collected from the brain."

Keaton smiles, "Ohh! There's a lot of T La Rock in there!"

The piece of paper I hand Keaton says: "That people are prone to bite: that biters may sometimes be bitten."

"What's this?"

I don't know—

"Ah-ha!"

—if it's true.

"I wouldn't call it biting," he says.

I'll leave it up to him.

Keaton chuckles.

"Maybe influenced. But not biting."

The quote belongs to Dickens, but right now it's ours.

"You shouldn't have done it," Keaton warns, scattering the silence outside his headphones. "I can't let you leave with this record!" He cups his headphones to keep it in mind. He can now remember things he couldn't prior to the injury. And somewhere in a Brooklyn nursing home, there are Alzheimer's patients who can't recognize their kin, but can sure as shit tell you who T La Rock is.

Some musical rhythms can mess with your head. ⊙

Originally appeared in Wax Poetics Issue 5, Summer 2003.

Check Your Bucket

Hip-Hop's Building Blocks

by Andrew Mason

It was 1987, and I was making my regular pilgrimage to Music Factory in Times Square, searching for goodies of the audible kind. Passing the Buddha-like figure of Stanley Platzer, the store manager who seemed permanently ensconced behind a small counter near the front of the store, I eagerly flipped through the latest releases on labels like Cold Chillin', Prism, Fresh, and First Priority. ¶ On the wall there were a few mysterious records that caught my eye. Looking over the titles, I saw things like "Apache," "Big Beat," "Honky Tonk Woman," but no artists were listed. Were these some Pickwick-style knock-offs by a no-name cover band? Why were songs by the Rolling Stones and Billy Squier, two bands that personified mainstream rock and roll, loitering in the prime real estate of wall space reserved for the hottest slices of the underground music then known as "new school rap"? I didn't know, and didn't give it much thought, quickly snatching up the "Pickin' Boogers" and "Juice Crew Dis" singles. ¶ Flashback to a few years before. Late at night, high up on the radio dial, I would occasionally hear weird collages of music that seeped into my subconscious and laid the foundation that would eventually explain this phenomena to me. Cheech and Chong talkin' some bullshit, suddenly a heavy beat pounded through (that made even a playin'-the-wall herb like me want to shake my pants), repeating and stuttering back on itself, then—wait, what's that weird electronic outer space-sounding noise…into something that sounds like "White Lines," but I know that's not Melle Mel. I rummaged through a shoe box to find a tape I could record over. »

Rap music had been sort of a novelty for me; I was not a b-boy from the Bronx, simply a kid into music. The popular rap hits of the early '80s were records I bought, but they didn't hold any particular prominence over the rest of the pop music of the day. But by the mid-'80s, things had changed. I had always been an avid taper of radio shows, and my ear steadily gravitated towards the sounds I was hearing. When I discovered stores like Music Factory, I made them my mecca, quickly becoming a fanatic of what were clearly the freshest sounds out there.

As sampling became more prevalent, I started to hear elements in the new jams that I recognized. I couldn't quite place most of them, but they were familiar as a Beatles melody. A friend hipped me to the fact that a funky cowbell riff I loved so much was in fact from a song called "Mardi Gras." I started examining those cheap-looking records that had SUPER DISCO BREAKS written in big block type across the front, and soon enough came across one with a song that fit the description. I placed the record with the off-center orange and black label on the turntable, dropped the needle on the first track, and, with that sensation that only vinyl can give, waited for the tune to kick in. Huh? The needle must've jumped, because there was my cowbell jam, but it wasn't playing right. Examining the record, I couldn't see anything wrong. I later found that every single pressing of that record had that skip in it (and still does; check out *Super Disco Brakes Vol. 1*). Thank you, Paul Winley.

In spite of this technical difficulty, a flame had been sparked which only gained in intensity. I quickly graduated to the superior pressings of Street Beat Records' *Ultimate Breaks & Beats* series, then in its prime—already to fourteen volumes or so by the time I got to them. *UBB #9* was my toe in the water, and I was immediately hooked. This article is a study, an attempt to get at why tunes on these records have such resonance, but above all a tribute to an essential ingredient of hip-hop.

There is a logical starting point when attempting to understand this culture that has grown from the roots of hip-hop and flowered into what we call beatdigging. When a fledgling beat maker is getting started there is essential 101 knowledge. You crawl before you walk, and when it comes to this game, crawling means learning the foundation: the beats and breaks that gave birth to hip-hop. These tunes are our music theory and history, the rules you need to know before you can break them.

If all this seems abstract and removed from where we're at these days, let me take you back. A party, just getting bubbling. The room is not too big, not too small. A few groups of ladies, some fellas maintaining neutral ground. The DJ has a stack of 45s in front of him and has begun cueing up the next. The groove sends a wave of bass up from your feet, meeting the highs and mids in your chest and causing an involuntary ripple of your torso. The fellas nod. The ladies swing heads appreciatively. All right. Suddenly a grin breaks out on one of your boys. He has heard the intro for the next song being brought in. *Bam!* The DJ brings the fader over and the rest of the room shares the joy as energy starts building up in the rapidly filling room. It doesn't stop there; feet begin shuffling as drums you have heard since childhood get worked out, snapping and splintering as the DJ gets busy with two copies of the same joint. The next jam comes in and by now somebody is going for theirs, body working in time to a groove as sweet and familiar as the fragrance of spring. The next record hits the spot like a perfect pick-and-roll, and you know you're in the right place. The room is full and the party is live, and it's just begun.

Beautiful, right? Don't think this is some late '70s flashback,

though. This scene took place less than a month ago, late 2001. The DJ was Spinna, the location a basement club in Manhattan, and nearly all the joints that got everyone so open can be found in one place: the *UBB* series.

Ultimate Breaks & Beats is essentially a catalog of rhythm. The 150-plus songs it compiles over its twenty-five volumes demonstrate an impressive array of 4/4 drum patterns and variations that form a textbook for any rhythmatist looking to generate motion, whether your kit is an Akai, Technics, or Ludwig.

To take it further, a case can be made that the breaks featured on Street Beat's *Ultimate Breaks & Beats* series form the basis for modern popular rhythm. This thesis does not seem so far-fetched when you trace the roots of contemporary electronic and dance styles and their indebtedness to rap music and its production techniques. It's a chronology that leads from community center parties in Harlem and the Bronx to the rise of sampling in the mid-'80s and onward to the creations of the dance music innovators who were inspired by the rhythm patterns of rap music.

Avant-garde experimentalists like Karlheinz Stockhausen, John Cage, and Steve Reich worked with primal "samples" (tape loops) in the '50s and '60s, and music professionals in the '70s used expensive machines like the Fairlight and the Mellotron to imitate various live instruments. It wasn't until the mid-'80s, however, that digital sampling equipment began to come within the reach of non-professional musicians.

As sampling became an option for more folks involved in making music, it was a natural step to take the funkiest pieces of party classics and loop them, thereby imitating the feel of a DJ running a break with two copies of the same record. Grandmaster Flash explains the concept: "My main objective was to take small parts of records…maybe forty seconds, keeping it going for about five minutes."[1] In fact, this strategy was employed well before samplers came into use. Keith LeBlanc, drummer on many of the early Sugar Hill records, related this story: "Sylvia [Robinson, Sugar Hill Records president] would be at Harlem World or Disco Fever, and she'd watch who was mixing what four bars off of what record. She'd get that record, and then she'd play us those four bars and have us go in and cut it better."[2]

In 1985, E-MU introduced the SP-12 sampling drum machine, and soon after that sampling started to pop up in rap music. Rick Rubin redid LL Cool J's "Rock the Bells" using a large chunk of Trouble Funk as its rhythmic bed (the original version of "Bells" was all drum machine), while Marley Marl hooked Biz Markie up with "The Biz Dance" (graced by drum hits chopped from Rufus Thomas's "Do the Funky Penguin") and "Make the Music with Your Mouth Biz" (Isaac Hayes, in fact, making much of the music with his piano via a nice sample). Ced Gee handled production for Ultramagnetic MC's and Boogie Down Productions, creating the amazing "Ego Trippin'" with little more than an SP-12 and a loungey-sounding 7-inch with a dope drum break. The usage of James Brown on BDP's "South Bronx" kicked off a long (unrequited) love affair between samplists and the Godfather of Soul (Double Dee and Steinski had also used liberal chunks of Soul Brother #1 as early as 1984 on their landmark remix of "Play that Beat Mr. DJ" by G.L.O.B.E. and Whiz Kid).

So where did folks go for their source material, the sure shot beats that would resonate with such power in their listeners? Some had access to record collections of their parents and the creativity to use them, but for many, the most convenient way to obtain these essential beats was through break compilations.

Street Beat Records, the company that distributed *UBB*, was incorporated in 1986 by a car service driver and part-time DJ named Lenny Roberts, aka Breakbeat Lenny. It was not the first or only label reissuing what was called B-Beat (Break Beat) music. There were plenty of one-off "Disco Mixer" 12-inches that edited up-tempo disco breakdowns together for the club jocks, and 12-inch bootleg reedits of anthems like "Scratchin'" (extended past eight minutes) and "Apache" that had been around since the late '70s. Paul Winley's infamous *Super Disco Brakes* series was in lo-fi effect straight out of 125th Street, and the equally infamous but more mysterious *Octopus* (as the no-named series is commonly referred to) records were coming out of Florida by way of the Bronx. Much more obscure, these direct predecessors of the *UBB* series date to 1980 and are the Pithecanthropus erectus to *UBB*'s Homo sapiens. The *Octopus* track listing is duplicated almost exactly on the first ten *Ultimate Breaks* records, raising questions about the relationship between the two.

In an article published in 1988, Lenny Roberts claimed that the *Octopus* records were put out by "some guy in the Bronx," and stressed that he (in contrast) "wrote away for all the licensing" on his comps. So where did the *Octopus* originate? I talked to a long-time employee of NYC's Downstairs Records who told me about a series of doo-wop bootlegs making the rounds in the mid- to late '70s, allegedly mafia sponsored. The compiler, apparently also an aspiring cartoonist, adorned these bootlegs with various anthropomorphic animal characters. Thus the *Octopus*—with its image cheerfully cueing up a couple of records under the words "Break Beats," a phone to one ear and headphones to the other—was likely just an attempt to diversify the market. This theory is supported by the location of the manufacturer of the *Octopus* boots: Hollywood, Florida, a well-known wiseguy ward.

Octopus #7 and *#8* became the *UBB* "mystery" LPs (SBR-507 and SBR-508), probably more available in *Octopus* form than on the rapidly discontinued Street Beat pressings of these two volumes (rumor has it that John Davis threatened lawsuits over the inclusion of his "I Can't Stop" on SBR-507 and that the master for SBR-508 was lost). Beyond these two and a song that appeared on some pressings of *Octopus #4* called "Get Up" (Pookie Blow rhyming over the "Dance to the Drummer's Beat" break), the *Octopus* survives to this day in the guise of *UBB*.

What sets Street Beat's *Ultimate Breaks* apart from all its competitors is its sheer longevity, its superior sound quality, and, most of all, being in the right place at the right time.

The series is fascinating on several levels. For one, the fusion of styles it contains demands the listener disregard notions of genre. This is a mind-set that is perhaps not as revolutionary as it once was, but at the time it was like lightning bottled, a roots tonic straight out of the witch doctor's apothecary. After all, playlists of these records were copped from party favorites spun by Bambaataa, Herc, even David Mancuso (by way of GM Flash). *UBB* was the series that really broke the original "wall of silence" surrounding breakbeat music and set a precedent in break compilations.

I spoke to David Mancuso about how he feels seeing records he introduced at his legendary Loft parties end up on break records. Although his attitude towards unauthorized copies of tunes isn't positive ("I don't like bootlegs!"), Mancuso has always been about spreading the love when it comes to hot tracks. He was one of the founders of the first record pool (the New York Record Pool, founded in 1974), a system devised to keep influential DJs stocked with the latest, greatest tunes. In exchange for new releases, members of the pool were required to rate records according to their personal reaction and to the floor reaction when it was played. One of the members of the record pool was Joseph Saddler, aka Grandmaster Flash.

Afrika Bambaataa was also in attendance at Loft parties, where records like "Woman" by Barrabas (originally picked up by Mancuso at a flea market in Amsterdam) and Lonnie Liston Smith's "Expansions" were in heavy rotation. These tunes quickly made their way uptown and from there eventually onto the *UBB* comps.

Both the *Octopus* and the Street Beat records share the sometimes useful, sometimes infuriating trait of looping breaks within certain songs. The idea was to make short breaks easier to catch, but in some cases this resulted in uncomfortably stiff edits such as on Lyn Collins's "Think" or Dyke and the Blazers' "Let a Woman Be a Woman, Let a Man Be a Man." Louis Flores, credited with editing the tracks, used another interesting technique that occurs a couple times in the series: the pitch change. "UFO" by ESG was originally issued by 99 Records on a 45 RPM 12-inch. The grinding, heavy groove heard on *UBB #9* is the result of hearing this record at the lower, wrong, turntable tempo setting (play your break record at 45 to hear it as it was originally recorded). Dexter Wansel's stately "Theme From the Planets" gets flipped by reversing this method, sending it into warp drive on 45. Even weirder is the edit on the Winstons' "Amen Brother." It sounds like Flores pitched down this crazy up-tempo drum break by simply tapping the 33/45 buttons once at the beginning of the break, then again at the end to bring the song back to its intended pitch.

Flores also tacked vocal phrases onto various cuts, these fall into the category of DJ tools. Most notable is "(Runaway) Wouldn't Change a Thing," an excerpt from a Thomas "Coke" Escovedo LP. On the original album, the last vocal shout of "Runaway" precedes the percussion intro to "Wouldn't Change a Thing" by several seconds—typical track spacing on an album. On *UBB #13* the gap is removed, making it easier for DJs to imitate the routine Flash used when he would scratch the vocal shout over the next tune's breakbeat intro.

The series combined the obvious with the unheard-of. It doesn't take long to find such unlikely comrades as Rufus Thomas and Gary Numan (*#22*) or the Rolling Stones rubbing shoulders with an obscure Italian disco band (*#2*). Long before folks like Gilles Peterson or Keb Darge were compiling impossibly rare 7-inches for mass consumption, Street Beat ensured that thousands of DJs and aficionados had copies of obscure cuts like "Impeach the President" by the enigmatic Honey Drippers or Please's Philipino funk version of "Sing a Simple Song."

Neither *Octopus* nor *UBB* listed artists for any of their songs, however. As Lenny Roberts said, the *UBB* series does include publishing information, but that's it. Whether the decision to not include artists' names was a result of publishing rights (or lack of them) or a code of honor is debatable. The legendary level of secrecy surrounding break records was tight, and, to this day, a big part of the competition that goes on among DJs is finding a record that your brethren are not up on. In the late '70s, when the Zulu Nation and the Herculords sound systems were battling, it was all about volume and coming up with that mystery joint that caught you out there and made you rush the decks to catch a glimpse of the label. First-wave innovators such as Kool Herc, Bam, Jazzy Jay, and Flash made a science out of unearthing these obscure rhythmic riffs that would not only move the crowd but confound their rivals as well. Many felt that it was out of bounds for anyone to be revealing ingredients. As Jazzy Jay said, "It took a little bit of that mystery out of it, 'cause it was hard to find these records. You didn't find them every day of the week. When Lenny made them available, it was like, anybody can have them now."[3]

But for a new generation of fans who never saw Bam rock the parks in the Bronx, these comps were gold. As Kenny "Dope" Gonzalez, told me, "I'm down with them, 'cause they taught a lot of us about breaks. They were key in a lot of people's collections, even though people knock them." Renowned breakbeat aficionado DJ Spinna related, "I picked up my first *Ultimate Breaks* in '85. There used to be a store on 42nd Street where cats went to get all the bootleg breakbeat 12-inches like 'Impeach the President' and 'Funky President,' which are even harder to get than the *Octopus* joints." For many contemporary masters, *UBB* was school—or, as Q-Bert put it in his barnstorming tour through the Street Beat series, preschool (DJ Q-Bert, *Demolition Pumpkin Squeeze – A Pre School Break Mix*).

Of course, fame will bring its share of biters. From the disco/electro-oriented Street Beat bootlegs with pre-*UBB* catalog numbers SBR-498, SBR-499, and SBR-500 (the actual Street Beat series started at SBR-501) to bootleg versions of the discontinued #7, there have been countless coattail-riding copycat compilations. The popular *Diggin'* series, now in double digits, started as a blatant *UBB* spin-off, shamelessly titling the inaugural LP *Ultimate Breaks & Beats #26*. Before you could say, "Yo, you could catch a smack for that," this blasphemy was corrected; on subsequent pressings, the brash upstart reverted to its proper moniker, *Diggin' (Vol. 1)*.

These days the shelves of record stores are littered with similar *spot-the-sample*-type break compilations and reissues seemingly intent on turning over every last funky rock. Looking at the role these comps play now, it may be hard to understand or remember the weight *UBB* held during its prime. The pinnacle of *UBB*'s influence was probably in 1987–88, when it was not uncommon for hip-hop tracks and even LPs to be based almost wholly on tracks contained in the latest *UBB*. Many classic singles released in that time, like "My Philosophy" (BDP), "It's My Thing" (EPMD), "I Know You Got Soul" (Eric B. and Rakim) and "It Takes Two" (Rob Base and DJ E-Z Rock), fit this description.

As the '80s came to a close, breakbeat culture had moved far from its roots. Innovative beat makers began disdaining the now well-known breaks on *UBB* and the series lost steam. Cuts began to be included *because* they had been sampled, rather than for their established fame with the b-boys (a group rapidly being overwhelmed in number by "rap" fans who often had little connection to the culture that gave birth to the music). All the People's "Cramp Your Style," the basis for BDP's "Still #1," found its way onto *#21* a year or so after BDP used it. AJ Woodson, better known as AJ Rok of JVC Force, told me, "I sampled Freda Payne's "Easiest Way to Fall" [the B-side of "Band of Gold"] off both her 45 and her album. It was added to the breakbeat album some two or three years after we used it, because we used it [on 'Strong Island']." The track appeared on *#23*, issued towards the end of 1989.

Street Beat would only release two more LPs in the series, *#24* and the final twentieth "Silver Anniversary" edition appearing in 1991. Over ten years have passed, but, to this day, the records are still available, still essential, still the king. ○

Originally appeared in Wax Poetics Issue 1, Winter 2001.

NOTES

1. David Toop, *Rap Attack* (London: Pluto Press, 1984), p.63.
2. *Village Voice* (Jan. 19, 1988).
3. *Ibid.*

Ultimate Breaks & Beats Discography

SONG	ARTIST	YEAR	LABEL	NOTES
SBR-501 (1986)				
Mary, Mary *	The Monkees	1967	Colgems/RCA	
Black Grass *	Wilbur "Bad" Bascomb	1972	Paramount	
Amen, Brother *	The Winstons	1969	Metromedia	Drum break is pitched down (switches from 45 to 33 RPM); the rest of the song is at normal pitch.
Daisy Lady *	7th Wonder	1979	Parachute	
Indiscreet *	D. C. LaRue	1976	Pyramid	Only 4:53 of the 12-inch version is used.
Do the Funky Penguin *	Rufus Thomas	1972	Stax	
SBR-502 (1986)				
Get Me Back on Time, Engine No. 9 *	Wilson Pickett	1970	Atlantic	
Catch a Groove *	Juice	1976	Greedy	12-inch version, 45 version does not have the drum break.
Honky Tonk Women *	The Rolling Stones	1967	London	
You'll Like It Too	Funkadelic	1981	LAX	
The Boogie Back	Roy Ayers Ubiquity	1974	Polydor	
Chella Ilá *	Orchestra Internationale	1974	Fiesta	Often referred to as "Disco Italiano," the title of the Orchestra Internationale LP.
SBR-503 (1986)				
Got to Be Real	Cheryl Lynn	1978	Columbia	
Apache	Incredible Bongo Band	1973	MGM/Pride	
Dance to the Drummer's Beat	Herman Kelly & Life	1978	TK	12-version, Jim Burgess remix.
Bongo Rock	Incredible Bongo Band	1973	MGM/Pride	
Give It to You	UPP	1975	Epic	
Pussy Footer *	Jackie Robinson	1977	Direction	
SBR-504 (1986)				
Different Strokes *	Syl Johnson	1967	Twinight	
I Know You Got Soul *	Bobby Byrd	1971	King	
I Think I'd Do It *	Z.Z. Hill	1972	Mankind	
Sing Sing	Gaz	1978	Salsoul	
Breakthrough	Isaac Hayes	1974	Enterprise	
Funky Music Is the Thing, Pt. 2	Dynamic Corvettes	1975	Abet	Part 2 of the 45 version.
SBR-505 (1986)				
Shifting Gears *	Johnny Hammond	1975	Milestone	
Hit or Miss *	Bo Diddley	1974	Chess	Listed as "Hit and Miss."
Soul, Soul, Soul	The Wild Magnolias	1974	Polydor	
Synthetic Substitution *	Melvin Bliss	1973	Sunburst	Listed as "Substitution."
Get Up and Dance	Freedom	1979	Malaco	12-inch version
Heaven and Hell	20th Century Steel Band	1975	Island	
Shack Up (part II) *	Banbarra	1975	United Artists	Part 2 of the 45.
SBR-506 (1986)				
Sing a Simple Song *	Please	1975	Philips	
Cold Sweat *	James Brown	1967	King	
Theme from 2001 *	Cecil Holmes Soulful Sounds	1973	Buddha	
Son of Scorpio *	Dennis Coffey	1973	Sussex	
Scratchin' *	Magic Disco Machine	1975	Motown	
Down on the Avenue	Fat Larry's Band	1976	WMOT	
I Like Funky Music	Uncle Louie	1979	Marlin	12-inch version
SBR-507 (1986)				
Give It Up or Turnit a Loose	James Brown	1969	King	The "live" version from the Sex Machine LP.
Street-Talk (Madam Rapper) Instrumental	The Funky Constellation	1979	Frozen Butterfly	
Let's Dance	Pleasure	1976	Fantasy	
I Can't Stop	John Davis	1976	Sam	12-inch version
Planetary Citizen *	Mahavishnu Orchestra/John McLaughlin	1976	Milestone	
Good Ole Music	Funkadelic	1970	Westbound	
You Are What You Are	William Ray	1977	Magic Touch	
SBR-508 (1986)				
The Mexican	Babe Ruth	1973	Harvest	Rereleased on SBR-513
Frisco Disco	Eastside Connection	1978	Rampart	Rereleased on SBR-513
Flip	Jesse Green	1977	Epic	12-inch version
Bring It Here	Wild Sugar	1980	TSOB	Rereleased on SBR-519
Hand Clapping Song	The Meters	1970	Josie	Rereleased on SBR-513
Midnight Theme	Manzel	1979	Fraternity	
Two Pigs and a Hog	Freddie Perren	1975	Motown	From the Cooley High Soundtrack
It's My Thing	Marva Whitney	1969	King	Rereleased on SBR-518
SBR-509 (1986)				
Easter Parade	Ingrid	1982	Polydor	12-inch version
UFO *	ESG	1981	99	Originally pressed on a 45 RPM EP, this version is pitched down (to 33 RPM).

* Song has been edited/manipulated

Big Beat	Billy Squier	1980	Capitol	
Cavern	Liquid Liquid	1983	99	
Long Red *	Mountain	1972	Windfall	From the Mountain Live LP.
Seven Minutes of Funk	Tyrone Thomas & the Whole Darn Family	1976	Amherst	The Amherst label version was used; there is different mix of the same song on Soul International Records.

SBR-510 (1986)

Funky President	James Brown	1974	Polydor	
Theme from the Planets *	Dexter Wansel	1976	Philadelphia Int'l	Track has been pitched up (from 33 to 45 RPM).
Theme from S.W.A.T	Rhythm Heritage	1978	ABC	
It's Great To Be Here *	The Jackson Five	1971	Motown	
Ain't We Funkin' Now	The Brothers Johnson	1978	A&M	12-inch version
Shangri La *	La Pregunta	1978	GNP Crescendo	12-inch 33 RPM version (12-inch 45 RPM version has a saxophone solo over the drum break).
Last Night Changed It All *	Esther Williams	1976	Friends & Co.	12-inch version; 7-inch version is identical but does not have the telephone ring on the intro.

SBR-511 (1986)

Impeach the President *	Honey Drippers	1973	Alaga	
God Make Me Funky *	Headhunters	1975	Arista	Listed as "God Make Me Funny," uses 3:00 of the LP version.
Gotta Get Out of Here	Lucy Hawkins	1978	SAM	12-inch version
Action *	Orange Krush	1982	Mercury	
Kool Is Back	Funk Inc.	1971	Prestige	
Love's Theme *	Fausto Papetti	1975	Durium	

SBR-512 (1986)

Granny's Funky Rolls Royce *	Junie	1975	Westbound	Uses only the vocal intro from the 3:41 original.
Funky Drummer *	James Brown	1970	Polydor	
The Champ	Mohawks	1968	Pama	
Walk This Way *	Aerosmith	1975	Columbia	
Johnny the Fox	Thin Lizzy	1978	Vertigo	
Ashley's Roachclip *	Soul Searchers	1974	Sussex	
Gangster Boogie *	Chicago Gangsters	1975	Gold Mind	
Groove to Get Down	T-Connection	1977	TK	

SBR-513 (1987)

The Mexican	Babe Ruth	1973	Harvest	
Keep Your Distance *	Babe Ruth	1976	Capitol	
I Wouldn't Change a Thing *	Coke Escovedo	1976	Mercury	Listed as "(Runaway) Wouldn't Change a Thing," the final seconds of Escovedo's "Runaway" has been tacked on as the intro.
Frisco Disco	Eastside Connection	1978	Rampart	
Phenomena Theme	In Search Of Orchestra	1977	AVI	
Hand Clapping Song	The Meters	1970	Josie	

SBR-514 (1987)

Sister Sanctified *	Stanley Turrentine	1972	CTI	
Willie Chase	J. J. Johnson	1974	MCA	
Uphill Peace of Mind	Kid Dynamite	1976	Cream	
Jam on the Groove	Ralph MacDonald	1976	Marlin	
Knock Him Out Sugar Ray	Experience Unlimited	1980	Vermack	
Blow Your Head	Fred Wesley & the J.B.'s	1974	People	

SBR-515 (1987)

Change (Makes You Want To Hustle)	Donald Byrd	1975	Blue Note	
Brother Green (the Disco King)	Roy Ayers	1975	Polydor	
Mr. Magic *	Grover Washington Jr.	1975	CTI	4:30 of the 9:11 LP version is used.
Main Theme from Star Wars	David Matthews	1977	CTI	
Jack and Diane *	John Cougar	1982	Epic	
Bouncy Lady *	Pleasure	1975	Fantasy	
Rock Music	Jefferson Starship	1979	Grunt	

SBR-516 (1987)

The Assembly Line	Commodores	1974	Motown	
I Walk on Guilded Splinters	Johnny Jenkins	1974	Capricorn	
Gimme What You Got *	Le Pamplemousse	1976	AVI	12-inch "Long" version
"T" Plays It Cool *	Marvin Gaye	1972	Tamla	
Think (About It) *	Lyn Collins	1972	People	
Space Dust *	Galactic Force Band	1978	Springboard	
Take the Money and Run *	Steve Miller Band	1976	Capitol	

SBR-517 (1987)

Listen to Me	Baby Huey	1970	Curtom	
The Lovermaniacs (Sex) *	Boobie Knight & the Universal Lady	1974	Dakar	
Yes We Can Can	Pointer Sisters	1973	Blue Thumb	
One Man Band (Plays All Alone)	Monk Higgins	1974	Buddha	
N.T.	Kool & the Gang	1971	De-Lite	The final 3:19 of the 6:29 LP version is used ("N.T. Pt. 2" off the 45 version).
Let a Woman Be a Woman, Let a Man Be a Man *	Dyke & the Blazers	1969	Original Sound	
Whiskey and Wine	Bram Tchaikovsky	1979	Radarscope	From the "Girl of My Dreams" single.
Feel Good [edit] *	Fancy	1974	Big Tree	Listed as "L.L. Bonus Beats," it's a loop of Fancy's "Feel Good" beat at 45 RPM.

* Song has been edited/manipulated

SBR-518 (1988)

Song	Artist	Year	Label	Notes
Let's Have Some Fun	Bar-Kays	1977	Mercury	
Conga	Lafayette Afro Rock Band	1976	Makossa	
Yellow Sunshine	Yellow Sunshine	1973	Gamble	
It's Just Begun *	Jimmy Castor Bunch	1972	RCA	The intro to "Troglodyte" ("What we gonna do right here is go back…") is edited onto the beginning of "Just Begun."
It's My Thing	Marva Whitney	1969	King	
I Believe in Music	Kay Gees	1976	Gang	
Ride Sally Ride	Dennis Coffey	1972	Sussex	

SBR-519 (1988)

Song	Artist	Year	Label
Rock Creek Park	Blackbyrds	1975	Fantasy
I Get Lifted	K.C. & the Sunshine Band	1975	TK
Cookies	Brother Soul	1975	Leo Mini
Misdemeanor	Foster Sylvers	1973	MGM/Pride
Bring It Here	Wild Sugar	1981	TSOB
Chicken Yellow *	Miami	1974	Drive
Put the Music Where Your Mouth Is	Olympic Runners	1974	London
Sport *	Lightnin' Rod	1973	United Artists

SBR-520 (1988)

Song	Artist	Year	Label	Notes
Lonesome Cowboy *	Roy Ayers	1976	Polydor	
Chinese Chicken	Duke Williams	1973	Capricorn	
I'm Gonna Get You *	Joe Quarterman	1974	GSF	
Reach Out of the Darkness *	Friend & Lover	1973	Verve Forecast	
House of Rising Funk	Chubukos	1973	Mainstream	Issued as a 45 under the Chubukos name, they were called Afrique on LP.
Hook and Sling (Part 1)	Eddie Bo	1969	Scram	
Kissing My Love *	Bill Withers	1973	Sussex	

SBR-521 (1989)

Song	Artist	Year	Label	Notes
Free Your Mind	The Politicans	1972	Hot Wax	
Papa Was Too *	Joe Tex	1966	Dial	
Hector	The Village Callers	1968	Rampart	
Devil with the Bust	Sound Experience	1974	Philly Groove	
Soul Pride	James Brown	1969	King	
Cramp Your Style *	All the People	1972	Blue Candle	
Shaft in Africa (Addis)	Johnny Pate	1973	ABC	
I'm Gonna Love You Just a Little Bit More Baby *	Barry White	1973	20th Century	
Dizzy [edit] *	Tommy Roe	1969	ABC	Listed as "L.L. Bonus Beats #2," it is a loop of the drum break from Tommy Roe's "Dizzy."

SBR-522 (1989)

Song	Artist	Year	Label
Woman	Barrabas	1972	RCA
Corazon	Creative Source	1974	Sussex
Save the World	Southside Movement	1974	Wand
The Grunt (part 1) *	The J.B.'s	1970	People
Do the Funky Penguin (part 2) *	Rufus Thomas	1972	Stax
Dynamite (the Bomb) *	Shotgun	1977	ABC
Films	Gary Numan	1979	Atco

SBR-523 (1989)

Song	Artist	Year	Label	Notes
The Breakdown (part 2) *	Rufus Thomas	1971	Stax	
Country Cooking	Jim Dandy	1975	Chrysalis	From the *Flash Fearless vs. the Zorg Women* soundtrack.
Joyous	Pleasure	1977	Fantasy	
Get Out of My Life Woman *	Solomon Burke	1968	Atlantic	
You Don't Know How Much I Love You	Alphonse Mouzon	1974	Blue Note	
Oh Honey	Delegation	1977	Shady Brook	
The Easiest Way To Fall *	Freda Payne	1970	Invictus	

SBR-524 (1990)

Song	Artist	Year	Label	Notes
Tramp	Lowell Fulson	1966	Kent	
(You) Got What I Need	Freddie Scott	1968	Shout	
You Can't Love Me if You Don't Respect Me	Lyn Collins	1975	People	
Blind Alley	The Emotions	1972	Volt	
Expansions	Lonnie Liston Smith	1975	Flying Dutchman	Listed as "Expansions - Part I," this is 3:07 of the 6:04 LP track (part 1 of the 45).
Hard to Handle *	Otis Redding	1968	Atco	
You and Love Are the Same	The Grassroots	1969	Atco	
Sneakin' in the Back	Tom Scott	1974	Ode	

SBR-525 (1991)

Song	Artist	Year	Label	Notes
I've Been Watchin' You	Southside Movement	1973	Scepter	
Pot Belly	Lou Donaldson	1970	Blue Note	
Mambo #5	Samba Soul	1977	RCA	12-inch version
Don't Change Your Love *	Five Stairsteps	1968	Curtom	
Take Off Your Make Up	Lamont Dozier	1973	ABC	
Love & Affection	Ike White	1976	LA	
The Payback *	James Brown	1973	Polydor	

* Song has been edited/manipulated

Twelve by Twelve

by Andrew Mason

The 12-inch single was born of happy serendipity. Mastering engineer José Rodriguez needed to cut an acetate for regular client Tom Moulton, an up-and-coming remixer, and had run out of 7-inch blanks. Pressing the song on a 10-inch blank, the duo was stunned by the deeper, louder sound the spread-out grooves produced. Although this seminal single never circulated, it wasn't long before their discovery was officially sanctioned. In late 1975, the first LP-sized singles were produced as promotional items for Scepter Records—a label not coincidentally guided by disco aficionado Mel Cheren—and in May 1976, the floodgates opened with Salsoul Records releasing Double Exposure's "Ten Percent," the first commercially available 12-inch. ¶ Nightclubs and discotheques featuring an individual playing pre-recorded music (as opposed to a band or jukebox) were just hitting their stride and the prolific TM/JR (as Moulton and Rodriguez tagged the runout grooves of their collaborations) led the movement by producing extended singles aimed straight at this blossoming club culture. The Gallery, the Loft, Better Days, the Paradise Garage, and other primal New York City nightspots became proving grounds for these records under the guidance of incorrigibly innovative musical selectors like Walter Gibbons, David Mancuso, Tee Scott, and Larry Levan. ¶ Below are some of the original shots that rocked these focal points, all released from 1977 to 1982, an undeniably magnificent era of club classics. Some of these are bona fide hits, some are little known, all have the potential to rip up the dance floor. »

Dinosaur L "Go Bang! #5" b/w "Clean on Your Bean #1"
(Sleeping Bag) 1982

This is the first release from Will Socolov's and insatiable eclecticist Arthur Russell's Sleeping Bag Records, curiously emblazoned with endangered/extinct species. The music released under the Dinosaur L name was performed by the Ingram family, a Philadelphia-based R&B unit who recorded extensively as session players as well as under their own name. An earlier session with Russell produced the Larry Levan–mixed "Is It All Over My Face," another Loft anthem. More dub-like with an expansive feel, "Go Bang!" was born from a unconventional twenty-four-bar song structure Russell devised, over which the band improvised (the "#5" in the title refers to the original tag the jam was given, pre-mixdown). François Kevorkian applied his dub-inspired mixing techniques to the resulting tracks, leaving us with a trancey 130 BPM groove with uneasy organ (sounding like someone was leaning on the keys), trumpet, and skittery electric piano dropping in and out. A particularly powerful moment comes towards the end of the tune when instruments gradually drop from the mix, tension building, until we are left with swirling dischordant Rhodes and light shaker. As your ear begins to tell you the song is fading out, *boom!*, the bass, organ, and vocals are slammed back in for a transcendent dance-floor firework. Male and female vocals alternate, chanting the direct lyric, "I wanna see all my friends at once… I wanna go bang!" and summing up the Loft experience in a succinct if offbeat phrase. The flip side has another off-kilter improvised groove, a nice little horn riff, and more head-scratching lyrics: "Gotta be clean on your bean."

Jeanette "Lady" Day "Come Let Me Love You"
(Prelude) 1981

A super breakbeat sure shot, idling smoothly at 115 BPM. Those uninterested in foreplay can skip Day's breathy come-ons and head for the B-side instrumental version, where mixer François Kevorkian has

placed the eminently cuttable breakdown in pole position at the intro. Any more-than-casual listener to early hip-hop radio in NYC would recognize this whistle/cowbell/timbales break from its cameos in DJ Red Alert's show on 98.7 KISS-FM, among others. In 1982, Prelude Records released *Kiss Mastermixes*, a double album comprised of KISS DJ Shep Pettibone's personal re-edits and remixes of various Prelude radio hits. The edit for "Come Let Me Love You" is particularly interesting in that it grafts the synth break from the 12-inch version of Ian Dury and the Blockheads' "Spasticus Autisticus" into the middle of the Prelude track, uncredited, and indisputably vicious.

Chicago "Street Player"
(Columbia) 1979

Yes, rock brontosaurus Chicago. This one is an unusual promo copy of Chicago's 1979 single, both sides identical. Though the label and sticker trumpet it as a "Special 12-inch Version," it seems no different than the version on the *Chicago 13* LP. The blowdried tale of a struggling musician who has "seen it all," "Street Player" was written by Rufus keyboardist David "Hawk" Wolinski and Chicago drummer Danny Seraphine, and debuted as the title track to Rufus's 1978 LP. Wolinski, also responsible for Rufus favorites "Ain't Nobody," "Any Love," and "Do You Love What You Feel," assisted on Chigago's retake, joined by two other auspicious guests: Maynard Ferguson and Airto Moreira. The souped-up result features an intense and twisting horn line, instantly recognizable as the hook from the Bucketheads' club smash "The Bomb (These Sounds Fall into My Mind)" (vocalist Peter Cetera is actually saying "street sounds swirling through my mind"). After the obligatory verses we're treated to a handclap-led percussion break that begins with a fantastic Ferguson brass smear spelunking into Moreira's polyrhythms, followed by a reharmonization of the main riff. As if they were saving the DJ the trouble of running doubles of the hottest part of the song, the percussion is given eight more bars to shine solo before the devious horn

chart returns. And the band isn't content to vamp as the song's last minute runs out; after a short guitar solo, a showy, rondo-like vocal chorus proves Chicago could flip many styles (listen here for the little "woo!" vocal stab Kenny Dope used to punctuate the Bucketheads' blast). A useful bootleg re-edit of "Street Player" that places the percussion break at the intro was issued on the notorious Rated "X" label, backed with Giorgio Moroder's "Evolution."

Buffalo Smoke "Stubborn Kind of Fella"
(RCA) 1978

You know about white labels, how about white vinyl? Here we have a Lou Courtney–produced update of the Marvin Gaye chestnut that some might call a prime example of a corny disco cover version to stay away from (see Amii Stewart's "Knock on Wood" or Frankie Avalon's "Venus"). Once you get past that preconception (and maybe the first minute or two), you're left with a joyous, uplifting gospel-influenced stormer. After the somewhat prosaic head, the tune builds steam to a killer conga-led breakdown. "Why don't somebody put their hands together right here!" shouts the vocalist and if you don't feel the spirit then I guess I can't help you. The white vinyl issue is relatively rare, with two different mixes. The David Todd remix on the A-side is my pick; the original version on the flip brings the snares a little higher while dropping the bass low in the mix.

Sergio Mendes and Brasil '88 "I'll Tell You" b/w "Lonely Woman"
(Elektra) 1979

Now, I won't argue that Sergio Mendes didn't release some awful schlock as his band slumped to octogenarian stature. But this single is a bouncy and respectable jam, if not quite a floor filler, and still gets regular club play from deeper-crated DJs. Uncredited on the 12-inch, "I'll Tell You" was mixed by beloved New York City DJ

legend Tee Scott (who sadly passed away in 1995). Naturally, he made sure there were plenty of snappy drum and percussion features (the intro's cowbell/drum break and stop-start groove are particularly inviting) and an up-front popping bass line. The female lead vocals may lack the personality of the vintage Mendes lineups, but they handle the stock R&B phrasing of bassist Nate Watts's composition with adequate sass.

Thelma Houston "I'm Here Again"
(Motown) 1977

Motown, likely seeking to capitalize on the incredible popularity of Houston's cover version of "Don't Leave Me This Way" (originally by Harold Melvin and the Blue Notes), recorded and released this boldfaced simalcrum. Aimed hungrily at the "disco market," it is a virtual retake of the previous hit, down to the subdued, schmaltzy intro and the "*ooohhh baby!*"'s leading to the choruses. What sets "I'm Here Again" apart, though, and what has made it into somewhat of a cult classic, is the back half of the song. After the band gets by the routine run through the verses, they (and Houston) throw down on a vicious groove reminiscent of the Originals' "Down to Love Town" (Motown; 1976). Houston seems to come to life at this point and delivers some energetic, soul-stirring ad libs as the band crackles with electricity behind her. The piano is tremendously entertaining, chasing a descending string riff so eagerly it almost trips over itself. Very tough in this white label promo manifestation.

Chas Jankel "Glad to Know You" b/w "3,000,000 Synths/Ai No Corrida"
(A&M) 1981

A monster long-playing single that contains three distinct jams. The A-side is given to "Glad to Know You," the lead single off Jankel's second solo LP, *Questionnaire* (though not on the British release

of the LP). Ian Dury wrote the lyric, and it follows that "Glad to Know You" is a funky/quirky pop tune similar to the (delicious) fare Jankel purveyed during his stint with Dury and the Blockheads, if slightly more discofied. The song is driven throughout by Chas's charismatic earthy-toned piano riff and features a thumping funk bass break. Jankel was well versed in the dub theory of his day (going on to record with Sly and Robbie in 1981), and utilizes many of these effects as the well-crafted tune wends its way through break and verse. The dub masterpiece on this particular piece of plastic however drops at the top of the B-side, where the title "3,000,000 Synths" captures only some of the over-the-top bombast of the tune. Fractionally slower than the 116 BPM A-side, the group disposes of conventional song structure and lets the Linn Drum beat keep on rocking while Chas and Oberheim programmer Chris Warwick trade twisted funk bombs from their high flying synths. As if this wasn't enough, the final song on this weighty 12-inch is "Ai No Corrida." Yes, the same tune Quincy Jones took top ten in mid-1980. As the story goes, A&M rookie Chas's top-ranking stablemate Q heard the song shortly after Jankel submitted it. Jones recorded a rearranged version with his all-star band that left the tune polished to a high sheen (neglecting, however, to include Jankel's dark synth and drum break). The clavinet player on Q's version, by the way, was none other than "Hawk" Wolinski.

The New York Community Choir "Express Yourself" b/w "Have a Good Time"
(RCA) 1977

The NYCC released two very solid albums on RCA; this single is taken from the first. RCA remixer of choice David Todd contributes luscious extended versions on both tracks, practically giving us entire soloed drum tracks over the course of his arrangements. "Express Yourself" is the choice cut here, another example of the venerable club formula of positive, gospel-styled vocals over a solid up-tempo funk groove. The song opens with a funky flangy electric bass bumping over "Sing Sing"–style drums (that's Gaz's "Sing Sing," check your *Ultimate Breaks*). Jazzy verses follow, anchored by more bass, finally settling into an absurdly long drum break. How long is absurdly long? About four minutes or so of reverby kick, snare, and hi-hat with hand claps and assorted percussion flying through. DJs beware, however: though the beat is delectably open, the tempo swings wildly—blend at your own risk. And make sure you flip the record and check the drum breaks in "Have a Good Time," guaranteed to put a stupid grin on your face.

Love Committee "Law and Order" b/w "Just as Long as I Got You"
(Gold Mind) 1978

Listening to the productions of Philly groove wizards Norman Harris, Earl Young, and Ron Baker (guitar, drums, and bass), one can't help being struck by how these are *songs*, with distinctive (if not always profound) lyrics, bridges, choruses, breakdowns. They have, in a word, dynamics, something in short supply in much dance music. This record is no exception, and both tunes are sparkling models of the well-crafted orchestral epic Salsoul was known for. The A-side was the hit, but to me the flip holds the hidden treasure. A bittersweet opus that manages to avoid collapsing under its own melodrama, it comes off as a goofy but heartfelt plea from a man "out there messing around with every girl that comes along" while his woman is home "washing the kids' clothes every night." A sepulchral tenor voice chanting the title provides the indelible hook, and Walter Gibbons gives it a full, extended treatment. (Norman Harris reportedly had a hard time accepting disc jockeys reconfiguring his careful arrangements, but Gibbons's knack for the danceable and dramatic is undeniable.) DJ/producer Dimitri Yerasimos (PKA Dimitri from Paris) dropped a potent re-edit of this cut on BBE in 2001.

Frank Hooker & Positive People "This Feelin'" b/w "Ooh Suga Wooga"
(Panorama) 1981

This unlikely goodie is a dope disco funk cut that has it all: hooky intro with a long open drum break, tight ensemble playing, soulful vocals, plus a nasty George Benson–esque scat/guitar solo. It works well as a transition record as the tempo gathers speed over the course of its seven-minute run, rising from a bumping 112 to 120 BPM. The same full-length version is available on the self-titled LP, a piece I'd passed over many times due to the cover's high cheese factor (the band decked out in matching shiny jackets and denim, bare chests and gold chains gleaming). Let that be a lesson to you! David Mancuso has ranked this one among his top one hundred classics, and it's not hard to see why, with its uplifting message, party vibe, and solid musicality—each a well-appreciated ingredient in the Loft sound.

Montana "Warp Factor II" b/w "A Dance Fantasy"
(Atlantic) 1978

Despite the *Star Wars*–influenced title, this cut cruises at a stately 94 BPM, leaving it in that awkward area, a little too disco-y for funk DJs, yet kind of slow for disco DJs. My advice? Forget about all that, and play the record. The sultry groove cooked up by bandleader and vibesman Vincent Montana is irresistible. A looming presence over Philly Soul and disco in general, Montana's is a name to look for when getting into disco 12-inches (peep his undisputed classic releases with the Salsoul Orchestra ["Love Break"], Philly Sound Works ["Heavy Vibes"], and Goody Goody ["It Looks Like Love"]). At 7:40, the 12-inch mix is a good two minutes longer than the album version, with the added material coming in the form of an elongated vibes solo—unavoidably reminiscent of Roy Ayers's *Lifeline*-era disco-jazz in spite of the widely different phrasing of the two vibraphonists. "Warp Factor II" begins with a flute flourish and a short open drum break before the theme is introduced. After a

perfunctory tenor sax solo the stringy theme gets one last shot before disappearing rapidly in the distance as the band settles into the business at hand. From here on out we have a pure organic groove from the small combo (drums, congas, electric bass, Fender Rhodes) with Montana's vibes swirling furiously above. What to say about the fifteen-minute flip side, a suite whose full (and fully ridiculous) title is "A Dance Fantasy Inspired by *Close Encounters of the Third Kind*"? Well, there are plenty of enticing grooves for the disco/house samplist, often overlayed with gimmicky, heavily panned sound effects and even some sitar, but the farther the band stays from the corny five-note theme the better. The finale is a downright bizarre take on "When You Wish Upon a Star" with vocals by Sister Sledge. "A Tom Moulton Mix," though not one of his defining moments.

Harvey Mason "Groovin' You" b/w "The Race"
(Arista) 1979

Drummer Harvey Mason weighs in to the disco scene with this nugget. It's a family affair, the A-side cowritten and produced by brother Kenny, and, as you might expect, there's a well-developed percussion element throughout. Guest Ralph MacDonald rocks a familiar jam on the groove, joined by a young Sheila Escovedo, ultimately exploding into what has got to be the funkiest tympani riff ever. Over this wall-rattling break comes a memorable highlight of the tune, the vocal chorus' insistent echoing of the descending tympani line. If it sounds strangely familiar, it's because Euro house practitioner Gusto based his pioneering filtered house hit "Disco's Revenge" on that very vocal riff. Watch the folks on the floor lose control of themselves when you blend the two records. "You *will* groove," as one of the voices puts it. ◗

Originally appeared in Wax Poetics Issue 3, Fall 2002.

12×12 with Louie Vega

by Andrew Mason

"My style is combined from a lot of different things I got growing up," veteran producer and DJ Louie Vega states. Not an uncommon circumstance, except that, for this kid from the Bronx, growing up was, well, a little different than most folks. Living down the street from Jazzy Jay in a household where uncle Hector LaVoe was a frequent guest, with older sisters who were dedicated club goers and record collectors, it was probably inevitable that his life would revolve around music. As a Latin freestyle guru, he worked on over a hundred records before shifting his attention to house music and a partnership with Brooklyn breakbeat ace Kenny Gonzalez. As Masters at Work, they have been one of the most prolific and respected mainstays on the dance-music scene for over ten years, anchoring their innovative and intricate productions with legendary DJ sets at clubs worldwide. ¶ "I got my real big break in 1986," remembers Vega. "At that time, I was playing hip-hop, reggae, freestyle, the classics; I used to give them everything." With that sentiment in mind, Louie gives Wax Poetics a little bit of everything in his choice of twelve of the many 12-inch singles that have particular meaning for him. I should note that he came prepared with around forty records, and it was only after much deliberation that he settled, with some reluctance, on these. Regrets to Level 42, Gwen Guthrie, George Benson, Jamiroquai, Klein and MBO, Baricentro, Deodato, Lonnie Liston Smith, and the other great cuts that didn't make it this time around. »

Time Zone "Wildstyle"
(Celluloid) 1983

"Wildstyle," or "Zulu Wildstyle" as it's shown on the cover, is a thumping 112 BPM electro track driven by a monstrous synth bass line. Afrika Bambaataa's frenzied shouts and a reverbed track of Chic's "Good Times" being cut up add to the intense vibe. The title is an homage to the nascent hip-hop scene documented in Charlie Ahearn's seminal 1982 film (graf legend Dondi is thanked on the sleeve), a scene in which Bambaataa and the Zulu Nation were towering figures. "Planet Rock" had been an enormous success the previous year (a certified gold single in 1982), and Bambaataa, along with his DJs, Jazzy Jay and Red Alert, were reaching the pinnacle of their influence. On Bill Laswell's Celluloid Records, home to many progressive rap tracks, they got the chance to to push the envelope further, fashioning a funky and uniquely Bronx take on Kraftwerk (the music on this single is credited to "Wunderverke").

VEGA: One of my mentors was Jazzy Jay. I grew up a couple blocks from him, and he knew I was a young aspiring DJ, so he took me under his wing. At that time, he was playing at the Roxy and we used to go check him out, Bambaataa and the whole crew. I was fifteen, sixteen and really learned a lot from him as a DJ. I loved the mixture at the Roxy, there was all sorts of different nationalities hanging out, and everybody was so into the hip-hop scene. We were all into Kraftwerk's music; *Trans-Europe Express* was a pivotal point in hip-hop music and dance music. One record revolutionized the scene, because it changed the sound. Bambaataa and that crew were really innovative and took hip-hop to a different place, incorporating those European electronic ideas but giving it a hip-hop flavor. I played this once at the Sound Factory Bar [in the mid-'90s] and bugged everybody out, pulling out my Soulsonic Force records and just cutting up all the jams. [*laughs*]

Ian Dury and the Seven Seas Players "Spasticus Autisticus"
(Polydor) 1981

"I dribble when I nibble, and I quibble when I scribble, I'm knobbled on the cobbles, 'cause I hobble when I wobble..." Dury, famously afflicted by polio, gives us a typically witty and unsentimental look at his affliction. This was recorded at Compass Point Studios in the Bahamas, concurrently with another influential session by AWOL U.S. funksters Tom Tom Club, who were recording their first LP. The two groups not only shared the studio but also a rhythm section (Jamaican powerhouse Sly and Robbie), keyboard player (Tyrone Downie), and engineer (Steven Stanley). The song begins on a mellow funk vibe, but develops several interesting moods as it progresses, climaxing in a cavernous, ping-pong panned synth break. Listen for the Tom Tom Club's Weymouth sisters in the chorus of shouts at the end of the tune.

VEGA: Bambaataa, Jay, and Red—they were playing all kinds of music. It wasn't just about one thing. They were playing the punk vibe too, the B-52's, the Clash. It was all about a good song, a good record, a good beat. This is a record that has a reggae element, plus an electronic element because of the synth sounds. It's got vocals that are very different, very out, kind of like David Byrne, or the B-52's: "Mesopotamia." And that synth break... I'll never forget hearing it in the Paradise Garage. Going from speaker to speaker, and everybody was freaking out! The whole groove was slamming, but when I heard that sound, the stereo going back and forth, I had to find out who did this record. That feeling, right there, you know you're about to hear [Liquid Liquid's] "Optimo" or "Cavern"!

ESG II "Standing in Line"
(Emerald Sapphire & Gold) 1987

Post–99 Records, the enterprising Scroggins girls released this four-song EP. The highlight is a thumping, swerving cut that belies its motionless title. The angry vocals, pinched guitar, and driving beat probably owe more to punk than funk, but that didn't stop this cut from packing the dance floor in many a dance club.

VEGA: ESG had these records that just stuck in your head. You all know "Moody" and "UFO," which we all played at the different tempo, and then there was this one, "Standing in Line." I used to call it the *Courageous Cat and Minute Mouse* bass line. Larry [Levan] used to tear this up at the Garage. ESG were from the Bronx, but they were so underground that nobody knew. When I found out later, I was like, "Yeah, that's my people!" 'Cause I'm from the Bronx too, but we really didn't know at the time. Their records worked in dance clubs, and they worked in rock areas, in the punk scene. The instrumentation is so minimal, yet it sounds so powerful, you can tell they were one-minded as a band. Self-produced too! I bought this when it came out.

The Hollies "Draggin' My Heels"
(Epic) 1977

An unlikely Loft anthem, this 1977 offering from British pop rockers the Hollies is a lush melancholy number with understated percolating percussion and tasty keyboard work. Though any vinyl hound has probably thumbed past untold expanses of Hollies LPs, this 12-inch is extremely elusive and the subject of heated Internet bidding amongst those in the know.

VEGA: I was at a flea market in the city on 6th Avenue with a friend of mine, [producer and Tribal Winds label founder] Antonio Ocasio, when he found this and told me it was a big David Mancuso record at the Loft. I took his word for it, and when I got it home and listened to it, it blew me away. I could just feel being in the Loft and feeling this vibe. This is what it's about. And you know the other songs the Hollies sing! I used to hear them on WABC and the other pop stations. The Hollies?! I would love to know how a group like that came to do a record like this. It's so cool that they would do this kind of thing; their usual style was totally different. In a way, this was inspirational to Masters at Work, because one of our goals is to bring in people from different genres of music and collaborate with them. Kenny and I actually did an updated version of this song, but we never put it out, because I didn't know who could sing something like this, but we did the track. These guys have an incredible tone; it reminds me a little of the Cyrkle.

It's not a record you can play everywhere, only because people are not educated enough [in dance music]. Or you really have to be playing for a long time in the night to take them on that journey. I played this in Japan, and the people screamed. Over there, the deeper, the better. Pull out your rare jams—they'll love it!

Joubert Singers "Stand on the Word"
(Next Plateau) 1985

A scarce release from an "all in the family" gospel group affiliated with the First Baptist Church of Crown Heights in Brooklyn, led by organist Joseph Joubert (look for his name and assured playing on other house records), this clearly illustrates the strong connections between the house and gospel genres. One of the primary forces behind this melding, and a name closely identified with the New Jersey house sound, was Club Zanzibar resident DJ Tony Humphries.

VEGA: My thing was going to hear the DJs who I liked spin. Tony Humphries was definitely on that list, and I used to go to Zanzibar religiously when he was rocking on KISS-FM. We would hear him on the radio, then be like, "We got to go hear him in person!" I went to the clubs as much as I DJed. This is really a gospel standard, but they put that four-on-the-floor thing on it, and it just happened. I always loved the little kid who sang on it; we used to mimic it, everybody would sing that part. Hearing it on that system at Zanzibar was something else. That was another Richard Long sound system, same as at the Garage. He was a sound genius. The places that he did were fantastic, because they had great DJs and a great sound system. There was the Roxy, the Garage, Studio 54, the Underground, the

Funhouse—I used play on that one! When Tony played this record at Zanzibar he inspired me to play it at my gigs.

Lamont Dozier "Going Back to My Roots"
(Warner Brothers) 1977

Dozier, best known as one of the primary songwriters for Motown ("Stop! In the Name of Love," "Jimmy Mack") and the cofounder of the Invictus/Hot Wax labels, wrote this soul searching epic for his second Warner Brothers LP, *Peddlin' Music on the Side*. Dozier's charismatic piano riff is worked to its fullest potential by Crusader Joe Sample, with assistance from bandmate Wilton Felder on bass and Hugh Masekela, who contributed the wonderfully dynamic and shifting arrangement. Also keep your eyes out for Richie Havens's powerful version, and a deliciously funked-up take from native New Yorkers, Odyssey.

VEGA: This was a big inspiration for my Nuyorican Soul project, and I have to pay tribute to Lamont Dozier, one of the greatest writers of all time. It starts with that incredible piano, goes into the song, there's a little African break, and it goes out with a chant, everybody releasing. This is a very spiritual record. It's one of those records that, when put on in the right setting, you're going to get people with their arms up in the air, people singing along, people sweating. If I was to pick one song that represented what I've learned musically over the years, what I've grown up with in New York, this would be it. Being able to go to the city, you could hear jazz when you want, you could hear soul when you want, Latin music, funk, hip-hop, rock. If I was born in a different place, I would never be what I am now; I know it. It had to be because I am from New York, what I experienced with my family, in the city, with my friends. This record symbolizes that for me.

There's a lot of ways you can bring this in [the mix], which is cool. Sometimes, I might bring it in from the middle, from the African breakdown, then bring it back to the beginning. Or keep running that part, and not let the piano break come in. Create anticipation, then, *bam!*, come right in. My style of playing can get very theatrical, I'll get into sound effects, or keyboard breaks, things that can break it down without everybody just stopping. That's the idea.

Endgames "Ecstasy (Centurion Mix)"
(Virgin) 1983

Second-tier British new-wavers Endgames had one full-length album release, from which two singles were drawn. This dubbish mix of "Ecstasy" was the B-side of one of them, and became another victim of early hip-hop's voracious appetite for nasty funk grooves, no matter the

complexion. The 105 BPM beat with bouncing synth bass and an addictive block chord hook was a natural for DJs in almost any venue.

VEGA: This goes back to my roller-skating days at the Skate Key [roller rink] in the Bronx. There's a DJ that spun there that had one of the best 12-inch collections I've ever seen. His name is Wayne Burgois; they call him Mad Wayne. He gave me a lot of great 12-inches, in fact he gave me [Barrabas's] "Woman." I was a real roller skater back in the day, from say '78 to '83, I was skating heavy. The scene was like break dancing but on skates. I would go to Skate Key, or I would go to Laces and hear Danny Krivit. That synth sound in here is terrific, and the Fairlight voice is dope. I just played this record at my monthly Dance Ritual party; I think I mixed it with Melba Moore's "You Stepped into My Life." It's a little down-tempo, but the open sax intro you can drop over something else, then when the keyboards come in, *whooo*! That's exactly what happened when I played it last week. People went nuts.

Malcolm McLaren "D'ya Like Scratchin'"
(Island) 1983

Impressario McLaren's collaboration with New York City radio icons the World Famous Supreme Team is an indisputable hip-hop landmark. Featuring "a special party mix" drawn from the full-length *Duck Rock* LP, this extended player has all the juice you could ask for, from sampling pioneer Trevor Horn's thunderous production to the now world-famous radio chatter from which the title was drawn. Even the cover art with its Keith Haring appropriations, dual Technics 1200s photo, and ridiculously tricked out boom box is a pastiche of archetypal hip-hop icons. Anne Dudley and Jonathan Jeczalik, along with Horn, the main synth and drum programmers on this project, would join forces to form the group Art of Noise, releasing their own hip-hop homage ("Beat Box") later the same year. Shout out to Supreme Team captains C-Divine the Mastermind and Just Allah the Superstar of WHBI, godfathers of all hip-hop radio shows to come.

VEGA: This brings back memories of Jellybean at the Funhouse; I think Afrika Bambaataa got in there at the end too. Nineteen eighty-three, man, it was an influential time for me. I guess this was Malcolm McLaren's interpretation of the hip-hop scene. This is really a Trevor Horn record. The drum machines and all sound like him...something's backwards in there, like a rock guitar. Trevor Horn's a genius. We worked in his studio in England once but never met him. This is another record that still gets people open. It's cool the way the rap comes in so naturally, like somebody just picked up the mic and started going. I always hated that little part towards the

end, where the beat drops and comes back in [on the wrong beat]. I used to mix this with "Funkbox Party" by Masterdon Committee.

The Coach House Rhythm Section "Time Warp/ Nobody's Got Time"
(Ice) 1977

Guyanese-born, British-bred superstar Eddy Grant was a founder of the successful soul/ska group the Equals and a prolific solo artist and producer, founding his own label, Ice, in 1972. The headquarters of all Ice recordings was the globetrotting Grant's Canadian studio, named the Coach House. "Nobody's Got Time" was a single from Grant's 1980 LP *My Turn to Love You*, distributed by Epic. The deep, futuristic electronic rhythm is topped by a searing harmonica solo and vocal from Grant, who played all the instruments on this cut except the drums (Jamaican music legend Lloyd Charmers contributes handclaps!). The Ice release seen here was backed by an instrumental workout on the same groove, titled "Time Warp," that was later used by Epic on the flip side of their 12-inch release of "Electric Avenue," a hit single from Grant's next LP. Grant also redid this in a slower, drum-heavy version that came out as a Torpedo Records 7-inch.

VEGA: I play this to this day, and people think it's a new record. He was really ahead of his time. Those handclaps! The sounds they got on these records, they got the deep bottom of reggae into the dance world. His voice sounded great, he had the hooks, and he had the songs. What a groove. Plus it has that realness in the mix, there's not a lot of effects on everything, it's all right in your face. When you hear it on a big system it's like he's singing right in front of you. This was another big Loft record, but the cool thing about this is that wherever it was played the dancers came out; they'd hear it and all get out on the floor. ["Time Warp"] was played in all the underground clubs, whereas the [Epic] A-side ["Electric Avenue"] was played in the mainstream spots. "Time Warp" is also cool 'cause you can ride it with other records, you could mix a vocal in there, do something different with it.

Bo Kool "(Money) No Love"
(Siamese) 1981

A mysterious low-budget release licensed from London's Tania Records that got huge play from New York City's underground DJ community. The "TW" in the credits is one Tony Williams—sometimes mistakenly thought to be the Miles Davis protégé and drum prodigy, but actually a London-based reggae producer of the same name. The one-time BBC radio presenter concocted an irresistible synth-funk masterpiece

here with the help of rapper Bo Kool, who quotes liberally from Dennis Brown's reggae smash "Money in My Pocket." With the heavily dub-influenced instrumental on the flip, this 12-inch has become increasingly scarce in recent years. The relentless minor key bass line has inspired untold numbers of imitators, notable among them Man Friday ("Love Honey, Love Heartache" on Vinylmania) and Mateo and Matos ("Love Style" on Spiritual Life).

VEGA: I first heard this on a tape my older sisters brought home. A lot of my schooling came from them; they had been going to the Loft since '72! I think the first time I heard it out was in a club called Ones, maybe in 1981. This, [Dinosaur L's] "Go Bang," "Time Warp," that whole flavor, they were tearing it up. And they used to play the vocal. It's a funny rap; I think it's a British dude. I play the vocal and the instrumental, depending on the mood. There's more of that reggae influence in here, with the hi-hat and the dubby delays. And that bass line! What can you say about this record? It's all about that groove.

ESP "It's You"
(Underground Records) 1986

An early Chicago house anthem, and one of the first releases on Rocky Jones's Underground Records (famously home to Steve "Silk" Hurley's British chart-topper "Jack Your Body").

VEGA: I've got to stick at least one house classic in here. At this time, I was DJing at the Devil's Nest in the Bronx and a place called Heartthrob, which used to be the Funhouse, in Manhattan. When I first heard house music, I was blown away. On a big system, those records—Mr. Fingers and all the Trax, Underground, DJ International stuff—they sounded amazing. We had records back then coming out of New York; they weren't labeled house music, but they were compatible with what was coming out of Chicago. It was a lot more vocal oriented, things like Billie's "Nobody's Business," the stuff on the Supertronics label [mostly mixed by Tony Humphries] like Touch and all that. But then you had these records coming from Chicago that had the bass lines of some of the Salsoul and disco classics, so from the beginning they were really familiar, though the drums were more powerful than the disco records. It was cool to play them with the old records; the crowd reacted really well when they heard it. Then there was also a darker, moodier side to it, like the Jungle Wonz and Mr. Fingers' "Can You Feel It."

Though the New York sound rose up at the same time as the Chicago scene, I do know that Marshall Jefferson and Mr. Fingers had a big influence on the producers and DJs here as well. We loved it,

we had open arms for it. I'm not going to say that house completely came from Chicago, because there was already a sound that we were developing. To me, Boyd Jarvis would be our Larry Heard. [Jarvis] came up with these funky bass lines, like "The Music's Got Me," "Somehow Someway" [both by Visual on Prelude Records]. There was Colonel Abrams [and] "You Don't Know" [by Serious Intention on Easy Street Records]. Those beats were different than the drum machines they were using in Chicago. Chicago used a lot of the [Roland] 909. The early '80s here were the 808 and the Linn Drum, then the [Ensoniq] SP-12.

Barrabas "Woman"
(RCA) 1972

Under-acknowledged Spanish rock and soul outfit Barrabas were responsible for several disco classics, the most prominent of which was probably "Hijack," famously covered by Herbie Mann (and more recently celebrated in its Beatnuts-sampled Enoch Light version). The group's popularity in New York can be traced directly to the influence of Loft leader David Mancuso, who turned his friends on after discovering their eponymous first LP in an Amsterdam flea market. "Woman," backed here, as on the 45, by "Wild Safari," is drawn from that LP. The 12-inch seen here is an extremely rare Mexican pressing.

VEGA: If I had to pick five records that represent me, this would be one of them. The first two [rim shot] sticks on the intro are wiped on my copy; they got burnt out from playing it so much! This record is dope, the way they meshed the rock and Latin sounds together. It wasn't the same way Santana did it. This became an anthem; you could play it at anytime for anybody. I heard this when my sisters brought it home on 45, another one they heard at the Loft. Mancuso broke this record in the States; I think he got this overseas somewhere. It reminds me of Rare Earth a little, too. Supposedly this 12-inch sold recently for $2,200. The person who sold it told me that I was partially responsible, because I've been playing this a lot lately, and somebody in the club saw that I was playing it off the original 12-inch and went looking for it. It's crazy how things start! ◗

Originally appeared in Wax Poetics Issue 4, Spring 2003.

Left-Field Americana

by Dante Carfagna

As a viable means of mechanical reproduction, the long-playing record joined the photograph and the printed word as an affordable format for the distribution of one's creative impulses from the late '60s onward. While nowhere near the sheer individual quantity of its smaller brother—the 7-inch, 45 RPM single—the LP offered a broader timescale and a larger graphic with its 12-inch size. It allowed the artists behind the sound a more spacious canvas in which to make their aural mark. The major record companies distributed thousands of popular works, yet the scope and spectrum of the self-produced LP record is an almost unfathomable preponderance. While the corporative music company's releases can be cataloged due to excessive paper documentation resulting from the business element, the privately pressed releases of the United States can never be totalized due to the gross locality and their restricted distribution. We scan the margins of American private-press LPs in all genres, bringing to light the seams and stitches of the American sound patchwork.

Order of Orpheus *A Trip Through the Planes from the Throne of God*
(Om Source 7083) 1977

Bearing a stock cover and subtitled "An Aquarian Ensemble Dedicated to Channeling Music from the Higher Forces through Improvisation," the Order of Orpheus is indicative of the quasi-religious and proto-New Age records that were prevalent in the U.S. throughout the '70s. The mastermind behind this Reston, Virginia organization was Joel Andrews, who, according to the wordy liner notes, has channeled some 1,500 Individual Attunement tapes and sixty General Healing tapes. In these tapes, Andrews would give a reading of a person's past lives through the world of music and offer some advice for their future paths. For a fee. At some point, the Order of Orpheus decided that as a result of the "rapid developments in musical healing," they should put out a record of their own "higher" musical works. In a group channeling in 1975, Andrews, along with Mahoteh on flute and clarinet, John McBride on guitar and protean conch (!), and John-David on percussion, created the music we hear on the LP. Sonically, we are talking engaging exotic cosmopalimpsest, random quotations from random holy books, a uniquely American improvisational sensibility, all hemmed up in some sort

of phenomenal transportation package. There is an account in the liners that when listening to the playback of the album, the musicians noticed an "expanded space resonance," and, after "technical investigation," the conclusion was reached that the added sonic dimension had been a blessing from the mighty Om Source. Ah, of course! Also on the back cover is the obligatory contact info necessary to bring the Order of Orpheus to *your* town, and the services they can offer while there—individual instruction, musical healing workshops, and full-blown concerts. This release bears a close resemblance to two other records discussed in this article, Arica and Ojas, but it lacks the organization of the Arica and the slovenly nature of the Ojas. An interesting document for those into underground metaphysical organizations of bygone eras who had the determination to manifest their philosophy in music. Buried for certain, with daylight nowhere to be seen.

Doug Snyder/Bob Thompson *Daily Dance*
(New Frontiers 1) no date

The unlikely town of Washington Court House, between Columbus and Cincinnati in southern Ohio, was obviously the atmosphere needed to generate a document of such solidarity and perspective.

Snyder and Thompson were a guitarist and drummer respectively, and this is their vibratory postcard from nowhere. A first glance one might mistake this LP for a C.R.I. label classical release, as they have a similar graphic feel, but make no mistake once the needle is placed on the record. Likely from the mid- to late '70s, this duet has nothing to do with anything that has gone before, as even today it seems to dodge categorization. To the untrained ear, it might initially sound like pure noise, akin to an avant-garde release or a wild free jazz excursion, but upon closer investigation one begins to realize the lack of pretension and sheer naivety of its being. The duo tear through seven "songs" with titles such as "Time Overlaps Itself," "Soul and Universe," and "Truth Is a Pathless Land." They generate waves of energy through cascading feedback squall and drumbo bash and shimmer. A few tracks will start with something vaguely resembling a "groove," before they quickly deteriorate into their lonely Buckeye din. "Daily Dance" has much more in common with '90s groups like Fushitsusha or the Dead C than any group operating in the U.S. in the '70s—Ya Ho Wa 13 and the likes included. This type of recording eventually achieves a sort of religious quality, not through the obliged philosophy of a release such as the Arica, but rather from the honest belief held by the two creators that, *this is what needs to be done*. An adventurous outing to say the least, and one that can only exist within the private press cosmos. New Frontiers, indeed.

Arica *Audition Plantar*
(Woo Soo 1001) no date

The Arica Institute was/is a group founded by Chilean expat Oscar Ichazo in an effort to promote higher self-awareness through his "psycho-calisthenics." Gaining visibility through the late '60s, the '70s found Arica owning a posh building in midtown Manhattan in order to accommodate its legions of followers. The ground floor contained a bookshop that was one of the few locations where this LP could be purchased. *Audition Plantar* is a double album containing four side-long trips into the ethereal and demonstrable world of psycho-calisthenics. Intended to be a musical accompaniment to the mental exercise regime put forth by Ichazo, the removal of any knowledge of ideology leaves the music to stand on its own. And it does so in a hypnotic and groovy fashion. Three of the four sides are muggy, percussive flights with funky bass figures propelling the interlocked haze forward. Times are few that one can remember bobbing their head to so-called "meditational music," but the Arica just might get the crowd open at the Windham Hill Club. The only LP comparable within religious-groove margins would be the Church of Scientology's funky Apollo Stars release. Apparently, the (uncredited) musicians appearing on this album had had it with the

chillum and their Amon Duul LPs, but even with the strict Arican discipline couldn't quite shake their modal stoner roots. The fourth side is a free blowout that would give the Muntu Ensemble a chill up the spine. The *Audition Plantar* LP was also issued in a pink cover with spoken meditation instructions over the instrumental tracks and a different fourth side. Such was the popularity of Arica's music that the open-minded A&R team at Just Sunshine Records decided the trance-groove of the Institute would fit snug against their last Betty Davis offering and promptly released an LP entitled *Sunshine*. Straight to the cut-out bins it went. All three of Arica's recorded documents are ripe for reissue and come highly recommended for those who like their sonic workouts long and deep in the bag. Ichazo is now known for being the copyright holder of the popular New Age icon, the enneagram.

David Lee Jr. *Evolution*
(Supernal 1973/74) 1974

David Lee Jr. was a talented drummer whose recorded output is scant, appearing on a few India Navigation and Strata-East LPs in the mid-'70s. Obviously, the space allotted to Lee on the Alan Braufman and Charles Rouse dates had the drummer nonplussed, for he chose to record this solo LP for his own Supernal concern. Even the seemingly unrestricted nature of the releases on Strata-East or India Navigation would be hard put to contain an effort as angular and precursory as demonstrated on "Evolution." While by and large a solo percussion record, it is Lee's imagination that bridges the drum chasm between a Milford Graves punch-and-paint and the free pocket of James Black's second-line distortions. Like most of the artists discussed in this column, Lee has a decidedly personal cosmic perspective, one without the ballyhoo trappings of Sun Ra or glossy New Age Unitarianism. Assisted on two tracks by "normal" players Bob Cranshaw and George Davis, the trio excursions are oblique jazz funk wobbles like an understandable and demure Cha Cha Shaw, but Lee's encompassing solo drum outings are the true focus here. After all, this is *his* record. Break dudes should duly note that the track "Cosmic Vision" is a 120-second boom-bapper with a close relative in Niagara. Also of note to potential appropriators is the descending funk oneness of "Second Line March." Lee dedicates his music to "peace and freedom," and there is no doubt to the earnestness of his dedication upon listening to this truly refined Black space document. And even when Lee sings a ballad that stretches into Ed Askew country, you have to dig it. Unsurprisingly, this long-player bears no sound resemblance to any private jazz or funk document in which it would be filed next to. While the Strata-Tribe–Black Jazz axis gets its umpteenth renewal via audiophile reissues, David Lee

Jr. is holding it down for those into the next. Cheers to "the Hatter" and his shaker plunk, keep on pushing.

Ojas *The Seven Levels of Man*
(no label 88-62) 1978

Nutshell: one-man-against-the-universe bludgeoned electronics LP from Oklahoma City, issued with two differently colored covers. Steve McLinn would be the guy in the crowd unanimously called "the lurker." McLinn is the sole proprietor of the Ojas enterprise, but unlike the Order of Orpheus or Arica, he neither has, nor needs, followers. In Oklahoma City, if you have an ARP, a Moog, an Oberheim, a Roland and some wind chimes, you don't need so-called followers, or at least that is what McLinn is out to solidify. With said bank of electronics, McLinn creates two sidelong, semi-aquatic portals into his idea of the consciousness of man. Sporting the required cosmic patina and banter, Ojas attempts to manifest "the sound which is the force that holds the physical octave." Whether or not he succeeds is anyone's call, but as we know, the Moog tends to drift and is *really* hard to tune. McLinn does succeed in making a purely electronic LP from the late '70s that sounds nothing like Tangerine Dream or their wayward hypnagogic ilk. The aural scenery created in OKC in 1978 has more in common with say, a post-kif fascination with a particular tetra in the college aquarium than a release on Brain, Perspectives Musicale, or the Japanese Voice label. This LP demonstrates the inherent beauty of the private press LP, in that it is a *real* demonstration of a particular person's view of the world, with no topical or industrial influences. This is the sound of self-preservation, an anthropological window in which there is no anthropologist, for the people in question *record themselves*. ◗

Originally appeared in Wax Poetics Issue 3, Fall 2002.

Reflections of Time feat. Padro *Sweet, Romantic and Sexy Joy*
(PLG 777) no date

At first glance, one may assume that this LP is your standard, rare, local soul LP from the mid- to late '70s. The undiscerning listener may even play the record and come to the same conclusion, as the twelve songs sound like honest falsetto ballads typical of the era.

Yet upon serious scrutiny, and with experienced soul knowledge, one realizes that this is something far more surreal and Delphian. Padro Gray is a Chicagoan and this, his only release, might be the largest red herring ever reeled in by the vinyl angling community. You see, none of the songs on the LP are originals, in fact, they are not even covers—they are direct transfers from other people's records. I believe what we have in this document is a custom mixtape set to

wax, only Padro disguises it with actual production and arranging credits made to fool the owner into thinking this was *his* music and voice. Where an arrangement allows, Padro whispers breathy sheet talk until the *real* vocalist begins his singing, at which time Padro disappears. All of the tunes have a similar cool falsetto lead, perhaps justifiable as the same vocalist. Where the vocalist sounds obviously different, Padro claims this to be another member of his group, the Reflections of Time, taking lead vocal duties. I have yet to confirm all of the track's rightful artists, but it is certain that Padro had a soft spot for the Moments, and member Harry Ray in particular, for he wholesale hijacks "Ride Your Pony Girl" from Ray's All Platinum 45. Once one gets over the stupefying dupe job at hand, you begin to appreciate the severe *privacy* of this LP, a work of intense personality and gall. I can imagine the group of friends around a bottle of wine: "*Man, we don't need no band to get the ladies, we only need a* record." So while the reader tries to make it out of the meta-modern, sample clearance, rightful collage aporia that this buried LP generates, remember that this LP somehow gained reissue in Japan in the early '90s. Padro even duped the experienced Japanese collectors. The only recorded evidence even vaguely similar is the Rearrangers Band 45 on the Life label, in which Al Green's "Love and Happiness" is recorded as it plays in a nightclub in south Chicago and is issued by a group as an original composition. The Reflections of Time LP may very well be the nadir of the private press aesthetic.

Ice Cold *Ice Cold*
(studio demo, no #) 1975

With its generic printed white sleeve drenched in utter ambiguity, this mysterious LP demands the seasoned collector's attention. Recorded in 1975 in Omaha, Nebraska, Richard McCain would seem to be the brain trust behind this musical enigma, as he produced and arranged the entire record. The material contained within the twelve inches of plastic is hard to pigeonhole within any one genre, as a large portion of the records discussed in this column will tend to do. The first side offers four excursions into paltry funky rock, with vocals supplied by the Real Is Soul vocal group, led by the 1975 Miss Black Nebraska, Jantha Whitmore. The four tunes are passable within their limitations, but when compared to the expanse that is the second side, the twenty-five minute "Cycles of Infinity," one will rarely return to these grooves. Spanning the horizon, "Cycles of Infinity" moves through a variety of different sounds, from percussive ambience to fuzzed psych to minor key trifles to a bizarre jazz vamp, all flowing seamlessly together.

The final coda mashes all of the movements gone through prior into a wild, noisy two minutes or so. Too jazzy for psych guys, too fuzzy for funk guys, this is music for wide open ears. Similar to the

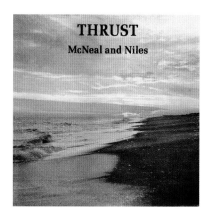  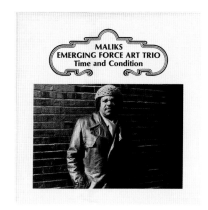

Loading Zone LP on Umbrella in approach, Ice Cold straddles and leaps sonic borders openly and with gusto. As the majors would get nowhere near the Cornhusker confidence exuded by McCain and associates herein, the "Not To Be Sold Or Released" disclaimer on the cover is perfectly prophetic. It says Nebraska, but certainly off the map in terms of recorded music as commodity.

McNeal and Niles *Thrust*
(Tinkertoo 5001) 1979

From Cleveland, Ohio, the McNeal and Niles LP demonstrates everything that is beautiful about the privately pressed record. A group of very talented musicians playing music of their own creation, pressing it up locally, and continuing on with their lives. No aspirations of fame or fortune will be found here; this is music by them for you. Though the label claims it as recorded in 1979, the sonancy begs to differ. Sounding like a ripe 1974 session, guitarist Wilbur Niles and keyboardist Machelle McNeal set a mellow, sophisticated funk down on all seven tunes on the LP. Highlights are hard to decide, as this record has something for everyone's tastes. The opening track, "Ja Ja," has heavy hookah ambience with McNeal skipping soul Rhodes across Niles's rippling guitar and Norman Wade's snapping drums. While an undecidedly lame title, "Punk Funk" actually brings the goods, venturing into "Cutting Room" regions like the Oceanliners working Lake Erie. Side Two finds the middle half of the side taken up by the extraordinary "Quiet Isle," a laid-back affair, again with some crisp drumming, that resembles a Black Steely Dan on funk Quaaludes. The album's closer, "One Slave, One Gun," leaves us with an up-tempo, cyclical dirge, vaguely Latin in modality. Niles would push into the '80s with two other LPs, "Thrust Is" (NRG 5001) and "Re-Entry" (Plum Place 1004), but with McNeal's immaculate keys replaced with a flaccid saxophone and a much cleaner, sterile sound all around, they do not come recommended. I have never met anyone who, upon listening to this record, wasn't pleasantly surprised to find out that music this listenable was still being made at the dawn of the '80s. The stock cover used on this release was one in great favor in the late '70s, especially with country and gospel artists. With this in mind, it is often that great local LPs slip under the buyer's radar due to the anonymity that arises from custom cover art.

Sweet Maya *Sweet Maya*
(no label 7091N8) 1977

Hailing from tiny Paw Paw, Michigan, and recorded at Brice Roberson's semi-famous Uncle Dirty studio in Kalamazoo (Rhythm Machine, Odyssey, etc.), this ensemble could be the blueprint for thousands of local bands in the U.S. in the '70s. Every town had bands that developed a significant following playing wholly original music, an alternative to the show band who played the hits of the day. Sweet Maya played original music, some of it tepid and typical mid-'70s fare, some of it adventurous and intricately arranged. And for every group that only played live, there exist many that pooled the resources at hand and issued a distributional object. These LPs are stripped of their associative trappings upon entering the world of the used record, and serve as a window to another environment and climate for the soul that happens upon them. One has surely said to themselves, "What were they thinking?" when encountering a sound that seems misplaced given the sonic quo of the particular era, and the Sweet Maya release certainly has one of those head scratchers lurking on its grooves. "People Suite," the last song on the second side (often the place where experiments are to be found), finds the group predicting the early '90s hip-hop era in an almost scary fashion. Drums bang about with SP1200-like precision, the bass loops just like someone loops a bass line, and a bridge is crossed that hears Pete Rock crying from below it, "I'd take the whole thing as an *interluuuuudde...*" It clocks in at seven minutes, and apart from a brief dodgy change, one might think that they were listening to a current chunk of well-made instrumental hip-hop that hasn't been made yet.

Now, if only to find a copy of this, or any other local LP, that *hasn't* been autographed by the entirety of the band. The challenge awaits, but in the meantime Sweet Maya languishes, fully signed, in the basements of hip divorcees and community college drop-outs all over central Michigan.

Malik's Emerging Force Art Trio *Time and Condition*
(EFAE RR-42479) 1982

The idea of free jazz being a marketable commodity is a topic that has been hotly denounced and defended for decades after the intial influx of out documents in the early to mid-'60s. Avant-garde jazz musicians and the notion of the artist-owned label are nothing but inseparable upon discussion of outlet and dissemination of an individual's art. Free players often find themselves being excluded from a musical form that they are fully present within and contribute to daily, and a privately pressed record is a natural product of this exclusion. Much has been written on larger scale cooperations like the AACM, the JCOA, and the Black Artists Group, but there are hundreds of additional self-directed movements that were quickly swallowed up by the passage of time and the tide of recorded musics. Maurice "Malik" King, a powerful and soulful alto player, is joined by fellow St. Louis natives Qaiyim Shabazz and Zimbabwe Nkenya, on percussion and bass violin respectively, on this, his sole vinyl

adventure. With certain loose ties to the B.A.G. (the poem on the back cover is by Floyd LeFlore's wife, Shirley), the Emerging Force Art Trio are in league with the Phill Musras and Abdul Hanans of the world as absolutely unknown giants of creative jazz. Time and Condition is the type of music that bears unbelievable amounts of honesty and dedication for the listener, regardless of their interest in jazz or any other type of sounds. This LP seems to disintegrate any collector-driven thoughts on pressing quantity, rarity, or value, for this is such a human effort it demands autonomy. If pataphysics were schooled, this album would be required listening for its excep-

tional qualities. The music herein is searching and moving, pictures of sound filtered through a Black Midwest experiential template, finally labeled "jazz." As King and Shabazz are now deceased, the self-produced long-playing record has given us the opportunity to live through thirty-seven minutes of sound that represent a lifetime of living, seeing, and breathing music. And we could not ask for much more than that. ◗

Originally appeared in Wax Poetics Issue 4, Spring 2003.

I want to lift the veil from the "normal," the unrecognized, unsuspected, incredible, enormous normal. The abnormal first acquainted me with it, disclosing to me the prodigious number of operations which the most ordinary of men performs, casually, unconcerned, as routine work, interested only in the outcome and not in the mechanisms... –Henri Michaux, 1966

Most people spend a great deal of time on their album covers. Major record companies have had art direction departments since the cockcrow of the LP era. Each cover is to distinguish its contents as different than another's. The front of the LP often has a photograph of the artist, often has a significant snapshot, some have wild, colorful paintings. In the larger recording world, uniformity seems intolerable, for the consumer needs to look at something new, something *different*. Certain labels had teams of artists developing a visual identity for their product, though careful to distinguish between one release and the next. Utilitarian or serial design seemed forbidden but for specialist (read: no sales) labels and institutional releases; imprints like Ocora, BYG Actuel, Folkways, and nearly every sound-library release are examples. The nature of the artwork, obviously harnessed to the musical content, can be seen as it changes through the eras. With major-label issues, one can usually tell a record from the '80s apart from a '60s release. It gets much trickier and sublime when dealing with the private-press sphere, as each artwork is distinctly individual rather than communal. For the semiotics major, think diachrony over synchrony.

Since the LP cover can hold a certain talismanic quality to its authors, which is subsequently deferred to the music buyer, most artists prefer to draw up visuals that resound with the sounds contained within. How then to determine difference in records that share the same cover art? The pre-designed stock cover has given the collecting world a common denominator, a qualitative equalizer where content supersedes context. In this world of the impersonal visual, a pious gospel recording can bear the same artwork as that of drug-addled psych release. High-school-sponsored taping of stage bands, choral groups, and lab bands almost indefinitely bear stock covers when found as LPs—a move made to please all parents, regardless of background, no doubt. It is this normality and benightedness that marks the stock LP cover and its contents as something worthy of investiga-

tion to the traveled collector. As the search for the obscure finds focus, one finds themselves drawn to the seemingly innocuous or bland, as perhaps this is the reason that the particular recording has languished undiscovered. The collector can imagine the immediacy that the particular artist felt upon completion of a full-length recording and the need to share his impulses: "No time for a picture, let's get this out there." Yet even then, they have the option to choose from a set of predetermined pictures one that might best suit their careful contents. One is forced to decompose the essence of their art to a simple statement—perhaps a landscape, perhaps an abstract design, maybe even a seasonal motif like a wreath or a snow-covered mailbox.

So the decision is made, the records are ordered from any number of custom record presses, more often than not Century Records in California, and the object is sold, or given away, or packed into an already crowded attic. When it resurfaces (and the entrance of the private LP into the used LP bin usually indicates that something happened to the original owner), it is rendered anonymous through its molting of a connected personality. And it has myriad cousins and uncles that it has never met, all wearing the same clothes but often speaking drastically different languages. It has become standard, normal, unable to distinguish itself from that of its identical ilk, dare we say a phono-eme. It takes the adventurous collector to sweep the stock LP from its basic environment, cast it in a new light and transform it into something exceptional, something abnormal. The removal of the veil of normality occurs at the site of the tone arm and platter. The surge of recent stage-band LP collecting is the tip of the iceberg when discussing this transformation, with many rare psych, soul, and jazz LPs bearing stock cover designs only now starting to breathe new air. ◗

Originally appeared in Wax Poetics Issue 5, Summer 2003.

Val Shively's Common Ground

by Cosmo Baker

A big DO NOT ENTER sign graces the front door of Val Shively's R&B Records. First-time customers have stood confused in front of that door in the freezing Philly winter air, not bothering to read the sign a little closer—handwritten in Magic Marker, it reads, "unless you know what you want." ¶ But anyone can see the huge sign on his roof that reads "Over 4,000,000 oldies in stock"; it's unmistakable when you're driving around Upper Darby, right outside of West Philadelphia. The first time I mustered up the courage to enter the store, I thought back to warnings of how the proprietors could "make you feel like you don't know anything." That's kind of how it is, though. When you walk in through that front door, you are living in their world, playing by their rules. But, oh, what a world it is. ¶ I had wanted to replace a record that had "mysteriously disappeared" after a gig in Las Vegas. Intent on getting another copy, I walked in, and, immediately, stacks and stacks of 12-inch vinyl surrounded me. Above the stacks of wax were walls that had old eight-by-ten glossy photos of bands I've never heard of, and gold records for songs that I didn't know existed. There was a counter that separated the front part of the store from the unbelievable rows of 7-inch wax in the back. Two guys were concentrating on pulling records from the walls and a third guy was talking on the phone, calling for records from the other two while trying to take notes and sort small stacks of 45s. The man, an average looking White guy in his mid-fifties, looks up at me with a cold gaze and says, "What do you need?" ¶ I felt as though my very presence in their store was fucking up their program, so I, not one to make waves at all, humbly cleared my throat. "Um, do you have Freddie Scott's 'You Got What I Need' on 45?" Without even batting an eye he calls back, "Chuck? John? Would one of you guys pull Freddie Scott? He's on the Shout label"—and goes right back to his phone call. They found it, I got it, and was gone. But that was it for me; I knew that I was hooked. And by the way Val looked at me as I left, he knew that I would be back. That was years ago. »

I started coming back on the regular. I've been a 45 hound for almost as long as I've been DJing, which is well over ten years, yet funk 45s—at least the real choice ones—never really made themselves available. So now I decided it was time to catch up on all that I had missed. My first goal was to replace all the songs that I had been playing out as a DJ on LP or 12-inch to 45. I've been doing this for way too long. I have bad legs and knees, and I don't feel like carrying these damn crates anymore. Plus, to be honest with you, it just looks so damn cool. My second goal was to grab all the records that I knew about but didn't have. These guys seemed to really know their music, so I figured that I'd start coming in with my want lists. The third goal, one that I never thought that I would be in a position to follow through with, was to get behind that counter and start getting my hands dirty in those immense piles of records, just looking for something, anything, everything.

I became a fixture around the shop to a degree. Customers were usually looking for one or two oldies: a Flamingos here, a Heartbeats there. I would watch as many a mobile DJ would come in and get records for weddings and anniversaries. Occasionally there would be the obvious beat-head asking for particular records, or some odd British cat with a laundry list of northern soul. I always wondered how in the hell they could keep track of anything. Val's desk is covered with a thousand little slips of paper, various 45s, and half-full soda bottles. He wouldn't have it any other way though, as it's a perfect organizational technique for him. He knows where everything is in a New York minute. This self-proclaimed control freak needs to always have his hands on every part of the business. I eventually learned that all the records on the shelves were sorted by label. If you didn't know what label the record you were looking for was on, it made the search for it that much tougher, no matter what other information you had on it.

I went up to Val's a couple of days after 9/11. I had stressed myself over the whole situation, especially since I spent the entire first day trying to get in contact with my brother, an NYU film student. One thing that calms me down and helps me forget my troubles is digging through old stacks of records, and I figured that Val's was the perfect place to partake in such meditation. Everybody was out of it that week, including Val, who I could see was visibly distracted when I walked in the store. With the lack of business, and the innate need for communication that the situation instilled in everyone at that time, we got to rapping. Under the stern gaze of his steely eyes there was a hell of a lot more to this man.

Val Shively grew up with stern parents in the Upper Darby neighborhood of Philadelphia, a working class neighborhood in the '50s. "Since I can remember, music was the thing," he says. "I started buying pop records in 1956, mostly listening to White pop stations like WIBG, which was the big station in this town. Everybody listened to that. When I heard something that I liked, like Bobby Darin's 'Splish Splash,' which came out in 1957, I would wait for them to come off of the jukeboxes. It would cost a dollar [for a new] record, which was a lot of money for me, especially back then. I knew where all the jukebox operators were, so I would wait until the records were dead and get them five for a dollar." Val bought up Bobby Darin records, Chuck Berry, Little Richard—"anything that was popular on the radio at the time," he says. "I started buying records like there was no tomorrow." Right then and there, all other hobbies went by the wayside.

"Pretty soon I had thousands and thousands of records, and I was into every aspect of collecting records. The groups, the labels, everything." He made the fledgling steps of his now empire by sell-ing the extra copies of the records that he amassed to his schoolmates. "Around 1959, I decided to curb my record buying by getting a reel-to-reel tape recorder and taping music from my transistor radio. I used to carry this big old transistor around with me all the time. Around the same time, I started to fool with the dial and see what was happening. I said to myself, "I wonder what's going on all the way to the right of the dial?" Black radio, which was relegated to the far end of the radio-wave spectrum, was what he found. "It blew my mind!" he remembers. "The music was far superior. So I spent the entire year of 1960 inside taping songs off the radio, effectively ruining any chance of having a social life.

"I graduated high school in 1961 and started attending Pierce Business School in downtown Philly. All the while I was still raiding the jukebox joints and selling records to kids I knew. But money wasn't the point of me doing it. I just wanted to have the best collection. I loved music, so I wanted to make sure that I had the records that were important to me in my collection." In 1962, a classmate suggested he tune into WCAM, a small radio station that was broadcasted out of Camden, New Jersey, to hear Jerry "the Geator with the Heator" Blavat's show. The Geator was a wild radio broadcaster who modeled his show and on-air antics after legendary radio broadcasters like Philly's Jocko Henderson from WHAT and WDAS AM. Jocko actually got his act from the radio DJ "Hot Rod," who broadcasted out of Baltimore, Maryland, and who is generally considered, by old school heads, as the first rhymer.

"The first night I tuned into the station I was disappointed," Val tells me. "Here was all this Latin crap. Then the kid told me, 'No, you have to tune in late night'—so I did. When I finally heard it, I was like, "What the hell is this?" I mean, I thought I knew shit. I had tons of records, more than anybody, and now all of the sudden I'm hearing records that made me say, "What is this music?" This changed my whole idea of things. So all the old pop records were done, and this was the music that I needed to have. The sound of Black vocal groups really was cemented as the sound of choice for me. The harmonies, the bass, the high notes, all of it."

"So this kid from my class joined me on my quest around the neighborhoods of Philadelphia in search of independent R&B records. We were going downtown to buy some record sleeves one day, and on the way back the kid saw a five-and-dime that had a sign in the window, 'Three records for a dollar.' So you know how that is, especially when your mind is always on the lookout for records. We went racing to get to the crates and start to scour through them." In these crates of wax, Val found two of his most wanted records at the time: "Footstomping, Pt. 1" by the Flares on Felsted and "Just a Lonely Christmas" by the Moonglows on Chance—red vinyl—written by the famous Harvey Fuqua.

Later they passed the Record Museum, a legendary store at 10th and Market Street, which is to this day Philly's best area to get the latest hip-hop and breakbeat records. "It was a Saturday afternoon, and the place was packed with kids raising a ruckus," he remembers. "They were mostly kids around my age and younger, and [on] the walls were lists and lists of records that they were offering money for. Now I thought of myself as Mister Records, and I'm looking over these lists, and I couldn't find almost any title that I recognized." But he did recognize one: the Moonglows—and the Record Museum was offering twelve dollars for it.

"So I said to the guy behind the counter, 'Hey, mister, I got that record.' The guy said to me, 'Yeah? You're full of shit.'" As Val argued with the clerk, who would only give twelve dollars in credit or six dollars in cash, someone kicked him from behind. The guy pulls him to the side and says, "I'll give you ten dollars for that record. Meet me outside in five minutes." Eager to do so, he went outside and completed the sale, elated at the profit margin. Val seemed to feel the adrenaline rush all over again as he told the story.

Six months later, he found out that Philadelphia was "nothing" and that all the activity—"insane craziness," as he calls it—was coming out of a store in New York called Times Square Records. TSR was owned by Irving "Slim" Rose and was located inside a NYC subway station at 42nd and Broadway. "They used to hold all the records on the wall with tape, because when the trains rolled by, the whole place would shake, and they would come falling on the floor." He had no money, but had an incredible drive to obtain new R&B records. Eighteen-year-old Val sold his three thousand records for ten cents apiece to buy these new records. He got on a bus and made the pilgrimage to Times Square and was amazed with how much more music they had. "Here were all these kids, just like in Philly but much more, and they're all packed in the store shouting out for records and writing down the names of the groups and the titles of the songs. It was a real madhouse. In all this madness, some guy looks at me and says, 'You look familiar.' Me, well, I puff out my chest and say, 'I don't think so, man. I'm from Philly!'

"And the guy says, 'That's it! Hey, Slim, here's the asshole from Philly that sold me the [Moonglows] record.'" After he had bought it off Val for ten dollars, he went back into the Record Museum and traded it for two hundred dollars in records.

Val spent the rest of his time at Times Square Records writing down the names and labels of these great records and went back to Philly, where he branched out to North and West Philly, all the way down to Chester and even over to Camden to find these records. Vinyl fever had infected his bloodstream.

Just as he began to rebuild his collection with strictly the choicest R&B records of the early '60s, he moved to Kentucky with his family. Val was being taken away from his friends and his music. "For what?" he asks. "To watch the corn?" But he moved, got a job as an accountant, and became a recluse, shut away from his passion for the world of music. After a year of scrimping and saving, Val made his escape back to Philly. On his arrival, he was greeted with the rude awakening of a changed world. The climate had changed from people being enraptured by the sweet serenades of the street corner symphonies to that of Beatlemania.

Val eventually got a job with wholesale distributor Norman Cooper, who bought all his records from Henry Stone's Tone Distributors out of Florida—home of the Alston, Marlin, Rockin, Cat, and TK imprints, and whose warehouse workers included Harry Wayne Casey, later of KC and the Sunshine Band. Cooper serviced most of the Philadelphia area. Val went from delivering all the latest hits to spots all around Funky North Philly—while doing his own searching and collecting of the finest in independent R&B and soul records—to handling all the duties of working at Cooper's one-stop, from buying the records and keeping the books to hiring help.

Val hired a young saxophone player as a favor to a client. During his lunch hour, the kid would practice on his sax in lieu of eating. "We would tell him, 'Hey, man, don't play that shit. We're trying to eat; you're gonna make us throw up!'" Val remembers treating everything as a big joke. A year later, Val's hired hand, a one Grover Washington Jr., got the opportunity to be a KUDU session player on Johnny Hammond's *Breakout*. Not long afterward, Washington was hired back for another session—but Hammond got arrested in Tennessee for drunk driving. Not to let the studio time go to waste, they recorded material for Washington—yielding the 1971 hit *Inner*

Photo by Bryan Hitch.

Photo by Beth Fladung.

City Blues. Washington worked with Val for about another year before he was able to make a good living on his music.

I sit in amazement of the stories from these long-forgotten times. I sit in awe of this character, and that's in the truest sense of the word "character." A couple of weeks ago Val slipped and broke a bone in his vertebrae. Against the urges of his doctor and his wife to stay in bed and recuperate, he's here in the store wrapping packages, stacking records and holding court for me and about five other people who came to shop and got wrapped up in these stories. It's mesmerizing to watch him move and gesture with his hands as he speaks. "I never thought that I'd work for myself, I always thought that I'd work for [Norman Cooper]," Val tells me.

"The summer of 1972, I went to see my mom down South. I was with this kid from London, who I liked. So I said that he should come with me, and maybe we would look for some records." Val and his British friend go to Nashville, all the while his friend nagging that "there's nothing in Nashville." The two end up at a store called Buckley's, which is filled with 78s. "I hate 78s," Val says. As his friend looks through the 78s, Val finds out that the upstairs holds vinyl. The manager tells Val that nobody has ever been upstairs. "I say, 'What's the price?' and she says, 'Whatever you want to pay. Just don't fall through the ceiling.' So I go upstairs—*tons of records...* records that are legendary. And I'm shaking." When the woman tried to interrupt Val's search—because she had to go home—Val promised her a steak dinner and a ride home to let them stay. "The whole car was full of records. I remember [driving] her home, we stuffed her in someplace!"

Upon his return he found his workplace to be in such disarray that he finally decided to quit and open up his own shop. The mother lode of records that he had just found in Nashville helped bolster his

collection enough so it was finally possible. "I did it for the first six months out of my house, which I thought would be cool. I figured that I could do mail order; I wouldn't have to pay no [store] rent. What do I need a store for? But two things happened. Number one was I never got dressed, I never shaved. I became a recluse. Working in my underwear, I don't have to do shit! So I started to lose sight of the world. And number two was some very shaky people started to come to my house. And my collection is up there, and that's what's really sacred to me—my record collection.

"My goal from the beginning was to have the best record collection. It's not about money. Once I started with the mail order thing I became pretty big with this. If you wanted old records, I was the guy." Around 1971, the old R&B scene exploded in New York. "The only problem," Val tells me, "was that no record shops carried this shit. See it's all timing. This is all happening around the same time. All of the sudden, I'm getting busloads of kids in from New York coming to see me here in Philadelphia. It's like what I used to do was now happening to me. There were two other guys in California. Their names were Henry and Art Mariano out of San Mateo. We were the game.

"I used to put out these mailing lists every now and then with what I had, what I would sell it for, and on the back what I was looking for. Now there was a guy from Detroit who interviewed me for a newspaper but the article never came out. A couple of months later, I went on a cruise with my now wife, and the Mariano brothers and their dates, and when I came back there was no mail in my post office box. The people at the post office pulled me into the back and showed me my mail. It was stacks and stacks and stacks up to the ceiling. I used to get maybe ten, fifteen letters a week."

The reporter had sold the article to the *National Inquirer*. "Old

Photo by Beth Fladung.

records are worth big money," it said. Val remembers reading, "'Everybody's probably got them in their basement. If you want to know what your records are worth, this guy [Val] makes millions of dollars.' It [was] all bullshit! It scared the shit out of me! Man, I thought I was going to jail." Val hired people to sort through the letters and do mail-outs. "My catalogs were free at first. It cost me a buck to make it. I didn't give a shit if you were gonna buy something or not. You might have something I'm looking for. So all these letters are people that wanted catalogs. I ended up getting a half a million letters [from] people with records, and I sent out probably a hundred thousand catalogs. So I did really unbelievably, and I've never had to do another catalog since," Val says.

"When I first started the store in 1972, it was going to be just what I loved, the vocal harmony groups. Then I thought that I should carry all the other stuff, funk, different stuff, so it just started growing. I've made some insane deals with radio stations, jukebox distributors for everything. This guy came by one day with a dump truck with the back filled with dirt and…records. The records were just shoveled in. A store in West Philly collapsed, and they just shoveled [the records] into the truck with the mortar and plaster and glass. All that shit was all funk, all that stuff that people are killing for today. See, back then it meant nothing, but now it's something. That's the way it is. Lawrence Welk could kick off tomorrow for all I know. I've seen it all," he says.

"I love all that oddball shit that nobody pays attention to. I pride myself by making a living off of the industry's mistakes. See, about all that funk stuff, when I see kids coming in—and, see, first of all it's a young thing, you guys are keeping it going. Just like I keep it going in my own world. You know what, young people, the funk, it's exciting to me. It's not where my head is, but you know what,

I can appreciate it, 'cause it's the same deal that I'm into. The same thing, just off-the-wall, oddball shit that nobody paid any attention to. And you guys are making something out of it."

At this point it was dark outside, and I could tell that Val was feeling the effects of such an animated conversation. I decided that I would wrap things up and get on the road. I had a show to do that night anyway so I handed my stack of 45s to Val. He thumbed through them—the Nu-Sound Express's "Ain't It Good Enough" on Silver Dollar; the Parliaments' "Good Old Music" on Revilot; Isley Brothers' "Keep on Doing" on T Neck; Syl Johnson's "Is It Because I'm Black" on Twinight; Minnie Ripperton's "Adventures in Paradise" on Epic—and gave me my price. It was a reasonable price, Val being very fair with me. You see, Val knows what he has; he's no fool. And he knows what he can get for the records that he sells. But he also knows that the value of these records is much more than any price that can be put on a piece of plastic. What he's selling is his passion, his memories and a view into his soul. It's funny how much we have in common. We both share a passion on the verge of madness. But it's a beautiful thang. Like he said to me before, "It's all about the music." A love for this old music—from a buck like me to an O.G. like Val—is truly the greatest common ground that there is. ◗

Originally appeared in Wax Poetics Issue 2, Spring 2002.

"You can only see the flip"
–Human League "Black Hit of Space"

For as Long as that Tick Is Followed by that Boom

by Dave Tompkins

That's it. "Are you an asshole?" That's the hook. That's what the guy at the Trucker's Center Truck Stop said. The 45 is called "The I-95 Asshole Song," cut in 1983 by August and the Spur of the Moment Band for Pantera Records, a Florida label that shared trembling walls with Miami bass imprint Joey Boy. ¶ That A-hole song probably had heavy burn on the Trucker's Center jukebox, which is just off I-85, not 95, in Concord, North Carolina. The restaurant's clientele moved this country novelty single up and across highways through the South, but when they hit North Carolina, I-85 South actually yaws eastward, a Charlie Brown frown across the map. ¶ To make things more dyslexic, the Trucker's Center is off Exit 58 on 85, though it's "tixE 85" in the rear-view mirror, since I missed it and almost got wiped off the road by a rig full of bald chickens, nearly plunging through a billboard advertising an empty promise ("This could be your space here!") but swerving in time to catch the bumper sticker too close to my grill: "Clear, you're behind." ¶ Eyelids peel out to the screech of tires, or the sound of Pharoahe Monch simulating the screech of tires in your tape deck. On Organized Konfusion's "13," Monch goes Truck Turner and burns rubber before yelling, "I'm comin' like a redneck truckah!" His partner Prince Po yells, "Asshole!" like a sideswiped hitchhiker. ¶ Go right off Exit 58 and there's Kannapolis, the small cotton mill town forsook by George Clinton in 1970's "Mommy, What's a Funkadelic?" Eight minutes in, a rust-warbled harmonica makes the humidity shudder as George, not one to watch the paint peel, heads north for Jersey to get his hair laid. »

Photos by Eothen Alapatt.

Whether it's George's flight or a rap blinker that's been on since the Flashformer, disconnection yields too many possibilities. An exit ramp could mean Mothership or Waffle House Theme Song. Take a left off Exit 58, cross the bridge, pass the waffle chunk chili and find yourself in Concord, North Carolina. Pop it out at chewgum speed and Concord sounds like "conquered." Like record.

Textile mills literally owned Kannapolis-Concord and the surrounding Cabarrus County area during the Depression, attracting one-way commuters from as far as Kentucky. Though the mills have since closed, the Phillip Morris plant keeps the sky ashy and nails yellow and clacking. A clip-on tie goes to P.M. and IBM for bringing in more congestion. Other than that, Concord is pretty much strip malls, parched lots, and fast food that'll give you days of thunder.

Trapped among the Drive Thru gut plastic is what used to be the Trucker's Center Truck Stop. Open its ratty screen door today and you'd be entering Ye Olde Clock Shoppe, its mead-sopped English a bit older than the forty-ounce beers sold at Lil' Bucks Mart across the street. When the Clock Shop was a Truck Stop, the floor was more grease licked than the parking lot. Rumor has it that some of this leftover lard sweat was later used to keep the clocks in beat.

The clocks are just a front for all of the used records anyway. There's also some dwarves made of pecan shells but the card says "Gnomes." Either way, all of them watch you look through records, and none tell you where the records came from.

The Clock Shop originally opened in Kannapolis in 1948 without a record to its name, seven years after electric war baby George Clinton was born. In 1971, I-85 opened up, broke the Kannapolis-Concord hyphen and diverted the Trucker's Center's business, forcing the popular restaurant to lock its doors for the first time, for good, in its 24-7-365 life. So the clocks moved across the Route 29

Bridge to Concord and into the Trucker's Center. Once the truck stop's owner finished doing time for tax fraud, he returned to the rheumatic clapboard house next to the Clock Shop and pretty much stayed there until one day he had a coronary and checked out in front of the TV. Still clutching the remote when they found him. His set had signed off too, hissing and bubbling like a deep fryer.

The Clock Shop is the best thing going in Concord, though the nearby Charlotte Motor Speedway would roar otherwise. But what's speed without time for its records? While the time/records thing is more played out than spelling school with a *k*, the Clock Shop is the one place where you can't escape it, the one place where *watch* means "take forever looking and even longer explaining where the hell you were in the first place." "Late for dinner, early for breakfast," as they say. "A clock on my chest proves I don't fess," as Flavor Flav says.

So poke in your nose.

The Clock Shop smells like moldy gold toe-up socks.

Like, creak a window or something.

As expected, the Clock Shop clocks don't do much. Most of them don't work, as if each clock stopped to gnaw a different moment and got its teeth stuck. The lamp cuckoo caught a migraine from the mad bird trapped in its forehead. Every hour, the cuckoo tries to headbutt its way out, softening its mad bird skull on the cute little door.

These mushy thumps recall a DJ from Detroit, Jeff Mills aka "The Wizard." He'd start his old-school electro show with coo-cooing, chiming, working clocks. Then Hashim's vocoder voice would bust out and repeat, "It's time!" Except Wizard would stop the turntable after "It's" so the consequent "t" would slightly drag. Like: "It's *tchw*! It's *tchw*! It's *tchw*!" Like someone was shoving a softball of used Chewels into a robot's mouth for every big league *tchw*!

It's now four *tchws* in the afternoon, and crickets in the back are not impressed. They taunt the cuckoo, feigning endless night with their EPMD cadence, "go-take-a-nap, go-take-a-nap." Meanwhile, the Fiddle Clock's been claiming last call since 1963.

None of this seems to bother the Perpetual Calendar Clock, flat on its back and ripping winks. Its face randomly twitches, dreaming about Waxhaw, maybe Jersey, unaware it may be sleeping on a copy of MC Tatiyana's "Back off Jack" on Clockin' ZZZs Records, mixed by some guy named McKasty from Queens. And Clock Shop clocks don't chime; they clonk, and they only clonk when shoved aside for the records.

The Clock Shop clocks share five thousand square feet with 162,000 used records. That's 150,000 45s, five thousand LPs, and seven thousand 78s. If you're one of the doomed, keep track. Not sure when the last count was, but chances are it was before that guy from PM Dawn came through.

Take a look around. Three-leveled shelves of 45s run along the entire perimeter, where people once sat sawing Salisbury steaks tough as baseball gloves. Now, it's clocks and records all over the damn place. Like a Pink Floyd song, an ELO record cover, a Morris Day group, a Boy George plea, a Leaders of the New School acronym, a bong hit ephiphany ("Duuude, the inner mind's eye!").

In the rear workshop, it's now quarter to cutthroat and clock viscera spills all over the cabinets and tables. Looks like the dwarves cut out a while ago. There are a few dead flies leftover from the kitchen days, but other than that, it's clockguts drawer to floor. Even the clocks on the far wall have been face-lifted, tinkered down to their bare mechanisms. They are "The Movements," the springs, verges, pendulums, and gears designed to run us into the dirt.

There was a day when the Second Movement 45, a breakneck blast of funk, could be found at Ye Olde Clock Shoppe. Even had its own section till some fool ran off with the divider. There was a time when you might catch the Second Movement themselves playing out in nearby Charlotte or Greensboro. Now, it'd drive you nuts in North Carolina looking for either, only to come up with a head rush and a handful of silverfish.

Squeak your eyes with a knuckle and scan the room for now. The sun makes a lazy afternoon play through the blinds and catches the air wiggling suggestively in the gold dust. Kool Keith once said, "I'm Fucking Flipping," and it sure would be good to find a 45 like Eddie Long's "It Don't Make Sense But It Sure Sounds Good." Any song with a three-legged toad riding a one-eyed mule getting bit by an egghead mosquito is a friend of mine.

There's a yellow issue of Famous Monsters of Filmland #105 on the floor, March 1974, Christopher Lee on the cover right after he starred and sang in The Wicker Man, a macabre folk fertility musical. In the back of FM, you could order a record of Ugo Toppo reading "Imp of the Perverse" while waiting for the Wicker Man soundtrack to come out.

If The Wicker Man isn't at the Clock Shop, at least the pecan people will point you to the world's unconfirmed largest pair of underwear, originally fitted for the song "Meet Me with Your Big Black Drawers On." These acrylic ogre undies are nailed to the wall just above the turntable, a sneeze away from a crop duster fashioned from Harley beer cans.

Of course, there's the obvious 45 clock on the wall behind the counter, and, of course, it's the only one here that actually works. It hangs above an old musket that once blew some Jeremiah's toe to tarnation, near a crumpled box of "patron privilege" 45s that includes "Alice, This Ain't Wonderland" and, Lordy, there's the "I-95 Asshole Song."

The 45 clockface is "60 Minute Man," the shag hit by Chairman

of the Board. For our purposes, it should be "There Was A--." Never mind. Wrong place, wrong everything.

Moving right along, watch your step and don't trip on the race car driver gnomes loitering around the vinyl bins. Fashioned from pecan shells and glue, these dwarves were created by a former Professor of Religion at Davidson College, about forty minutes west of Concord and Ye Ole Black Spindle Hole.

Black Holes should recognize White Dwarves, those dense beards of collapsible stars preceding the void, before you fall head over heels for an infinity because all clocks mechanical and biological appear to have stopped. Time is based on light, so you'll be feeling your way around and down forever. Though the Black Hole's time-traveling feature has been analyzed out the Asimov, all astrognomes should go to Concord.

Some Clock Shop stars have collapsed, while others fell off the wagon and passed out in the parking lot: warped, scratched, sleeveless, and mildewed. Forgotten for G-minus-good, because the Clock Shop doesn't give a rip about time and light. Stooping all day at the Clock Shop hurries the dedicated record digger toward his golden years. Some might walk out of there with nothing but a pair of shot kneecaps. One futuristic toymaker would call it "accelerated decrepitude."

With the Clock Shop's sheer vastness, hope and despair run neck and cricked neck, often passing familiar comforts like Black Sabbath's first album. The peach light on its cover blends with the arctic orange glow on the cover of Human League's second and best album, 1980's Travelogue. Each jacket is dusky in different parts of the world. The former has a witch, the latter: a guy on a dog sled.

The dog sled isn't as weird as the cover of Human League's first album, Reproduction, where infants squirm beneath a cracked-glass dance floor. The idea was "nicked" from Samuel R. Delaney's 1967 sci-fi book, The Einstein Intersection, in which a maternity ward appears beneath a polarized dance floor as reminder to restock the population. The droid bop of "Path of Least Resistance" and quantum electrodynamics of "Zero as a Limit" make Reproduction worth the artwork, even to the punks who spit their own blood on the Human League at their gigs.

Travelogue is funkier, allowing you to dance, or stomp, in its cynical face. With deeply affected Korgs and Rolands, the Sheffield quartet's dark sense of humor is cloaked in the midnight dour of their synthesizers. This was before the girls and too many guys joined the group, before the sound went poofier than an exploding seagull. (Though Martin Rushent's later instrumental remix of "Things That Dreams Are Made Of" deserves Big Bird status.)

Along with Mick Ronson ("Only After Dark") and Solzhenitsyn, TV was the muse of Travelogue. An ad for Gordon's Gin, a children's show about a crow and a hamster, a documentary about boiling silk worms, and "James Burke's Connections"—a late-night BBC science-history program that inspired "Black Hit of Space," Human League's song about a song that swallows up all the songs and record stores in the universe. You'd think the Black Hit would've swallowed the gadzillion copies sold of Human League's hit "Don't You Want Me," a hit yet to happen from Dare, the last album Lester Bangs heard before he died. Nonetheless, a temporal eating disorder shouldn't keep the Black Hit from its repast. Our former truck stop must've given it some serious reflux ticker burn.

It doesn't say anything about this in Phil Oakey's lyrics printed on the back cover of Travelogue. It does say, "Someone stopped the clock when they should've started early," but that's four tracks down from "Black Hit" on "Dreams of Leaving," a cut that runs on Gulag time, vanishing into itself as Stalin filled his black hole of a soul with the blood of his people.

"Black Hit of Space," on the other hand, is about being paranoid of one's record player. For reasons none other than "space," Phil's spoken part is missing from the back sleeve. According to the song, Phil is just trying to eat a sandwich and listen to a record when suddenly the lights go out and the blandest song ever goes on forever. Then, in a hungover pallbearer's voice, Oakey reaches for a turntable arm "one micron long weighing more than Saturn."

"I don't know if that's heavy enough to make it a White Dwarf," wonders Phil Oakey, now sucked into this mess through a phone box in Sheffield, England. "The turntable arm might not be heavy enough to be a Black Hole. I've always been wary of people who put science fiction in their records. Especially synth records, because it seemed a bit too obvious."

Serious words coming a guy whose "all-time favorite monster" is Creature from the Black Lagoon, "the fishiest folk-hero from the '50s," according to *Famous Monster* editor Forrest J. Ackerman.

Recorded in an old veterinary building full of empty hutches and brown bugs, "Black Hit of Space" begins with stark clap echo and meteor pebbles plunking into a well of pet bones. You then spiral into synthesizer feedback, not new wave but a tarn dark one that pulls you under with a warbling Stranglehold undertow. The song was originally "I Held You Underwater," and, save for the draconian electro of "Being Boiled," (same album, other side, evil trumpet), "Black Hit" may be the group's funkiest cut. The frazzled stabs during the sandwich part suggest El-P's robot cat hissing on the fritz.

"It's one of the most powerful records, rhythmically, that we ever did," says Phil, a man who once wished he had wing mirrors on his mic stand. "I still feel very proud of it—though why I should, I don't know, because I didn't do the rhythm—that was Ian Marsh. But it was before digital reverbs, so it must've been the room we were in. Or something." So Phil started sleeping at the old vet while maintaining his orderly gig at a plastic surgery hospital.

The notion for "Black Hit of Space" came over pancakes at the Nameless Restaurant in Sheffield, not far from the forsaken animal lab. "The restaurant was like the Human League in that it had slides. We were very boring onstage, so we had slides. They had equally random upside-down slides. We were talking to Giovanni Dadomo [English journalist and member of punk group Sniveling Shits] about a BBC science program we'd seen. Peter Ustinov was trying to explain the quantum world, using his twin brother as a special effect. One took off in a spaceship, and one stayed on Earth. And they tried to describe the things that would happen with time slowing down. Ideas about the collapse of space were coming up. As you approach the speed of light, you can see the back of an object before you see the front of an object. I thought that would be good. I wouldn't mind seeing the back of things before I saw the front. But I never liked Peter Ustinov really."

At the end of the song, the Black Hit continues to gorge, and Phil wants out, saying, "*Every time I tried to flee, the record was in front of me,*" perhaps trying to escape that waitress in the cocktail bar he's yet to meet. "Right," he recalls. "You're moving so fast that instead of going away from something, you end up going towards it. Like one of those songs you can't stand that's all over radio, no matter how fast you switch the dial."

With its oafish silver knobs, the clock shop stereo looks like a throwback from Dr. Who's stoop sale. *Travelogue* is safely in the hutch, and I'm now faced with "Black Hole Bop," a 1983 electro 12-inch by X-25. Projected from speakers on opposite walls, "Black Hole Bop" sounds good in the Clock Shop, two android pilots con-

versing across a room of decay. A vocoder crackles from the far right: "I am now proceeding toward my destination: the Black Hole." Then the beat drops and bounces off the Busch beer drum clock.

Then a voice dragged by Winston smoke says, "I think we're from different eras, son."

It doesn't come from the speaker but behind the counter near the musket. There's Clock Shop/Black Hole "operator" Bill Arey. Bill ain't no pecan-shell race-car driver gnome. He has a dog, and he's never done the "Black Hole Bop." Bill says he hasn't heard a real tune since Glenn Miller did "In the Mood," before Glen Miller's plane mysteriously vanished in the English Channel in 1944.

Bill knows I've entered the Clock Shop equivalent to a Black Hole's irresistible "Schwartzshield Radius," meaning the hope of pulling another X-25, or a Section 25, or anything on 25 Ta Life, pulls me in for good.

Bill snickers, "Even a blind pig can find an acorn now and then." I cough a mummy's stale air. "Be careful, Dave. That's ain't dust. That's real estate."

At seventy-eight, Bill can make lore out of stories, and his Winston Light's been burning longer than the vinyl itch that got us here. His pollen golf shirt fades like filtered afternoon, while a red windbreaker suits his face and good-natured saltiness. The snarl of gray fishing twine on his head seems partially blown off. Bill looks like the kind of man who rides with the windows down, petting the wind, making waves, and thinking about the girl who said she liked the ocean.

Stick the whole arm out, and the wind winds it counterclockwise. Bill will tell you that, every Saturday, he used to wind every clock in the Clock Shop until his arm fell off.

When the Clock Shop moved to Concord, Bill turned the business over to his son Reid, who then started buying out record collections whenever possible. A "blue baby" born with a rare congenital heart defect, Reid Arey passed in April of 2000, at the absurd age of twenty-six. Doctors called his condition a "Tetralogy of Flow." "He couldn't play outside with other kids, but he never complained," says his father. "He was inside taking things apart and putting them together. When he was twelve, I bought him a Wall Regulator Clock advertising Orange Crush. Next thing I knew, it was in pieces on his bed. Reid said he wanted to see what made it tick. About an hour later, he had it back on the wall running."

In addition to playing doctor with clocks, Reid Arey bought a lot of records. "His thing was shag music," says Bill, remembering when his son would sell 45s outside Ducks, a beach club in South Carolina. "People would bring in collections, or Reid would go out and find them. He knew what to do with every record."

Somehow, in between making shag bootlegs and making people's collections disappear, Reid ran across one of the most innovative Miami bass records ever, Ladi Luv's "Good to the Last Dub." Fifteen-year-old Salenthia "Ladi Luv" Clayton recorded for Joey Boy Records in 1989, right next to the label that released "The I-95 Asshole Song," and above the plant that pressed Luke Skyywalker records by the truckload. This B-side peach was scrambled and quadified by Joey Boy engineer Carlos Santos, an outdoor enthusiast who accidentally shot up the private game reserve of Salenthia's daddy, Sheriff Clayton, while under the influence of some species of moonshine that made the flies fall dead from the sky.

As I hold my Ladi Luv, Bill Arey talks about some guy from Rhonda, North Carolina, the birthplace of stock car racing and moonshine. Apparently, he once came into the Clock Shop with a box of bluegrass records and a case of 160-proof corn liquor. "He said, 'I got somethin' for you,' and unloads a case of moonshine flavored with

apricots and cherries. Nice guy. Almost lost his foot from diabetes."

Bill sighs some smoke. "But we can't sell that stuff."

So you gave it back?

"No. I said we just can't sell it."

Bill also had to take down the fluorescent beer signs in the Clock Shop's window, because people would come in expecting a bar. "I'd say, 'No, but I'll give you a beer if you want one.'"

A guy who smells like the bar that wasn't there comes in looking for Southern rock videos, preferably the Outlaws or Rossington-Collins. A few seconds later, the door jingles with his empty-handed departure, and Bill shrugs. Bill's helped many people get to their grits and some digging extremists have asked to be locked in the Clock Shop overnight. How long do we have, anyway?

"When I unlock the door, I'm open," he flattens. "When I lock the door, I'm closed." Bill doesn't recognize Truck Stop hours.

Ask Bill Arey if he can tell time and, in a voice gravellier than his

parking lot, he'll answer, "Nope."

Nope?

"And I don't buy green bananas, because I don't know if I'm gonna be here tomorrow."

More smoke, more silence, and no ticks. Arey stares at Lil' Bucks across the street, where Outlaw is now slumped by the ice machine.

"You know, after four surgeries had kept him alive, Reid's body started failing, and he had to stay in bed. One time, his sister and mother were in the room talking and Reid got out of bed and stared at the clock on the wall. He crooked his neck and was concentrating really hard. They kept talking, and Reid kept staring. Finally, he said, 'Would you please be quiet. I'm going to put this clock in beat.' So Reid set the beat right. And that was the last time he got out of bed. You see, that clock was going *ticka-tocka-ticka-tocka-ticka-tocka*." ❍

Originally appeared in Wax Poetics Issue 5, Summer 2003.

Home Improvement

written and illustrated by Alberto Forero

It starts out small enough: a record here, two records there. First you make a pile near your turntables. Then, the pile gets pretty big and you look for a crate. It seems like the milk company finally got hip to the popularity of milk crates for holding things other than milk, and now all you can find are 10" crates behind your grocery store. I once considered hiring a carpenter to build some wooden shelves or boxes. I mean, how complicated or expensive could that be? Cut the wood, nail it together; you're done, right? Wrong. I called half a dozen places and ended up with quotes from $250 to $800—for six, no frills, 13" plywood cubes. I thought, there has to be a better way. And there is: you do it yourself. I haven't done a lot of carpentry, but I was able to make some nice record cube shelves for about $10 apiece, and here's how.

CHECKLIST OF SUPPLIES (ENOUGH FOR SIX RECORD CUBES)

- Hammer
- One 8 oz. tube of "PL Premium Wood Glue" or similar ($5)
- One box of "Grip-Rite Fas'ners" 4d or similar 1½" nails. ($1.50)
- Three 4' × 4', ½"-thick plywood sheets ($15 each)
- One 2' × 4', ½"-thick plywood sheet ($8)
- An old sheet

THE DESIGN

I decided on cubes because they are modular, move around easily, and can form together for different-shaped shelving units. Also, with cubes I could have a platform for my tables and mixer as well. And one cube will comfortably fit eighty-five LPs.

I drew out a plan. This was pretty easy, since they're just cubes. I figured I'd need a little extra space at the top to easily get records in and out, so I designed a space 14" high and 13" wide and 13" deep. The side pieces fit between the top and bottom of the cube in a "post and lintel" form [**fig. 1**], able to support a lot of weight. I designed a cube that had a top, bottom, and back made from 14" × 14" pieces, and the two sides made from 14" × 13" pieces [**fig. 2**].

A TRIP TO THE HARDWARE STORE

I went to Home Depot and saw that wood is nice, but it's expensive and heavy. That's when I checked out the plywood: cheap, sturdy, relatively light, and not bad looking, especially when you're basically seeing only the edges of it. I used ½"-thick plywood—you can buy a 4' × 4' sheet for $15, or a 2' × 4' sheet for $8. If you get three of the 4' × 4' sheets and one of the 2' × 4' sheets, you will have enough plywood to make six record boxes, plus have a few extra pieces in case you mess up. That works out to twenty 14" × 14" pieces and thirteen of the 14" × 13" pieces once cut. Home Depot charges fifty cents per cut, so for six boxes, you're looking at about $12 in cutting charges. Bring a diagram showing exactly how you want the wood cut [**fig. 3**].

PUTTING THE CUBE TOGETHER, STEP BY STEP

When you're constructing the cubes, it's good to lay an old sheet or towel on the ground so that you don't get the glue all over the place. But watch that the boxes don't dry connected to the sheet. I also found it helpful to mark the connecting ends of the pieces with an X. The pieces look pretty similar, so it's good to put the box together methodically. Once you make one, however, it's pretty obvious.

When attaching each piece, I picked the better-looking side, one with less splinters or dirt, and placed it facing outside. Don't worry if you hammer a nail in and see it start to come out the side of the wood—just pull it out and start over a ¼" from where you

Figure 1

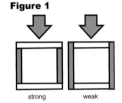

strong   weak

Figure 2

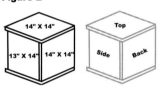

Figure 3

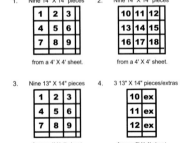

1. Nine 14" X 14" pieces from a 4' X 4' sheet.
2. Nine 14" X 14" pieces from a 4' X 4' sheet.
3. Nine 13" X 14" pieces from a 4' X 4' sheet.
4. 3 13" X 14" pieces/extras from a 2' X 4' sheet.

Figure 4

(back)

Figure 5

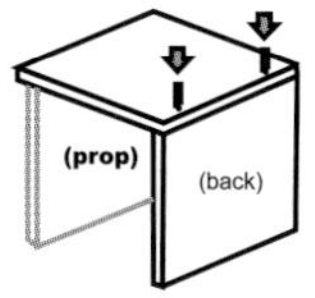

Figure 6

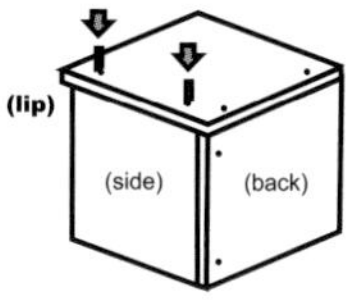

Figure 7

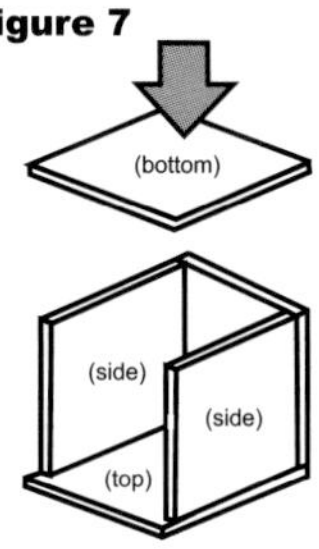

Figure 8

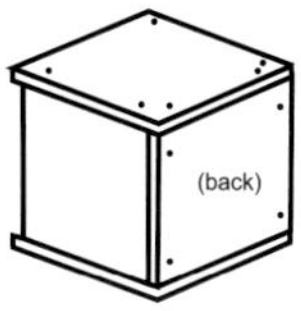

Figure 9

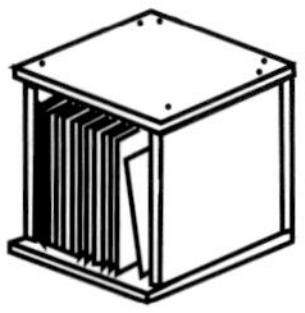

were hammering—you probably won't see the original hole because you're not looking at the inside or the side of the cube. And if you leave that sharp nail sticking out on the inside, you run the risk of slicing up that mint copy of *Afro-Harping* you just found for fifty cents at a garage sale.

Make sure that the edges of your box are as level as possible and line up at nice tight corners. The guy who was cutting my wood cut a few of pieces a ½" off or so, but I found that with a little careful positioning, almost all of my boxes were solid (no gaps at edges), and, again, if your box is slightly off, no one's ever going to notice.

1. Take the back piece (14" × 14") and hold it vertically [**fig. 4**].
2. Add a thin line of glue on the top edge of the back piece.
3. Place the top piece (14" × 14") on top of the back piece and line it up with the back edge. To keep the top piece level, temporarily prop another 14" × 14" piece under the front edge [**fig. 5**].
4. Holding the top piece perpendicular to the back piece, hammer one nail through the top into the center of the back piece, about 2" from each side.
5. Place a side piece (14" × 13") against the top and back. There should be a ½" lip of the top reaching over the side; that's fine—it will be a little dust cover on the front of your box. Add a thin line of glue on the top and the side of this piece, press it into the top and back, and then hammer in nails 2" from each edge on top, watching to make sure that things stay lined up [**fig. 6**]. Then turn the box with the back side up, and hammer two more nails to connect the back and side piece.
6. Do the same thing for the other side.
7. Flip your box on its top, and add glue around the three edges [**fig. 7**].
8. Take the bottom piece (14" × 14") and place it opposite the top to complete the box [**fig. 7**].
9. Hammer two nails in each of the three sides [**fig. 8**].
10. Now that you have the box put together, apply a thin line of glue on every inside edge of the box, just to make it extra sturdy.
11. Set the box aside. Once the glue is relatively dry (thirty minutes), put a pile of records or books on top of the box, just to make sure that the pieces dry firmly together.
12. The finished box [**fig. 9**].

NOTES

Don't put the records in before the glue has completely dried or they'll never leave the box; let the glue dry overnight. I found that I put a bit too much glue on the first time, which then left hard bumps on the insides of the box, making it harder to slide records in easily. I recommend using a minimum of glue (the nails will suffice). You could always sand off excess glue later—but this is supposed to be a simple project. It took me about an hour to put together the first box, but the others went faster. If the hammering gets too noisy, you can put an old towel or sheet in the box, drummer style, to muffle the sound a bit. (Unfortunately, this didn't stop me from getting a noise complaint.) And you can stain or paint the cubes if you are more ambitious. ◉

Originally appeared in Wax Poetics Issue 1, December 2001.

Appendix

IDRIS MUHAMMAD SELECTED DISCOGRAPHY

Black Rhythm Revolution! (Prestige) 1970

Peace and Rhythm (Salam Wa Nagama) (Prestige) 1971

Power of Soul (Kudu) 1974

House of the Rising Sun (Kudu) 1975

Turn This Mutha Out (Kudu) 1977

Boogie to the Top (Kudu) 1978

You Aint No Friend of Mine (Fantasy) 1978

Fox Huntin' (Fantasy) 1979

Make It Count (Fantasy) 1980

Kabsha (Theresa) 1980

My Turn (Lipstick) 1993

Right Now (Cannonball) 1998

Nat Adderley *Calling Out Loud* (A&M/CTI) 1968

Gene Ammons *Black Cat* (Prestige) 1970

Gene Ammons *My Way* (Prestige) 1970

Gene Ammons with Sonny Stitt *You Talk That Talk* (Prestige) 1971

Amiri Baraka *It's Nation Time* (Black Forum) 1972

George Benson *Other Side of Abbey Road* (CTI) 1970

Walter Bishop, Jr. *Coral Keys* (Black Jazz) 1971

Luiz Bonfá *Jacaranda* (Ranwood) 1973

Rusty Bryant *Soul Liberation* (Prestige) 1970

Rusty Bryant *Fire Eater* (Prestige) 1971

Rusty Bryant *Wildfire* (Prestige) 1971

Rusty Bryant *Friday Night Funk for Saturday Night Brothers* (Prestige) 1973

Gary Chandler *Outlook* (Eastbound) 1972

Merry Clayton *Keep Your Eye on the Sparrow* (Ode) 1975

Hank Crawford *Help Me Make It Through the Night* (Kudu) 1972

Hank Crawford *Wildflower* (CTI) 1973

Hank Crawford *Don't You Worry 'Bout a Thing* (CTI) 1974

Paul Desmond *Summertime* (CTI) 1968

Lou Donaldson *Alligator Bogaloo* (Blue Note) 1967

Lou Donaldson *Mr. Shing-A-Ling* (Blue Note) 1967

Lou Donaldson *Midnight Creeper* (Blue Note) 1968

Lou Donaldson *Say It Loud!* (Blue Note) 1968

Lou Donaldson *Everything I Play Is Funky* (Blue Note) 1969

Lou Donaldson *Hot Dog* (Blue Note) 1969

Lou Donaldson *Pretty Things* (Blue Note) 1970)

Lou Donaldson *Cosmos* (Blue Note) 1971

Lou Donaldson *Sassy Soul Strut* (Blue Note) 1973

Lou Donaldson *Scorpion: Live at the Cadillac Club* (Blue Note) 1995

Charles Earland *Black Talk!* (Prestige) 1969

Pee Wee Ellis *Home in the Country* (Savoy) 1976

Fania All-Stars *Social Change* (Fania) 1981

Roberta Flack *Feel Like Makin' Love* (Atlantic) 1975

Dean Fraser *Big Up!* (Island) 1998

Ceasar Frazier *Hail Ceasar!* (Eastbound) 1972

Eric Gale *Forecast* (Kudu) 1973

Grant Green *Carryin' On* (Blue Note) 1969

Grant Green *Alive!* (Blue Note) 1970

Grant Green *Green Is Beautiful* (Blue Note) 1970

Grant Green *Visions* (Blue Note) 1971

Gene Harris and the Three Sounds *Self-Titled* (Blue Note) 1971

Andrew Hill *Grass Roots* [previously unreleased] (Blue Note) 1969

Richard "Groove" Holmes *Good Vibrations* (Muse) 1977

Richard "Groove" Holmes *Shippin' Out* (Muse) 1978

Freddie Hubbard *New Colors* (Hip Bop) 2001

Bobbi Humphrey *Flute In* (Blue Note) 1971

J & K *Betwixt & Between* (A&M/CTI) 1969

Willis "Gator Tail" Jackson *Bar Wars* (Muse) 1977

Willis "Gator Tail" Jackson *Single Action* (Muse) 1978

Bob James *One* (CTI) 1974

Bob James *Touchdown* (Columbia) 1978

Bob James *Lucky Seven* (Columbia) 1979

Bob James *All Around the Town* (Columbia) 1981

Rodney Jones *Soul Manifesto* (Blue Note) 2001

Charles Kynard *Wa-Tu-Wa-Zui* (Prestige) 1970

Ron Levy *Zim Zam Zoom: Acid Blues on B-3* (Bullseye Blues) 1996

Ron Levy's Wild Kingdom *Greaze Is What's Good* (Cannonball) 1998

Wilbert Longmire *Champagne* (CBS) 1979

Harold Mabern *Wailin'* (Prestige) 1969

Harold Mabern *Greasy Kid Stuff!* (Prestige) 1970

Galt MacDermot *Woman Is Sweeter* (Kilmarnock) 1969

Galt MacDermot *Haircuts* (Kilmarnock) 1969

Galt MacDermot's First Natural Hair Band *Self-Titled* (United Artists) 1970

Galt MacDermot *Up From the Basement* (Kilmarnock) 2000

Bill Mason *Gettin' Off* (Eastbound) 1972

David "Fathead" Newman *Concrete Jungle* (Prestige) 1976

David "Fathead" Newman *Keep the Dream Alive* (Prestige) 1977

Don Patterson *Why Not* (Muse) 1978

Houston Person *Person to Person* (Prestige) 1970

Houston Person *Real Thing* (Eastbound) 1973

Pharoah Sanders *Jewels of Thought* (Impulse!) 1969

Pharoah Sanders *Journey to the One* (Theresa) 1980

Shirley Scott *Lean On Me* (Cadet) 1972

Horace Silver *That Healin' Feelin'* (Blue Note) 1970

Lonnie Smith *Turning Point* (Blue Note) 1969

Melvin Sparks *Sparks!* (Prestige) 1970

Melvin Sparks *Spark Plug* (Prestige) 1971

Melvin Sparks *Akilah* (Prestige) 1973

Melvin Sparks *Texas Twister* (Eastbound) 1973

Melvin Sparks *'75* (Westbound) 1975

Leon Spencer *Sneak Preview* (Prestige) 1970

Leon Spencer *Louisiana Slim* (Prestige) 1971

Leon Spencer *Where I'm Coming From* (Prestige) 1972

Leon Spencer *Bad Walking Woman* (Prestige) 1972

Sonny Stitt *Turn It On* (Prestige) 1971

Sonny Stitt *Black Vibrations* (Prestige) 1971

Sonny Stitt *Goin' Down Slow* (Prestige) 1972

Fats Theus *Black Out* (CTI) 1970

Stanley Turrentine *Common Touch* (Blue Note) 1968

Stanley Turrentine *Don't Mess with Mister T.* (CTI) 1973

Stanley Turrentine *The Man with the Sad Face* (Fantasy) 1976

Grover Washington Jr. *Inner City Blues* (Kudu) 1971

Grover Washington Jr. *Soul Box* (Kudu) 1973
Reuben Wilson *Love Bug* (Blue Note) 1969
Various Artists *Hair (The Original Broadway Cast Recording)* (RCA) 1968
Various Artists *The Lost Grooves* (Blue Note) 1995
Various Artists *Blue Note Rare Grooves* (Blue Note) 1996

BERNARD "PRETTY" PURDIE SELECTED DISCOGRAPHY

Soul Drums (Date) 1967
Purdie Good (Prestige) 1971
Stand by Me (Whatcha See Is Whatcha Get) (Mega) 1971
Soul Is...Pretty Purdie (Flying Dutchman) 1972
Shaft (Prestige) 1972
Lialeh (Original Movie Soundtrack) (Bryan) 1974
Coolin' 'n Groovin' (West 47th) 1995
In Tokyo (West 47th) 1995
Master Drummers, Volume I (Luv N' Haight) 1995
Master Drummers, Volume 2 (Ubiquity) 1996
Bernard Purdie's Soul to Jazz (Act) 1996
Bernard Purdie's Soul to Jazz II (Act) 1997

Harold Alexander *Sunshine Man* (Flying Dutchman) 1971
Harold Alexander *Are You Ready?* (Flying Dutchman) 1972
Gene Ammons *The Boss Is Back* (Prestige) 1969
Gene Ammons *Brother Jug!* (Prestige) 1970
Louis Armstrong *Louis Armstrong and His Friends* (Flying Dutchman) 1970
Roy Ayers Ubiquity *Change Up the Groove* (Polydor) 1974
Roy Ayers Ubiquity *A Tear to a Smile* (Polydor) 1975
Roy Ayers *Ubiquity Vibrations* (Polydor) 1976
Albert Ayler *New Grass* (Impulse!) 1968
Bama the Village Poet *Ghettos of My Mind* (Aware) 1974
Gato Barbieri *El Gato* (Flying Dutchman) 1971
Salome Bey *Sings Songs from Dude* (Kilmarnock) 1973
Michael Bolotin *Self-Titled* (RCA) 1975
Randy Brecker *Score* (Solid State) 1969
Charlie Brown *Why Is Everybody Always Pickin' on Me* (Contact) 1972
James Brown *It's a Man's Man's Man's World* (King) 1966
Oscar Brown *Movin' On* (Atlantic) 1972
Rusty Bryant *Night Train Now!* (Prestige) 1969
Rusty Bryant *Until It's Time For You to Go* (Prestige) 1974
Buari *Self-Titled* (RCA) 1975
Gary Burton *Good Vibes* (Atlantic) 1970
Billy Butler *Plays Via Galactica* (Kilmarnock) 1973
Charlie Byrd *The Great Byrd* (Columbia) 1969
Charlie Byrd *Aquarius* (Columbia) 1971
Bobby Callendar *Rainbow* (Boston Sound) 1969
Larry Coryell *Coryell* (Vanguard) 1969
Larry Coryell *Fairyland* (Mega) 1971
Joe Cocker *Luxury You Can Afford* (A&M) 1978
Hank Crawford *It's a Funky Thing to Do* (Atlantic/Cotillion) 1970
Hank Crawford *Help Me Make It Through the Night* (KUDU) 1972
Hank Crawford *Don't You Worry 'Bout a Thing* (KUDU) 1974
Hank Crawford *I Hear a Symphony* (KUDU) 1975
Wild Bill Davis *Doin' His Thing* (RCA) 1967

Miles Davis *Get Up With It* (Columbia) 1975
Wayne Davis *A View From Another Place* (Atlantic) 1973
Lou Donaldson *Sweet Lou* (Blue Note) 1974
Cornell Dupree *Teasin'* (Atlantic) 1974
Pee Wee Ellis *Home in the Country* (Savoy) 1977
Roberta Flack *Quiet Fire* (Atlantic) 1971
Roberta Flack & Donny Hathaway *Self-Titled* (Atlantic) 1972
Ronnie Foster *Sweet Revival* (Blue Note) 1973
Aretha Franklin *Young, Gifted & Black* (Atlantic) 1971
Aretha Franklin *Let Me in Your Life* (Atlantic) 1974
Aretha Franklin *With Everything I Feel in Me* (Atlantic) 1974
Caesar Frazier *'75* (Westbound) 1975
Nikki Giovanni *The Way I Feel* (Niktom) 1975
Benny Golson *Tune In, Turn On* (Verve) 1967
Daryl Hall/John Oates *Abandoned Luncheonette* (Atlantic) 1973
Herbie Hancock *Fat Albert Rotunda* (WB) 1969
Ellerine Harding *Ellerine* (Mainstream) 1972
Eddie Harris & Les McCann *Second Movement* (Atlantic) 1971
Richard "Groove" Holmes *Night Glider* (Groove Merchant) 1973
Richard "Groove" Holmes *New Groove* (Groove Merchant) 1973
John Lee Hooker *Simply the Truth* (One Way) 1969
Freddie Hubbard *A Soul Experiment* (Atlantic) 1969
The Insect Trust *Self-Titled* (Capitol) 1968
The Insect Trust *Hoboken Saturday Night* (Atco) 1970
Dizzy Gillespie *Cornucopia* (Solid State) 1970
"Boogaloo" Joe Jones *Boogaloo Joe* (Prestige) 1969
"Boogaloo" Joe Jones *Right On, Brother!* (Prestige) 1970
"Boogaloo" Joe Jones *No Way!* (Prestige) 1971
"Boogaloo" Joe Jones *What It Is* (Prestige) 1972
Quincy Jones *Walking in Space* (A&M) 1969
Quincy Jones *Body Heat* (A&M) 1974
King Curtis *Live at Fillmore West* (Atco) 1971
King Curtis *Everybody's Talkin'* (Atco) 1972
B.B. King *Completely Well* (ABC) 1970
B.B. King *Guess Who* (MCA) 1972
Rahsaan Roland Kirk *Blacknuss* (Atlantic) 1971
Al Kooper *You Never Know Who Your Friends Are* (Columbia) 1969
Charles Kynard *Reelin' with the Feelin'* (Prestige) 1969
Charles Kynard *Afro-Disiac* (Prestige) 1970
Charles Kynard *Wa-Tu-Wa-Zui* (Prestige) 1970
The Last Poets *Delights of the Garden* (Douglas/Casablanca) 1977
Yusef Lateef *Yusef Lateef's Detroit* (Atlantic) 1969
Yusef Lateef *The Diverse Lateef* (Atlantic) 1970
Lightnin' Rod *Hustler's Convention* (Douglas Collection/UA) 1973
Love Child's Afro Cuban Blues Band *Self-titled* (Roulette) 1975
Herbie Mann *Push Push* (Embryo) 1971
Masters of Groove *Masters of Groove Meet Dr. No* (Jazzateria) 2001
Les McCann *Invitation to Openness* (Atlantic) 1972
Freddie McCoy *Funk Drops* (Prestige) 1965
Freddie McCoy *Listen Here* (Prestige) 1968
Galt MacDermot *Shapes of Rhythm* (Kilmarnock) 1966
Galt MacDermot *Hair Pieces* (Verve) 1967
Galt MacDermot *Woman Is Sweeter* (Kilmarnock) 1969

Galt MacDermot *Cotton Comes to Harlem* (UA) 1970

Galt MacDermot *Two Gentlemen of Verona* (Kilmarnock) 1970

Galt MacDermot *The Nucleus* (Kilmarnock) 1971

Galt MacDermot *Ghetto Suite* (Kilmarnock) 1972

Galt MacDermot *Isabel's a Jezebel* (Cast Recording) (UA) 1972

Galt MacDermot *Take this Bread/A Mass in Our Time* (Kilmarnock) 1973

Galt MacDermot *Dude/The Highway Life* (Kilmarnock) 1973

Galt MacDermot *Karl Marx Play* (Kilmarnock) 1973

Galt MacDermot *La Novela* (Kilmarnock) 1976

Galt MacDermot with Pretty Purdie & Bad Bascomb *Live in Nashville* (Kilmarnock) 2000

Galt MacDermot *Up from the Basement* (Kilmarnock) 2000

Galt MacDermot *More from the Basement* (Kilmarnock) 2002

Gary McFarland *America the Beautiful* (Gryphon) 1968

Jimmy McGriff/Groove Holmes *Come Together* (Groove Merchant) 1973

Jimmy McGriff *Supa Cookin'* (Groove Merchant) 1973

Fergus MacRoy *Almost an Hour with Fergus MacRoy* (Kilmarnock) 1973

John Murtaugh *Blues Current* (Polydor) 1970

Oliver Nelson *Swiss Suite* (Flying Dutchman) 1971

David "Fathead" Newman *Bigger & Better* (Atlantic) 1968

David "Fathead" Newman *The Many Facets of David Newman*(Atlantic) 1969

David "Fathead" Newman *Captain Buckles* (Atlantic) 1971

David "Fathead" Newman *This Is the Weapon* (Atlantic) 1973

Frank Owens *Brown'n Serve* (Encounter) 1973

Ralfi Pagán *I Can See* (Fania) 1975

Johnny Pate *Outrageous* (MGM) 1970

Houston Person *Houston Express* (Prestige) 1971

Esther Phillips *From a Whisper to a Scream* (KUDU) 1972

Esther Phillips *Alone Again, Naturally* (KUDU) 1972

Esther Phillips *Performance* (KUDU) 1974

Sonny Phillips *Sure 'Nuff* (Prestige) 1969

Sonny Phillips *Black on Black* (Prestige) 1970

Seldon Powell *Messin' with Seldon Powell* (Encounter) 1973

Profile *Sands of Time* (Encounter) 1973

Pucho & the Latin Soul Brothers *Heat!* (Prestige) 1968

Pucho & the Latin Soul Brothers *Jungle Fire!* (Prestige) 1970

Chuck Rainey Coalition *Self-Titled* (Skye) 1972

The Charlie Rouse Band *Cinnamon Flower* (Douglas/Casablanca) 1977

Mongo Santamaria *Stone Soul* (Columbia) 1969

Mongo Santamaria *Workin' on a Groovy Thing* (Columbia) 1969

Mongo Santamaria *Soul Bag* (Columbia) 1969

Mongo Santamaria *Mongo's Way* (Atlantic) 1971

Mongo Santamaria *Afro-Indio* (Vaya) 1975

Mongo Santamaria *Sofrito* (Vaya) 1976

Shirley Scott *Soul Song* (Atlantic) 1969

Shirley Scott *Shirley Scott and the Soul Saxes* (Atlantic) 1969

Stars of Faith *Self-Titled* (Vanguard) 1978

Gil Scott-Heron *Small Talk at 125th & Lenox* (Flying Dutchman) 1970

Gil Scott-Heron *Pieces of a Man* (Flying Dutchman) 1971

Gil Scott-Heron *Free Will* (Flying Dutchman) 1972

Gil Scott-Heron *The Revolution Will Not Be Televised* (Flying Dutchman) 1974

Archie Shepp *For Losers* (Impulse!) 1970

Archie Shepp *Cry of My People* (Impulse!) 1973

Archie Shepp *Kwanza* (Impulse!) 1974

Horace Silver *Silver 'n Brass* (Blue Note) 1975

Nina Simone *Sings the Blues* (RCA) 1967

Jimmy Smith *Respect* (Verve) 1967

Johnny "Hammond" Smith *Here It 'Tis* (Prestige) 1970

Johnny "Hammond" Smith *Soul Talk* (Prestige) 1969)

Johnny "Hammond" Smith *Black Feeling!* (Prestige) 1969

Johnny "Hammond" Smith *Wild Horses/Rock Steady* (KUDU) 1971

The Soul Finders *Sweet Soul Music* (Camden) 1967

Dakota Staton *Madame Foo Foo* (Groove Merchant) 1972

Steely Dan *Royal Scam* (ABC) 1976

Steely Dan *Aja* (ABC) 1977

Cat Stevens *Foreigner* (A&M) 1973

Sonny Stitt *Never Can Say Goodbye* (Cadet) 1975

Gabor Szabo *Jazz Raga* (Impulse!) 1966

Leon Thomas *Blues and the Soulful Truth* (RCA) 1972

Leon Thomas *Full Circle* (Flying Dutchman) 1973

Eddie "Cleanhead" Vinson *You Can't Make Love Alone* (Mega) 1971

Grover Washington Jr. *All the King's Horses* (KUDU) 1972

Marion Williams *Standing Here Wondering Which Way to Go* (Atlantic) 1971

Reuben Wilson & the Cost of Living *Got to Get Your Own* (Cadet) 1975

Jimmy Witherspoon *Spoonful* (Blue Note) 1975

Fritz the Cat (Original Soundtrack Recording) (Fantasy) 1972

Hair (The Original Cast Recording) (RCA) 1967

CLYDE STUBBLEFIELD SELECTED DISCOGRAPHY
courtesy of Cherryl Aldave and Alan Leeds

James Brown & the Famous Flames *Sing Christmas Songs* (King) 1966

James Brown *Sings Raw Soul* (King) 1967

James Brown & His Famous Flames *Live at the Garden* (King) 1967

James Brown & His Famous Flames *Cold Sweat* (King) 1967

James Brown & His Famous Flames *I Can't Stand Myself When You Touch Me* (King) 1968

James Brown Nothing But Soul (King) 1968

James Brown *I Got the Feelin'* (King) 1968

James Brown *Live At the Apollo Vol. 2* (King) 1968

James Brown *A Soulful Christmas* (King) 1968

James Brown *Say It Loud – I'm Black and I'm Proud* (King) 1969

James Brown *James Brown Plays & Directs the Popcorn* (King) 1969

James Brown *It's a Mother* (King) 1969

Marva Whitney *It's My Thing* (King) 1969

James Brown *Ain't It Funky* (King) 1970

James Brown *It's a New Day—Let a Man Come In* (King) 1970

James Brown *Sex Machine* (King) 1970

Bobby Byrd *I Need Help* (King) 1970

Ben Sidran *I Lead a Life* (Blue Thumb, 1972)

Ben Sidran *Puttin' in Time on Planet Earth* (Blue Thumb) 1972

Ben Sidran *Don't Let Go* (Blue Thumb) 1974

James Brown *Motherlode* (Polydor/Polygram) 1988

Clyde Stubblefield *The Funky Drummer* (WC Music Research) 1992

Clyde Stubblefield *Call Him Mr. Funk* (WC Music Research)

Garbage *Garbage* (Almo, 1995)

Clyde Stubblefield *Revenge of the Funky Drummer* (Interaction) 1997

Clyde Stubblefield *Original Funky Drummer Breakbeat Album* (Mol) 1998

James Brown *Say It Live and Loud: Live in Dallas 1968* (Polygram) 1998

The J.B.'s *Reunion Bring the Funk on Down* (ZYX) 1999

The FunkMasters *Find the Groove* (JCK&BPC) 2001

The B3 Bombers *Live! At the Green Mill* (Alltribe) 2002

The J.B.'s Reunion *Bring the Funk Down* (Instinct) 2002

James Brown and the Famous Flames "Cold Sweat, Pt. 1/ Pt. 2"(King 6110) 1967

James Brown and the Famous Flames "There Was a Time (Live)"(King 6144) 1967

James Brown "I Got the Feelin'" (King 6155) 1968

Marva Whitney "Things Got to Get Better" (King 6168) 1968

James Brown "Say It Loud – I'm Black and I'm Proud, Pt. 1/ Pt. 2"(King 6187) 1968

Marva Whitney "I'm Tired, I'm Tired, I'm Tired" (King 6193) 1968

James Brown "Let's Unite the Whole World at Christmas/ In the Middle, Pt. 1" (King 6205) 1968

James Brown "Santa Claus Go Straight to the Ghetto/ You Know It (Inst.)" (King 6203) 1968

Marva Whitney & James Brown "You Got to Have a Job" (King 6218) 1969

Marva Whitney "It's My Thing" (King 6229) 1969

James Brown "The Popcorn/ The Chicken" (King 6240) 1969

James Brown "Soul Pride, Pt. 1/ Pt. 2" (King 6222) 1969

James Brown "I Don't Want Nobody to Give Me Nothing (Open Up the Door, I'll Get It Myself), Pt. 1/ Pt. 2" (King 6224) 1969

James Brown "Mother Popcorn (You Got to Have a Mother for Me), Pt. 1/ Pt. 2" (King 6245) 1969

James Brown "Lowdown Popcorn" (King 6250) 1969

Marva Whitney "I Made a Mistake Because It's Only You, Pt. 1/ Pt. 2" (King 6268) 1969

James Brown "Ain't It Funky Now (Inst.), Pt. 1/ Pt. 2" (King 6280) 1970

Marva Whitney "He's the One" (King 6283) 1969

James Brown "Funky Drummer, Pt. 1/ Pt. 2" (King 6290) 1970

James Brown "Brother Rapp, Pt. 1/ Pt. 2" (King 6310) 1970

Bobby Byrd "I Need Help (Can't Do It Alone), Pt. 1/ Pt. 2" (King 6323) 1970

The J.B.'s "These Are the J.B.'s, Pt. 1/ Pt. 2" (King 6333) 1970

Myra Barnes (Vicki Anderson) "The Message from the Soul Sisters, Pt. 1/ Pt. 2" (King 6334) 1970

Bobby Byrd "If You Don't Work You Can't Eat" (King 6342) 1970

James Brown "Get Up, Get Into It, Get Involved, Pt. 1/ Pt. 2"(King 6347) 1970

Bobby Byrd "If You Got a Love You Better Hold onto It" (Brownstone 4206) 1972

JOHN "JAB'O" STARKS SELECTED DISCOGRAPHY
courtesy of Cherryl Aldave and Alan Leeds

Bobby Bland *Two Steps from the Blues* (Duke DLPS-74) 1961

Bobby Bland *Here's the Man* (Duke DLPS-75) 1962

Little Junior Parker *Driving Wheel* (Duke DLP-76) 1962

Bobby Bland *Call on Me* (Duke DLPS-77) 1963

Bobby Bland *Ain't Nothing You Can Do* (Duke DLPS-78) 1964

Joe Hinton *Funny (How Time Slips Away)* (Back Beat BLP-60) 1965

James *Brown James Brown Plays New Breed (The Boo-Ga-Loo)*(Smash S67080) 1966

James Brown *James Brown Sings Raw Soul* (King 1016) 1967

James Brown *James Brown Live at the Garden* (King 1018) 1967

James Brown and the Famous Flames *Cold Sweat* (King 1020) 1967

James Brown and the Famous Flames *Live at the Apollo, v. 2*(King 1022) 1967

James Brown *James Brown Presents His Show of Tomorrow*(King 1024) 1968

James Brown *I Can't Stand Myself When You Touch Me* (King 1030) 1968

James Brown *I Got the Feeling* (King 1031) 1968

James Brown *James Brown Plays Nothing But Soul* (King 1034) 1968

James Brown *A Soulful Christmas* (King 1040) 1968

James Brown *Say It Loud – I'm Black and I'm Proud* (King 1047) 1969

James Brown *It's a Mother* (King 1063) 1969

Marva Whitney *Live and Lowdown at the Apollo* (King 1079) 1970

James Brown *Ain't It Funky* (King 1092) 1970

James Brown *Sex Machine* (King 1115) 1970

Bobby Byrd *I Need Help* (King 1118) 1970

James Brown *Super Bad* (King 1127) 1971

James Brown *Revolution of the Mind* (Polydor 3003) 1971

James Brown *Hot Pants* (Polydor 4054) 1971

James Brown *Get on the Good Foot* (Polydor 3004) 1972

James Brown *There It Is* (Polydor 5028) 1972

The J.B.'s *Food for Thought* (People 5601) 1972

The J.B.'s *Doing It to Death* (People 5603) 1973

James Brown *The Payback* (Polydor 3007) 1974

James Brown *Black Caesar* (Polydor 6014) 1973

James Brown *Hell* (Polydor 9001) 1974

Fred Wesley and the J.B.'s *Damn Right I Am Somebody*(People 6602) 1974

Maceo *Us* (People 6601) 1974

James Brown *Sex Machine Today* (Polydor 6042) 1975

James Brown *Hustle* (Polydor 6054) 1975

Fred & the New J.B.'s *Breakin' Bread* (People 6604) 1975

James Brown *Love Power Peace Live at the Olympia* (Polydor) 1992

The J.B.'s Reunion *Bring the Funk on Down* (ZYX) 1999

The Funkmasters *Find the Groove* (Funkmasters) 2001

Bobby Bland "I'll Take Care of You/ That's Why" (Duke 314) 1959

Bobby Bland "Lead Me On/ Hold Me Tenderly" (Duke 318) 1960

Bobby Bland "Cry, Cry, Cry/ I've Been Wrong So Long" (Duke 327) 1960

Bobby Bland "I Pity the Fool/ Close to You" (Duke 332) 1961

Little Junior Parker "Driving Wheel/ Seven Days" (Duke 335) 1961

Bobby Bland "Ain't that Loving You/ Jelly, Jelly, Jelly" (Duke 338) 1961

Bobby Bland "Don't Cry No More/ St. James Infirmary" (Duke 340) 1961

Little Junior Parker "How Long Can This Go On/ In the Dark" (Duke 341) 1961

Bobby Bland "Turn on Your Love Light/ You're the One (That I Need)" (Duke 344) 1961

Little Junior Parker "Annie Get Your Yo-Yo/ Mary Jo" (Duke 345) 1962

Bobby Bland (w/ Ike Turner) "Who Will the Next Fool Be/ Blue Moon" (Duke 347) 1962

Bobby Bland "Yield Not to Temptation/ How Does a Cheating Woman Feel" (Duke 352) 1962

Bobby Bland "Stormy Monday Blues/ Your Friends" (Duke 355) 1962

Bobby Bland "That's the Way Love Is/ Call on Me" (Duke 360) 1963

Bobby Bland "Sometimes You Gotta Cry a Little/ You're Worth It All" (Duke 366) 1963

Bobby Bland "The Feeling Is Gone/ I Can't Stop Singing" (Duke 370) 1963

Joe Hinton "Funny/ You Gotta Have Love" (Back Beat 541) 1964

Litle Junior Parker "I'm Gonna Stop/ Strange Things Happening" (Duke 371) 1964

Bobby Bland "Ain't Nothing You Can Do/ Honey Child" (Duke 375) 1964

Bobby Bland "Share Your Love With Me/ After It's Too Late" (Duke 377) 1964

Bobby Bland "Ain't Doing Too Bad, Pt. 1/ Pt. 2" (Duke 383) 1964

Bobby Bland "These Hands (Small But Mighty)/ Today" (Duke 385) 1965

Bobby Bland "Blind Man/ Black Night" (Duke 386) 1965

Little Junior Parker "Crying for My Baby/ Guess You Don't Know (the Golden Rule)" (Duke 389) 1965

Bobby Bland "Dust Got in Daddy's Eyes/ Ain't No Telling"(Duke 390) 1965

James Brown "New Breed, Pt. 1/ Pt. 2" (Smash 2021) 1965

James Brown and the Famous Flames "Money Won't Change You, Pt. 1/ Pt. 2" (King 6048) 1966

James Brown and the Famous Flames "Don't Be a Drop-Out/ Tell Me that You Love Me" (King 6056) 1966

Vicki Anderson "You Send Me/ (Something Moves Me) Within My Heart" (King 6066) 1966

James Brown and the Famous Flames "Bring It Up/ Nobody Knows" (King 6071) 1967

James Brown "Let Yourself Go" (King 6100) 1967

James Brown "America Is My Home, Pt. 1/ Pt. 2" (King 6112) 1968

James Brown "Get It Together, Pt. 1/ Pt. 2" (King 6122) 1967

James Brown "If I Ruled the World" (King 6155) 1968

James Brown "Licking Stick Pt. 1/ Pt. 2" (King 6166) 1968

James Brown "Goodbye My Love, Pt. 1/ Pt. 2" (King 6198) 1968

James Brown "Ain't It Funky Now, Pt. 1/ Pt. 2" (King 6280) 1969

James Brown "Get Up (I Feel Like Being a) Sex Machine, Pt. 1/ Pt. 2" (King 6318) 1970

James Brown "Super Bad, Pts. 1 & 2/ Pt. 3" (King 6329) 1970

Myra Barnes (Vicki Anderson) "Super Good, Pt. 1/ Pt. 2" (King 6344) 1970

James Brown "Spinning Wheel (Instrumental), Pt. 1/ Pt. 2" (King 6366) 1971

James Brown "Soul Power, Pt. 1/ Pt. 2" (King 6368) 1971

Bobby Byrd "I Know You Got Soul" (King 6378) 1971

James Brown "Escape-ism, Pt. 1/ Pts. 2 & 3" (People 2500) 1971

James Brown "Hot Pants Pts. 1 & 2/ Pt. 3" (People 2501) 1971

James Brown "Make It Funky, Pt. 1/ Pt. 2" (Polydor 14088) 1971

James Brown "I'm a Greedy Man, Pt. 1/ Pt. 2" (Polydor 14100) 1971

Vicki Anderson "I'm Too Tough for Mr. Big Stuff" (Brownstone 4202) 1971

Bobby Byrd "Hot Pants – I'm Coming, Coming, I'm Coming" (Brownstone 4203) 1971

Bobby Byrd "Keep on Doin'" (Brownstone 4205) 1971

The J.B.'s "Gimme Some More" (People 602) 1971

James Brown "My Part/ Make It Funky, Pts. 3 & 4" (Polydor 14098) 1971

James Brown "Talkin' Loud & Sayin' Nothin', Pt.1/ Pt. 2" (Polydor 14109) 1972

James Brown "There It Is, Pt. 1/ Pt. 2" (Polydor 14125) 1972

James Brown Soul Train "Honky Tonk, Pt. 1/ Pt. 2" (Polydor 14129) 1972

James Brown "Get on the Good Foot, Pt. 1/ Pt. 2" (Polydor 14139) 1972

Bobby Byrd "Never Get Enough" (Brownstone 4208) 1972

Bobby Byrd "Sayin' It and Doin' It Are Two Different Things, Pt. 1/ Pt. 2" (Brownstone 4209) 1972

The J.B.'s "Hot Pants Road/ Pass the Peas" (People 607) 1972

Lyn Collins "Think (About It)" (People 608) 1972

The J.B.'s "Giving Up Food for Funk, Pt. 1/ Pt. 2" (People 610) 1972

Sons of Funk "From the Back Side, Pt. 1/ Pt. 2" (King 6398) 1972

Lyn Collins "Me and My Baby Got a Good Thing Going" (People 615) 1972

Lyn Collins "Mama Feelgood" (People 618) 1972

Fred Wesley and the J.B.'s "Doing It to Death/ Everybody Got Soul" (People 621) 1973

Maceo and the Macks "Parrty, Pt. 1/ Pt. 2" (People 624) 1973

Lyn Collins "Take Me Just as I Am" (People 626, 633) 1973

Lyn Collins "You Can't Beat Two People in Love" (People 630) 1973

Maceo and the Macks "Soul Power '74, Pt. 1/ Pt. 2" (People 631) 1973

James Brown "I Got Ants in My Pants, Pt. 1/ Pt. 2" (Polydor 14162) 1973

James Brown "Stone to the Bone, Pt. 1/ Some More" (Polydor 14210) 1973

Fred Wesley & the J.B.'s "You Can Have Watergate, Just Gimme Some Bucks and I'll Be Straight/ If You Don't Get It the First Time, Back Up and Try It Again" (People 627) 1973

Fred Wesley and the J.B.'s "Same Beat, Pt. 1/ Pt. 2" (People 632) 1973

Fred Wesley and the J.B.'s "Damn Right I Am Somebody, Pt. 1/ Pt. 2" (People 638) 1974

James Brown "The Payback, Pt. 1/ Pt. 2" (Polydor 14223) 1974

James Brown "Papa Don't Take No Mess, Pt. 1/ Pt. 2"(Polydor 14255) 1974

James Brown "Coldblooded" (Polydor 14258) 1974

Fred Wesley & the J.B.'s "Rockin' Funky Watergate" (People 643) 1974

Fred & the New J.B.'s "Breakin' Bread/ Funky Music Is My Style" (People 648) 1975

James Brown "Sex Machine, Pt. 1/ Pt. 2" (Polydor 14270) 1975

James Brown "Dead On It, Pt. 1/ Pt. 2" (Polydor 14279) 1975

SWEET CHARLES SHERRELL SELECTED DISCOGRAPHY
courtesy of Matt Rowland and Alan Leeds

Mary Queenie Lyons *Soul Fever* (King/DeLuxe DLP-12001) 1968

James Brown *Soulful Christmas* (King 1040) 1968

James Brown *The Popcorn* (King 1055) 1969

Marva Whitney *It's My Thing* (King 1062) 1969

James Brown *It's a Mother* (King 1063) 1969

Marva Whitney *Live and Lowdown at the Apollo* (King 1079) 1969

James Brown *Ain't It Funky* (King 1092) 1970

James Brown *It's a New Day – Let a Man Come In* (King 1095) 1970

James Brown *Sex Machine* (King 1115) 1970

Maceo & All the King's Men *Funky Music Machine* (Excello EX-8022) 1972

The J.B.'s *Doing It to Death* (People 5603) 1973

Maceo Parker *Us* (People 6601) 1973

James Brown *The Payback* (Polydor 3007) 1974

James Brown *Hell* (Polydor 9001) 1974

Fred Wesley & the J.B.'s *Damn Right I Am Somebody* (People 6602) 1974

Sweet Charles Sherrell *For Sweet People from Sweet Charles* (People 6603) 1974

Fred Wesley & the New J.B.'s *Breakin' Bread* (People 6604) 1974

James Brown *Sex Machine Today* (Polydor 6042) 1975

James Brown *Everybody's Doin' the Hustle and Dead on the Double Bump* (Polydor 6054) 1975

Lyn Collins *Check Me Out If You Don't Know Me By Now*(People 6605) 1975

The J.B.'s *Hustle with Speed* (People 6606) 1975

James Brown *Get Up Offa That Thing* (Polydor 6071) 1976

James Brown *Bodyheat* (Polydor 6093) 1976

James Brown *Mutha's Nature* (Polydor 6111) 1977

James Brown *Jam/1980's* (Polydor 6140) 1978

The J.B.'s *Rock Groove Machine* (Drive 111) 1979

James Brown *Hot on the One* (Polydor 6290) 1980

James Brown *Live in New York* (Knockout 1501) 1981

James Brown *In the Jungle Groove* (Polydor) 1986

James Brown *Live at Chastain Park* (Charly JAM1984 – U.K.) 1988

James Brown *Say It Live and Loud* (Polydor CD 314-557668) 1998

Maceo Parker *Funk Overload* (What Are Records? 60032) 1998

Maceo Parker *Dial M-A-C-E-O* (What Are Records? 60038) 2000

James Brown "Give It Up or Turnit a Loose" (King 6213) 1969

James Brown "You've Got to Have a Job" (King 6218) 1969

James Brown "Soul Pride, Pt. 1/ Pt. 2" (King 6222) 1969

James Brown "I Don't Want Nobody to Give Me Nothing (Open Up the Door and I'll Get It Myself), Pt. 1/ Pt. 2" (King 6224) 1969

James Brown "The Popcorn (instr.)/ The Chicken (instr.)" (King 6240) 1969

James Brown "Mother Popcorn Pt. 1/ Pt. 2" (King 6245) 1969

James Brown "Lowdown Popcorn (instr.)/ Top of the Stack (instr.)" (King 6250) 1969

James Brown "Let a Man Come in and Do the Popcorn, Pt. 1" (King 6255) 1969

James Brown "Let a Man Come in and Do the Popcorn, Pt. 2" (King 6275) 1969

James Brown "Ain't It Funky Now, Pt. 1/ Pt. 2 (instr.)" (King 6280) 1969

James Brown "Brother Rapp, Pt. 1/ Pt. 2" (King 6285 W) 1970

James Brown "Funky Drummer, Pt. 1/ Pt. 2" (King 6290) 1970

James Brown "It's a New Day, Pts. 1 & 2" (King 6292) 1970

James Brown "If You Don't Work You Can't Eat" (King 6342) 1970

James Brown "Stoned to the Bone Pt. 1" (Polydor 14210) 1973

James Brown "The Payback Pt. 1/ Pt. 2" (Polydor 14223) 1974

James Brown "Sex Machine, Pt. 1/ Pt. 2" (Polydor 14270) 1975

James Brown "Dead On It, Pt. 1/ Pt. 2" (Polydor 14279) 1975

James Brown "Dooley's Junkyard Dog (long version)/ (short version)" (Polydor 14303) 1976

James Brown "Get Up Offa That Thing/ Release the Pressure" (Polydor 14326) 1976

James Brown "Bodyheat Pt. 1/ Pt. 2" (Polydor 14360) 1976

James Brown "Kiss in '77/ Woman" (Polydor 14388) 1977

James Brown "Summertime/ Take Me Higher and Groove Me" (Polydor 14433) 1977

James Brown "People Who Criticize/ If You Don't Give a Doggone About It" (Polydor 14438) 1977

James Brown "Love Me Tender/ Have a Happy Day" (Polydor 14460) 1978

James Brown "Eyesight/ I Never, Never, Never Will Forget" (Polydor 14465) 1978

James Brown "The Spank/ Love Me Tender" (Polydor 14487) 1978

James Brown "Nature Pt. 1/ Pt. 2" (Polydor 14512) 1978

James Brown "Get Up Offa That Thing (Live)/ It's Too Funky in Here (Live)" (Polydor 2129) 1980

Past, Present and Future "Bones to Bones/ I Don't Want to Go On Without You" (Mecca 101) 1967

Marva Whitney "I'm Tired, I'm Tired, I'm Tired" (King 6193) 1968

Alfred "Pee Wee" Ellis "Little Green Apples/ Come on in the House" (King 6199) 1969

Marva Whitney "What Do I Have to Do to Prove My Love to You/ Your Love Was Good For Me" (King 6202) 1968

Marva Whitney "You Got to Have a Job (If You Don't Work – You Can't Eat)" (King 6218) 1969

Marva Whitney "It's My Thing (You Can't Tell Me Who to Sock It To)" (King 6229) 1969

Marva Whitney "I Made A Mistake Because It's Only You, Pt. 1/ Pt. 2" (King 6268) 1969

Marva Whitney "He's the One" (King 6283) 1969

Fred Wesley & the J.B.'s "You Can Have Watergate, Just Gimme Some Bucks and I'll Be Straight/ If You Don't Get It the First Time, Back Up and Try It Again" (People 627) 1973

Fred Wesley & the J.B.'s "Same Beat Pt. 1/ Pt. 2" (People 632) 1973

Lyn Collins "Take Me Just as I Am" (People 633) 1974

Fred Wesley & the J.B.'s "Damn Right I Am Somebody Pt. 1/ Pt. 2" (People 638) 1974

Sweet Charles "Soul Man/ Why Can't I Be Treated Like a Man" (People 639) 1974

Fred Wesley & the J.B.'s "Rockin' Funky Watergate" (People 643) 1974

Sweet Charles "Dedicated to the One I Love/ Give the Woman a Chance" (People 645) 1974

The J.B.'s "Breakin' Bread" (People 648) 1974

Sweet Charles "I Won't Last a Day without You/ I Never Let You Break My Heart" (People 653) 1974

The First Family "Control (People Go Where We Send You) Pt. 1/ Pt. 2" (Polydor 14250) 1974

Lee Austin "I'm a Man" (Polydor 14251) 1974

Fred & the New J.B.'s "(It's Not the Express) It's the J.B.'s Monaurail Pt. 1/ Pt. 2" (People 655) 1975

Sweet Charles "Hang Out & Hustle/ Together" (People 656) 1975

The J.B.'s "Thank You for Lettin' Me Be Myself and You Be Yours, Pt. 1/ Pt. 2" (People 660) 1975

Lyn Collins "Mr. Big Stuff/ Rock Me Again & Again & Again" (People 662) 1975

The J.B.'s "All Aboard the Soul Funky Train" (People 663) 1975

The J.B.'s with James Brown "Everybody Wanna Get Funky One More Time, Pt. 1/ Pt. 2" (People 664) 1976

J.B.'s Wedge "Bessie, Pt. 1/ Pt. 2" (Brownstone 7072) 1976

J.B.'s International "Nature, Pt. 1/ Pt. 2" (Brownstone 7073) 1977

The J.B.'s "Rock Groove Machine, Pt. 1/ Pt. 2" (Drive 6277) 1979

The J.B.'s "Just Wanna Make You Dance/ Rock Groove Machine" (Drive 6282) 1979

Charles Sherrell "If I Only Had a Minute" (Muscle 5007) 1981

Charles Sherrell & the Chimpanzees "Do the King Kong/ Funky Fantasia" (Crazy Mama's) [Unknown year]

MARVA WHITNEY SELECTED DISCOGRAPHY
courtesy of Dante Carfagna

It's My Thing (King 1062)

Live and Lowdown at the Apollo (King 1079)

I Sing Soul [Unreleased] (King 1053)

"Your Love Was Good for Me/ Saving My Love for My Baby" (Federal 12545)

"Your Love Was Good for Me/ Saving My Love for My Baby" (King 6124)

"Unwind Yourself/ If You Love Me" (King 6146)

"Your Love Was Good for Me/ What Kind of Man" (King 6158)

"Things Got to Get Better (Get Together)/ What Kind of Man" (King 6168)

"What Do I Have to Do to Prove My Love to You/ Your Love Was Good for Me" (King 6202)

"I'm Tired, I'm Tired, I'm Tired (Things Better Change Before It's Too Late)/ You Got to Have a Job (If You Don't Work–You Can't Eat)" (King 6218)

"Ball of Fire/ It's My Thing" (King 6229)

"Things Got to Get Better (Get Together)/ Get Out of My Life" (King 6249)

"I Made a Mistake Because It's Only You, Pt. 1/ Pt. 2" (King 6268)

"This Girls in Love With You/ He's the One" (King 6283)

"This Is My Quest/ Giving Up on Love" (T-Neck TN-922)

"Daddy Don't Know About Sugar Bear/ We Need More (But Somebody Gotta Sacrifice)" [B-side with Ellie "Gripey" Taylor] (Forte 1114/1115)

"Daddy Don't Know About Sugar Bear/ We Need More (But Somebody Gotta Sacrifice)" (Excello 2321)

"Don't Let Our Love Fade Away/ Live and Let Live" (Excello 2328)

Marva W. Taylor "(Hey, You and You and You and You) I've Lived the Life/ Nothing I'd Rather Be than Your Weakness" (Forte 11151)

M-W-T Express featuring Marva Whitney Taylor "I've Lived the Life/ Nothing I'd Rather Be" (Forte 6045)

Marva and Melvin with the M.W.T. Express "All Alone I've Loved You/ (Get Ready For) The Changes" (Forte 1117)

JOEL DORN SELECTED ATLANTIC RECORDS PRODUCER DISCOGRAPHY

Mose Allison *Western Man* (1971)

Black Heat *Black Heat* (1972)

Black Heat *No Time to Burn* (1974)

Oscar Brown *Movin' On* (1972)

Ray Bryant *MCMLXX* (1970)

Gary Burton *Good Vibes* (1970)

Gary Burton and Keith Jarrett *Throb* (1969)

Gary Burton *Alone at Last* (1971)

Gary Burton and Keith Jarrett *Gary Burton & Keith Jarrett* (1971)

Roberta Flack *First Take* (1969)

Roberta Flack *Chapter Two* (1970)

Roberta Flack *Quiet Fire* (1971)

Roberta Flack *Roberta Flack & Donny Hathaway* (1972)

Roberta Flack *Killing Me Softly* (1973)

Eddie Harris *The Electrifying Eddie Harris* (1967) [not producer; see story]

Eddie Harris *Silver Cycles* (1968) *co-producer

Eddie Harris *Plug Me In* (1968)

Freddie Hubbard *High Blues Pressure* (1967)

Freddie Hubbard *A Soul Experiment* (1969)

King Curtis/Champion Jack Dupree. *Blues at Montreux* (1971)

Rahsaan Roland Kirk *Here Comes the Whistle Man* (1965)

Rahsaan Roland Kirk *Inflated Tear* (1967)

Rahsaan Roland Kirk *Left and Right* (1968)

Rahsaan Roland Kirk *Volunteered Slavery* (1969)

Rahsaan Roland Kirk and the Vibration Society *Rahsaan Rahsaan* (1970)

Rahsaan Roland Kirk *Blacknuss* (1971)

Rahsaan Roland Kirk *Natural Black Inventions: Root Strata* (1971)

Rahsaan Roland Kirk *Meeting of the Times* (1972)

Rahsaan Roland Kirk *I, Eye, Aye: Live at the Montreux* (1972)

Rahsaan Roland Kirk *Bright Moments* (1973)

Rahsaan Roland Kirk *The Man Who Cried Fire* (1973)

Rahsaan Roland Kirk *Art of Rahsaan Roland Kirk* (1973)

Rahsaan Roland Kirk *Prepare Thyself to Deal with a Miracle* (1973)

Rahsaan Roland Kirk *The Case of the 3-Sided Dream in Audio Color* (1975)

Rahsaan Roland Kirk *Other Folks' Music* (1975)

Yusef Lateef *The Complete Yusef Lateef* (1967)

Yusef Lateef *The Blue Yusef Lateef* (1968)

Yusef Lateef *Yusef Lateef's Detroit* (1969)

Yusef Lateef *The Diverse Yusef Lateef* (1969)

Yusef Lateef *Suite 16* (1970)

Yusef Lateef *Part of the Search* (1971)

Yusef Lateef *The Gentle Giant* (1972)

Yusef Lateef *Hush 'N' Thunder* (1973)

Yusef Lateef *The Doctor Is In and Out* (1976)

Hubert Laws *Laws' Cause* (1969)

Hubert Laws *Wild Flower* (1972)

Junior Mance *I Believe to My to My Soul* (1966)

Junior Mance *Harlem Lullaby* (1966)

Junior Mance *With a Lotta Help from My Friends* (1970)

Les McCann *Comment* (1969)

Les McCann *Much Les* (1969)

Les McCann/Eddie Harris *Swiss Movement* (1969)

Les McCann *Invitation to Openness* (1972)

Les McCann *Talk to the People* (1972)

Les McCann *Live at Montreux* (1973)

Les McCann *Layers* (1973)

Les McCann *Another Beginning* (1974)

Eugene McDaniels *Headless Heroes of the Apocalypse* (1971)

Bette Midler *Divine Miss M* (1972)

Bette Midler *Songs for the New Depression* (1976)

David "Fathead" Newman *House of David* (1967) *co-producer

David "Fathead" Newman *Bigger & Better* (1968)

David "Fathead" Newman *The Many Facets of David Newman* (1969)

David "Fathead" Newman *Captain Buckles* (1970)

David "Fathead" Newman *Lonely Avenue* (1971)

David "Fathead" Newman *The Weapon* (1973)

The Jimmy Owens–Kenny Barron Quintet *You Had Better Listen* (1968) *co-producer

Max Roach Members *Don't Git Weary* (1968)

Max Roach *Lift Every Voice and Sing* (1971)

Mongo Santamaria *Mongo '70* (1970)

Mongo Santamaria *Mongo's Way* (1971)

Mongo Santamaria *Mongo at Montreux* (1971)

Shirley Scott *Soul Song* (1969)

Shirley Scott *Something* (1970)

Don Shirley *The Don Shirley Point of View* (1972)

Sonny Stitt *Deuces Wild* (1967)

Luis Gasca *The Little Giant* (1969)

Joe Zawinul *Zawinul* (1970)

 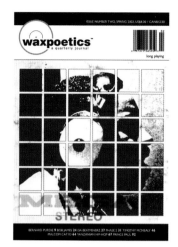  

  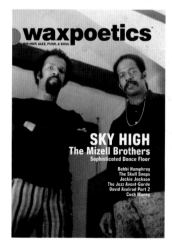 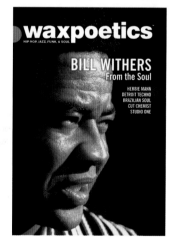

waxpoetics
HIP-HOP, JAZZ, FUNK, & SOUL

DILLA
THE HIP-HOP ISSUE

PUBLIC ENEMY &
THE BOMB SQUAD

KOOL HERC VS.
PETE DJ JONES &
GRANDMASTER
FLASH

BAY AREA HIP-HOP

QUESTLOVE ON DILLA

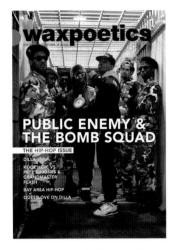

waxpoetics

PUBLIC ENEMY &
THE BOMB SQUAD

THE HIP-HOP ISSUE

DILLA

KOOL HERC VS.
PETE DJ JONES &
GRANDMASTER
FLASH

BAY AREA HIP-HOP

QUESTLOVE ON DILLA

waxpoetics
HIP-HOP, JAZZ, FUNK, &

PARLIAMENT
FUNKADELIC

GEORGE CLINTON • BERNIE WORRELL
BOOTSY COLLINS • GARRY SHIDER
BILLY "BASS" NELSON • THE PARLIAMENTS
PEDRO BELL • OVERTON LLOYD

waxpoetics
HIP-HOP, JAZZ, FUNK,

PARLIAMENT
FUNKADELIC

GEORGE CLINTON
BERNIE WORRELL
BOOTSY COLLINS
GARRY SHIDER
BILLY "BASS" NELSON
THE PARLIAMENTS
PEDRO BELL
OVERTON LLOYD

waxpoetics
HIP-HOP, JAZZ, FUNK, & SOUL
NY STAND UP!

BOOGALOO
BAD BOY
Joe Bataan

FANIA RECORDS AND SALSA
COLLECTOR PHOTO SPREADS!

BRAZIL'S AZYMUTH
COLOMBIAN DANCE FLOOR
NEW YORK'S KOOL DJ RED ALERT

HUGH MASEKELA
RICHARD PRYOR
DR. ALIMANTADO
BALTIMORE CLUB

waxpoetics
NY STAND UP!

NEW YORK'S
KOOL DJ
RED ALERT

BOOGALOO BAD BOY JOE BATAAN
FANIA RECORDS AND SALSA
COLLECTOR PHOTO SPREADS!
BRAZIL'S AZYMUTH
COLOMBIAN DANCE FLOOR

HUGH MASEKELA
RICHARD PRYOR
DR. ALIMANTADO
BALTIMORE CLUB

DJ RED ALERT

NEXT
RECORDS INC.

THE WAX POETICS FIVE-YEAR ANNIVERSARY

waxpoetics
HIP-HOP, JAZZ, FUNK, & SOUL

THE UPSETTER
LEE "SCRATCH" PERRY

THE SOUL SYNDICATE + LLOYD "BULLWACKIE" BARNES
EIGHTBALL & MJG + KING CURTIS + DENNIS COFFEY

THE WAX POETICS FIVE-YEAR ANNIVERSARY

waxpoetics
HIP-HOP, JAZZ, FUNK, & SOUL

*Eightball
& MJG*

waxpoetics
HIP-HOP, JAZZ, FUNK, & SOUL

JAMES BROWN
MAY 3, 1933–DECEMBER 25, 2006

waxpoetics
HIP-HOP, JAZZ, FUNK, & SOUL

THE STORY OF
PLANET
ROCK

JAMES BROWN

CHARLES STEPNEY
AND CHESS RECORDS

MINNIE RIPERTON
TERRY CALLIER
PAZANT BROTHERS
ED BLAND

waxpoetics
HIP-HOP, JAZZ, FUNK, & SOUL

LIBERATED FUNK
BETTY
DAVIS

TOO SHORT
KING ERRISSON
ORNETTE COLEMAN
JOÃO DONATO
STEVE REID
PHAROAHE MONCH
MARVA WHITNEY

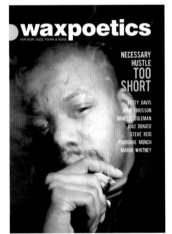

waxpoetics
HIP-HOP, JAZZ, FUNK, & SOUL

NECESSARY
HUSTLE
TOO
SHORT

BETTY DAVIS
KING ERRISSON
ORNETTE COLEMAN
JOÃO DONATO
STEVE REID
PHAROAHE MONCH
MARVA WHITNEY

waxpoetics
HIP-HOP, JAZZ, FUNK, & SOUL

*Rick
James*
Ghetto Symphony

THE LATIN QUARTER
BUNNY LEE
CHICO HAMILTON
ARTHUR RUSSELL
RAMP
DJ SHADOW

waxpoetics
HIP-HOP, JAZZ, FUNK, & SOUL

HIP-HOP'S CELEBRITY WAREHOUSE
THE LATIN
QUARTER

RICK JAMES • BUNNY LEE
CHICO HAMILTON • ARTHUR RUSSELL
RAMP • DJ SHADOW

waxpoetics
HIP-HOP, JAZZ, FUNK, & SOUL

MANDRILL

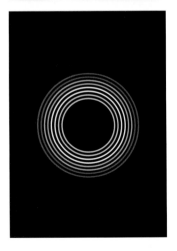